Praise for Stephen Sestanovich's

Maximalist

"Sestanovich provides a comprehensive view of the past seventy years of U.S. foreign policy and offers a useful and often original look at the strategies of the last twelve American presidents. . . . This book will reward both the specialist and the novice; anyone interested in the past or the future of U.S. policy and power would benefit from its insights."

—Walter Russell Mead, *Foreign Affairs*

"In his engaging and richly anecdotal new book, *Maximalist*, Stephen Sestanovich applies [his] understanding [of the desire to dominate and the impulse to pull back] as a framework for reexamining post–World War II U.S. history to find the persistent truths and lessons that he believes can inform our understanding of the present. . . . He is at his best in describing the Johnson and Nixon administrations, capturing the infighting among those presidents and their senior advisers as they grappled with America's role in the world." —*The Washington Post*

"*Maximalist* . . . makes clear that the U.S. has never achieved strategic continuity. American strategy has frequently shifted, sometimes over the course of a single administration, and these disruptions have often proved beneficial to our national security. . . . [An] excellent book." —*The Wall Street Journal*

"Among the many virtues of *Maximalist* is the mathematical elegance of its thesis. . . . Compelling. . . . Refreshingly nonpartisan."

—Michael Doran, *Commentary*

"*Maximalist* is a highly readable account of American engagement during the Cold War and the War on Terror. It provides a commonsense means to assess American military and diplomatic policy without the fog of political rhetoric."

—*New York Journal of Books*

"A leading voice. . . . Offers a provocative reassessment of America's global dominance. . . . Sestanovich finds fresh lessons in the past that clarify our chaotic present."

—*The Record*

"In his excellent study of post-1945 American foreign policy, Stephen Sestanovich asks us to take a 'long view' of America's place in the world. . . . Offers valuable glimpses behind the veiled face of diplomacy. . . . Sestanovich has given us an engaging testament to original thinking. And he's done so on an issue of profound and durable importance."

—*The Washington Free Beacon*

"Americans routinely need to be reminded that our past was not as smooth and rosy as we like to remember it; Stephen Sestanovich provides a masterful and entertaining corrective. *Maximalist* is beautifully written, with engaging anecdotes woven throughout. Most important, it will change your view of Obama's foreign policy."

—Anne-Marie Slaughter,
President and CEO, New America Foundation;
Bert G. Kerstetter '66 University Professor Emerita
of Politics and International Affairs,
Princeton University

Stephen Sestanovich

Maximalist

Stephen Sestanovich served as ambassador-at-large for the former Soviet Union during the Clinton administration, as a senior staff member at the National Security Council and the State Department during the Reagan administration, and before that as senior legislative assistant to Senator Daniel Patrick Moynihan. He is currently the Kathryn and Shelby Cullom Davis Professor of International Diplomacy at Columbia University's School of International and Public Affairs, and the George F. Kennan Senior Fellow for Russian and Eurasian Studies at the Council on Foreign Relations. He and his wife, Ann Hulbert, live in Washington, D.C.

MAXIMALIST

MAXIMALIST

AMERICA IN THE WORLD FROM TRUMAN TO OBAMA

Stephen Sestanovich

VINTAGE BOOKS
A Division of Random House LLC
New York

FIRST VINTAGE BOOKS EDITION, OCTOBER 2014

Copyright © 2014 by Stephen Sestanovich

All rights reserved. Published in the United States by Vintage Books, a division of Random House LLC, New York, and in Canada by Random House of Canada Limited, Toronto, Penguin Random House companies. Originally published in hardcover in the United States by Alfred A. Knopf, a division of Random House LLC, New York, in 2014.

Vintage and colophon are registered trademarks of Random House LLC.

The Library of Congress has cataloged the
Knopf edition as follows:
Sestanovich, Stephen.
Maximalist : America in the world from Truman to Obama /
Stephen Sestanovich. — First Edition.
pages cm
1. United States—Foreign relations—1945–1989.
2. United States—Foreign relations—1989– I. Title.
E744 .S5473 327.73009'04—dc23 2013030396

Vintage Trade Paperback ISBN: 978-0-307-38830-8
eBook ISBN: 978-0-385-34966-6

Author photograph © Michael Lionstar
Book design by Betty Lew

www.vintagebooks.com

Printed in the United States of America
10 9 8 7 6 5 4 3 2

For

Ann, Ben, and Clare

CONTENTS

Prologue: "We Do Big Things" 3

Part One: 1947–1960

1. Truman at the Creation: "The United States Must Run This Show" 17
2. Truman at War: "Victory Is a Strong Magnet" 39
3. "Enough Is Enough": Eisenhower and Retrenchment 65

Part Two: 1961–1980

4. "Boy Commandos" of the New Frontier: Kennedy's Anxious Activism 93
5. "Mainly Violins, with Touches of Brass": Johnson Against His Advisers 121
6. "We Have Not Been Divided": Johnson at War 145
7. Retrenchment and Vietnam: "Get Going, Take Risks, Be Exciting" 167
8. Retrenchment and Détente: "A Nihilistic Nightmare" 191

Part Three: 1981 to the Present

9. "Outspend Them Forever": Reagan and the End of the Cold War 221
10. "No One Else Can Do This": Bush, Clinton, and the Retrenchment That Wasn't 243

11. "Things Related and Not": Bush and September 11 — 273

12. "No Wiggle Room": Obama and Retrenchment — 301

Epilogue: "If It's Worth Doing, It's Worth Overdoing" — 325

Acknowledgments — 337

Notes — 339

Index — 379

Illustration Credits — 403

MAXIMALIST

PROLOGUE

"We Do Big Things"

In 2003, forty years after [President Kennedy's] death, when America's reputation abroad was in tatters, I was in Rome for a speaking engagement, and invited by a local foreign policy group to give an address. "On what subject?" I asked the chairman. "Tell us about the good America, when Kennedy was president," he said. I did. I talked about an America admired for its values, respected for its principles, not feared for its might or resented for its success; an America that led by listening, worked with the rest of the world, and respected international law; an America that stood for peace, not one that started wars.

—Ted Sorensen[1]

IT IS HARD TO THINK of any country that has ever put a larger stamp on its time than the United States of America in the second half of the twentieth century. In the wake of two world wars, which left other major powers severely crippled, America made the decisive contributions to global recovery. During the Cold War and long afterward, it was an anchor of security, an agent of prosperity, an advocate of national independence and political modernization. The most valuable institutions of international cooperation were, directly or indirectly, inspired by the United States. Its impact, moreover, extended far beyond high politics. American ways of doing things encouraged economic, social, cultural, intellectual, and technological innovation around the world.

That, at any rate, was the twentieth century. The twenty-first has already been different. Its early years brought terrorist attacks, diplomatic isolation, a burst of global anti-Americanism, and military campaigns that the United States found easy to start, impossible to win, and extremely difficult to end. To these travails were added a global financial crisis, widely blamed on American mismanagement, and a shake-up in the international economic pecking order. The United States is now on track, some say a fast one, to lose its position as the world's largest economy. Scholars and pundits argue that its central role in international politics is also at risk. And with Washington policy making blocked by partisan gridlock, many question the country's ability to cope with significant new challenges.

America's past and present, in short, have rarely seemed so different from each other. One result of this mismatch has been a surge of interest in the ingredients of our previous success. What was it that once enabled the United States to deal so effectively with so many international problems—to give the world so much while also getting so much in return? Military power and economic growth are essential ingredients of a large global role, but many find the real secret of America's large achievements in its readiness to create equal partnerships with other nations, to take their interests and ideas into account, and to play by mutually agreed rules. For others, the key lies in policy continuity over long periods, the kind of steadfastness across decades that—to take the most glorious example—produced victory in the Cold War. Still others point to the importance of national consensus. In the past, it is said, when Americans agreed on how to handle big problems, they were able—in Barack Obama's words—to "do big things."[2]

IT IS THE ARGUMENT of this book that there is much to learn from the history of American foreign policy, but that we can't learn it from the sepia-tinted versions of the past that have dominated public discussion in recent years. Play well with others; make sure the country is united; find a good strategy and stick to it: our history has a more interesting story to tell us than these homilies suggest. The reason that the past can help us chart the future is that it was just as confused and chaotic as the present. It reminds us how often we have clashed with our friends and misunderstood our enemies, how often policy makers have miscalculated what they could accomplish, how rarely they kept commitments in balance with available resources, and how often they acted in full knowledge that public opinion was against them.

To take even a half-serious look at the history of American alliances is to learn how ambivalent Washington policy makers have been about working with others. Yes, they always aspired to join with like-minded governments in a spirit of give and take. They sincerely believed in the value of multilateral institutions and the advantages of observing accepted rules of the road. Yet in tackling the toughest problems, our leaders have—with some justice—usually come to doubt that collaborative approaches would succeed. Consulting with allies is one thing; letting their interests, not to mention their chronic indecision and feebleness, undermine American policy is something else entirely. It is no exaggeration to say that the history of American foreign policy is the history of what presidents and their advisers do once they conclude that others, at home and abroad, are not likely to help them very much.

No president illustrates this point better, as it happens, than the hero of Ted Sorensen's "good America" story. John Kennedy's exceptionally difficult relations with allied governments were captured in the title of Henry Kissinger's 1965 book on the subject, *The Troubled Partnership*. As we will see, the animosity between Kennedy, on the one hand, and the leaders of France and West Germany, on the other, exceeded any case of transatlantic discord until the presidency of George W. Bush. Charles de Gaulle and Konrad Adenauer complained that Kennedy, when not simply deceiving them, was pursuing policies that put the security and independence of their countries at risk. Adenauer had a special reason to resent the young U.S. president, who openly maneuvered to oust him from his job. And De Gaulle may have known that American officials thought he needed "a psychiatrist."[3]

John Kennedy was usually able to count on greater support from the British prime minister, Harold Macmillan, than from the leaders of France and Germany. (So, of course, was George W. Bush.) But the Anglo-American "special relationship" had many lapses of understanding and outbursts of bad feeling. When the United States decided, in August 1962, to breach an international embargo on major arms sales to Israel, Macmillan sent Kennedy a furious protest. The prime minister expressed his personal "disgust and despair" at what he called a "disgraceful piece of trickery." As always, when British and American priorities in the Middle East diverged, Washington insisted on taking its own approach and left London to adjust as best it could. (Macmillan had long been unhappy with Britain's subservience to America. Early in his career, he compared relations between the two countries to the way "Greek slaves ran the operations of the Emperor Claudius.")[4]

Relations between the United States and its close allies have evolved since Kennedy's day, but the problems that frustrated him have not gone away. American policy makers still find it difficult to get others to work with them as productively as they would like. In July 2009, in her first major speech as secretary of state, Hillary Clinton explained why. Multilateral cooperation, she said, often fails because other countries are so heavily influenced by things like "history, geography, ideology and inertia." Even when a common interest is at stake, uncooperative governments "sit on the sidelines or sow discord and division."

Speaking for a new administration committed to treating other countries with greater respect, Clinton expressed a dilemma that has vexed American policy makers for decades. She set forth principles of liberal internationalism with verve and conviction, but she was also clear-eyed about how much stood in the way of making these principles a reality. Obstacles to cooperation—which she gave their correct academic name, "collective action problems"—could only be overcome, Clinton insisted, by American leadership. "No challenge," she said, "can be met without America."[5]

Hillary Clinton's predecessors, and presidential advisers of both parties, shared her view, and they were often far less polite about it. John Connally, Nixon's treasury secretary, said of the economic disputes he handled, "The foreigners are trying to screw us, but I intend to screw them first." John Foster Dulles, who served Eisenhower as secretary of state, dismissed Europe's leaders as a group of "shattered 'old people.'" Allied governments, complained Dean Rusk, who served Kennedy in the same job, had grown too accustomed to having all problems addressed by "an American plan put together as a complete plan from A to Z." (Rusk's exasperation showed when he snapped at a British journalist: "When the Russians invade Sussex, don't expect us to come and help you.") With other countries able to contribute so little, Walt Rostow, Lyndon Johnson's national security adviser, thought the United States had to act on "a relatively lonely stage." It had to play this solitary role for years, "without throwing our sheriff's badge in the dust."[6]

Because working with others has been so maddeningly hard for the United States, we cannot look to the past for ready-made solutions to "collective action problems." For those who have convinced themselves that the troubles of the past decade were caused by simple neglect of some well-established collaborative tradition, this will be a disappointment. We don't really have such a tradition. (And our doubts go way back. Consider Emerson: "We believe in ourselves as we do not believe in others. We permit all things to ourselves, and that which we call sin in others is experiment to us.") All the same, the difficulties faced by past presidents and policy makers also mean that their experiences were closer to ours than we think. They too dealt with allies who couldn't agree on much, with semifunctional multilateral institutions, and with the thankless consequences of trying to solve every problem through American "leadership."[7]

The lessons of this story can aid our thinking now and in the future. To learn them, we have to look closely at what past administrations accomplished and failed to accomplish. We will not get the answers right if we think we know them in advance.

A QUICK SCAN of our history also makes it impossible to believe that the global role of the United States was based on strategic continuity from one decade to the next. We are not wrong to consider American diplomacy in the second half of the twentieth century a gigantic success story, but it usually didn't feel that way at the time. Until the very last years of the Cold War, every president leaving Washington at the end of an administration was widely condemned for his foreign policy record. Some were virtually run out of town. Almost every new occupant of the Oval Office thought the world had changed in some fundamental way that his predecessor either totally misunderstood or failed to manage effectively.

This was how Truman viewed Roosevelt, how Eisenhower viewed Truman, how Kennedy viewed Eisenhower, and so on. Twenty years later, when Ronald Reagan took over from Jimmy Carter, his verdict was harsher still. Reagan believed that America had been losing the Cold War for at least the previous three presidencies.

Some of these claims were unfair and partisan, but they were not mere campaign rhetoric. They shaped the outlook and actions of most new administrations. The story of American foreign policy, we will see, is not one of dogged continuity but of regular, repeated, and successful efforts to change course.

What pushed presidents to seek a new foreign policy direction? The short answer is, two different types of failure. The first was the kind usually associated during the Cold War with the word *crisis*—some alarming new challenge that raised the prospect of a major American setback and required an urgent response. These moments of crisis included Western Europe's seeming economic collapse in the winter of 1947, North Korea's attack on the South in 1950, the launch of Sputnik in 1957, Nikita Khrushchev's threat to strangle West Berlin in 1961, the Cuban Missile Crisis a year later, the Soviet invasion of Afghanistan in 1979, martial law in Poland in 1981, Iraq's seizure of Kuwait in 1990, Balkan mass murder later in the decade, and of course the attacks of September 11, 2001. Time and again, Washington's response was, to use George Kennan's description of the debate triggered by the Korean War, like "a stone thrown into a beehive."[8]

At such moments, amid frenzied debate about what to do next, American policy makers usually concluded that a large response was the only way to turn back the threat at hand—and the still larger ones probably lurking behind it. The United States would have to develop new ideas, generate new resources, make new commitments, shake up the status quo. Our leaders typically had just one answer to such problems: Do more. Think big. Pedal to the metal.

"Maximalist" presidents, of course, heard from some of their advisers that the United States was overreacting, that the crisis reflected local conditions rather than a global challenge, or that doing too much might well worsen the situation and even undermine American interests. But they usually rejected such balanced advice. These presidents—Truman, Kennedy, and Reagan are the most obvious examples—wanted a big package of countermeasures. Maximalist policy making did not necessarily mean taking reckless or mindless action, and the most extreme imaginable responses were generally ruled out. But any plausible idea about how to push back usually got a sympathetic hearing.

We find a very different pattern when we look at presidents who had to cope with a second type of failure: that of overcommitment. Here Eisenhower and Nixon are the classic examples. Both were Cold War presidents charged with closing down stalemated wars at bearable cost. Their job was to unwind a disaster and to put American policy on a more sustainable foundation. They sought to calm an angry public, to shift responsibilities to friends and allies, to explore accommodation with adversaries, to narrow commitments and reduce costs. They too faced dissenters within their own ranks—advisers convinced that the global position of the United States could not survive any scaling back—and they too overruled them. The motto of America's "retrenchment" presidents was the opposite of the one adopted by our "maximalists." Do less, they said, not more. Think harder, not bigger. Hit the brakes, not the gas.

Strategies of "maximalism" and "retrenchment" bear an obvious cyclical relation to each other. Again and again, one has provided a corrective to the other's mistakes. When the maximalist overreaches, the retrencher comes in to pick up the pieces. Then when retrenchment fails to rebuild American power, meet new challenges, or compete effectively, the maximalist reappears, ready with ambitious formulas for doing so.

Since the 1940s, we have seen this cycle played out at least three times. The first cycle began with the activism of the early Cold War—for many, American policy's "golden age." It ended with the seeming drift of the late Eisenhower administration. The second began with the activism of the New Frontier and ended with the abandonment of détente in the late 1970s. The third cycle opened with Ronald Reagan's claim that America had the ability to "begin the world over again."[9] Whether this third cycle ever really ended—and if so, when; if not, why not—is one puzzle in the story ahead of us.

Most presidents are admittedly uncomfortable thinking of themselves as either pure maximalists or pure retrenchers. John Kennedy was an activist by instinct. He was also acutely aware of the risks to which his own instincts, and those of his activist advisers, exposed him. Richard Nixon, by contrast, knew that he had to pull back, to get the war in Vietnam "off his plate." But he worried that withdrawal would turn into an across-the-board American retreat. Kennedy was a maximalist always looking around for a safe exit. Nixon was the opposite: a reluctant retrencher always trying to whip himself into an activist lather.

Maximalists aren't madmen. They know that they risk overdoing things. Retrenchers aren't simply passive. They understand that pulling back can be dangerous. Both kinds of presidents have tried to fine-tune their strategies, to find the extra ingredient that would produce better long-term results. But they have usually not succeeded very well. Kennedy oversaw an enormous surge in American power, and he sometimes found it hard to control. Nixon oversaw a drawdown of American power, and he sometimes found it hard to check. Their successors—for Kennedy, Lyndon Johnson; for Nixon, Gerald Ford, and Jimmy Carter—found it even harder.

Neither maximalist presidents nor retrenchment presidents have devised a successful and sustainable formula for managing America's role in the world. Both have regularly yielded to blindness, inertia, and overconfidence. It is easy to think of maximalists as more likely to "overdo" it, but retrenchers have overdone things too—in the opposite direction. As we will see, neither has had much luck trying to change course. Each has instead had to be rescued from error by the other. This is what makes their stories so important to understand. In worshipping at the shrine of foreign policy continuity, Americans ignore what may be the single most important lesson that our history teaches: that discontinuity has been the source of our greatest success.

BECAUSE A SINGLE WORD, *containment,* was used for so long to describe U.S. strategy—even though that strategy was always changing—our foreign policy is sometimes thought to have reflected broad national agreement. In fact, no issue of American politics has been more consistently divisive or more emotionally charged than our relations with the outside world. Maximalism and retrenchment have started some nearly endless arguments.

Every president from the 1940s on knew that how well he handled major issues of national security would decide his political survival. Military disaster in Korea "destroyed the Truman Administration," recalled Dean Acheson, who—though we remember him as a giant of American diplomacy—was all but put on trial by congressional committees. When Vietnam began to bring down Lyndon Johnson's presidency, commentators compared the turmoil generated by the war to a national nervous breakdown. Some of Johnson's advisers worried about a breakdown in the American political system too.[10]

This record of discord is so strong that the myth of foreign policy consensus, which ruled for many years, has had to be repackaged. The new version has it that for over half a century and more, politicians and policy makers were obliged to implement a single set of ideas about American global primacy, lest they look weak and ruin their careers. Johnson gave classic expression to this view when he described right-wing anti-Communism as the "great beast" that would destroy him if he accepted defeat in Vietnam. For some, candidate Barack Obama's embrace of the war in Afghanistan proved the point. Because he was against the war in Iraq, he had to find some other war to be for. The Cold War may be over, but the "beast," it seems, lives on. Our leaders have been so afraid of populist nationalism that they supported policies they didn't believe in, even wars they knew would end badly.[11]

American politicians do often pick their policies to make themselves look tough. Yet liberals' fear that conservatives will attack their patriotism and manhood is just one example of how partisan disagreements shape American foreign policy. Liberal politicians and policy makers have had their own ambitious ideas about how to employ the vast power of the United States—and they will surely continue to do so.

Of this, there is again no more convincing proof than the Kennedy administration. George Ball (who was Dean Rusk's deputy) wrote that the president and his advisers wanted to fashion a global strategy in keeping with America's "revolutionary" traditions. He wasn't talking about the Peace Corps. Liberal activism led the United States to encourage the overthrow of South Vietnamese president Ngo Dinh Diem in November 1963. Hearing of this, Dwight Eisenhower was so shocked by the thought that Washington might depose a friendly leader (he had, of course, ordered covert operations, but only against adversaries) that he asked John McCone, the director of the CIA, to explain what was going on. Kennedy, McCone answered, was surrounded by "liberals in his government who want to reform every country" in the world.[12]

McCone had worked for Eisenhower and may have been playing to his old boss's prejudices. But he was absolutely right about Diem's overthrow. The most liberal members of Kennedy's team were the most single-minded advocates of the coup. They considered Diem a retrograde figure who was blocking the emergence of modern politics in South Vietnam and making it harder for the United States to prevail there. Even though the coup ended in bloodshed and murder, John Kenneth Galbraith (who had wanted to get rid of Diem for years) wrote Averell Harriman to praise the affair as "another great feather in your cap."[13]

Thirty years later it was liberals who pressed Bill Clinton hardest to stop the genocidal Balkan wars of the 1990s. With the Cold War over, the "beast" of right-wing anti-Communism had largely fallen silent as a factor in foreign policy debate. The most vocal supporters of what came to be called "humanitarian intervention" were instead human rights advocacy groups, international relief organizations, even the media. Madeleine Albright, ambassador to the U.N. at the time, spoke for them when she challenged Colin Powell, then the chairman of the Joint Chiefs of Staff. "What's the point," Albright asked Powell across the table at the White House, "of having this superb military you're always talking about if we can't use it?"[14]

Liberals, in short, have not always been on the defensive when it comes to the use of American power. Nor have conservatives always treated foreign policy downsizing as weak and unpatriotic. Playing to the public's interest in "peace" has been a prominent part of every single Republican administration's political strategy since the 1970s. Richard Nixon led the way in such maneuvering. His opening to China, he exulted, would be "good to hit the Democrats with at primary time." Running for reelection two decades later, George H. W. Bush seemed almost embarrassed by his foreign policy accomplishments. The congressional Republicans who opposed Barack Obama over Syria in September 2013 were not the first to think doing less might be good politics.[15]

Presidents and policy makers of both parties have long wrestled with this same problem—how to advance America's international interests in the face of unreliable public support. Expecting their policies to be unpopular, they looked for ways to adjust. Some sought success on the cheap, or misrepresented the costs of the actions they proposed. Others favored a spasm of all-out, expensive effort—to get a big job done quickly, before the public changed its mind. Still others sought to avoid controversy by operating in secret.

Most administrations—whether maximalists or retrenchers—have been deeply divided about how best to deal with the vagaries of domestic politics. When Colin Powell advised presidents that military interventions should have prior legislative approval, he was giving one answer: put the burden on Congress. Dick Cheney and Donald Rumsfeld had different advice: keep Congress out of national security decision making in the first place. This one disagreement alone helped to shape American foreign policy over much of the past three decades.

As the United States disengages from the wars of the past ten years and rethinks its international involvements, we are beginning to hear that the country is on the verge of a restored foreign policy consensus. There can be no better time to understand both how rare such a thing has been in the past—and how often it has produced error and calamity.

FOREIGN POLICY SETBACKS and controversies usually lead Americans to take a stronger interest in the history of our foreign policy. The war in Vietnam suggested to many scholars, politicians, and pundits—and much of the public too—that policy had been on the wrong track for decades. They decided that its motivating ideas and deepest impulses were mistaken and perhaps even evil. The result was the most severe loss of confidence in its international purposes that the United States has ever experienced.

It says something important—and healthy—about America's changing idea of itself that in recent years discontent with our foreign policy has taken the opposite course. The more one criticized current policy, the more likely one was to believe that past policy had been good. Both of these responses—looking for the "good America" or the bad—have been right about the importance of the past, but neither has gotten us much closer to the truth. We won't fully understand today's choices unless we explore the ideas and impulses that over many decades defined America's way in the world—where they came from and why they lasted, what they have done for us (and to us), which ones are ready for the scrap heap, and which can be put to work again.

Part One

1947–1960

I

Truman at the Creation

"THE UNITED STATES MUST RUN THIS SHOW"

Dean Acheson, Harry Truman, and George Marshall

WHEN GEORGE MARSHALL came to work on Monday morning, February 24, 1947, after a couple of days out of town, he had been secretary of state for barely a month. His deputy, Dean Acheson, quickly briefed him on a problem that had kept the department's senior staff busy over the weekend. The U.S. government, Acheson felt, would soon be forced to make "the most major decision with which we have been faced since the war."[1]

For Harry Truman, Acheson's description was an understatement. In not quite two years as president, he had, among other things, overseen the end of the most destructive war in human history, negotiated face to face with Joseph Stalin, given the order to drop atomic bombs on Japan, and persuaded the Senate to ratify the UN Charter. The challenges he faced so early in his presidency eventually led Truman to devote the entire first volume of his memoirs to 1945 alone—a "year of decisions," he called it. But all that seemed mere preparation for a larger drama. What was now before him, he told his cabinet, was a "decision more serious than had ever confronted *any President*."[2]

Over time Truman's sense of what America had taken on grew more expansive still. "We are faced," he said, "with the most terrible responsibility that any nation ever faced. From Darius I's Persia, Alexander's Greece, Hadrian's Rome, Victoria's Britain, no nation or group of nations has had our responsibilities."[3]

In the first half of 1947, America's leaders concluded that they had to go beyond the case-by-case, slightly improvisational approach to international problems that they felt they had been following since the end of World War II. Their concerns about Soviet aims and actions had steadily increased. So had their readiness to push back when necessary against the expansion of Moscow's influence. But there was not yet agreement within the U.S. government to make the containment of Soviet power the central organizing principle of foreign policy. There had been no public presentation of such a strategy, nor any focused effort to join with other nations in implementing it.

As Dean Acheson and his colleagues worked overtime on the last weekend of February, American policy was about to change. The British government had officially informed the State Department that, for budgetary reasons, it was curtailing its presence in the eastern Mediterranean. Someone else would have to keep the Greek government from falling to a Communist insurgency, bolster Turkey against the Soviet Union, and provide for regional stability. In March, Truman went before Congress to seek emergency economic and military support for both countries. The United States, he announced, must be ready to help "free peoples" defend themselves against armed insurgencies and foreign pressure.[4]

This declaration, which became known at once as the Truman Doctrine, was just one of the landmark initiatives taken in early 1947 by the president and his advisers. Also in March the foreign ministers of the "Big Four"—Britain, France, the Soviet Union, and the United States—convened in Moscow to discuss reparations, the future of Germany, and other contentious issues. After six weeks of fruitless talks, George Marshall basically gave up on cooperation with the Soviet Union. The Moscow meetings, as one member of Marshall's party put it, "rang down the Iron Curtain." America would now take a different approach, one that focused on rebuilding the western half of a divided Europe. On his way home from Moscow, the secretary of state instructed the U.S. military governor in Germany, General Lucius Clay, to accelerate the economic integration of the American and British occupation zones.[5]

A third new policy of 1947 was the most celebrated of all. Visiting Europe during its coldest winter in half a century, a succession of American officials, including Marshall himself, had come back shaken by what they saw. Millions, they feared, were starving. The United States had to act. Otherwise economic hardship would surely produce political chaos—and probably soon. Truman administration planners were urgently instructed to consider possible U.S. responses to this danger. Even before their ideas were fully formulated, Marshall wanted to signal that help was on the way. Speaking at Harvard's commencement in June, he expressed America's readiness to help Europe avert disaster. Truman, hoping to win congressional support by associating foreign aid with a national hero, and perhaps satisfied that he already had a "doctrine" of his own, made it known that the new program would be called the Marshall Plan.

THESE WERE ALL SIGNIFICANT initiatives, and many equally creative measures were to follow. But what was it about America's expanding international "responsibilities"—other than presidential hyperbole—that filled Truman and his advisers with such anxiety? And what called forth comparisons to ancient monarchs like Alexander and Darius? It wasn't really the scale of the resources that the United States had to mobilize. Between 1948 and 1952, it ended up providing $13 billion in aid to Europe under the Marshall Plan. (The equivalent number in 2012 dollars would be $125 billion.) Large as it was, this amount was actually less than the assistance—$16.25 billion, according to the Bureau of the Budget—that the United States had already made available since the war ended. Between 1945 and 1947, it had put up 75 percent of the UN Relief and Rehabilitation Administration's $10 billion budget; loaned $4.4 billion to Great Britain and over $3 billion to other European countries; and renegotiated trade agreements intended to help European industries get back on their feet.[6]

The primary concern that ran through the deliberations of American policy makers in this period was not the size of the reconstruction bill; it was their awareness that the United States had to bear the cost alone. Europe had been far more gravely damaged by the war than Americans had realized. Will Clayton, the State Department's number-three official, responsible for economic policy, described the British as gamely "hanging in by their eyelashes." Acheson's judgment was more brutal. They were "finished," he said. "They are through." In addition to Greece and Turkey, Britain soon announced its departure from Burma, Palestine, and India. This retreat, *The New York Times* observed, left "a void in the economic and political universe." By the fall of 1947, the Royal Navy was canceling maneuvers just to save fuel.[7]

Even more than destitution, however, it was Europe's dysfunction that worried American officials. They believed that selfish and parochial views and broken political processes kept the governments of the Old World from dealing constructively with their own problems. This concern came up in countless diplomatic encounters. When, in the course of his March–April meetings in Moscow, Marshall asked French foreign minister Georges Bidault whether the United States could count on France, he got a revealingly unconfident answer. Oh, yes, Bidault promised, France could definitely be counted on—assuming it managed to avoid civil war! Understandably, Marshall was not fully reassured. He doubted that the French would play a positive role under any circumstances and scorned their views of how to handle Germany as "outmoded and unrealistic."[8]

The paralysis of other European governments was even more complete. On the eve of Truman's March 12 speech to Congress, American diplomats trying to put together an assistance package for Greece realized that they themselves would have to draft the Greek government's request to Washington for help. (Acheson later referred to this as the friendly "guidance of a feeble hand.") Later, when aid started arriving, the same Americans wrote the Greek thank-you note as well. George Kennan, the thoughtful and increasingly influential foreign service officer whom Marshall hired in early 1947 to create a new policy-planning staff in the State Department, used the same word as Acheson in delicately summarizing the broader problem. The Europeans, he said, were seeking "guidance rather than responsibilities."[9]

With weakness and disorganization the norm across Europe, Marshall and his colleagues began to fear that the Soviet Union would dominate the continent without having to do anything more aggressive than wait. The secretary of state's alarm was heightened by the private meeting he had with Stalin in April, at the end of the long foreign ministers' conference in Moscow. The Soviet leader had a soothing message for his visitor. All disagreements, he insisted, could be worked out with patience and goodwill. Marshall felt he could see through this seeming reasonableness. While negotiations continued, Europe's crisis would deepen and Soviet opportunities to make trouble would increase. Kennan's assessment was even more dire. The Russians, he warned, "feel . . . that Europe is in reality theirs, although Europe may not know it."[10]

Europe falling apart, the Russians poised to pick up the pieces—all this was disturbing enough, but American policy makers were anxious about a third part of the picture too. Was their own country fit for the large role that history had seemingly assigned to it? Acheson had been brooding on this problem for some time. He addressed it in late 1945, in remarks to the Maryland Historical Society, saying that the American people's views about foreign policy could be reduced to three short and simple sentences: "1. Bring the boys home. 2. Don't be a Santa Claus. 3. Don't be pushed around." He repeated his doubts about American staying power when he addressed the Harvard Club in Boston in June 1946: "We have got to understand that all our lives the danger, the uncertainty, the need for alertness, for effort, for discipline will be upon us. This is new to us. It will be hard for us."[11]

Acheson voiced the same concern again in February 1947, on the very day that he briefed Marshall about the need for aid to Greece and Turkey. "This hits us too soon," he worried over lunch, "before we are ready for it." As of January, Congress had had a Republican majority for the first time in fourteen years. Its first order of business had been to vote a tax cut; Acheson doubted that Republicans, in their present mood, would embrace foreign aid. Even the president's party had its reservations. As word spread that the administration was considering new commitments in the eastern Mediterranean, members of the Democratic Congressional Conference sent word that they did not want to prop up either the British or the Greek monarchy.[12]

In the late 1940s, Americans with a strong internationalist outlook on foreign policy tended to share Acheson's unease about their country's readiness for new international responsibilities. Some, of course, welcomed the challenge. It would, George Kennan believed, subject Americans to a valuable "test of national quality." To pass it, they would have to overcome the skepticism of many foreign governments, friend and foe alike. One of the reasons, Kennan suspected, that Stalin and his colleagues were so confident of being able to dominate postwar Europe was their scorn for America. The Russians doubted (and Kennan clearly shared the doubt) that the United States would "be able to muster, as a nation, the leadership, the imagination, the political skill, the material resources, and above all the national self-discipline necessary" to manage the process of global recovery. Kennan worried that countries threatened by Soviet power had the same doubt about America, that they were "skeptical as to our mastery of our own fate and our ability to cope with the responsibilities of national greatness."[13]

Kennan and Acheson were soon at odds over how to handle this new vocation. But they and other policy makers agreed that it could not be rejected. "Today," Kennan wrote, "we Americans stand as a lonely, threatened power on the field of world history." Standing apart from others would only increase the danger ahead. "We would be placing ourselves in the position of a lonely country, culturally and politically. To maintain confidence in our own traditions and institutions we would henceforth have to whistle loudly in the dark. I am not sure that whistling could be loud enough to do the trick."[14]

THESE THREE INTERLOCKING ANXIETIES—about Europe's viability, Russia's aims, and America's fitness—left Harry Truman and his advisers feeling they were in a deep hole in the spring of 1947. And unless the United States acted soon, it might find itself in a far deeper one, with the world's major industrial centers falling inexorably under Soviet control. Washington, Kennan feared, had "already delayed too long." A shy and cerebral man, he disdained hot political rhetoric, but others were less cautious. Complacent democracies, it was widely thought, needed a jolt in order to recognize danger. Will Clayton expressed a common sentiment when he argued that the president simply had to "shock the country."[15] The sharp ideological edge of Truman's March address to Congress, asking for economic and military aid to Greece and Turkey, showed how the administration would apply this shock. A global struggle was under way, and "the free peoples of the world," said the president, "look to us for support in maintaining their freedoms." He did not single out the Soviet Union as the threat to American security, or even refer to Communism as such, but his meaning was unmistakable. Marshall worried that the speech, while not naming names, might be too strident. Reacting to a draft sent to him in Europe for his comments, he passed back a mild caution about its "flamboyant anti-Communism."[16]

The secretary of state's advice was ignored. Truman, who expected his proposals to require "the greatest selling job ever," later wrote that he wanted "no hedging in this speech." Marshall, in any case, soon showed he could use strong rhetoric too. When he returned from his marathon meetings in Moscow at the end of April, his own vocabulary was at least as fierce as the president's and his accusations were much more explicitly anti-Soviet. Moscow's proposals, Marshall said in a nationwide radio address, were clearly "adapted to the seizure of absolute control." They could only lead to "dictatorship and strife."[17]

As Truman and his advisers gauged the public response to such rhetoric, they were clearly encouraged to make their portrait of a predatory adversary ever more lurid. But they did not overstate their assessment of Soviet strength nearly as much as they understated their assessment of Europe's weakness. And that judgment they did not share with the American people at all.

History, culture, and popular attitudes put such a burden on European governments, American officials believed, that they were likely to waste much of the aid they received. The idea at the heart of Marshall's Harvard speech—that Europeans should first consult among themselves and prepare a request for assistance—reflected a suspicion that unless obliged to work together, they would produce padded, duplicative, and contradictory proposals. Aid offered on this basis would only perpetuate Europe's rivalrous parochialisms—and its dependence on the United States.

The State Department officials who outlined a European assistance program for Marshall agreed that success was possible only if the Old World adopted a new framework. America's goal, one argued, had to be to get "Europe on its feet and off our back." This would never happen, wrote Undersecretary Clayton, as long as Europe's economy "continues to be divided into many small watertight compartments as it is today." Kennan insisted that the United States had to "*force* the Europeans to begin to think like Europeans, and not like nationalists."[18]

America's task, in other words, was not merely to help Europe but to change it. The job called for great sternness, even with close friends. The Europeans, Kennan stressed, had to see that the United States would not help them unless it was confident that the plan they came up with would do "the whole job." This was their last chance: there could be no further requests. European governments had to agree, explicitly and in advance, to American terms for using assistance "carefully and economically." For someone schooled in European history, deeply sympathetic to European culture and traditions, and acutely conscious of the scale of Europe's problems, Kennan's words bristled with anger. "If the peoples of Western Europe," he wrote, "were to reject American aid on those terms, then that in itself would be equivalent to a final vote for Russian domination."[19]

When Marshall told his Harvard audience that a large assistance effort had to offer the prospect of a "cure rather than a mere palliative," his words were meant as a challenge to European governments. But regular scoldings and rigid ultimatums might not be enough to get Europeans to change their ways. To make assistance work, American officials were convinced that they would have to control it themselves. In interagency meetings before Marshall's speech, Acheson had concluded that Europe's role would be somewhat less than publicly advertised. A request for help, he felt, should "come . . . *or appear to come*—from Europe." But appearance was not reality. The responses to Marshall's speech, acknowledged

Robert Murphy, the senior American diplomat in Germany at the time, "were not quite as spontaneous as they were made to seem." In all the planning memos and documents, the one sentence that seemed to make the greatest impression on Acheson—he italicized it and cited it twice, with enthusiasm, in his memoirs—was the last line of Will Clayton's May trip report: "*The United States must run this show.*"[20]

Acheson had already made it clear, when he oversaw preparation of the Greek-Turkish aid package, that he did not want multilateral institutions involved in any way in implementing American policy. Through nine drafts of Truman's March speech to Congress, he had crossed out all references to the United Nations until he found language sufficiently meaningless that he could live with it. In May he accepted an amendment from Senator Arthur Vandenberg—which envisioned the termination of U.S. aid once the UN was able to take responsibility for it—only because he was absolutely sure this could never happen. Acheson was not alone in seeing large multilateral mechanisms as unlikely to advance American interests. Even Kennan (who favored disbursing European aid through the UN) called the idea of peace through international institutions a "grandiose form of day-dreaming."[21]

Because so many more countries had to be involved, American officials considered multilateral waste and inefficiency as an even bigger problem for the Marshall Plan than they had been for the Truman Doctrine. Clayton warned Acheson that "we must avoid getting into another UNRRA." The UN relief agency (whose establishment Acheson, then serving as assistant secretary of state for economic affairs, had himself negotiated during the war) had cared for millions of people in the war's aftermath. But what American officials remembered—and resented—was not the humanitarian success story. It was the reports of "taxpayer dollars" benefiting new Communist regimes in Yugoslavia, Romania, and elsewhere. If this happened again, it would discredit the entire idea of aid.[22]

Convincing Congress that the U.S. government could avoid a repetition of the UNRRA pattern would not be easy. In an early memorandum for Robert Lovett (who succeeded Acheson as Marshall's number two in midsummer 1947), Kennan admitted that the design of the effort was moving slowly. About the Marshall Plan, the memo said simply, "We have no plan." It was a "rather embarrassing situation," recalled Paul Nitze, who had been recruited by Kennan to work on the aid program, later becoming his deputy and then his successor as director of the Policy Planning Staff. To win support for the effort, Marshall himself insisted on a four-year time limit for disbursing aid. Congress would never vote for anything big that it feared might last forever. As to how much everything was going to cost, Nitze admitted that no one had any idea. All he could say was, "[We] knew it would be expensive."[23]

Because so much money was under discussion, American policy makers were immensely relieved when Stalin ordered all Eastern European diplomats to pull out of the assistance talks. Marshall's offer of Europe-wide aid without invidious ideological distinctions had been intended to make his proposal look statesmanlike, not to be accepted. Even so, Soviet withdrawal left the far harder problem still unsolved—how to get Western European governments to come up with a workable proposal. To make sure that their requests were not "out of line" with what the United States could support, Washington supervised their consultations closely. Officials from participating European countries were summoned to a late summer conference in Paris to finalize their ideas, at which Clayton and others exhorted them to be practical.[24]

Kennan, who also attended the meeting, was depressed by what he saw. Successful European cooperation now seemed almost inconceivable to him. The delegates to the conference could hardly create a consensus any stronger "than the political and psychological fabric of the war-torn, fear-wracked, confused and maladjusted" countries they represented. Britain's situation Kennan found particularly desperate—"tragic to a point that challenges description." He predicted that its policies would, as a result, be "unrealistic, erratic, slap-happy." France too was "deteriorating with terrifying rapidity."

How then was Europe—in its desperate state—going to fashion a credible proposal? For Kennan, the answer was obvious. The United States, he recommended, would have to "decide unilaterally" on a plan to present to Congress. "This would mean that we would listen to all that the Europeans had to say, but in the end we would not *ask* them, we would just *tell* them what they would get."[25]

And that was more or less what happened. European consultation yielded a request for $28 billion. Under American review, this was pared to $17 billion before being presented to Congress in December 1947. Almost a year passed between Marshall's Harvard speech and final congressional passage. (In the interim, almost $600 million in emergency relief was approved.) The $13 billion that was eventually paid out was less than half the European proposal, but it proved adequate. In the four years of the Marshall Plan, Western European GDP growth was 30 percent. The key problem that it was designed to address—the fact that Europe's economies could not produce enough for export to buy the goods that fed its people and kept its industry working—all but disappeared. In just three years German exports grew sixfold. The European trade deficit with the United States—$8.5 billion in 1947—shrank to $1 billion in 1950.[26]

The praise and acclaim for American aid, and for the visionary generosity behind it, have never let up. Marshall himself applauded Congress's vote to fund the plan as "an historic step in the foreign policy of this country." For Winston Churchill, it was "a turning point in the history of the world." Georges Bidault declared that history knew no "finer, more far-sighted gesture." Sixty years after the aid began to flow, an admiring reexamination of the effort carried the title *The Most Noble Adventure.*[27]

But the most telling judgment about the Marshall Plan's impact on American foreign policy was the one passed on it at the time by Joseph Jones, a member of Acheson's staff, who described the emergence of the program in *The Fifteen Weeks,* for years the definitive study. Success, he concluded, showed "not the limits but the *infinite possibilities of influencing the policies, attitudes, and actions of other countries* by statesmanship in Washington."Anxious as they were about their own country's fitness for a global role, and deeply skeptical of what others might contribute, American policy makers were discovering how much could be accomplished if they ran the show.[28]

IN 1947 THE UNITED STATES HAD—through policies of security assistance, economic recovery, and German reconstruction—made clear that it would put its power, resources, and determination behind an effort to "contain" the Soviet Union. To do so, it had paid attention to the most conspicuous and worrisome vulnerabilities of "the free nations" (a phrase beginning to come into widespread usage). American policy sought to overcome these weaknesses, by creating what Acheson called "situations of strength"—a new strategy that commanded strong support in both the United States and Western Europe. But neither the policy makers nor the publics on either side of the Atlantic had yet coped with the rigors of Soviet retaliation. In the year after the Marshall Plan began, Stalin did retaliate, and the tensions he created subjected America's new strategy to its first and most demanding Cold War test.[29]

In answering the challenge of "containment," the Soviet Union exploited the many levers and pressure points available to it. In September 1947 it established the Cominform as a latter-day reincarnation of the Comintern, reasserting the unity and centralization of the international Communist movement. Moscow directed Western European Communist parties to abandon the coalition governments of which they had been members. The result was social and political polarization in key Western countries, especially France and Italy. Walter Bedell Smith, the American ambassador in Moscow, charged that the Soviet Union had "declared war on European recovery." By bringing down the democratic government of Czechoslovakia through a Communist coup in February 1948, Stalin demonstrated that vulnerable governments of Eastern Europe could be brought to heel. Finally, in trying to choke off Western access to Berlin in June, he brought international tensions to their highest level since the war.[30]

All these actions made 1948 utterly different from the year before. In 1947 the dominant American fear had been of economic unraveling and social disintegration. This now gave way to fear of active subversion and military confrontation. Shaken by Stalin's counterchallenge, Western governments began to focus on creating institutions and policies of collective defense. On March 17, just weeks after the Czech coup, Britain, France, and the Benelux countries formed the Western Union. By prearrangement, Truman addressed Congress on the same day, associating the United States with the new grouping. In June, Congress adopted the so-called Vandenberg resolution, which formally endorsed the idea of American participation in a regional security pact covering Western Europe. These steps, taken in an atmosphere of crisis in 1948, laid the groundwork for the formation of the North Atlantic alliance in 1949. Having withstood Soviet pressure in 1948, the Western occupying powers were also able to go forward with the revival of the German economy and the restoration of German self-government, steps that led to the creation of the West German state in 1949.[31]

Many decades later, these results remain remarkable achievements. Much more than the Marshall Plan, they were the political and military initiatives that defined and sustained Western strategy through four decades of Cold War. They are all the more remarkable because they were not, as often remembered, the product of a strong and unshakable consensus. How the United States should cope with the new tensions of 1948 was in fact a matter of ongoing dispute within the American foreign policy establishment. It was not just the far left and the isolationist right that were unhappy with containment; the Truman administration was itself deeply divided. To achieve the results he did, the president had to ignore the analysis of some of his leading diplomatic experts, override the near-unanimous objections of his highest-ranking military officers, and brush aside the preferences of America's uneasy allies.

No dissent from the containment strategy of 1948 was more vehement than that of the man who had authored the term in 1947, George Kennan himself. His much-discussed *Foreign Affairs* article, "The Sources of Soviet Conduct," had—despite the use of a pseudonym, "X"—made him a genuine policy celebrity, better known than many higher-ranking officials. In subsequent decades, Kennan complained that containment had over time been understood and implemented in too narrowly military terms. In fact, however, his disenchantment with the direction of policy happened almost immediately and had nothing to do with a misinterpretation of the concept. It was a disagreement about the facts. The State Department's best-informed and most brilliant Soviet expert believed that there was no real Soviet military threat to speak of. There was, in turn, no need to do anything about it.

The same Kennan who had in 1947 been highly sensitive to the distress of European leaders and publics now, just one year later, found their anxieties "a little silly." There was, he thought, "nothing unexpected, nothing out of the ordinary, in any of the Communist behavior—the strikes in France and Italy, the Czech coup and the Berlin blockade—that caused so much alarm in the Western capitals." He claimed to have seen it all coming, said he had told Marshall to expect it, and even considered it an unpleasant, backhanded acknowledgment of Washington's success. The West had simply mustered more unity of purpose than Stalin expected. The result was a completely predictable "baring of the fangs" by Moscow, to which the West did not have to bother responding. End of story, he seemed to say.[32]

Kennan admitted to an instinctive unease with the influence of democratic politics on the policy making of trained professionals. For him, a danger privately anticipated by the experts should not have alarmed the public once it materialized. In explaining why he thought a full-blown alliance or even American security guarantees for Western Europe were unnecessary, he frequently compared the situation of Western societies to that of someone cornered by a dog with very sharp teeth. The sensible thing to do in such a case, he argued, was to tell Soviet leaders that "teeth have nothing whatever to do with our mutual relationship." Kennan did not make clear whether this strategy had ever helped him deal with an actual dog. But he was convinced that Moscow's teeth—meaning Soviet military power—could safely be dismissed as "neither here nor there." It was the Soviets, he insisted, who were "overextended."[33]

THE IDEA THAT the United States could ignore Soviet military capabilities was held, Acheson later recalled, by "some liberals and some Kremlinologists." The State Department's leading Soviet hands—not just Kennan but also Charles ("Chip") Bohlen, later ambassador to Moscow—tended to downplay the risk of a full blockade of Berlin. "The real threat, they said, lay in the weakness of the West European social, economic, and political structure." Correct that, and the Russian danger would disappear. "This," Acheson declared, "I did not believe."[34]

Nor did many others in the Truman administration. In 1948 Europe was in the middle of a yearlong, on-again-off-again "war scare" (a "dither," in Kennan's view), and in considering how to respond, Washington did not take its cue from its regional specialists. Lovett, who served as Marshall's deputy for a year and a half while Acheson was back in private practice, rejected the idea of doing nothing. The United States had already tried the strategy of what he called "peace through weakness" (a surprisingly harsh summary of the Truman administration's strategy between 1945 and 1947). Now the goal was "to deter aggression by proof of determination. For him, the "only question" was how this determination should be proved.[35]

Lovett answered his own question by seeking the support of Senator Arthur Vandenberg for a congressional resolution that endorsed the idea of a transatlantic alliance. This successful collaboration between a Democratic administration and a Republican Congress has ever since been treated as a classic instance of foreign policy bipartisanship. But Kennan took no satisfaction in what Lovett had done. It made him "very unhappy."[36]

The increased international tensions of 1948 also brought to the surface disagreements between Truman and the professional military. When in late March the Soviet occupation authorities first obstructed deliveries of food, fuel, and other goods to West Berlin, the resulting confrontation—lasting only two weeks—was no more than a foretaste of the later blockade. But the episode persuaded generals in Washington that the time was right to begin a unilateral withdrawal from Berlin. General Omar Bradley, the army chief of staff, suggested that by pulling out of Berlin voluntarily, the United States would be able to "minimize the loss of prestige" that a forced retreat would entail.[37]

For Truman, this was unthinkable. When the Soviets imposed a full blockade in June, cutting off both rail and truck supplies, he fully backed his senior representative in Germany, General Lucius Clay, against the Pentagon brass. We are "going to stay, period," the president told his advisers. The generals in Washington were undeterred. Bradley insisted that a long-term airlift to keep West Berlin going was simply not "feasible." His colleague, General Hoyt Vandenberg, the air force chief of staff, objected to diverting the large numbers of aircraft necessary to supply the city. As a group, the chiefs again suggested that some way be found to pull out "without undue loss of prestige."[38]

Such counsels irritated Truman. (To his wife, he complained about the useless performance of his "muttonhead Secretary of the Army.") Ignoring Pentagon recommendations, he approved Clay's request to enlarge the airlift. Deploying nuclear-capable B-29 bombers to airfields in Great Britain, he reminded Stalin who had the bomb. For Truman, there was no point in worrying about spreading American power too thin to deal with some hypothetical future contingency—not when the immediate threat was so serious. Yet the generals remained unhappy. The operation, they felt, risked planes that would be vitally important in the event of all-out war. In October, just weeks ahead of the 1948 presidential election, the chiefs tried again to put the president on the spot. Privately, they challenged Truman to declare that the defense of Berlin was so important that all-out preparations for war should be authorized. If, however, holding on to this isolated outpost in the middle of the Soviet occupation zone was *not* that important, then the United States should begin to find a way to get out.

Easily dodging the generals' trap, Truman accepted neither of their options. He was willing to pay the price of East-West confrontation in increased tension with Moscow but not in increased spending. And with an election at hand, he was not prepared to alarm the voters with new talk of war, no matter what the military wanted. In his memoirs, General Bradley called the president's decision "outrageous."[39]

Apart from setting Truman against the military and diplomatic professionals, the Berlin blockade and airlift also produced the most emotional disagreements since the war, between the United States, on the one hand, and Britain and France, on the other. American officials had hoped that the lure of Marshall Plan aid would take the edge off French opposition to rebuilding Germany—and it did, at least in part. When the American, British, and French foreign ministers met in early 1948, they agreed on an economic plan for their German zones, which also included proposals for increased German self-government. The French, however, rejected the details of the plan, and through the spring fought against implementing it. The rising fear of war actually gave French officials a new argument against speeding up German reconstruction. There was no telling, they said, how the Soviet Union might respond to such provocations. Having proposed steps that Moscow angrily opposed, the United States should explain how it would deal with violent Soviet countermeasures.[40]

These were not small disagreements. In early 1948 American policy makers saw no way to revive the West German economy except by creating real money. Without it, inflation and the black market would rule supreme. (The price of a carton of Lucky Strikes—the surrogate currency of the occupation—reached $2,300 at midyear.) Still the French resisted—and did so until the United States resolved the disagreement by calling their bluff. The currency reform, Washington now informed Paris, would go ahead in the unified Anglo-American zone, no matter what the French did in their own zone. New banknotes were secretly printed and prepositioned in Frankfurt. On the eve of the announcement of the new currency, the French Chamber of Deputies—threatened with a cutoff of Marshall Plan funds—yielded and embraced American policy.[41]

Before the Berlin blockade, the French were the main source of Western disunity. Once the Soviets actually cut off ground access to the city, the British also began to wobble. Foreign Secretary Ernest Bevin's public rhetoric was firm, but a month into the crisis—working on comparatively routine issues like the precise language of diplomatic approaches to Moscow—American officials found his ideas "redolent with appeasement." The U.S. ambassador in London, Lewis Douglas, gently reassured his anxious Washington colleagues that Bevin was simply trying to "maintain a united front" with "a fearful and bankrupt France." But Marshall's own contacts suggested that the British themselves were also fearful. Bevin, he said, "kept referring constantly to the fact that 'they were in the front line.' " On his return from Europe after an October visit, Marshall told Truman and others that he found all the Western Europeans "completely out of their skins, and sitting on their nerves."[42]

Before and during the blockade, both the British and the French remained aware of their critical dependence on American military power. But dependence did not by any means give them confidence that the United States would use its power wisely. And it did not make them willing to defer to Washington. To the contrary, Chip Bohlen, who had been dispatched to Europe early in the crisis to calm allied opinion, found the Europeans convinced that the United States was "hell-bent for war." It was hard to persuade them otherwise. Even Bevin suspected the worst of Washington. "I know all you Americans want a war," he blurted out to Bohlen, "but I'm not going to let you 'ave it."[43]

DESPITE SUCH DIVISIONS—and despite the doubts of senior American diplomats and military officers—the West emerged from the Berlin blockade almost completely victorious. By January 1949, Stalin was hinting that he was ready to back down, and by May 11, trains and trucks were again bringing the city food, fuel, and other supplies. The months of confrontation had been costly for Soviet diplomacy. Even as the Red Army held Berlin hostage, Western governments had put in place the policies and institutions that would guide them for decades.[44]

Stalin did salvage one tiny, face-saving scrap from the standoff: Western agreement to hold yet another meeting of the foreign ministers of the Big Four for yet another discussion of Germany. But even this "conference"—a tedious month-long affair in Paris—proved to be a further humiliation for Moscow. Before leaving Washington for the meetings, Dean Acheson, whom Truman had picked to replace the ailing Marshall as secretary in January 1949, told the press that if he found the Soviets uncooperative, he would simply "pack up [his] marbles and go home." Sure, German reunification would be nice if it could be achieved on Western terms. If not, he said, well, "to hell with it."

Acheson's odd, taunting rhetoric made no concession whatever to diplomatic niceties on the eve of a major negotiation. And he did not let up in the conference that followed. For four weeks in May and June 1949, the Soviet foreign minister and his delegation heard a united Western position so unyielding that there was nothing to talk about. Enjoying the spectacle, Truman told a cabinet meeting, "It looks like Dean has got Mr. Vyshinsky on the run."[45]

American policy was now harvesting the results of its activism the previous two years. Having first devised a strategy for restabilizing Western

Europe, and having then stood fast against Soviet retaliation, Truman and Acheson were—as the secretary of state's braggadocio suggested—no longer even pretending to seek compromise.

For George Kennan, all this was deeply distasteful. The division of the continent that was taking shape he considered neither sustainable nor desirable. It would be far better to find a compromise formula that allowed German reunification on acceptable terms and undermined Soviet control of Eastern Europe. While the Berlin blockade was still under way, and East-West tensions were still at their peak, he had therefore begun to think through an alternative diplomatic strategy that might be pursued when the crisis was finally over. The plan that he came up with, a scheme known internally as Program A, was the first significant proposal to end the Cold War by negotiation. It never had much chance of becoming official policy, but its rejection—just as Acheson was reimmersing himself in the complexities of East-West diplomacy—made the premises of American strategy clearer than ever.

Program A was a sober, balanced, well-thought-out effort to call off the East-West confrontation in Europe. It provided for an end to the occupation of Germany, both East and West. Foreign forces would withdraw (in the case of the United States, to coastal enclaves from which they could easily return in the event of trouble). Germany would be unified, neutralized, and demilitarized. Eastern European states would regain their autonomy.

In Kennan's mind, the main advantage of the plan was that it would end the "abnormal political-military responsibility" that the United States had assumed for the security of Western Europe. To him, everything about this outsize role was wrong—and unlikely to last. Indefinite "paternal tutelage" would eventually be rejected by the Germans. It sapped the national will of the British and French. And it called on the United States to perform a role for which it was ill suited. Far better, he argued, would be an agreement with Moscow that would leave "large areas" of the world—including both Germany and Japan—"uncommitted as between the two worlds." Soviet receptiveness to such arrangements could not be known for certain, but Kennan was hopeful. "A readiness on our side to withdraw would," he conjectured, "eventually stimulate a disposition on the Soviet side to do likewise."[46]

In Western Europe, Kennan knew, such ideas were anathema—a warning sign of American fickleness and a step toward the revival of an independent and dangerous Germany. When French officials heard of Program A—and related proposals on which he worked during the remainder of the year—they "reared up like a frightened horse." Such reactions, Kennan recollected,

> filled me with impatience. What in the world did they think we had been doing in Europe these last four or five years? . . . What did they suppose the Marshall Plan was all about? Could they not see that we were well aware of the real dangers with which Western Europe was faced and that we were acting, as generously and effectively as we could, to combat them?[47]

In his irritation with European governments, Kennan thought that the right answer was to challenge them to develop their own strategy. "This is our best suggestion," he wanted to tell them, "if you don't like it, it is up to you to name the alternative . . . ; the main responsibility is now yours." Because he felt that negotiated solutions would at some point become possible, he opposed Western actions that he felt would prevent serious bargaining with Moscow. Among such actions, he included the formation of a West German state and even the formation of NATO—the two most significant Western successes in withstanding Soviet pressures.[48]

Acheson was first exposed to Program A as he prepared for the foreign ministers' meeting in Paris. He was impressed by Kennan's presentation and thought it deserved "the most careful study." The characteristic elegance of the proposal was one part of its appeal. (Kennan's writing, the secretary of state once observed, had a "sad lyrical beauty about it which drugs the mind.") More important, Acheson and Kennan shared a keen appreciation of Europe's weakness. But they disagreed completely on what to do about it.[49]

In Kennan's view, the decline of the Western European powers argued for a strategy that would shake them out of their abject dependence on the United States. To Acheson, Europe's weakness simply increased the risk of what he called "settlements by default"—the slow accommodation of demoralized governments and societies to Soviet military superiority. To avert this, there must be no doubt about American commitment. "The threat to Western Europe," he wrote in *Present at the Creation,* "seemed to me singularly like that which Islam had posed centuries before, with its combination of ideological zeal and fighting power." Then, Europe had prevailed through a "great outburst of military power and social organization." But "this time it would need the added power and energy of America."[50]

Facing such an adversary, Acheson was not ready to offer up two of the world's most advanced societies—the defeated powers of the war just past—as "uncommitted" areas. "Western Europe and the United States," he believed, "could not contain"—here Acheson used Kennan's own word against him—"the Soviet Union and suppress Germany and Japan at the same time. Our best hope was to make these former enemies willing and strong supporters of a free-world structure." The "structure" that he envisioned would not be, as Kennan seemed to imagine, some copy of an earlier European balance of power but a united front firmly led by the United States. This goal would surely be endangered by offering to negotiate the status of Germany and Japan. It could only be realized by the most stubborn and unyielding American policy. Kennan wanted these issues on the table so that they were ready to be discussed. Acheson wanted them off the table so that they would never be compromised.[51]

Kennan and Acheson's disagreement defined two antithetical approaches to dealing with America's principal adversary. At the very moment when the Soviets had thrown in the towel and ended the Berlin airlift, Kennan wanted to pursue a complex design that might over time allow Moscow to recoup its losses. He conceived of the Cold War as a temporary spike of tension, which could be kept from becoming permanent by the right diplomatic compromises. The purpose of containment was, as he put it, to "tide us over" until these compromises could be achieved. (Years later Henry Kissinger expressed his agreement with Kennan. "We lost our opportunity.")[52]

When Acheson sat down with his British and French colleagues to frame a common position on the future of Germany before the "face-saving" conference in Paris, compromise was the furthest thing from their minds. Offering Moscow absolutely nothing, they put forward a self-confident, even aggressive plan for reunification. East Germany was to be governed by the West German constitution, reparations were to stop, and four-power decisions would henceforth be made by majority vote (in which the Soviets would, of course, always be outnumbered). This package offered the Soviets so little that when the American delegation caucused before the first meeting at the Palais Rose, a leading member of the team that had come to Paris actually criticized it as much too one-sided to be credible. The dissenter: John Foster Dulles, who four years later succeeded Acheson as secretary of state. He participated in the Paris conference as an outside consultant and symbol of bipartisanship.

If the U.S. position was too one-sided for John Foster Dulles, of course, there was not much chance that Joseph Stalin would find it worth discussing. But that was Acheson's point. Agreement with Moscow was not the goal of American policy in 1949. If anything, signs of hesitation in Soviet policy were a reason to make Western diplomacy more demanding. As for Dulles, once he saw how unreasonable the Soviet position was, and how easily—effortlessly, really—the British and French could be persuaded to support the toughest U.S. line, he sheepishly asked that his earlier objections be struck from the American delegation's records.[53]

Several months later Acheson spoke at Berkeley about the international situation and American strategy, and he used the occasion to explain how he thought negotiations with the Soviet Union might eventually become meaningful. The list of ten conditions that he set out—beginning with German reunification and free elections and ending with a cessation of Soviet propaganda—demanded even more than the allies' package had in Paris the previous spring. Critics said the speech showed that the United States was asking Moscow to surrender—a criticism that was not so much wrong as, to Acheson's mind, irrelevant. "I see no evidence," he told his Berkeley audience, "that the Soviet leaders will change their conduct until the progress of the Free World convinces them that they cannot profit from a continuation of these tensions."[54]

IN THE MIDDLE OF 1949, Harry Truman and his advisers were entitled to look back with satisfaction on the previous two years. They had shown what the president (praising Acheson) called "a genius for bold design." In place of an ad hoc, case-by-case opposition to Soviet policy, they had developed a more comprehensive and focused strategy. The United States had pulled Europe back from the brink of economic collapse, established an alliance structure for Western collective defense, and moved steadily toward rehabilitating West Germany as a core ally. This was an impressive record of achievement by any standard but especially when measured against the trio of anxieties that had burdened policy makers just two years earlier: fear of dysfunction at all levels of European society, fear of the Soviet Union's ability to exploit these weaknesses, and fear of America's inexperience as a global leader.[55]

Success had hardly made these anxieties disappear. In 1949 American policy makers still disdained Europe's weakness and still worried that the Soviet Union had fundamental advantages in its competition with the West. They still saw their own traditions as obstacles to effective policy and still believed their country was "not ready" for its large new role.

Yet the president and his advisers had also begun to discover what "the added power and energy of America" could accomplish. It allowed them to develop a maximalist strategy that scorned halfway measures in favor of doing "the whole job." It emboldened them to ride out Soviet pressures and rising tensions, to override allied doubts and internal division. Truman, Marshall, Acheson, and others saw they could push their own preferences and policies forward without yielding anything to the other side. Nothing did more to shape American foreign policy in the years that followed than the well-learned lessons of this success.

2

Truman at War

"VICTORY IS A STRONG MAGNET"

General MacArthur and President Truman

AT THREE IN THE MORNING on May 22, 1949, James Forrestal, whom Harry Truman had picked two years earlier to be the first secretary of defense, threw himself from the sixteenth floor of the Bethesda Naval Hospital outside Washington. A day later the foreign ministers of the Big Four sat down to discuss Germany at the Palais Rose in Paris. By the time it was over, the Paris conference offered abundant proof of the success of American diplomacy. The president was delighted with the results and greeted the returning Acheson at the airport with an enthusiastic "Well done!" Forrestal's suicide, by contrast, was a reminder of problems that Truman almost always handled badly: the management of America's defense establishment, its use as an instrument of policy, and the growing cost of fighting the Cold War.[1]

The Truman administration's internal battles over military issues climaxed in a near-disaster for U.S. forces halfway around the world, putting the president's entire foreign policy at risk. But they started as something more mundane—a fight about money. Forrestal had taken a leading part in the Pentagon's long dispute with Truman over the defense budget, which continued to escalate after the president removed him in March 1949. The so-called revolt of the admirals showed that the new secretary, Louis Johnson, could not manage the military either. He spent barely a year on the job trying to cut spending before war in Korea made the entire effort irrelevant. By September 1950, Johnson was also fired. And worse was ahead. Truman was challenged next by the legendary general who was running the war. "Mr. Prima Donna, Brass Hat, Five Star MacArthur," the president had called his antagonist—"a play actor" and a "bunco man." In April 1951, Douglas MacArthur was fired too.[2]

Forrestal, Johnson, and MacArthur were among the strangest people ever to hold high positions of military authority in the U.S. government. Omar Bradley, who served under Forrestal as army chief of staff, described him as "reclusive, brooding," "shy, introverted," a man of "cold intensity." Truman went to the other extreme in picking Johnson, a political crony who had served as his finance chairman in the 1948 campaign. With this choice, the president had, in Bradley's view, "unwittingly . . . replaced one mental case with another." As for MacArthur, his personal impact on the Korean War is captured in two words that dot Dean Acheson's retelling of the story: "manic" and "depressive."[3]

FOR ALL THESE PATHOLOGIES and quirks, Truman's real problems at the Pentagon were not psychiatric. His goals simply conflicted with one another. Fiscal prudence, personal preference, and partisan politics all led him to favor a small defense budget. "No military man," he fulminated, "knows anything at all about money. All they know is how to spend it, and they don't give a damn whether they're getting their money's worth or not." Even so, Truman wanted to marry tight spending to an extremely ambitious foreign policy. He sought to assist allies, deter adversaries, and enlarge American influence, all without enlarging the armed forces.[4]

For Omar Bradley, these impulses—a smaller budget but a bigger policy—meant that the administration's strategy didn't add up. "No one," he argued,

> had fully thought through [containment's] long-term military implications. Getting tough with the Russians, holding them in check around the globe, fighting fire with fire, clearly demanded a concurrent buildup of our conventional military forces, especially the U.S. Army. It may seem hard to believe, but exactly the opposite was taking place.

By 1948, with the Cold War escalating, Bradley found that tight budgets had "reduced the Army to a shockingly deplorable state." Two years later, when American forces were called on to fight in Korea, their condition was—as General Matthew Ridgway, MacArthur's successor, put it—one of "shameful unreadiness."[5]

When he became secretary of defense in 1947, Forrestal had accepted a tight military budget. Keeping spending low made it easier to fund the Marshall Plan and help Europe rebuild. But the deepening Cold War changed his mind. In pushing for more resources, he expressed a consensus of the nation's leading military figures. In a February 1948 memo, written just before he retired from the army to become president of Columbia University, Dwight Eisenhower warned Forrestal that postwar demobilization had gone too far. Without a reversal, he argued, the

United States would have to abandon Europe and the Far East "to chaos and communism." That same month Secretary of State Marshall worried to the cabinet that "we are playing with fire while we have nothing with which to put it out."[6]

Energized by the "war scare" that followed the Czech coup of February 1948, Truman responded favorably to these appeals. He asked Congress to increase the Pentagon's budget above the $10 billion already requested. (The 2012 equivalent: approximately $100 billion.) He called for universal military training and a reinstatement of the draft. When the Berlin blockade further raised fears of Soviet aims, the president asked for money to help European governments strengthen their armed forces.

But if Truman was always ready to give the military a budgetary boost in time of crisis, he usually backtracked once tensions eased. The $3.5 billion increase for defense that he approved when war fears peaked in February 1948 (the joint chiefs told him they really needed $9 billion more) was trimmed to just $2.5 billion in May. Telling his advisers he actually preferred $1.5 billion, the president said he would approve no more increases for at least two years. By the fall he was again talking about cuts. Before the November election, he publicly expressed the hope that improvements in the international situation would allow reductions in defense spending of $5 billion to $7 billion—a cut of roughly 50 percent.[7]

Forrestal knew how hard it would be to change the president's mind. In October he had privately advised Truman that after the election he would send him two budgets. The first would fit under the president's $14.4 billion cap, while the second—perhaps $4 billion higher—would reverse cuts in manpower and, in the event of war, give the United States military options other than an all-out nuclear attack on the Soviet Union. Truman had a blunt answer. He did not want to see the second budget. Even considering it "would be interpreted as a step toward preparation for war."[8]

When Forrestal told the chiefs what Truman had said, they squeezed him just as much as the president had, informing the secretary of defense that they "could agree on no program within the $14.4 billion limit." What followed was, in Bradley's words, a process of "bloody committee combat." Forrestal begged the chiefs not to reject Truman's budget outright but to help him show the president how little "usable military power" it would buy. He believed Truman would recognize the "absurdity" of the spending cap if he were sure that "we have taken every drop of water" out of the budget. The secretary was prepared to squeeze the drops out himself, one by one. (Sailors, he ruled, did not need seven pairs of pants each; soldiers would do without new automatic rifles.)[9]

Forrestal also sought to enlist Marshall as an ally and regularly peppered the secretary of state with leading questions about whether military weakness might not lead to diplomatic "embarrassment." Knowing Truman's views, Marshall was noncommittal. No matter what question Forrestal posed, he "made no comment," suggesting only that the outlook might brighten after the coming election.[10]

Instead it darkened. After his famous surprise victory over Dewey in the 1948 election, Truman proved that his tight budget talk was no electoral pose. Forrestal, the service secretaries, the chiefs, and the senior budget officials were called before him on December 9 to review the Pentagon budget. The president politely described their presentations as "interesting" but again rejected an increase—and, as Bradley recounted, "after a mere thirty minutes dismissed the group."

Forrestal despaired, telling the chairman of the House Armed Services Committee that Truman was "a hard-money man if I ever saw one." He joked bravely about the president's buck-stops-here decision-making style. "In the person of Harry Truman," he declared, "I have seen the most rocklike example of civilian control the world has ever witnessed."

What Truman wanted, however, was not simply a defense secretary who accepted control. He wanted one who exercised it too. When the president's State of the Union message on January 5 included a tax increase but no increase for defense, a new round of warfare between the White House and the Pentagon seemed about to begin. Just three days later the secretary of the air force, Stuart Symington, openly challenged the president's budget caps, issuing a report that called for an increase in aircraft of almost 50 percent. In reply, Truman criticized Symington at his next press conference.[11]

With the president publicly battling one of Forrestal's own subordinates, it was obvious that the secretary of defense had lost control of his job. In late January Truman, who for more than two and a half months had refused to tell Forrestal whether he wanted him to stay on, finally said he didn't. But "Give 'em Hell" Harry never made such breaks cleanly. He had fired a key member of his cabinet without making a public announcement, receiving a formal resignation, or setting a departure date. (Truman's subsequent firings of Johnson and MacArthur were also slow-motion affairs.) By March, Forrestal still hadn't quit, and another White House phone call was needed to dislodge him. By the end of the day, he had resigned. By the end of March, he had left the Pentagon. By the end of April, he was in psychiatric care. A month later he was dead.[12]

JAMES FORRESTAL'S STORY had its elements of tragedy. Louis Johnson's was closer to farce. Omar Bradley considered his new boss—a "big 250-pound bear"—to be "the worst appointment Truman made during his presidency." Dean Acheson described the behavior of his new colleague as evolving over time from merely "peculiar" to completely "impossible." Others felt the same way. The president himself noted that Johnson eventually "offended every member of the cabinet." Lesser officials turned against him too. Truman's young naval aide thought Johnson "a criminal."[13]

Criminal or not, the new secretary quickly made himself the un-Forrestal. He set out, in Bradley's words, to "bash heads [and] cut budgets." In his first month on the job, he canceled the navy's prize procurement project, the long-planned "super-carrier." When the navy secretary resigned in protest, Johnson replaced him with another big campaign contributor (who publicly admitted he knew nothing about naval matters). In mid-May the secretary administered a further shock, lowering the $14.4 billion Pentagon spending cap, which Forrestal had lobbied to lift, to $13 billion. And in July—after ratification of the North Atlantic treaty, which now obliged the United States to defend ten new European allies and Canada—came Truman's announcement that he foresaw further "adjustments downward" in national security spending.[14]

The president's mandate to cut the defense budget kept Johnson in a permanent state of war with the military. Though he seemed to relish it, nothing could have prepared him for the admirals' "revolt." The most extreme struggle of its kind in the history of the American military was fought out almost entirely in public. In August 1949 senior admirals voiced their alarm at rumors of deep cuts in the number of aircraft carrier groups. Testifying before the House, the commander of the Pacific fleet, Admiral Arthur Radford, charged that Johnson's plans, which gave the air force the primary role in deterring war, would effectively "eliminate" the navy. Admiral Ralph Ofstie, the navy's man on the Atomic Energy Commission, joined in, declaring that Johnson's strategic bombing doctrine was "militarily unsound, . . . morally wrong, and . . . decidedly harmful to the stability of a postwar world." The "random mass slaughter of men, women, and children" that would result was, he said, "ruthless and barbaric" and "contrary to our fundamental ideals."[15]

Truman did not mind overheated talk about the West's vulnerability as long as someone else was blamed for it and no expensive solutions were needed. He had himself tried to shock European leaders, at the April 1949 signing of the NATO treaty, by saying that the only way the United States would be able to stop a Soviet invasion was by conducting a strategic bombing campaign—on the territory of its new allies. But the admirals were not, as the president was, demanding that Europe address its own military weakness. They wanted Harry Truman and Louis Johnson to address *America's* weakness.

When the president and the secretary of defense counterattacked, they did not spare the admirals' competence, integrity, or loyalty (or even their manliness). Their point man was Omar Bradley, who a month earlier had become the first chairman of the joint chiefs. Exploiting his reputation as a mild-mannered straight arrow, Bradley delivered blistering congressional testimony against his navy colleagues—challenging, inter alia, the professional qualifications of Admiral Louis E. Denfeld, the chief of naval operations. (Denfeld was fired a week later.) In his memoirs, Bradley denounced the admirals' conduct as "insubordinate, mutinous," "utterly disgraceful," "completely dishonest," and proof of a "crybaby attitude."[16]

Truman and Johnson had put down an internal challenge. External challenges were more difficult to manage. The fall of 1949 was marked by two events widely considered to have changed the global balance of power. American intelligence confirmed in late September that the Soviet Union had tested an atomic bomb, breaking the U.S. nuclear monopoly. Within days came a second blow, long anticipated but equally momentous: the proclamation by Mao Zedong on October 1 of the People's Republic of China. Overnight, it seemed, America's most formidable adversary—already plenty dangerous—had gained control of the world's most advanced weapons and of the most populous nation on earth.

Events of this magnitude plainly required significant policy adjustments. Although Congress had earlier halved a request for military assistance to new European allies, it now changed course and quickly approved the full amount. In Asia, the administration accelerated its preparations for a peace treaty with Japan. To keep ahead of the Soviet Union militarily, Truman also agreed to consider whether to proceed with development of the hydrogen bomb—a technological advance expected to increase the destructive potential of existing nuclear weapons a thousandfold. The president's advisers were ready to debate the issue's complex moral, military, political, and budgetary implications, but their boss had little patience—and less time—for their agonizing. At a much-anticipated meeting of the National Security Council, at which these thorny issues were to be aired, Truman had only one question: "Can the Russians do it?" Assured that they would eventually be able to build the new weapon, he signed the necessary papers and adjourned the meeting—after seven minutes.[17]

The one thing these policy adjustments did not include was a new push for a bigger defense budget. Had it been up to Truman and Johnson, that issue would not have been raised at all. But before he put down his pen, the president signed one more piece of paper, agreeing to let the State Department lead a government-wide review of national security policy. Dean Acheson wanted his boss to face up at last to James Forrestal's old question: was the United States spending enough to prevent future conflict—and enough to prevail if conflict could not be prevented? Out of the bureaucracy's examination of this question came the document that has ever since been considered the fullest expression of American strategy in the Cold War. Known as NSC-68, it once more challenged Harry Truman's idea that the United States could run a large policy on a small budget.

ACHESON ASKED PAUL NITZE, Kennan's successor as director of the State Department's planning staff, to lead the new policy review. In the years since 1975, when NSC-68 was declassified, much discussion of Nitze's report has focused on its assessment of Soviet power, which was clearly based on unrealistic assumptions. But the document's recommendations were not driven primarily by the way it saw the Soviet threat. Its drafters were more alarmed by a problem within the new Western alliance. They argued that the twentieth century's many convulsions—"two global wars of tremendous violence, . . . two revolutions—the Russian and the Chinese—of extreme scope and intensity, . . . the collapse of five empires, . . . and the drastic decline of two major imperial systems, the British and the French"—had left the major European powers unable to resume their role as linchpins of global order. Yes, American policy had restored a measure of economic stability. Even so, Nitze and his planners shared the assessment of Chip Bohlen who, on a short visit to Washington from his post at the American embassy in Paris, stopped by to offer them his views. Europe, he reported, should be seen as "a patient whom we have been treating and who we can now say will not die but who, during the convalescent period, is showing decided tendencies to drift back into its former bad habits of disunity."[18]

The same outlook had, of course, shaped American policy making in 1947. For the authors of the Truman Doctrine and Marshall Plan, the weakness of other countries was a source of growing danger for the United States. In 1950 Nitze's team came to an even grimmer conclusion. "Our friends," they declared, "will become more than a liability to us; they can eventually become a positive increment to Soviet power."[19]

This astonishing forecast was based on a psychological analysis of how Western societies might lose their resolve to resist Soviet pressure.

> The risk that we may . . . be prevented or too long delayed in taking all needful measures to maintain the integrity and vitality of our system is great. The risk that our allies will lose their determination is greater. And the risk that in this manner a descending spiral of too little and too late, of doubt and recrimination, may present us with ever narrower and more desperate alternatives, is *the greatest risk of all.*

The fear of a cascading loss of resolve drove the entire analysis of NSC-68. Nitze and his colleagues believed that "the rest of the Free World is almost certain to become demoralized." They paid particular attention to a scenario they called "withdrawal under pressure"—pressure, that is, from allies who had lost confidence in the United States and sought illusory safety in accommodation with the Soviet Union.[20]

Couldn't Washington solve this problem by getting other countries to straighten up and shoulder a larger part of the burden of preserving international order? The drafters of NSC-68 said no. At least in the short run, allies could not do much; to think otherwise was to indulge what Nitze and his staff called the "native impetuosity" of Americans—the tendency to ask too much of others with different histories, cultures, and political problems. Only the United States could relieve the current global crisis. It had to provide the "power, confidence, and a sense of moral and political direction." The twentieth century had left America alone unscathed. "This fact imposes on us, in our own interests, the responsibility of world leadership."[21]

With this declaration, NSC-68 aimed straight at a confrontation with Truman and Johnson over the budget. Nitze thought the budgetary implications ran toward tens of billions of dollars, but Acheson steered him away from cost estimates. "Don't get into that hassle at this stage," he said. As with the Marshall Plan, he first wanted a presidential green light. Haggling about the price would come later. Even so, the document openly assaulted Truman's old-fashioned spending principles. It concluded with a blunt warning about where a "hard money" national security policy might lead: "Budgetary considerations will need to be subordinated to the stark fact that our very independence as a nation may be at stake."[22]

Before sending this inflammatory document to the president, of course, Acheson had to have it out with Louis Johnson. And so, with the project well advanced, he invited the secretary of defense to the State Department on March 22, 1950, to review its conclusions in the presence of officials, from many government agencies, who had prepared the document. In a much-recounted outburst, Johnson broke up the meeting after just a few minutes, pounding the table ("scaring me out of my shoes," Acheson recalled) and shouting that the entire effort was "contrary to his orders." He stormed out of the building, declaring that he had been "insulted." Staying behind, his principal military aide, Major General James H. Burns, "put his head in his hands and wept in shame."

Such behavior made it easy for Acheson to claim the secretary of defense was "mentally ill." ("His conduct became too outrageous to be explained by mere cussedness.") But Johnson had not conceded defeat—nor had Truman. After Acheson and the chiefs endorsed the finished document, Johnson dodged a direct confrontation over it. He blithely signed NSC-68, allowing it to go forward to the president on April 7. For his part, Truman praised the analysis, just as he had in deflecting Forrestal's proposals. Having received a study of America's national security predicament that he had himself requested, he now asked the bureaucracy to study its implications—a study of a study, in effect. The president did not approve the document, he did not sign it, he did not agree to make a declassified version public, and he did not endorse the budget increase that was its primary—in a sense, its *only*—practical recommendation. Just a month later, in May, Truman actually went back to saying that he wanted to reduce national security spending through increased economies. A dire assessment of how the Cold War was going was one thing.

He embraced that. Paying for it was something else. This the president still refused to do.[23]

Truman's advisers found him resistant to other policy adjustments that they considered necessary to waging the Cold War. The most explosive of these recommendations came to the president's desk on June 8, 1950, when the chiefs sent him their views on German rearmament. A credible defense against a Soviet invasion, they declared, required additional troops. The time had come, therefore, to make "the energy and resources of the German people become a source of constructive strength to the Free World." "As soon as feasible," the chiefs argued, West Germany should be brought into "Western European and North Atlantic regional arrangements."[24]

There was, of course, a Pentagon budget issue lurking in this proposal too—since the only way to allay European fears at the revival of German military power was through a permanent American troop presence on the continent. But once again Truman dodged the question of resources, criticizing the chiefs' proposal in more visceral terms. In a quick note to Acheson asking for his views, the president said he found their ideas "decidedly militaristic and . . . not realistic with present conditions."[25]

Such divisions were deepening the tensions in American national security policy. Although senior military officers—with the full backing of the secretary of state—believed that the capabilities of the U.S. military were inadequate to the tasks it faced, Truman would not make available the resources and the manpower to fix the problem. He had a maximalist moment—and a maximalist document—before him. He was not ready to back a maximalist policy. Seeing this discord and the growth of Soviet power, newly minted allies of the United States felt their own anxiety rise. Some weighed the advantages of charting their own course. Dean Acheson had waged a skillful campaign against current policy, but he had completely failed to turn the president around.[26]

IN JUNE 1950, Louis Johnson and Omar Bradley took a break from Washington's bureaucratic warfare and, accompanied by their wives and staff, embarked on a flying tour of American forces in the Pacific and East Asia. They visited Hawaii, Manila, Tokyo, Okinawa, and Alaska. Korea was not on the itinerary. For at least three years, it had been American policy to minimize military involvement in that country. In

1947 the JCS had seen "little strategic interest" in keeping troops there. For Dwight Eisenhower, then the army chief of staff, budget pressures made withdrawal an easy call. A long-term occupation would serve no purpose other than "preventing disease and disorder." The State Department agreed. George Marshall considered an American presence there "untenable." "Our main task," George Kennan concluded, "is to extricate ourselves without too great a loss of prestige."[27]

The Soviet Union also showed little desire to occupy Korea. Its troops left for home in 1948, and the remaining American soldiers did the same in June 1949. The thirty-eighth parallel, the line that demarcated Soviet- and U.S.-occupied territory at the end of World War II, became the hostile border between a Western-leaning regime in the south and a Communist-run "people's republic" in the north. The United States offered its client weapons and training but not (despite several requests) security guarantees. When Acheson, in his famous National Press Club speech of January 12, 1950, left Korea outside the "security perimeter" of American defense policy, the omission had a very simple explanation: the Truman administration did not see invasion as the real threat South Korea faced. Washington policy makers worried more about the Seoul government's ruinous economic policies and authoritarian politics, regularly lecturing it about inflation and free and fair elections. Some of them were actually pleased when Congress rejected aid for Korea in January. Only tough measures, they thought, would force Korean leaders to put their house in order.[28]

Washington's near-indifference to Korea vanished on June 24, 1950, mere hours after Johnson and Bradley returned home from their trip. Like other surprise moves by America's adversaries—Pearl Harbor, the Cuban missile crisis, the Soviet invasion of Afghanistan, September 11—North Korea's attack on the South sparked what Omar Bradley called "an intense sense of moral outrage." This was not garden-variety Communist subversion but "raw, naked aggression . . . with blazing tanks and artillery." The next day Truman flew back from Missouri to Washington to meet with his national security team. On the way he pondered the risks of doing too little. The democracies had failed to stand up to small-scale aggression in the 1930s, and the result had been world war. The United States now faced the same challenge in Korea. "This was the test of all the talk of the last five years," he believed. "The Reds were probing for weaknesses in our armor."[29]

The president and his advisers did not try to prove that the Soviet

Union had—as Acheson charged—"mounted, supplied, and instigated" the attack. Moscow's role seemed too obvious to require proof. Acheson considered it "an all-out attack on the leadership of the United States"—"an open, undisguised challenge," he called it on another occasion. "The Soviet leaders recognized that their policy might bring on a general war and"—for Acheson, this was the most disturbing part—"they were prepared to run that risk."[30]

Once more the government's best experts disputed this picture of Soviet intentions, but they were, in Chip Bohlen's understatement, "in the minority." He and Kennan believed South Korea had been invaded because it was "available for the taking." The invasion had to be resisted, of course, but there was no reason to think a global offensive was under way. "The Soviet action in Korea," Bohlen held, "was limited strictly to Korea."[31]

Truman disagreed. Successful aggression in Korea "would mean a Third World War," and he steadily increased American military involvement. After a first meeting with his advisers, he okayed the rapid supply of arms and equipment to the South Korean army. A day later he approved the use of offshore airpower to slow the attack. On day five, he authorized bombardment of North Korea itself, and on day six, fearing a rout, he ordered U.S. occupation forces from Japan into the fight.[32]

Consultations with members of Congress, who expressed strong support, convinced the president and his advisers that they could go to war in Korea without seeking new legal authority. Truman believed his power as commander in chief was all he needed to defend what suddenly seemed a clear American interest. (To back him up, Acheson sent over a list of eighty-five instances in which presidents had sent troops into battle.) And if a congressional consensus and legal precedents were not enough, a UN Security Council resolution, which called on members to support South Korea's defense, bestowed further legitimacy.[33]

Yet repelling the attack on South Korea was from the beginning only one part of the administration's response to the crisis. If general war was a more immediate danger than previously thought, then policy had to be reexamined across the board. Risks that had been considered acceptable before the invasion were less acceptable now. Precautions that had earlier seemed adequate now looked inadequate. And ideas that had failed to win support in the past were about to get a second chance.

HARRY TRUMAN HAD long resisted paying the price for maximalism. Now he gave up. The first policy casualty of the war in Korea was, not surprisingly, his resistance to higher defense spending. American boys were on the firing line, and Acheson wanted to be sure this new opportunity was fully exploited. It wasn't enough to secure Korea itself, he told the cabinet on July 14. The United States "must do more now," and it didn't seem to matter exactly what. "Prompt action is worth more than perfect action," he insisted. The president "must ask for money, and if it is a question of asking for too little or too much, he should ask for too much."[34]

The next week Truman asked Congress for an immediate $10 billion increase in the Pentagon budget—74 percent above his proposed $13.5 billion ceiling for 1951. The money, he said, was needed to meet the new dangers of "the world situation"—an elastic standard that justified a stream of new requests. As Acheson described it, "Appropriations and powers tumbled over one another, sometimes in such haste that supplemental appropriations virtually accompanied the regular fiscal-year bill they were supplementing." By the end of September, the National Security Council approved a completely new budget for 1951. The army would have 17 divisions (up from 10 envisioned in June); the navy, 322 combat ships (up from 238 in June); the air force, 70 "wings" of planes (up from 48 in June).

All this was only the start. By year's end, the JCS wanted 95 wings, not 70, and 18 divisions, not 17. Six months later the numbers had become 138 wings and 21 divisions. By June 1951 more Americans were serving in the armed forces than in June 1942.[35]

The second big policy change triggered by Korea involved German rearmament. Here Truman and even Acheson had been at odds with the chiefs before the war. Now they abandoned their hesitations. "My conversion," Acheson recalled, "was quick." Earlier he had believed that bringing Germany into the defense of Europe should involve a "process of evolution." No more. "Korea had speeded up evolution." The United States could no longer indulge the fears and animosities of Germany's neighbors. Two weeks after the North Korean attack, Truman told Acheson he was ready to approve an idea that, just one month earlier, he had labeled "as wrong as can be."[36]

Both the Pentagon and the State Department understood that European governments would never accept German rearmament without a stronger American commitment to Europe. At the beginning of September 1950, Truman announced that the United States would for the first time send combat divisions to Europe in peacetime. He and his advisers also recognized that American allies needed help building up their own strength. When the president asked Congress for $10 billion more for defense, he proposed a parallel $4 billion for security assistance for NATO.

American policy makers naturally suspected that the Europeans would, as always, pocket these historic initiatives and then fail to do their part. For this reason—and at the "united and immovable" insistence (Acheson's words) of the Pentagon—Truman decided to present the new troops and the new aid as an all-or-nothing "single package." Acheson was to advise NATO foreign ministers, who were about to arrive in New York, that they would get American troops—plus a high-profile American general to command them (it was expected to be Eisenhower)—*only* if they first accepted German rearmament.[37]

For the French, this "package" proved once again that the United States did not understand their difficult history and domestic politics. They called Acheson's plan the "bomb in the Waldorf" (after the hotel where the meetings took place). Jules Moch, the defense minister, declared that France would agree to it "over his dead body." Robert Schuman, the foreign minister and an Acheson favorite, said he could agree to the American proposal privately—but not, alas, in public. The problem was not simply that French voters would hate the idea. The French government claimed to be worried about pushing East-West relations beyond mere tension into outright war. French diplomats had raised this concern at least since the Berlin blockade. Again Acheson dismissed it. He told Schuman this was no moment for haggling. He demanded "an answer now."[38]

ACHESON BELIEVED THE Korean crisis had "broken inertia of thought on many critical matters"—a welcome and invigorating turn of events. Kennan, by contrast, found the result to be American policy making at its worst. The war had filled the air with all kinds of quickly formulated proposals. "People went buzzing and milling around, each with his own idea of what we were trying to do." His August 1950 diary entry described

> utter confusion in the public mind with respect to U.S. foreign policy. The President doesn't understand it; Congress doesn't understand

> it; nor does the public, nor does the press. They all wander around in a labyrinth of ignorance and error and conjecture, in which truth is intermingled with fiction at a hundred points, in which unjustified assumptions have attained the validity of premises, and in which there is no recognized and authoritative theory to hold on to.[39]

The months that followed seemed to vindicate Kennan's alarm. In September, American forces achieved a brilliant victory at Inchon that drove the North Korean invaders out of the South. Then, in an attempt to reunify the entire country, they squandered almost everything they had gained. Pushing beyond the thirty-eighth parallel and far to the north, they were surprised in late November by a huge Chinese army whose presence they had barely detected. The president, having lauded General MacArthur's "splendid leadership" in late 1950, fired him in early 1951. Public opinion, which had been overwhelmingly supportive of the war in the fall, now turned overwhelmingly negative. Allied governments had contributed troops when they thought Korea was a winning effort. Now, alarmed by what Americans were saying, they feared an overreaction—and a wider war.[40]

This was an unquestioned disaster—the biggest setback for U.S. policy since World War II. Yet it was the result of a far more orderly and thoughtful process than Kennan admitted, shaped less by mass hysteria or individual folly than by systematic strategic choice. As soon as American ground forces went into Korea at the end of June, Washington policy makers began to deliberate on the goals of the operation. On July 17, Truman asked his NSC advisers how far U.S. troops should go and what they should try to accomplish. Most policy makers were counting on a "limited engagement"—a "police action," it was called—that would end once North Korean forces had been chased back to the thirty-eighth parallel. At first Acheson shared this expectation. He saw no need to "shoot the works for victory." But as early as July 10, he started to worry about the viability of a halfway outcome. If American forces re-created a divided Korea, he ruminated to Nitze, they would have to stay there for a long time. It made no sense "to repel the attack and then abandon the country" all over again. Acheson had not yet made the leap to the goal of unifying Korea, but he told Nitze, who favored stopping at the old boundary, that he was troubled. He could not "see the end of it."[41]

To Acheson's worries, Pentagon planners had a radical answer. If stopping at the thirty-eighth parallel involved excessive long-term costs and prolonged vulnerability, the solution was a "maximum effort" to reunify the country. This would put Korea on a sounder, democratic footing and have a positive regional impact as well. The invasion would be America's "first opportunity to displace part of the Soviet orbit." Success would have "incalculable" significance across Asia. Best of all, it would spare the army a costly and protracted deployment in Korea, one for which it had no appetite. As MacArthur explained to Truman, "All occupations are failures."[42]

Acheson later treated this Pentagon paper as the source of the over-reaching that followed. But at the time his own Asia specialists embraced it. In fact, repackaged as a State Department analysis, it became the basis of a government-wide strategy document designed to answer Truman's questions about goals. The State Department agreed with the Pentagon that the United States should seek "the establishment of a free and united Korea and the elimination of the North Korean Communist regime." And it too was enthusiastic about the geopolitical payoff of victory. "Throughout Asia," it declared, "those who foresee only inevitable Soviet conquest would take hope." The State Department still worried about Soviet intervention, but it argued that Moscow could not possibly want "all-out war" and might accept an outcome backed by a "large [UN] majority."[43]

All this was exactly what the White House wanted to hear. Weeks earlier the president had sent Averell Harriman, who had recently taken over as Truman's new assistant for national security, out to Tokyo to confer with MacArthur. Harriman had returned a convert. MacArthur, he told the president, felt that success in Korea would turn the entire region around. "Victory is a strong magnet in the East," the general had said, and painted the future in broad, oracular strokes. A unified Korea would "become a strong influence in stabilizing the non-communist movement."[44]

With the whole government in agreement, the paper presented to the president on September 8—known as NSC 81/1—provoked little debate. Acheson and others later criticized it as muddled and confusing; Bradley called it a "masterpiece of obfuscation." But on the key issues, NSC 81/1 was utterly clear. The United States sought "the complete independence and unity of Korea"—without "general war." Its goal was "liberation rather than retaliation." MacArthur was to move north of the thirty-eighth parallel, with full UN authorization, so as to "destroy the North Korean forces." Planning was now to begin for "the possible occupation of North Korea," but the United States wanted to keep its stay brief. Early elections would allow American forces to withdraw "as soon as practicable."[45]

The only question not answered by NSC 81/1 was how to do all this, and here there *was* disagreement. MacArthur had devised an unconventional plan for an amphibious landing at Inchon on Korea's west coast that would enable American forces to encircle the North Korean army. It was a complete roll of the dice, dependent on tides, timing, and countless unknowables. MacArthur himself called it a "5,000 to 1" shot. Back in Washington his military colleagues didn't like the odds. Bradley considered the scheme "the riskiest military proposal I had ever heard of."

Yet the chiefs did not veto MacArthur's Inchon plan. What kept them from doing so was not simply traditional deference to the commander in the field, or the arrogance of this particular commander. MacArthur had gotten the White House to do what it had started doing on many issues: overrule the Pentagon. The general had used Harriman's August visit to lobby for his plan. Liking its boldness, Harriman immediately raised it with the president on his return. Truman was also enthusiastic, but knowing the military's doubts, he told Harriman to "get over to the Pentagon as fast as you can to convince Bradley and Johnson." By the time Harriman arrived, Louis Johnson—furious at the interference—had already heard from Truman himself that he "want[ed] this plan of MacArthur's supported." Soon Johnson and Bradley were summoned to brief the president on a plan they both opposed. Truman responded grandly to their play-acting. He found the plan "a daring strategic conception" and had "the greatest confidence that it would succeed."[46]

Three days before the Inchon landing came further proof that the president would impose his own preferences on policy. Ending weeks of backstage maneuvering, Truman announced that George Marshall would return to government service, replacing Louis Johnson as secretary of defense. The change was universally welcomed. Acheson heard about it in New York, in a meeting with European diplomats. His face lit up at the news, Nitze remembered. The secretary of state gathered aides around him and called for champagne to toast his rival's fall.[47]

MACARTHUR'S DAZZLING SUCCESS at Inchon made it harder than ever for Washington to second-guess him. He had never, to say the least, taken direction well, and now he was fortified by worldwide acknowledgment of his strategic genius. He had become, Acheson groused, "the sorcerer of Inchon." For decades, analyses of what went wrong in Korea have focused, understandably, on MacArthur's headstrong personality. The magic of a great victory certainly meant that when he let North Korean forces escape one trap after another, no one upbraided him. He devised an invasion of the North that Bradley considered the "worst possible solution"—one that would have been "laughed out of the classroom" if submitted by a young War College student. But no one told MacArthur to start over. Acheson described the senior policy makers, himself included, who failed to restrain the great general, as "paralyzed rabbits." Even George Marshall, newly back at the Pentagon, was deferential. As American forces neared the thirty-eighth parallel, the new secretary of defense—no less a national hero than his field commander—cabled MacArthur that he should feel "unhampered tactically and strategically" in the war's next phase. Truman personally approved the message.[48]

Yet the deeper reason that MacArthur had a free hand to pursue maximalist goals after Inchon was that Washington had embraced the same goals *before* Inchon. Over the course of the summer, the U.S. government had unequivocally rejected restoration of the status quo ante as its goal. It wanted the benefits that came with complete victory. Bradley supported the switch, but he also called it—correctly—a "drastic change" from the thinking that had first guided U.S. policy after the North Korean attack. The new strategy was, he thought, "bold and aggressive," even "dangerous."[49]

Acheson himself set out the new, broader conception of what the war was about when he told the cabinet in late September that the United States would soon demonstrate "what Western Democracy can do to help the under-privileged countries of the world." Truman was still more ebullient when he spoke to the nation on October 17, after his meeting with MacArthur on Wake Island in the middle of the Pacific. The progress of the war was "spectacular," the president declared. The United States would do its part "to help build a free, united and self-supporting Korean Republic." He warned against any "let-down" after this success. The "false revolution of communism" remained a global threat, and to meet it, "we seek full partnership with the peoples of Asia, as with all other peoples . . . a partnership for peace with all the world."[50]

Expansive goals shaped military decision making in the weeks between Inchon and the Chinese attack on MacArthur's forces. But even in this period MacArthur was hardly exempt from oversight. In early

November, as Washington began receiving intelligence reports of large-scale Chinese infiltration, the chiefs held around-the-clock discussions to consider an alternative strategy. (In his role as JCS chairman, Bradley considered the situation serious but not urgent enough to interrupt his "book leave." He kept in touch with colleagues by phone while working at home on his World War II memoir, *A Soldier's Story*.) Although the generals and admirals were "punchy" by the time they finished talking over the situation, they had convinced themselves—and Bradley too—that MacArthur should change course at once. The chiefs prepared orders telling him to pull his troops back from the Chinese and Soviet borders to the so-called waist of North Korea. There, still in control of 90 percent of the country's population, he would not be vulnerable to surprise attack.[51]

Documents from the archives of all the parties suggest that the chiefs were on the right track. The redeployment they envisioned would not, to be sure, have kept the Chinese from attacking. The invasion of the north had by itself probably made a Sino-American clash inevitable. But the chiefs' plan would have given U.S. forces more warning of an attack and made it harder for China to gain the upper hand in the early fighting.[52]

What prevented this happy (or, at least, less disastrous) ending? The day after the draft order was written, Bradley reconsidered and decided not to send it. His reason was not deference to the great "sorcerer," MacArthur, but unwillingness to give up on the full achievement of American goals. Bradley and his colleagues sought regime change in Korea. Not occupying the whole country would be "an admission of failure . . . with perhaps dire long-term consequences."[53]

This was what the chairman of the joint chiefs thought—and the president too. Because they did, the fact that MacArthur was a military legend, a manic-depressive, and a bad listener cannot be considered the main explanation of America's brush with disaster. The "sorcerer of Inchon" had many apprentices—the secretaries of state and defense among them—who were just as eager as he for a momentous victory. Senior policy makers had spent the months since the start of the war insisting that the United States had to exploit its huge strategic opportunity. Maximalism's origin was collective, not personal. On November 21, 1950, four days before the Chinese attacked, Marshall convened a meeting in his private dining room at the Pentagon, attended not only by the top brass but by Acheson and Harriman as well, to review MacArthur's proposed offensive. They were "unanimously in favor of letting him go ahead."[54]

WHEN CHINESE FORCES made their surprise entry into the Korean War, all the ingredients of America's success to date—an aroused public, confident generalship, a unified government, forces with global reach, international legitimacy, an allied consensus—seemed to collapse at once. Robert Lovett, who had been Marshall's deputy at State and now resumed the same role at the Pentagon, reported what he heard from members of the House Armed Services Committee: "that our entire entry into Korea had been a mistake and that we ought to pull out as rapidly as possible." The chiefs themselves were acutely conscious of how thin their resources were stretched and feared "the loss of what was practically our entire ground establishment." Some wanted to "come home and just forget the matter." (Bradley broached the idea with Acheson, who had a crisp reply: "Certainly not.")[55]

The possibility that the United States might be driven out of Korea was a severe blow to international confidence in American policy. At the UN, Acheson heard, there was a "state of panic." "Complaints were being made that U.S. leadership had failed." In Europe he found his counterparts "puzzled and worried about our country's state of mind." Anxiety about Washington's good sense spiked when Truman declared, at a November 30 press conference, that the United States would take "whatever steps are necessary" to cope with the deteriorating military situation—even, if necessary, the use of nuclear weapons.

The world had over time become familiar with Truman's blunt Missouri talk, but this was too much. British troops were endangered by Chinese troops and now, it seemed, by American leaders as well. With Parliament in an uproar, Prime Minister Clement Attlee had to address the matter face to face with Truman. When he announced a quick trip to Washington for an Oval Office showdown, there were, Truman sheepishly acknowledged, "cheers from both sides of the House."[56]

Attlee arrived in Washington on December 4, 1950, for a five-day summit, hoping—like many allied leaders over subsequent decades—to show colleagues and constituents back home that he could restrain the dangerous impulses of American policy. Uneasy at how little say they had had in the conduct of the war to date, the prime minister and the members of his party said they were determined to keep it from widening. They hoped for American agreement to pursue a cease-fire. They reminded the United States not to let the war become too costly, inasmuch as Europe was far more important than Asia to Western security interests. They urged their hosts to think about rapprochement with the Chinese Communists, all the better to divide them from the Soviet Union. Above all, Attlee sought personal assurances against any rash use of nuclear weapons.

Despite their own "deepening gloom" over the war, Truman and his advisers received the British delegation with conspicuous hospitality, professions of common purpose, and daily press releases proclaiming the value of the talks. But the bonhomie of the "special relationship" did not conceal the fact that the Americans gave their visitors virtually nothing of what they came for.[57] At the Pentagon, American generals closed ranks, defending MacArthur and lecturing the British that "a war could not be run by a committee." Truman went further, declaring that he was determined to keep fighting until the situation on the ground improved. The United States would do so even if other countries that had contributed to the UN effort gave up. "If we have support from the others, fine," he said. If not, "we would stay on anyway." Acheson concurred: "If we now give up in the Far East, we are through."[58]

The Americans rejected other British ideas with equal energy. Washington had no problem with a cease-fire if it could be achieved without unacceptable conditions. But Beijing was certain to want much in return, Truman insisted, and making concessions to the Chinese would only make them "increasingly aggressive." Acheson put the point more picturesquely: "We can't buy our way into this poker game; the cost of coming in is too high." The president also dismissed Attlee's claim that Mao might "wear the Red flag with a difference." The idea, popular in Britain, that China's rulers sought good relations with the West was, he said, pure illusion. As for the Russians, the president was unyielding. They "only understand the mailed fist, and that is what we are preparing for them."[59]

Even on issues where the two sides were not far apart, the Americans took the offensive. Yes, a military buildup in Europe was vital, but it would happen only if Washington and London subjected other allies to greater "bullying and cajolery." Acheson warned Attlee that Americans would not support resoluteness in Europe while retreating in Asia: "The public mind was not delicate enough to understand such opposing attitudes." The United States was "the only source of power" for countering the global Soviet threat, and its allies should do nothing to undermine American commitment. (Here Attlee ventured a small demurral, noting blandly that it was also "important to consider the UN and the importance of Asian opinion." Acheson would not let this pass. The one truly important thing, he shot back, was not "to weaken the security of the United States.")[60]

Shut down in this way, Attlee had only one more issue to raise before returning home. In a private session with Truman, he took up the question that had occasioned his visit in the first place: the possible use of nuclear weapons. Away from his advisers, the president was unexpectedly sympathetic to the prime minister's appeal. Rejoining the two delegations, Truman proudly announced that they had just agreed that "neither of us would use these weapons without prior consultation with the other." This small example of personal diplomacy left other American officials speechless. Nervous whispered conversations were followed by a small Oval Office caucus in which Acheson explained to the president and the prime minister that their breakthrough was a major change of U.S. policy. It would excite the "most vicious" political attacks and would inevitably be reversed. Deflated, Attlee settled for feeble communiqué language expressing an American "desire to keep [him] at all times informed" of developments that might lead to nuclear war.[61]

No other country in the world was considered more important to the United States in 1950 than Britain. And no government tried harder to support American policy—in this case, with combat troops. Even so, American policy makers saw high-level British unhappiness as a minor factor in solving their Korea problem. If Attlee had political difficulties at home, he would have to solve them himself—and leave real decisions to the United States. His meetings in Washington were the most significant and revealing extended encounter between the president of the United States and a major allied leader during the early years of the Cold War. Yet they had a completely predictable result. Truman sent his friend home with mere scraps for his trouble.

DESPITE THE PANIC that ensued when Chinese forces drove the United States out of North Korea, the Truman administration was able before long to stabilize the military situation and to protect the broader goals it had set for itself since the start of the war. Under their new commander,

General Matthew Ridgway, American troops fought their way back to the thirty-eighth parallel within a few months. They did so without nuclear weapons, without bombing China, and—because the president had imposed a strict manpower ceiling—without any reinforcements. The danger that the United States might be chased off the peninsula passed. Cease-fire talks began in July 1951.

Nor were other policy priorities sacrificed. When South Korea was first attacked, Truman and his advisers had rallied support for spending more—much more—on defense. This consensus remained strong. In 1950 the Pentagon budget was 5 percent of GDP. With the war, it surged into the teens and stayed high for decades. Defense spending did not come down below 10 percent of GDP until 1960 and did not return to 5 percent until 1977.[62]

In 1951, Congress also approved the most important elements of the administration's European policy: the deployment of U.S. combat divisions to NATO's front lines, and the appointment of an American general as supreme allied commander. And although Acheson predicted "much sorrow and anxiety" in future relations with Europe, his record in preserving allied unity was good. In 1951 and 1952 the United States, Britain, and France—with minimal dissent—turned back two successive Soviet diplomatic offensives, both of which aimed to dislodge West Germany from its place in the Atlantic bloc.

Outside Europe, the enlargement of America's global role gained speed. As Bohlen put it, "it was the Korean war and not World War II that made us a world military-political power." The United States, which before Korea had a small network of permanent installations outside the Western hemisphere, now began the steep climb to a mid-1960s peak of 450 bases in thirty-six countries. The war also led American policy makers to take a new look at the strategic significance of other parts of Asia. Soon the United States was giving France more military assistance—bombers, transports, fighter planes—in Indochina than in Western Europe. Other regions received equally keen attention. In 1951, the Egyptian government asked the United States to show that it intended to be a permanent player in the Middle East. Because the post-Korea spending surge had widened policy possibilities in all regions, the United States promptly responded to the Egyptian request by creating a Middle East command.[63]

For all these achievements, Acheson was not wrong when he said that the damage done by the Korean debacle was "impossible to overestimate." At home, charges leveled against Truman and his principal advisers ranged from incompetence to treason. The old bipartisanship of Vandenberg had perhaps already passed its peak, but now it became a rarity. Foreign policy turned into a divisive and emotional issue of domestic debate. It was in part to wait out these controversies that Acheson delayed writing his memoirs for fifteen years after he left office. Even then, despite the ebullience of its title, *Present at the Creation* was the melancholy story of how the Korean War "destroyed the Truman administration."[64]

Such was the war's impact on partisan politics. The impact it would eventually have on national strategy could only be guessed at in the closing years of Truman's presidency. He and Acheson—and for that matter, MacArthur—had treated Korea as an opportunity to put U.S. foreign policy into overdrive. They had had a chance to pursue, if only in one small country, what Kennan saw as the only goals that made sense to Americans in time of conflict—"total enemy defeat, total destruction of the enemy's armed forces, his unconditional surrender, the complete occupation of his territory, the removal of the existing government and its replacement by a regime that would respond to our concepts of 'democratization.'" These maximalist goals were now out of reach. In Korea and elsewhere, a new administration had to decide what would take their place.[65]

3

"Enough Is Enough"

EISENHOWER AND RETRENCHMENT

John Foster Dulles and Dwight Eisenhower

DWIGHT EISENHOWER and John Foster Dulles, who became president and secretary of state in January 1953, seem at first glance to be American history's strongest case of foreign policy continuity. Amid rancorous partisan debate, Republicans had won the White House for the first time in twenty years. They promised a new direction. And yet the diplomacy of the new administration was in the hands of two men who had, at high levels, served the old one. Before he sought the presidency, Eisenhower had been picked by Truman to be the first commander of NATO; Dulles had recently negotiated the U.S. peace treaty with Japan.

The new president and the new secretary both felt personally obliged to check their party's harshest critics of Truman's record. Eisenhower claimed he had decided to run when he realized that Republican "isolationists" opposed the very policy with which he was most closely identified—sending combat troops to Europe to steady America's new allies. He wanted a strategy, he once said, that would unite "the truculent and the timid, the jingoists and the pacifists." Consensus building came naturally to him, and he knew he couldn't achieve his goal by antagonizing people. "I'll tell you what leadership is," Eisenhower told aides. "It's *persuasion*—and *conciliation*—and *education*—and *patience*. It's long, slow, tough work. That's the only kind of leadership I know—or believe in—or will practice."[1]

Dulles, a more combative figure, had definitely criticized Truman during the campaign. Yet in a public review of foreign policy after a year as secretary of state, he lavished praise on the prior administration. It was no casual grace note. Dulles listed every landmark policy of the previous eight years—the Truman Doctrine, the Marshall Plan, the Berlin airlift, the formation of NATO, the defense of Korea, and more. He called them "precious values to be acclaimed."[2]

With the president and secretary of state holding such views, it was no surprise that the new administration left many of its predecessor's policies in place. Decades later George W. Bush treated continuity between Truman and Eisenhower as a retort to his own critics. Hadn't the former's policies been vindicated when the latter decided to stay the course? The review that Eisenhower conducted early in his term seemed to say yes. In 1953 he charged three task forces to make the best case they could for different national strategies. The one that emerged victorious was the very same approach that the incoming party had run against: containment.[3]

Even so, treating Eisenhower as an example of policy continuity is a mistake. The new president believed that Harry Truman's approach to national security was neither successful nor sustainable. Dulles described it as "emergency action imposed on us by our enemies." Such measures did "not necessarily make good permanent policies." In his inaugural address, Eisenhower said the same thing—and with a sharper rhetorical edge. The United States, he argued, had to go beyond a mere "spasmodic reaction to the stimulus of emergencies."

An effective strategy for the long haul, the new president and his team believed, had to start by fixing the many problems their predecessors had mishandled. It had to escape a hopeless military stalemate, cut the cost of defense, shift burdens to allies, replace stale ideological rhetoric with more hopeful initiatives, and shore up domestic support. Then, Dulles said, the United States could let "time and fundamentals work for us."[4]

Retrenchment hardly meant that Eisenhower thought the Cold War was over. While extricating themselves from failing efforts, he and his advisers believed that they continued to face a worldwide struggle with a dangerous adversary. America's allies remained at risk. Decolonization was opening up new realms for East-West competition. These realities complicated the new administration's choices. It had to pull back without abandoning critical interests. If the United States looked weak, it would only invite future conflict.

Squaring this circle proved as difficult for Eisenhower as it did for those of his successors who undertook retrenchment. When he left office, many close associates felt he had failed. Eisenhower's own speechwriter, Emmet Hughes, described his boss sadly as the "most popular—and the most criticized—of modern Presidents." His record, said Hughes, offered only "the half-solace of a series of truces."[5]

Truces, cease-fires, tense and unresolved standoffs, futile negotiations, grand proposals that went nowhere, growing popular anxiety—these were the emblems of Eisenhower's presidency. He was extremely skillful, even innovative, in scaling back from overextension. He saw clearly how the nation's institutions distorted policy outcomes and hemmed in policy makers. But he became less sensitive over time to the loss of dynamism in American diplomacy. There was a reason he eventually turned the White House over to a new president who promised to get America "moving again." Truces, it seemed, were not much solace after all. Nor were appeals to his long experience and unquestioned skill.

When he became president, Eisenhower had thought his job was to define and implement a foreign policy for the long haul. Few people have ever had a better grasp of what such a policy might be. We need to understand better why he did not succeed—why retrenchment proved so hard, and why it eventually gave way to maximalism again.

EISENHOWER'S HANDLERS thought his election victory was sealed by the speech he gave at the Masonic Temple in Detroit on October 24, little more than a week before the vote. "All of us," recalled Sherman Adams (soon to be White House chief of staff), "agreed that an extra-spectacular message would be needed that night to bring the campaign to an exciting climax." Their solution was a one-sentence pledge. "I shall go to Korea," Eisenhower declared. He also proposed to speed up the training of South Korean soldiers but said little more about how he would end the war.[6]

The trip that made good on this promise was also brief. In December, while his New York staff pretended he was tied up in meetings, the president-elect flew secretly to Korea. He met with President Syngman Rhee, listened to American commanders, had a cold breakfast with GIs at the front, and made a cryptic departure statement. The United States, he said, could not "continue to accept casualties without any visible results."[7]

At the new National Security Council's first meeting on Korea in early February 1953, the issue on the table was whether to try to break the military stalemate or negotiate a diplomatic compromise at the armistice talks, then in recess. Eisenhower had no use for a plan General MacArthur had suggested, to threaten China with nuclear attack unless it gave up all of North Korea. This, he thought, risked "offending the whole world." The president also disdained Truman's effort to gain the upper hand through "small attacks on small hills." He told his advisers that "we cannot go on the way we are indefinitely."[8]

Eisenhower drew on each of these strategies to develop his own plan. Insisting (incorrectly) that the United States had never aimed to unify Korea by force, he was ready to accept the border at the thirty-eighth parallel. But he wanted the Chinese and the Soviets to understand that he was ready for nuclear war to secure this compromise. If diplomacy failed, the United States would attack—"without inhibition in our use of weapons." It would not be limited by what Eisenhower, somewhat sneeringly, called a "world-wide gentleman's agreement."[9]

The new president did not worry that America's allies might object to the use of nuclear weapons. As long as the attack was a quick success, Eisenhower judged, "the rifts so caused could, in time, be repaired." But he saw no point in stirring public discord over the issue. While doing his best to alarm Moscow and Beijing, he kept London and Paris—not to speak of the American public—in the dark. The United States, he said, would keep its options to itself. There should be no discussion "with our allies of military plans or weapons of attack."[10]

These quiet threats worked. China returned to the negotiations, and an agreement was soon ready for signing. Getting South Korea to accept it was another matter. The South Korean parliament unanimously voted to reject any deal that left Kim Il Sung in power. President Rhee declared that if American troops would not fight to unify Korea, they should leave at once. To provoke Beijing, he freed thousands of North Korean prisoners who would otherwise have been sent home after a cease-fire.

Eisenhower marveled at this defiance. He liked to say that "you do not lead by hitting people over the head," but that seemed precisely what was needed to achieve peace in Korea. Eisenhower sent a State Department diplomat, Walter Robertson, to Seoul to "force Rhee back to rationality." While listening patiently to the Korean president's rants and protests, Robertson carried a blunt message: if South Korea blocked a deal, all American pledges of support would be "nullified." Rhee demanded unconditional guarantees, not promises. Eisenhower ignored him, and the South Korean leader backed down.[11]

While settling for a cease-fire, Eisenhower still hoped to salvage something meaningful from the war. Retrenchment, he felt, had to have its inspiring side. With the Marshall Plan in mind, he wrote the secretaries of state and defense and the new U.S. commander in Korea with ideas for rebuilding the country. The effort he envisioned, in which American military forces would play a central role, would be "almost unique in history" and have an "electrical" effect on world opinion. But despite many follow-up notes, the president found it difficult to generate funds and enthusiasm for his plan. A little deflated, he told a meeting of his advisers at year end that, when it came to putting their country back together, "the Communists were actually doing a much more impressive job."[12]

PEACE IN KOREA was only one element of retrenchment. The new administration's top foreign policy goal was to bring down the cost of the Cold War. On the return leg of his Asia trip, Eisenhower commandeered the cruiser USS *Helena* so that he and his top advisers could review global strategy at leisure. His spokesman called the three-day floating bull session "the mid-Pacific conference"—a chance for the new team to settle on its approach.[13]

Everyone saw defense spending as the most urgent problem. For Dulles, it threatened "huge budget deficits, a depreciating currency, and a feverish economy." To change this "ruinous" course, the Republicans had promised to cut taxes and lift wage and price controls. "Two more years of Truman budgets," said George Humphrey, the incoming treasury secretary, "would have meant Communism in America." Eisenhower was no ideologue, but his views produced equally heated rhetoric. The United States, he said, risked becoming an "armed camp," a "garrison state," or (even) a "police state." National "bankruptcy" was a possibility. The United States had to cut costs, or risk losing what Dulles called "the stamina needed for permanent security."[14]

Even before the Korean armistice, Eisenhower put defense spending on a steep downward slope. He cut Truman's last Pentagon budget proposal—$41.2 billion—to $35.8 billion, a reduction of more than 13 percent. With Soviet military strength rising, government planners had expected 1954 to be a year of "maximum danger," but the new president scoffed at this. "I am not going to be stampeded by someone coming along with a damn trick formula of 'so much by this date.'" His advisers amplified the theme. Humphrey said the first round of cuts had only "scratched the surface"—the real "surgery" was ahead. For fiscal 1955, his first real defense budget, Eisenhower proposed $30.9 billion, a cumulative cut of 25 percent. The end of the Korean War produced a quicker peace dividend than either the Vietnam War or the Cold War.[15]

Deep reductions were possible, of course, precisely because Truman's buildup had been so big. He had used Korea to adopt a new strategy that, among other things, would make the United States less reliant on nuclear weapons. For Eisenhower, this goal was too expensive. Deterring the Soviets, he thought, had to depend on being able to "blow hell out of them in a hurry if they start anything." The United States could not prepare for war, as Dulles mockingly described Truman's policy, "in the arctic and in the tropics; in Asia, the Near East, and in Europe; by sea, by land, and by air; with old weapons and with new weapons."[16]

The idea that nuclear weapons could keep the peace—and win any war—became an article of faith for budget-minded policy makers. At Treasury, Humphrey was an unabashed nuclear enthusiast. "All the rest of these soldiers and sailors and submarines and everything else," he said, "you could drop in the ocean and it wouldn't make too much difference." Eisenhower was only slightly more guarded. "Instead of conventional forces," he told his cabinet, "we must be prepared to use atomic weapons in all forms." The United States had to concentrate on "those things which can deter the Russians." The army, it seemed, no longer measured up. Believing that it had "expanded far beyond its necessary peacetime size," the new president forced his generals to shed fully one-third of their troops between 1953 and 1955.[17]

Eisenhower considered using nuclear weapons more often, and in response to a wider range of problems, than any other president. Yet one element of this nuclear dependency did bother him: the toll that anxiety about all-out war took on American morale. The new president spoke often of a widespread "hunger for peace"—a popular weariness with the cost of defense and the risk of war. Dulles said the administration wanted to "lift a great weight of fear" from the public mind. The United States, he mused to the president, should think about making "a spectacular effort to relax world tensions" on a global basis.[18]

Truman, to be sure, had also worried about the psychological stresses of the Cold War, but in a different way. NSC-68 had focused on the debilitating impact of Soviet military superiority on Western publics. For Eisenhower, the real problem was fear of nuclear war as such, no matter who was stronger. He believed people wanted the great powers to resolve their differences. Truman had worried about where talks would lead; Eisenhower, about not getting them started. To ease the fear of unending Cold War, he issued a series of would-be "spectacular" proposals.

In April 1953, after Stalin's death, the new president urged Soviet leaders to seize the "chance for peace" through joint cuts in military spending. That fall, in his first speech to the UN, he tried again, putting forward a plan that became known as "Atoms for Peace," under which the superpowers would provide fuel for Third-World nuclear reactors. In 1955, at his first meeting with Soviet leaders, Eisenhower proposed a global monitoring system—"Open Skies," he called it—to build East-West confidence and reduce the danger of surprise attack. All these initiatives fizzled, but the president was undaunted. More proposals followed. He would go anywhere, he said, from "Timbuktu to the North Pole, to do something about this question of peace."[19]

Eisenhower's commitment to reduce East-West tensions reshaped other elements of policy as well. He had launched his presidency with standard-issue Republican rhetoric about the Soviet leadership. ("They tutor men in treason. They feed upon the hunger of others. Whatever defies them, they torture, especially the truth.") Yet he tired of such talk. He felt people were not drawn to America's side by hearing how "wicked" Communism was. Few problems were solved by "table-pounding and name-calling." As diplomatic tools, they were "tragically stupid and ultimately worthless."[20]

When the president-elect and his team first discussed the Cold War's economic burden aboard the *Helena,* they had focused on questions of cost. Yet their choices eventually led to more radical revisions of policy. Tighter budgets meant greater reliance on nuclear weapons. This seemed to heighten international dangers and public anxiety and inspired the new administration to show that it was trying to make the world safer. Slowly but inexorably, the United States began to pull back from ideological confrontation. Containment may still have been American strategy, but retrenchment was giving it a very different look.

"DESTINY," EISENHOWER CLAIMED in his inaugural address, "has laid upon our country the responsibility for the Free World's leadership." The day before, he had written a more somber diary note to himself. Friends and allies who relied on U.S. resources should, he believed, understand a painful truth: "the American well can run dry."[21]

For the new president, leadership of the Free World meant pushing others to defend themselves. Eisenhower was more committed to the idea of European unity than any American president of the twentieth century, for one simple reason—burden sharing. A "United States of Europe," he once told his cabinet, would enable the United States of America to "sit back and relax somewhat."[22]

Harry Truman, of course, had also wanted Europe to spend more on defense, and he had achieved real results. Britain, which devoted 5.7 percent of GDP to defense in fiscal 1949–50, increased it to 9.9 percent by fiscal 1952–53. In the same period, French spending rose from 6.5 percent of GDP to 10.1 percent. These increases were enormous—but not good enough for Eisenhower. Once in office, he sent Dulles on a European trip to convey American impatience. Without more progress toward unification, a "rethinking" of American policy—meaning, less assistance or even withdrawal—would be unavoidable.[23]

Dulles's brief was a hard one. When Truman called for more allied spending, his own budget had also been growing rapidly. He had announced unprecedented peacetime deployments of combat forces to Europe and had gotten Congress to approve increased aid for allied militaries. Now the United States was again demanding greater European effort—while going in the opposite direction itself.

Eisenhower knew that "leadership" of the Western alliance rested on give-and-take. "This business of saying we are out in front, we know all the answers, you boys come along," he warned his staff, " . . . they are just not going to do it, that I can tell you just from the knowledge of people I have." Here was America calling big budgets "ruinous"—a threat to social and economic health—while telling its friends to spend more and more. The administration wanted to reduce security assistance to Europe too—and Congress voted for still deeper cuts.[24]

In 1953 the transatlantic debate about who should spend how much centered, as it had since Acheson's 1950 "bomb in the Waldorf," on the issue of German rearmament. The French had devised a scheme—creation of the so-called European Defense Community (EDC)—to keep West Germany from being able to field its own military forces. Eisenhower urged European governments to go forward with this plan even though he had, like many American officials, long ridiculed it. While at NATO, he had told George Marshall that the EDC embodied "every kind of obstacle, difficulty, and fantastic notion that misguided humans could put together in one package." Churchill agreed: the scheme was a "sludgy amalgam."[25]

One thing, however, was expected to make this odd design workable: the presence of U.S. forces in Europe. France asked the United States and Britain in late 1953 to guarantee that they would keep troops in Germany for at least twenty years. Eisenhower said no. He wanted Europe to provide for its own security—and soon. That the French could not even stand by their own proposal infuriated him. They seemed, in their indecision, a "hopeless, helpless mass of protoplasm."[26]

Eisenhower had deepened French indecision by refusing to promise that U.S. forces would stay in Europe. When the French National Assembly voted down the EDC scheme in August 1954, he was ready to retaliate. West Germany, he now said, had to be accepted as an equal member of NATO and full contributor to the common defense. If Paris resisted, the United States would sign a separate defense agreement with the Germans—excluding France.[27]

Having rejected its own plan, France had little choice but to accept Eisenhower's. (To ease French anxiety, Britain pledged to keep forces stationed on the mainland as long as others wanted them to stay.) The dispute over German rearmament that had divided the alliance for five years was finally being settled. Yet even at this historic juncture, Washington and Paris found it difficult to work together. The fits and starts of French decision making—and recurrent threats of backsliding—confirmed Eisenhower in his views about what could be expected of France. "Damn those French!" he said when it seemed that the Assembly might veto commitments made by the government. "It's their old game of diplomatic doodling to see how much they can get out for themselves, and never mind the rest of the world."[28]

IN THE 1950S, the United States and its allies repeatedly clashed over the conduct of the Cold War in Europe, but their most severe disagreements were about how to wage it beyond Europe. In the Third World, American policy makers had long believed that Britain and France were deeply misguided and doomed to fail. The Eisenhower administration took this attitude a step further: it wanted them to fail.

Dulles explained why on his first trip to the Middle East as secretary of state. He and Eisenhower expected the "hot breath" of Soviet policy to help them build a solid anti-Communist phalanx in the region. But the Europeans' "old colonial attitude toward the natives" was bound to "drive them into the hands of the communists." The United States had to avoid associating too closely with Britain in the region. Even when they worked together—as in the covert effort to bring down the government of Iran in August 1953—Washington and London saw things very differently. The United States feared Soviet influence in Iran, Eden told Churchill, but it did not share Britain's prime goal, which was to restore its oil rights. The Americans, he complained, wanted a quick solution and were not willing "to take second place even in an area where primary responsibility was not theirs." Washington was so uncomfortable about working with the British that in 1954 it decided at the last moment not to join the Baghdad Pact—long envisioned as a kind of mini-NATO for the Middle East—simply because Britain was also a signatory. It would support the pact but keep its cosponsors at arm's length.[29]

American policy was even more hostile toward France. It was clear by 1954 that the French would be driven out of Indochina unless the United States intervened. To relieve insurgent pressure on their troops in Vietnam (which were concentrated—foolishly, in Eisenhower's view—in a remote rural fortress known as Dien Bien Phu), Paris asked for nuclear bombing strikes. The Pentagon was sympathetic, but the president was not, and in April 1954 he overruled the chiefs. "You boys must be crazy," he exploded. "We can't use these awful things against Asians for the second time in less than ten years. My God!"[30]

Eisenhower, fearing enormous American losses in Indochina, aimed to stay out until France was defeated. He thought a French success would be bad for the Free World. When the French were beaten at Dien Bien Phu, Dulles called it "a blessing in disguise" for the United States. With the Europeans out of the way, new regimes—"free of the taint of French colonialism"—could at last be helped to become modern, functioning states. American military aid that had gone through Paris now went straight to Saigon; trainers were dispatched to help create and support an army to fight the Communists. Eisenhower saw such assistance as a way of avoiding the direct intervention that had stymied the French. "There are plenty of people in Asia," he said, "and we can train them to fight."[31]

Because the French were leaving Indochina, while the Americans were expanding their presence, the two allies' diplomatic interests frequently diverged. For France, the Geneva agreements of July 1954—under which Vietnam would be temporarily partitioned between the Communist north and the Western-backed south—were a convenient political cover for withdrawal. But to Eisenhower and Dulles, Geneva's terms seemed likely to undermine South Vietnam, requiring early national elections that its leaders could not win. As it had in Baghdad, Washington again refused to sign.[32]

Eisenhower's disagreements with Paris and London extended to other regions as well. In 1954 Washington gave covert military aid to opponents of the Guatemalan government of Jacobo Árbenz, whom it saw as advancing Communist goals. To block a Soviet foothold in the Western hemisphere, the United States intercepted ships that it said were carrying weapons to Guatemala. The British and French viewed such action as a gross violation of international law and prepared to express their opposition in the UN Security Council. To keep the issue off the agenda, Eisenhower had to threaten to use America's veto—for the first time ever. It stunned him that things had come to this. Washington had clearly "been too damned nice" to its allies. U.S. officials warned that they might retaliate against Britain's interests elsewhere in the world. Now it was the allies' turn to be outraged. Dulles, Churchill complained, "said a couple of things to Eden that need not have been said."[33]

The United States and its allies were further divided by Eisenhower's idea that Communist advances in the Third World could be prevented by threats to use nuclear weapons. Such threats, the president knew, reinforced a European view of Americans as "reckless, impulsive, and immature." So when the tiny offshore islands of Quemoy and Matsu (controlled by Chiang Kai-shek's Nationalist forces) were shelled from the Chinese mainland in September 1954, Churchill advised Eisenhower to simply write them off. They weren't worth the risk of war with China's Soviet patron, he thought. Eisenhower ignored him. He deepened his commitment to Chiang—first, in December 1954, signing a mutual defense treaty, and then in early 1955, winning advance congressional authority to go to war to implement it. Administration spokesmen emphasized that nuclear weapons were available to turn back a Communist attack. "I see no reason," the president told reporters, in words more inflammatory (and more carefully chosen) than any Truman had ever used, "why they shouldn't be used just exactly as you would use a bullet or anything else."[34]

After months of tension, the shelling of Quemoy and Matsu abruptly stopped in April 1955. The Chinese Communists had blinked, and the crisis was over. Zhou Enlai, China's foreign minister, explained that China did "not want to have a war with the United States." What Dulles called "brinkmanship" had apparently worked again. Yet it had also exposed a deep gulf between Washington and its allies. Eisenhower had threatened global war over a peripheral interest, insisting that he would carry out the threat without consulting anyone else. He had avoided war, but the lessons were disturbing even for him. The United States, he admitted to Dulles, might soon find itself waging "a life-and-death struggle under very great handicaps . . . [and] isolated in world opinion."[35]

THE EISENHOWER ADMINISTRATION wanted to find a steady and sustainable formula for waging the Cold War. Even so, in the Third World, its policies grew more unpredictable, estranging old allies and new partners alike. No event brought out these tensions more dramatically than the Suez crisis of 1956. Suez was no mere transatlantic disagreement, but a strategic defeat from which Britain and France never recovered. This was, in a sense, Eisenhower's goal. He and Dulles now went beyond merely wanting American allies to fail. The United States actively and decisively promoted their failure.

Although the Suez crisis was a climactic moment in the drama of European decolonization, it was American policy that touched it off. In 1955, hoping to counter growing Soviet influence in Egypt, Eisenhower and Dulles had offered to finance construction of the vast Aswan High Dam on the Upper Nile. At a total anticipated cost of $1.3 billion, it was the largest development project the United States had ever supported—and a symbol of a new approach toward Third-World regimes. The administration failed, however, to win support for the project in Congress, where the usual opponents of foreign aid were joined by cotton growers and the American Jewish community. Having claimed that the lure of aid would turn Egypt toward the West, Dulles was embarrassed by Nasser's recognition of Communist China in May 1956—and by his continuing rejection of peace with Israel. In mid-July, seeing how unpopular the project had become, the secretary of state decided to give up. If he didn't cancel funding himself, he admitted privately, the Senate would "chop it off tomorrow."[36]

Having abruptly reversed himself, Dulles now mounted a bizarre and unconvincing effort to make his decision look like a strategic initiative. He summoned the Egyptian ambassador to inform him of the cancellation, claiming—falsely—that the United States considered the project too big for Egypt to handle. He insisted—also falsely—that other members of the aid consortium (the World Bank and the British) agreed. Most peculiar was Dulles's boast that the move was part of a bold design. The termination of Aswan aid, he told Henry Luce, the publisher of *Time,* was "as big a chess move as U.S. diplomacy had made in a long time." By forcing Nasser and his Soviet patrons to find a way to pay for the project, American policy had put them "in a hell of a spot."[37]

In reality, of course, it was America's allies who were in a bad spot—as Nasser promptly demonstrated by nationalizing the canal. Anthony Eden, Churchill's successor as prime minister, told Eisenhower that in meeting this challenge, the British government had no choice but to "break" the Egyptian leader. From both Paris and London came the claim that, if they did not defend their interests, they would cease to be great powers. Harold Macmillan, Eden's chancellor of the exchequer, who knew Eisenhower well from the war years, told American diplomats that any compromise would make Britain "another Netherlands." (The United States, he groused to Dulles, might understand the Europeans' predicament "in [another] two-hundred years.")[38]

Eisenhower and Dulles condemned the seizure of the canal, but their allies' melancholy appeals did not move them. American policy makers *already* saw Britain as more or less another Netherlands; the United States simply wanted its friends to accept reality. In long letters to Eden—a correspondence that he wearily described as a "transatlantic essay contest"—the president sketched the negative consequences of using force to take back the canal. "Unless," he argued, "the occupying power was ready to employ the brutalities of dictatorship, local unrest would soon grow into guerrilla resistance, then open revolt, and possibly, wide-scale conflict." Worse, the entire Third World "would be consolidated against the West to a degree which, I fear, could not be overcome in a generation and, perhaps, not even in a century." The United States, Eisenhower wrote Eden, would condemn the use of force even by its closest allies. "I assure you that this could grow to such an intensity as to have the most far-reaching consequences."[39]

The centerpiece of American efforts to defuse the crisis was a hastily called multinational conference in London, beginning August 18, to discuss future management of the canal. It did not bring the United States and its allies closer together. To the contrary, Chip Bohlen, a member of the American delegation in London, considered his boss's performance at this meeting to be Dulles "at his worst." The secretary of state "shaded the edge of downright trickery and even dishonesty . . . . He talked out of both sides of his mouth," assuring the British and the French that he was with them, then telling the Russians that he wasn't. America's allies, said Bohlen, "felt tricked." They believed that the United States "had no clear policy."[40]

EISENHOWER AND DULLES did have a policy. They thought (wrongly, it turned out) that stalling would be enough to prevent war. Egypt was now running the canal without mishap, and the president felt that the idea of using force to restore European control had become "almost ridiculous." Dulles agreed: military options "were withering on the vine." In thinking that the crisis was almost over, American officials failed to see what was really happening. The British and French were "behaving," as the president's speechwriter Emmet Hughes put it, "suspiciously like people careful not to answer their phone till they were sure who was calling." Only when, together with Israel, America's allies launched their attack on the canal did Eisenhower and Dulles realize that they had been deceived.[41]

The reaction at the White House was immediate. It combined outrage with undisguised pleasure at the chance to join world opinion against old-fashioned imperialism. "Nothing," Eisenhower told the British, "justified double-crossing us." The tongue-lashing he gave Eden on the phone left the prime minister in tears.

> I don't see the point in getting into a fight to which there can be no satisfactory end, and in which the whole world believes you are playing the part of the bully, and you do not even have the firm backing of your entire people.

The president could not believe the allies' clumsiness. "I've just never seen," he told Hughes, "great powers make such a complete *mess* and *botch* of things . . . . My God!"[42]

The public American reaction was even harsher. Washington announced sanctions against Israel; in the UN Security Council it condemned the use of force and called for international peace-keepers. Henry Cabot Lodge, the UN ambassador, told Eisenhower that global praise for the United States was "absolutely spectacular." On national television, the president stayed on the high road. There could not be one law for the strong and another for the weak, he said. The United States had to stick to this principle even with close friends "or there will be no peace." Vice President Richard Nixon took a lower road, glorying in the split with U.S. allies. This "bold American declaration of independence" had had, he claimed, "an electrifying effect throughout the world."[43]

Washington's disapproval went far beyond rhetoric. When Eden asked for a face-to-face meeting, the president agreed, then publicly reneged. When the pound began to slide, the United States would not support it. The administration also refused to implement its plan for emergency sharing of oil supplies until British and French forces began to withdraw from the Suez. American policy makers saw what the crisis meant for their allies. For Britain and France, Dulles told the NSC, it was a virtual "death knell."[44]

Only one thing gave Washington pause: the Soviet opportunities created by the conflict. The British and French attack on Egypt had kept the West from exploiting the Red Army's bloody suppression of the Hungarian revolution, a popular uprising that further delegitimized Communist rule in Eastern Europe. Nikita Khrushchev, the new Kremlin leader, should have been on the ropes in late 1956. Instead, he threatened Paris and London with nuclear devastation, then proposed joint Soviet-American intervention to retake the canal. Eisenhower and his colleagues feared they had emboldened their main adversary. Reflexively, the president reached for the same nuclear threats he had used in the Asian crises of the last four years. Putting U.S. strategic forces on alert to deter Soviet intervention, he told his advisers, "If those fellows start something, we may have to hit 'em—and, if necessary, with everything in the bucket."[45]

HAD SUEZ BEEN A TRIUMPH or a disaster? Eisenhower was buoyant: "Everyone in the world says that in the last six weeks the U.S. has gained a place it hasn't held since World War II." Yet he and his advisers were also uneasy. With the Europeans marginalized for good, the United States had to assume new responsibilities. The president called for a quick review of foreign aid programs. He wanted to offer economic, military, and political benefits to governments that could keep the Soviets at bay. The Third World should see Western democracies as "a better group to hang with than the Communists." Still, he worried that others considered Washington long on talk—and short on real support for its friends.[46]

To dispel any image of passivity, Eisenhower summoned congressional leaders on New Year's Day 1957 and told them he needed a new grant of authority, this time "to sustain Western rights"—undefined—in the Middle East. The vacuum in the region, he told them, "must be filled by the United States before it is filled by Russia." Unless "ambitious despots" (he meant Nasser) knew U.S. forces could act on a moment's notice, the president warned, they might miscalculate. Both House and Senate granted his request.[47]

For more than a year and a half, American policy makers looked for an opportunity to apply the new Eisenhower Doctrine. The president wanted to make a decisive show of American power without bogging himself down. In July 1958, the overthrow of the Iraqi monarchy seemed at last to offer an opening. Military officers of a Nasserist type had murdered the king, and the whole region was on edge. The Lebanese government told Washington it feared Egyptian meddling, exercised through Syria. This concern was enough for Eisenhower. He summoned his advisers to the White House for a show of deliberation.

> My mind was practically made up regarding the general line of action we should take, even before we met. The time was rapidly approaching, I believed, when we had to move into the Middle East, and specifically into Lebanon, to stop the trend toward chaos.[48]

Virtually everyone hated the president's plan and its flimsy rationale. Not even Dulles saw any "hard evidence implicating Nasser" in Lebanon's troubles. He feared a Suez-like "wave of feeling against us throughout the Arab world." Congressional leaders insisted that Lebanon did not fit the "doctrine" they had endorsed a year earlier: it was threatened by civil war, not by foreign interference. Others doubted that the conflict was "Communist-inspired" and pointed out that UN inspectors had found no flow of arms from Syria. Intelligence reports warned of "terrorist attacks against American troops." Arab regimes would not support the United States publicly, and European opinion was also against. (In the House of Commons, Labor MPs cried "Shame!")[49]

Near-universal opposition did not deter Eisenhower. "The issue was clear to me—we had to go in." At the White House meeting, General Nathan Twining, the new JCS chairman, said troops could be ordered ashore as soon as he got back to the Pentagon. "Well, what are we waiting for?" the president demanded. He authorized Dulles to tell UN officials that they could take over once the United States restored order, and called Harold Macmillan, who had replaced Eden as prime minister after Suez, to give him a heads-up. Macmillan (who sighed, "You are doing a Suez on me") offered British troops, but the president brushed him off. No one else was to play a role.[50]

Once U.S. troops were on the ground, it quickly became clear that Eisenhower's public rationale for intervention—he compared it to Truman's support for Greece and Turkey—made no sense. There was no doubting Lebanon's disorder. Robert Murphy, the veteran diplomat whom the president dispatched as his personal emissary, said he had "not been in a more trigger-happy place than Beirut" since Berlin in 1945. But what was the disorder about—and could the United States calm things? The government Eisenhower proposed to help seemed powerless against the rebel factions it faced. Lebanon's army was split on sectarian lines, and its commander was afraid to act against insurgents. Doing so, Murphy learned, would "split [Lebanese forces] asunder . . . . [The] army would melt away."[51]

Amid this chaos, American diplomats, CIA operatives, and military commanders could not agree on what to do. The U.S. landing had actually increased factional violence, and the modest American fighting force—14,000 men at its peak—was too small to impose order. U.S. military commanders thought they might have to occupy the entire country. Murphy set himself a more limited goal: create a semblance of political calm and get out quickly. Early elections, he hoped, would allow a graceful exit. After three and a half months of occupation—during which Murphy visited one factional leader's hideout after another, mainly offering assurance that the United States meant them no harm—American forces left Beirut.

It was not easy to say what they had accomplished. Before the United States intervened, the new prime minister installed by Murphy had been a rebel leader trying to bring down the government. Now he *was* the government. In accepting a $10 million American check to repair damage done during the occupation, he denounced the very "doctrine" by which Eisenhower had justified intervention. The senior CIA man in Beirut was gloomy about the entire region. "No Arab state east of Suez," he judged, "could any longer be called pro-Western in the sense we'd once envisioned."[52]

Eisenhower acknowledged these concerns. The region's weak states guaranteed near-permanent tumult. "Until stable governments are set up and supported locally," he believed, "the Middle East will never calm down." America's own clients were hopelessly vulnerable. "If our policy is solely to maintain the kings of Jordan and Saudi Arabia in their positions, the prospect is hopeless, even in the short term."[53]

For all these worries, the president considered his Lebanon intervention—the most significant Cold War military operation between Korea and Vietnam and the first in the Arab world—a success. He had wanted to make up for Suez, to send Nasser and the Soviets a message, and he thought he'd made his point. Murphy agreed. No further intervention was needed. Touring the region after his departure from Lebanon, he met with General Kassim, the new Iraqi leader whose coup had triggered American action in the first place. Was the United States, Kassim asked, planning to strike Baghdad next? No, no, Murphy replied, that was out of the question. He challenged Kassim to give him "one good reason why Eisenhower would want to send American troops to invade the God-forsaken stretches of Iraq."[54]

LEBANON WAS EISENHOWER'S entire foreign policy in a (very small) nutshell. Do just enough, and no more, to deter threats as the president himself perceived them, without explaining his thinking to others or even caring whether they agreed. In the Middle East, this approach had seemed to work. On other issues, however, a debate was starting.

To make containment more sustainable, Eisenhower had by 1958 brought Pentagon spending down to 10 percent of GDP (from more than 14 percent when he took office). It began to be said, in fact, that the president was doing too little to meet military needs. The accusation enraged him. "The *idea,*" he said, "of *them* charging *me* with not being interested in *defense*! Damn it, I've spent my whole life being concerned with defense of our country."[55]

For the remainder of his presidency, this debate over defense spending and national security was Eisenhower's biggest headache. It had started with the Soviet Union's launch of the first man-made earth satellite, Sputnik, in October 1957. Suddenly, a controversy that Eisenhower had been able to dominate easily became one that he could not control at all. Fears of a "missile gap" were widespread. Isolated calls for more spending grew into a mainstream chorus. A year earlier the president himself had commissioned a blue-ribbon panel, led by the chairman of the Ford Foundation, H. Rowan Gaither, to study the costs and benefits of fallout shelters. Alarmed by Sputnik, the group hurriedly put forward a much broader set of recommendations, including a 25 percent increase in the Pentagon budget. Senior administration officials were themselves anxious. Christian Herter, Dulles's new deputy and his eventual successor, confided his fears to Emmet Hughes. "I am more worried than I have ever been," he said. "We—in the State Department—are only now learning serious things we never knew before about the limits of our military capacities."[56]

For many Americans, Sputnik was a new maximalist moment—a challenge to which the only appropriate response was a burst of policy activism. Eisenhower would have none of it. He rejected most of the Gaither Commission's recommendations and refused to declassify its report. (The casualty estimates for nuclear war were, he thought, too terrifying for public consumption.) He countered the group's proposed

$10 billion defense spending increase with one of just $1.5 billion—and said no increase at all would be even better. Reprising his old critique of Truman, the president insisted that the United States faced "not a temporary emergency . . . but a long-term responsibility." With Gaither and his colleagues in the Oval Office, Eisenhower mocked the nation's sudden mood changes. "Americans," he said, "will carry a challenging load only for a couple of years." The spending increases Congress was discussing he found purely symbolic—"more to stabilize public opinion than to meet any real need."[57]

The "missile gap" controversy was a classic case of national anxiety stoked by bad information presented as solid intelligence. Eisenhower, we now know, was a prisoner of his own supersecret information. Pictures produced by high-altitude U-2 spy flights told him there was no "missile gap." The president railed against the "demagogues and special interests" who alarmed the public, but until the Soviets shot down a U-2 in 1960, he could not even hint at what he knew. Unable to refute his critics, he seemed, in Hughes's own words, a "faltering force."[58]

Yet Eisenhower's declining credibility on national security issues had other sources too. He had, after all, argued—forcefully, publicly, repeatedly—that American military power was, as he put it, "awesome." And even without using sensitive data, he backed his case with specifics. In a nationwide address of March 1959, he pointed to no less than 41 different missile programs that the United States had under development. All the same, he was clearly losing the argument.[59]

Why was Eisenhower—a beloved war hero recently reelected president in a landslide—unable to reassure the public? Part of the problem was clearly the ongoing worldwide surge of East-West confrontation. In 1958 the Soviet Union, through its allies and clients, seemed to be putting pressure on one exposed Western position after another. That spring the president himself had identified a "trend toward chaos" in the Middle East. (Why else had he intervened in Lebanon?) During the summer, the Taiwan Straits standoff turned violent again. In the fall, Khrushchev renewed his threats against West Berlin, challenging Allied access to the city.[60]

Each of these crises—which followed one another, in Eisenhower's apt phrase, like "beads on a string"—seemed to raise the danger of war. The administration's responses were meant to look neither too passive nor too reckless, but to many critics they were either one or the other or both. The president's delphic utterances about defending Quemoy and Matsu were typical: he reminded the nation that nuclear weapons were at the ready, calling them "an almost routine part of our equipment." He hadn't decided whether to commit American forces but certainly "wouldn't hesitate" to do so.[61]

Not everyone was reassured by Eisenhower's approach. The joint chiefs found his brinkmanship stressful and confusing and told him they considered the islands indefensible. From retirement, Dean Acheson warned that the United States was heading toward "a war without friends or allies and over issues which the administration has not presented to the people and which are not worth a single American life." Shocked by his isolation, Eisenhower observed to Dulles that "as much as two-thirds of the world, and fifty percent of U.S. opinion, opposes the course which we have been following."[62]

If the Taiwan Straits crisis made American policy seem rigid, even reckless, Berlin raised the opposite fear. The chiefs worried that Eisenhower was doing too little to uphold the U.S. position there. In March 1959, after the president told Congress he wanted to reduce U.S. troop strength in Europe by more than 20 percent, General Twining asked for a meeting to present his colleagues' concerns. Was this any way to stand up to Moscow? In the Oval Office, Eisenhower cut him short. Remind the chiefs, he told Twining, that they are "not a policy-making body."[63]

Across the political spectrum, there was similar alarm. Even William Fulbright, the liberal senator from Arkansas, told the president that he found it hard to explain to constituents why the administration was reducing military manpower. "It looks strange," he said. Eisenhower was as curt and patronizing with Fulbright as he had been with Twining. Just tell your voters, he snapped, how deterrence works.[64]

EISENHOWER HAD MADE cooling the East-West nuclear competition one of the earliest themes of his presidency. Beginning in 1958, he returned to it constantly. While puzzled that Americans had become so "panicky," he was convinced that arms control initiatives were the right response. All earlier initiatives having failed, he now asked the secretary of state for new ones with at least "the appearance of something new." The United States couldn't, the president said, keep "hammering away on exactly the same keys." Dulles was sympathetic. "I feel desperately," he said, "the need for some important gesture in order to gain an effect on world opinion."[65]

Out of this frustration came the main policy innovation of the late Eisenhower administration: the effort to restrict nuclear weapons tests. In April 1958 the president wrote to Khrushchev to propose a system of comprehensive inspections to monitor a ban. The Soviet leader accepted, and formal talks opened at midyear.

In the negotiations that followed, Eisenhower found Soviet positions "completely ridiculous." Still, he told congressional leaders, he was determined to "soften up" the Kremlin leadership, if only "a little bit," before he left office. The administration's disarmament achievements, he admitted, were "negligible." The United States had made no "chip in the granite" of Soviet diplomacy. But the goal of opening up the Soviet Union was so important, the president said, that he would accept any inspection system its leaders would agree to.[66]

Eisenhower's pursuit of a test ban reflected his growing dissatisfaction with America's own nuclear strategy. In his view, it had become dangerous, expensive, and unnecessary. When the country woke up to this fact, he thought, "we will try to retrench." Dulles seconded the president's judgment. Long the administration's strongest anti-Communist voice, he was now just as relaxed about Soviet technological advances as Eisenhower. Some people, he told an NSC meeting in April 1958, thought the right military strategy was to "have the most and the best of everything." No, he countered, "enough is enough." The United States "*should not attempt to be the greatest military power in the world.*"[67]

This was an absolutely astonishing statement from Dulles. It went beyond retrenchment to retreat and resignation. But not even the conversion of an old Cold Warrior could help Eisenhower win Soviet cooperation. The president pursued East-West compromise in large multilateral forums, in smaller sessions of the Big Four foreign ministers, and in still smaller meetings, including one-on-one conversations with Khrushchev at Camp David in 1959—all without discernible result. During his last year in office, he hoped the four-power summit scheduled for Paris in May 1960 might offer a "ray of light." To improve the chances of success, he persuaded the British and French to make nuclear testing the only item on the summit agenda, and he told his own advisers that he would accept terms for a treaty that he knew many of them opposed.[68]

To hold his own administration together, Eisenhower tried to match conciliation with shows of vigilance. He authorized a U-2 flight over the Soviet Union on the very eve of the Paris meetings—even though he had earlier ruled out flights at such delicate political moments. When the plane was shot down, Khrushchev enjoyed a propaganda windfall, and Eisenhower fumbled in response. First denying any espionage, he then took personal responsibility for it, then rejected Khrushchev's demand for an apology.

In this atmosphere, the Paris summit could not possibly fulfill the president's high hopes for it. At the first session, Khrushchev delivered a tirade against Eisenhower and then stormed out. Clearly negotiation would continue only if the United States and its allies begged for it. Macmillan—"with tears in his eyes"—proposed to follow after Khrushchev and ask him to return. Eisenhower was sympathetic. Only De Gaulle saw that pleading could not produce a viable agreement. "Icy and contemptuous" of his colleagues' confusion, the French president adjourned the meeting—and the summit collapsed.[69]

After this disaster, Eisenhower had no choice but to strike a tougher pose. Even the Europeans had started complaining. The secretary-general of NATO, Paul-Henri Spaak, visited the president in the Oval Office and told him that U.S. leadership of the alliance had become "too kind, too indulgent." Eisenhower scorned meaningless, morale-boosting additions to the defense budget; he had even said that cutting it 20 percent would do no harm. Now, at last, he announced an increase. The decision pained him. How could building missiles and nuclear weapons do "more to restore a feeling of Western confidence in a stable future than had all the disarmament talks" he had tried to energize? The result was, he believed, a "wry and sad commentary on human intelligence."[70]

EISENHOWER'S HANDLING of the presidency had become regretful, disengaged, even passive. Yet there was one set of issues on which he took a different approach: he wanted to grapple with policy problems in America's own backyard. In May 1958 he pushed Nixon to tour Latin America. (The president had never done so himself.) Although the vice president was reluctant to make the trip—much too boring, he thought—the two-and-a-half-week journey that followed was anything but. In Peru, Nixon and his wife were "shoved, stoned, and booed"—and showered with saliva. In Venezuela, he faced a "howling and ugly mob [that] smashed [his] car . . . and threatened to overturn it and drag its occupants into the street." Nixon felt he "had come as close as anyone could get, and still remain alive, to a firsthand demonstration of the ruthlessness, fanaticism, and determination of the enemy we face in the world struggle." Not everyone saw Communism's hand in these events. Everyone, however, recognized that the United States could "no longer get by with fancy words and little action."[71]

This spasm of anti-Americanism put Latin America back on Washington's map. Policy makers argued for "sweeping changes" in U.S. strategy—trade liberalization, increased foreign aid, and more. Eisenhower told his advisers that "the most critical question before us is what the rich countries are going to do with their wealth." He asked "what could be done about the revolutionary ferment in the world." After Nixon's bruising trip, he began to formulate some answers. The president authorized the creation of the Inter-American Development Bank (and U.S. capital contributions to it); he proposed a new $500 million aid program to promote economic progress in Latin America; and he launched his own belated trip through the hemisphere in February 1960.[72]

Before these initiatives could bear fruit, however, U.S. policy faced a new challenge, which it has had to grapple with ever since. On New Year's Day 1959, Fidel Castro entered Havana as the victorious leader of the Cuban revolution. Alarmed, Eisenhower and his advisers began to explore ways of "restraining Castro if he should develop into a menace." By the end of the year, seeing the steady growth of Cuba's ties with the Soviet Union, they agreed that "something would have to be done." The United States began training a paramilitary force of Castro's opponents and explored formation of a government-in-exile.[73]

The administration was hardly dealing with Latin American radicalism for the first time. But squeezing Castro in 1960 proved far more difficult than bringing down Árbenz in 1954. The politics of the hemisphere had changed. Other governments were no longer ready to endorse campaigns to topple one of their own. Eisenhower concluded that to persuade other governments to oppose Castro, he needed a more comprehensive strategy. The United States had to reconsider its own support for the hemisphere's right-wing dictators.

In the course of 1960, the United States led an unprecedented assault on the most notorious (and most vulnerable) of these dictators, Rafael Trujillo of the Dominican Republic. In June, Washington joined other members of the Organization of American States (OAS) in finding Trujillo guilty of "flagrant and widespread violations" of human rights (among them, an assassination attempt against the president of Venezuela). In August it broke relations with Santo Domingo, and Eisenhower began to ready other levers of American power against Trujillo. He asked the military to be ready to intervene in the event of a coup, and the CIA began supplying small arms to Trujillo's opponents—historically, a key step toward support for a new government.[74]

These developments were a seismic shift in U.S. policy. As Eisenhower described it, "non-intervention" (the traditional demand by Latin American states that the United States stay out of their affairs) "had given way to a new idea—the idea that *all* American nations had an interest in ending feudalism."[75] He was betting that regime change against a left-wing adversary like Castro would be easier if he challenged a recognized right-wing retrograde like Trujillo at the same time. The gamble did not pay off. Herter, secretary of state since Dulles's death in 1959, confessed to Eisenhower that the United States had not persuaded the OAS either that Cuba was becoming a Soviet base or that its new leaders were Communists. (On Herter's memo, the president gave his own testy grade of State's performance: "Almost a zero!")[76]

Yet the resistance of other governments was only part of the problem. Eisenhower himself seemed undecided about how hard to lean on Castro. He set out a long list of criteria that had to be met before he would approve a covert operation in Cuba. The most demanding of these was the formation of a "responsible and unified" exile government. When the planners came back to him in December 1960—having made no progress toward this goal—he stonewalled. "Boys," the president said, "if you don't intend to go through with this, let's stop talking about it."[77]

Eisenhower always qualified his readiness to use American power with so many limits and conditions—some sensible, some all but impossible to meet—that his true aims were usually known only to him. So it was with Cuba. Through his last days in office, he kept goading his advisers to meet his criteria, so that an offensive could be put in motion. His final advice, on the eve of handing power to John Kennedy, was a warning not to be too cautious. Fear of "shooting from the hip," Eisenhower said, could be carried too far. To achieve large goals, the United States "should be prepared to take more chances and be more aggressive." Just for a moment, the old president sounded more like his successor than the author of eight years of retrenchment.[78]

DWIGHT EISENHOWER REMAINS a puzzle. One of the best qualified, most thoughtful, clear-headed, and practical-minded of our presidents, he was increasingly off balance in the national security debates that dominated his last years in office. Long after he left the White House, his stubborn, almost visionary good sense continued to attract admirers. He was a leader of extraordinary balance and reasonableness. How was it, then, that he came to seem so out of touch?[79]

Many factors—partisanship, ideology, the national boredom of the late 1950s, the media, the president's advancing age, even the interests of the "military-industrial complex" that he warned against—played a part in this story. But the puzzle should not be overstated. One explanation is more important than any other. Eisenhower took office offering a corrective to what he described as the politics of emergency. His consistent theme was that there had to be a way to manage foreign policy that avoided sharp swings between over- and underengagement. This was the counsel of his January 1961 farewell address, in which he warned Americans not to think that "some spectacular and costly action could become the miraculous solution to all current difficulties." The United States, he said, needed a strategy that would not promise too much, a mind-set that would "enable us to carry forward steadily, surely, and without complaint the burdens of a prolonged and complex struggle."[80]

Prizing sustainability as he did, Eisenhower was extremely resistant to changes of course. He was reluctant even to acknowledge new circumstances. As long as the task at hand was to climb down from the exposed positions created by Truman, his strategy had few challengers. Retrenchment did not, at least for a while, really have to explain itself. In the early 1950s, it seemed a self-evident necessity (much as Nixon and Kissinger's détente did in the early 1970s). Yet as memories of defeat and overcommitment faded, as technological change accelerated and geopolitical competition intensified, Eisenhower's strategy needed a better defense, and a better payoff, than he could give it. Americans were not satisfied with a policy that had no larger horizons at the end of the decade than it had had at the beginning. They began to think that policies designed for the long haul were blind to the needs and opportunities of the moment. They became more receptive to the argument that they had to, and could, do better. And they picked a new president who was eager to try.

Part Two

1961–1980

4

"Boy Commandos" of the New Frontier

KENNEDY'S ANXIOUS ACTIVISM

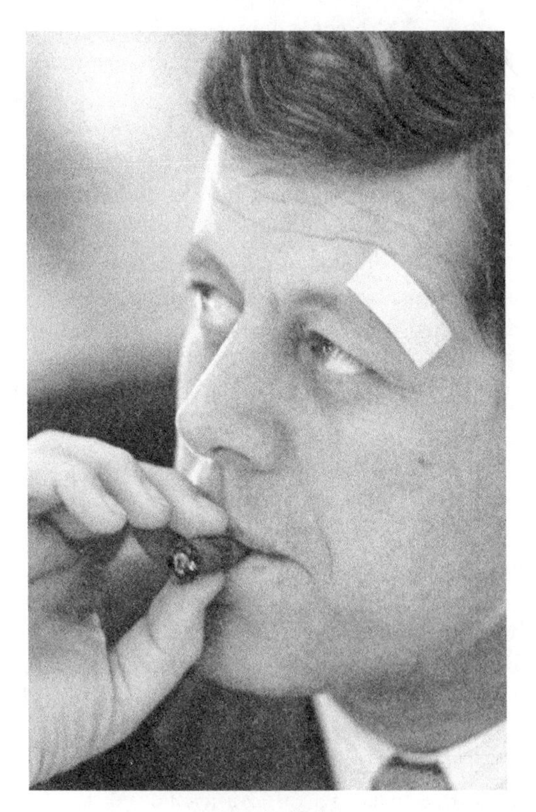

John Kennedy

WHEN ADLAI STEVENSON, twice the Democrats' losing candidate against Dwight Eisenhower, visited 1600 Pennsylvania Avenue early in the Kennedy administration, he was unhappy with what he found there—"the damnedest bunch of boy commandos running around," he told a friend afterward. He may not have been referring only to junior members of the White House staff. John Kennedy was the youngest man ever elected president—at forty-three, he was more than a quarter century younger than Eisenhower (and seventeen years younger than Stevenson). At forty-one, McGeorge Bundy, who had been dean of Harvard College since he was thirty-four, became the youngest national security adviser ever. Robert McNamara, forty-four, previously the youngest president of the Ford Motor Company, now became the youngest secretary of defense. The new administration was run, as the wife of Bundy's deputy Walt Rostow described them, by "the junior officers of the Second World War come to responsibility."[1]

The New Frontier's "junior officers" disparaged their elders' record with invective matched by few incoming administrations. Kennedy had argued on the campaign trail that America's security had "declined more rapidly than over any comparable period in our history." He belittled Eisenhower's presidency as "eight years of drugged and fitful sleep" and said history might eventually judge "that these were the days when the tide began to run out for the United States. These were the times when the Communist tide began to pour in."[2]

Fear of a changing nuclear balance—the "missile gap" that experts had worried about since Sputnik—was one part of Kennedy's indictment, and once in office, he launched the largest peacetime defense buildup in American history to date. But his call for new policies went far beyond military affairs. Unprecedented change was under way around the world, the new president said. To hold its own, the United States had to compete effectively in areas it had neglected under Eisenhower—"in social inventiveness, in moral stamina, in physical courage." American policy had not risen to this challenge. Instead, it "allowed the Communists to evict us from our rightful estate at the head of this world-wide revolution. We have been made to appear as the defenders of the *status quo*."[3]

The claim that global trends were leaving America behind had long been part of Kennedy's rhetoric. As a first-term senator, he had described the support he wanted to extend to developing nations (in this case, South Vietnam):

> What we must offer them is a revolution—a political, economic, and social revolution far superior to anything the Communists can offer—far more peaceful, far more democratic, and far more locally controlled.

In seeking the presidency, Kennedy expressed open disdain for those who, while sharing this goal, did not understand how to achieve it. "Attitudes, platitudes, and beatitudes"—his dismissive description of Eisenhower's empty talk—were no match for the rough ways of Communist power. The United States, he warned, had "allowed a soft sentimentalism to form the atmosphere we breathe." The onetime PT boat commander mocked the man who had organized D-Day. "A diffuse desire to do good," he said, "has become a substitute for tough-minded plans and operations."[4]

Scornful rhetoric is familiar enough in partisan politics, but Kennedy did not spare members of his own party. Stevenson he considered a "weeper." (Joking about a speechwriter's draft, he called it "good copy for Adlai," meaning too soft to be effective. "My style," he bragged, "is harder.") Even Clark Clifford—Kennedy's personal lawyer, the overseer of his presidential transition, and a veteran of the Truman White House—found that previous experience in government counted for little with the new team. They treated their predecessors, he lamented, "with something bordering on contempt." They "behaved as though history had begun with them."[5]

NO PART OF THE Kennedy administration's self-portrayal has been more durable than personal "vigor"—its confident readiness to act. Robert McNamara, described by David Halberstam as "the can-do man in the can-do society, in the can-do era," was a famous exemplar of this outlook. With no foreign policy experience, he came to Washington declaring that it was better to "have a wrong decision made than no decision at all." Those who worked closely with Kennedy saw that the activist bent came straight from the president. He liked to interrupt discussions of long-term strategy, said George Ball, who became the number-two man at State, by asking, "Let's not worry about five years from now, what do we do tomorrow?" For Walt Rostow, Kennedy's body language said it all. When an adviser wasted briefing time on an idea with which he was already familiar, the president "would tap his teeth and fuss with his tie." The ideas that appealed to him were those he could put to work right away. (Numbers confirm the point. In less than three years, John Kennedy authorized almost as many covert operations as Dwight Eisenhower had done in eight. And it was he who ordered the navy to create the elite commando unit that in 2011 found and killed Osama bin Laden.)[6]

This hyperactive "boy commando" style has regularly stimulated second thoughts about the Kennedy years. Decades after he served as a White House adviser, Arthur Schlesinger, Jr., bemoaned the "addiction of activism," calling it the "besetting sin of the New Frontier." The Kennedys were "not planners," he felt; "they were improvisers" and "impatient with systems." Others agreed that the price of impulsive policy making was high. It left the president, Paul Nitze concluded, "in a perpetual state of reaction to one crisis after another rather than working toward long-term goals."[7]

Yet some members of the new team thought the administration had a bigger problem than too much activism. Eminent scholars of American politics—among them, Richard Neustadt, Harvard's foremost authority on the presidency—had persuaded Kennedy that effective leaders kept their options open and did not commit themselves before they had to. George Ball thought the president had overlearned such maxims. For Ball, the decision-making theorists "provided too facile a rationalization for postponing unpleasant decisions on major issues where results would not be immediately apparent."[8]

Others shared this judgment. Although regularly invited to the White House to offer his views, Dean Acheson grumbled to Truman that the meetings were "strangely depressing. Nothing seems to get decided." Walt Rostow felt the same frustration. Early on he was asked to prepare a document defining the new administration's national security strategy. Though endlessly discussed, the ever-expanding draft was never adopted. No one cared to resolve the disagreements it provoked.[9]

By instinct, by ideology, by what many of them saw as strategic necessity, John Kennedy and his team were probably the most activist group ever put in charge of American foreign policy. After retrenchment under Eisenhower, they favored a more purposeful use of national power. At the same time, they were exceedingly indecisive managers of policy, given to protracted and inconclusive deliberation. Kennedy did prize vigor. But in a world of nuclear-armed rivals, he also feared, as Rostow put it, "convulsive and excessively energetic American actions." Neither of these qualities was more the administration's "besetting sin" than the other. Together—hyperconfident ambition shadowed by concern about getting in too deep—they shaped the New Frontier.[10]

Both traits were on display in Kennedy's inaugural address, which joined hot rhetoric with a call to reduce Cold War tensions. They were evident too in the administration's very first foreign policy crisis—the failed attempt to incite a popular insurgency against Castro by landing Cuban émigré fighters in the Bay of Pigs. The new president had been willing to go along with the CIA's operation in part because the idea matched his own instincts. But the reason the Bay of Pigs became a fiasco was not simply that Kennedy and his advisers had a weakness for decisive action. The entire affair also dramatized the cost of deferring decisions and splitting differences. Although the president was skeptical of the CIA plan, he did not reject it—he wanted it improved. For weeks Bundy assured him that the strategy was being refined. Only on the eve of the operation did Kennedy and his national security adviser conclude that the process had failed to produce a viable plan. And even then they did not call it off. They vetoed U.S. air cover for the émigré fighters who were trying to establish a beachhead. The operation was doomed without direct support, but it went forward anyway.[11]

Every major foreign crisis of the Kennedy administration—those that ended successfully and those that did not—showed the same counterpoint. Activist aspirations were adjusted by sensitivity to risk. The president and his advisers came to office convinced that better policy outcomes required bold leadership. But they were understandably fearful of having no way out of dangerous confrontations, and they found it excruciatingly hard to strike the right balance. Long deliberation often led them to postpone choice, to seek alternatives to direct action. Tough talk was followed by a secret search for compromise.

The key to understanding John Kennedy's maximalism is to see that it was designed from the beginning with an escape hatch. This strategic combination shaped the U.S. approach to the Berlin crisis in his first year as president. His handling of the Cuban missile crisis late in his second year repeated the pattern. His struggle to find a viable Vietnam policy, which dominated the last days of his presidency, showed how deeply it had become ingrained.

THE PROBLEM THAT preoccupied Kennedy more than any other in his first months was a Cold War perennial—Berlin. He saw it as a "dangerous mess" and, like Eisenhower, believed that dividing up the city after World War II had been a terrible mistake. But mishandling the issue could lead to disaster. Belligerence could spark a nuclear war; hesitation would signal defeatism. Berlin was the issue he most needed to get right when he met Nikita Khrushchev in Vienna in June 1961. It was, his advisers told him, the true "bone in the throat of U.S.-U.S.S.R. relations."[12]

For decades the encounter between Kennedy and Khrushchev at Vienna has been seen as a gross mismatch. A tough-talking old Bolshevik allegedly bested a well-meaning Yankee greenhorn—and concluded that he could push him around. Vienna's many meetings and social events were definitely full of combative, exhausting, and largely pointless argument. Every effort Kennedy made to start a constructive discussion with the Soviet leader was a failure. When he voiced the hope that neither superpower would upset the strategic status quo by challenging the other in the Third World, Khrushchev harangued him about socialism's inevitable triumph. When Kennedy worried about conflicts arising through "miscalculation," the Soviet leader ridiculed the idea. The Soviet Union would never go to war by mistake. To a plaintive question—did he not admit making mistakes?—Khrushchev answered with another boast: he was the man who had exposed Stalin's crimes to the world! A friend found the president "dazed" by all this. The Soviet leader, Kennedy told Harold Macmillan in London on the way home, was "much more of a barbarian" than he had expected.[13]

Sterile back-and-forth did not, however, keep the Yankee greenhorn from conveying his one crucial message: Kennedy wanted Khrushchev to know that the United States would not under any circumstances let itself be ousted from West Berlin. Here his language grew hard. "We are in Berlin not because of someone's sufferance," he said. "We fought our way there." Before signing a separate peace treaty with East Germany, as he threatened to do, Khrushchev should see that the denial of American occupation rights would be "a most serious challenge, and no one can foresee how serious the consequences might be." To be "expelled" from Berlin would put Washington's alliances at risk. He had not become president, said Kennedy, to preside over this result. The Soviet Union would not accept a similar loss; nor would the United States.[14]

The gravity and directness of Kennedy's warnings make it hard to think that, on this issue, he came off second best at Vienna. Yet he worried he hadn't gotten through—that Khrushchev did not believe the United States would risk war over Berlin. Back in Washington, in a state of agitation recalling the first days after the invasion of South Korea, the president and his advisers asked themselves how to make their resolve more credible. Dean Acheson, brought in for consultations, reached for the same answers he had pressed on Harry Truman in June 1950: a bigger defense budget, more troops to Europe, a state of emergency, a nuclear alert, and more. Because, as Acheson put it, the question "was essentially one of U.S. will," it was crucial to convey almost mindless determination. Even more important was to show that the United States could counter a Soviet challenge in Berlin without blowing up the world. The United States, Acheson argued, needed troops and planes that could actually hold off a Soviet attack. Western forces might not be able to win, but they had to fight long enough to make Moscow worry that "the danger of escalation was getting out of hand." McNamara agreed. At the edge of the nuclear abyss, the Soviets had to have the "motive and the opportunity for changing their course."[15]

Acheson counseled Kennedy, just as he had Truman, not to count on diplomacy to defuse the crisis. "An attempt to solve the Berlin issue by negotiation," he told the president, "is worse than a waste of time and energy. It is dangerous." Khrushchev "cannot be persuaded by eloquence or logic, or cajoled by friendliness." As long as the Soviet leader doubted Western resolve, Acheson insisted, "negotiation should be regarded purely from the propaganda point of view." It was merely a tool to shore up public support for tough military measures.[16]

Kennedy's advisers considered the former secretary of state a tiresome old dinosaur, but they too believed that forceful measures were needed. Even the ever-sober Chip Bohlen told the president that if Soviet forces tried to cut off Berlin, the United States had "to react swiftly and decisively and, indeed, to *overreact* if necessary." In a grim nationwide TV speech on July 25, Kennedy called for the formation of six new army divisions, emergency improvements in airlift capability, standby authority to triple draft calls and mobilize reserves, and new funding for fallout shelters. His language was just as categorical as it had been in Vienna: "We cannot and will not permit the Communists to drive us out of Berlin."[17]

The Berlin crisis of 1961—created by Khrushchev's threats to cut off Western access—followed the same trajectory as every previous crisis over the city. It inflamed East-West tensions and fears of nuclear war; it inflated the U.S. defense budget; and finally, it exposed the hollowness of Soviet threats. In August, Khrushchev built a wall through the middle of Berlin, at great cost to Communist prestige. But he did not try to push the United States as far as he had repeatedly said he would. A peace treaty with East Germany that would end Western rights in Berlin—which Soviet officials had called inevitable—never materialized. Despite tense moments between Soviet and American units on the Autobahn, the status quo remained intact.[18]

What followed this familiar East-West standoff, however, was a second and very different crisis—between the United States and its allies. Just eight days after Khrushchev put up the wall, Kennedy told Secretary of State Dean Rusk that he wanted "to take a stronger lead" in talks with Moscow. The president did not buy Acheson's argument that diplomacy could only help manage public opinion. He told Rusk that he was even ready to yield the strong legal pillar of the West's policy in Berlin—its "occupation rights"—as long as "strong guarantees" took their place. In this way, the Berlin problem could be solved for good. It would cease to be a possible trigger for war. Kennedy intended to be bold. "I am talking about a real reconstruction of our negotiating proposals," he told Rusk, "and not about a modest add-on."[19]

ONE OF THE MOST famous lines of John Kennedy's inaugural address—suggested to him by John Kenneth Galbraith—was the exhortation that the United States "never fear to negotiate." About Berlin, however, the president knew that America's friends completely disagreed with him. De Gaulle thought it a mistake to talk just because "Mr. Khrushchev has whistled." His outlook did not discourage Kennedy. It was time, he said sternly, to tell the allies "that they must come along or stay behind."[20]

The French and German response surprised the president: they preferred to stay behind. When Maurice Couve de Murville, De Gaulle's foreign minister, hosted his colleagues to discuss Berlin in December 1961, he informed them that France refused to take part even in exploratory talks with the Soviets. Rusk, a man for whom a bland calm was integral to diplomacy, responded with incredulity—and anger. He was "appalled," he said. If the alliance could not agree on this issue, he was "obliged to wonder whether there is, in fact, an alliance." When Couve de Murville said Khrushchev should be told that his own conduct made negotiations impossible, Rusk shot back that Western disunity would only embolden the Soviets. France was forcing the United States to ask whether the allies really "had the same objectives."[21]

After such a stormy meeting, the usual American response would have been to try to mollify the Europeans. Instead, the Kennedy administration stopped telling them the truth. Rusk left Paris pledging that the United States would offer no concessions that its allies found unacceptable, but the president overrode his commitment. The British and Germans, Kennedy explained, must not stop the United States from showing Moscow how flexible it was prepared to be. In mid-February 1962 he wrote Khrushchev again to propose what he called "a considerable departure from normal diplomacy"—in plain language, an offer to keep America's own allies in the dark. As Rusk flew off to meet with Andrei Gromyko in March, Kennedy acknowledged that the secretary of state's formal instructions were not especially innovative, but that was because "we must not put on paper things which might shock our Allies if presented without prior consultation." Rusk was to convey the real U.S. position to Gromyko orally and hint at further concessions if the Soviets were ready to sign an agreement.[22]

Kennedy's scheme was too devious, too disingenuous, and too far from previous policy to last. In April, Adenauer added his own dissent to De Gaulle's, writing Kennedy that he too now opposed talks with Moscow. Worse, he leaked his grievances to Daniel Schorr of CBS News. But the president did not yield. He ordered the American ambassador to call on Adenauer with a blistering complaint. (He worked on the language personally, Bundy noted, "to communicate sharply with the old gentleman.") Kennedy's message to Adenauer was that policy disagreements should be aired directly, not via "offensive" leaks. He could "hardly be expected to look with good humor on hints that these things were all done better by John Foster Dulles." After all, the president of the United States asked, hadn't he pushed back firmly against Khrushchev's threats? Hadn't he done more for Germany than De Gaulle? Adenauer should understand that "President Kennedy and not John Foster Dulles is now in charge of foreign policy."[23]

German defiance annoyed Kennedy, but France offered the more frontal challenge. So when the president received André Malraux, Nobel laureate and French minister of culture, in May, he did not mince words. De Gaulle, he complained, was making a "conscious . . . effort to eliminate us from the affairs of Europe"—without helping to solve common problems. "We feel like a man carrying a 200-pound sack of potatoes, and other people not carrying a similar load, at least in potatoes, keep telling us how to carry our burden." Kennedy said he was "getting tired of it." The United States hadn't taken on a large international role out of any "sense of *grandeur*" and would—here his frustration led him to stretch the truth—"be glad to get out of Europe."[24]

After this conversation, the president instructed the U.S. ambassador in Paris to make the same points to De Gaulle face to face, telling him—"with emphasis"—that France "cannot have both our military presence and our diplomatic absence" on major issues. De Gaulle gave no ground. He told the ambassador that he didn't fear America's withdrawal. What worried him was its "excessive role in European affairs." Kennedy, he complained, had tried to commit France and West Germany to policies they opposed. As for security guarantees, De Gaulle noted that the United States hadn't even entered World War II until France was already defeated! Rusk had this exchange in mind when, soon thereafter, he complained to Adenauer that "when we send envoys to some capitals, we are doubtful whether to send an ambassador or a psychiatrist."[25]

The nastiness of this second Berlin crisis—between the United States and its allies—revealed the gap in their strategic outlook. It was triggered by Kennedy's desire to break the pattern of recurrent East-West confrontations, even if doing so divided the alliance. The United States saw the status quo as dangerous and unsustainable and felt secure enough to handle the risks created by diplomatic experimentation. The French and the Germans did not. The status quo might be unsatisfactory, but they preferred to live with it. Kennedy and his advisers were frustrated by this clash of perspectives, but they understood its meaning. Whether waging the Cold War more vigorously or trying to reduce its dangers, the United States, as Rostow put it, would find itself on a "relatively lonely stage."[26]

EVEN MORE THAN in Europe, Kennedy and his team wanted a fundamental makeover of Eisenhower's strategy in the Third World. "America," said George Ball in describing the new outlook, "should not think of itself as a *status quo* country; its own traditions were revolutionary." Overemphasizing "political stability," he argued, ignored a potential American advantage. The United States should "stop trying to sustain traditional societies and ally itself with the side of revolution." The right place for American policy was on the side of change, even if that meant "transient instability."[27]

Such views made Kennedy and his team eager to explore diplomatic opportunities across the Third World. The desire to reach out to young leaders and changing societies spawned the Peace Corps and the Alliance for Progress. It also produced impatience with many of America's traditional clients. In the Middle East, the United States—hoping to broaden its policy beyond the Arab monarchies—now pursued a rapprochement with Nasser too.[28]

The new approach was most visible in policy toward South Vietnam. After Vice President Lyndon Johnson visited Saigon in May 1961, his report to Kennedy condemned the government of Ngo Dinh Diem for failing "to maintain and intensify its responsiveness to the social, economic and political needs of the people of Vietnam." Building popular support, Johnson told the president, was hard for "men in white linen suits whose contact with the ordinary people is largely through the rolled-up windows of a Mercedes-Benz." American aid would help, but what South Vietnam really needed was a new kind of politics. The United States had to "encourage the Saigon government, from the President down, to get close to the people, to mingle with them, to listen for their grievances, and to act on them. Handshakes on the streets of Vietnamese leaders and people": that, the vice president enthused, "is the concept that has got to be pursued."[29]

Johnson assured Kennedy that South Vietnam was "not in danger of imminent collapse," but the next few months shook American complacency. By October, Vietcong attacks had tripled, and the president's military adviser, General Maxwell Taylor, returned with Walt Rostow from their own inspection tour with a far grimmer message. The outlook, Taylor felt, was "the darkest" since the French withdrew in 1954. Rostow foresaw "slow but total defeat." Their report recommended the first deployment of U.S. troops to South Vietnam—a force of 8,000 soldiers who would be available to fight if needed, but whose immediate mission would be publicly announced as flood relief in the Mekong delta.[30]

Taylor later recalled that his and Rostow's proposal enjoyed wide support until the president shot it down. Kennedy certainly did not like it, but outside the White House staff no one else did either. The Pentagon wanted to know what the troops were supposed to do. "We must have a clear statement of the military objective before we recommend a force to accomplish it," said General Lyman Lemnitzer, the JCS chairman. The State Department focused on the inadequacy of South Vietnam's leaders. Dean Rusk said the big question was whether Diem could "give us something worth supporting." His answer was no—and would remain no "until Diem makes a 100% effort."[31]

Other State Department officials were even more hostile to Diem. Averell Harriman, whom Kennedy had charged with negotiating a cease-fire in neighboring Laos, said the United States could not stake its prestige on a "repressive, dictatorial and unpopular regime." George Ball forecast an ever-rising American military commitment to back an incompetent government. (Ball shocked his colleagues by mentioning 300,000 troops. Kennedy's famous response was "George, you're just crazier than hell.") Even John Kenneth Galbraith, newly named ambassador to India, weighed in. There was no overcoming Diem's "ineffectuality," he wrote after a stopover in Saigon, but the United States should not fear a military take-over. Young generals in power might offer a "fresh dynamic."[32]

To the "boy commandos" on the president's staff, all this was deeply frustrating. They saw greater American involvement as a way to overcome Diem's defects. Rostow had argued for months that the South Vietnamese needed a "radical push in the right directions." He and Taylor had largely won over their White House colleagues. Like those who had convinced Truman of the benefits of regime change in North Korea, Bundy told the president that victory in Vietnam "would produce great effects all over the world." The most committed NSC activist was Robert Komer, known as "Blowtorch Bob." Komer found the threat to South Vietnam so dire that "overreacting" was the only viable response. (This was the same word Bohlen had used in advising the president on Berlin.)[33]

Kennedy's staff did not sway him. He agreed to increase the U.S. military presence but wanted no combat units, only more advisers. The president also resisted the urgings of his senior advisers to make a public commitment to defend South Vietnam; he preferred to stay vague. And he certainly did not tell Diem that increased assistance depended on making his government more popular and inclusive.

The administration had had its first real debate about Vietnam, but, as Rostow complained to Kennedy, the finely balanced result didn't quite add up. The president himself seemed uneasy. After rejecting Taylor and Rostow's proposal, he marked the completion of a year in office with odd historical reflections to the National Security Council. "The record of the Romans," he mused, "made clear that their success was dependent on their will and ability to fight successfully at the edges of their empire." Despite his determination to invigorate American policy, "it was not so clear that we were yet in a position to do the same."[34]

Having rebuffed his advisers on the issue of troops, Kennedy felt the need for a more coherent Vietnam policy. The next time around, he wanted a senior member of his own staff to provide in-house advice on Southeast Asia. The top candidate for this new job was Michael Forrestal, son of the late secretary of defense (and a not-quite-adopted son to Averell Harriman). There was just one problem, as Forrestal admitted to the president when they met: he didn't know a thing about Southeast Asia. He had not studied it or even been there. "That's just what we want," Kennedy replied. "Somebody without preconceptions and prejudices."[35]

IN THE LATE SUMMER of 1962, John Kennedy remained eager to achieve some understanding with Moscow on Germany or nuclear testing. He did not want to be deflected by needless flare-ups on secondary issues. So when intelligence analysts poring over U-2 photographs from Cuba at the end of August discovered Soviet surface-to-air missiles, the kind that could keep U.S. spy planes from monitoring a military buildup, the president did not instantly ask what Khrushchev and Castro might be hiding. He told the CIA official who had briefed him to keep the new information to himself: "Put it in the box and nail it shut." McGeorge Bundy echoed his boss, insinuating that anyone favoring more flights over Cuba must want "to start a war." Dean Rusk was adamant that the president's European initiatives had to come first: "How do you expect me to negotiate on Berlin with all these incidents?"[36]

The decision not to find out what was going on in Cuba produced a "photo gap" of more than six weeks. In mid-October, when Kennedy finally learned what had taken place while he was looking the other way, the result was the most dramatic East-West confrontation of the entire Cold War. Launch pads for nuclear-armed missiles able to reach most of the United States were nearing completion. A quick, covert doubling of Soviet strategic forces was at hand, right in America's backyard.

For almost two weeks after this shocking news, the president and a small group of advisers known as the ExComm (for Executive Committee) debated the U.S. response virtually around the clock. Few of them doubted that the missiles would change the global balance of power. To accept them would be to leave both friends and enemies unsure of what to expect from the United States. The ExComm's firm conviction was that all the missiles had to go. The president never wavered from this maximalist goal (he changed his mind about how to achieve it).[37]

In debating what to do, Kennedy's advisers bounced from one position to another, sometimes from one day to the next. Many of them did so more than once. Even when they agreed on what to do, their reasons often differed. Many favored a quick strike on the missiles. Some opposed it because they thought it would not succeed; others, because they feared a negative international reaction; still others, because of likely Soviet retaliation in Europe. No one wanted to be, in the president's words, "the trigger-happy Americans who lost Berlin."[38]

Yet of all the members of the ExComm, no one traveled a greater distance between the approach that he supported at the start of the crisis and the one he favored at the end than John Kennedy. When he turned to the secretary of state to open the discussion at their very first meeting on the missiles, Rusk framed the choice around which the debate of the next thirteen days would revolve: relying mainly on military action or mainly on diplomacy. The president did not at first treat this as much of a choice. He focused almost entirely on the details of a strike against Cuba—should it be massive or selective, followed by an invasion, preceded by a warning, or not? As for the fear that defined the crisis in the public mind at the time and ever after—the fear that any use of force might spiral into a nuclear holocaust—Kennedy downplayed the danger. "Why," he asked dismissively, "would the Soviets permit nuclear war to begin under that sort of half-assed way?" The new crisis did make him reflect ruefully on an old one: "It shows the Bay of Pigs was really right. If we had done it right."[39]

Kennedy and his advisers have long been hailed—and justly—for their skill in salvaging a diplomatic solution in the face of extreme danger. Even so, the record makes very clear that most members of the ExComm—and the president in particular—doubted that the crisis could, or should, be resolved by negotiation. Talking, they feared, would only help Moscow. Bundy favored a quick military strike precisely because he expected global public opinion to be hostile to American policy. Given a chance to weigh in, friends and allies would surely urge the United States to live with the new threat. "The prospect of that pattern," he observed, "is not an appetizing one."[40]

The president shared these concerns. On Cuba, he admitted, the Europeans think "we're slightly demented." He doubted that the United States could gain much by mobilizing the Organization of American States or even the Atlantic alliance: "I don't think we ought to do the OAS. I think that's a waste of time. I don't think we ought to do NATO." The Soviet Union had been caught in a reckless move, Kennedy thought, and that put the burden of averting war on Khrushchev, not on Washington: "He's initiated the danger, really, hasn't he? He's the one playing God, not us."[41]

As the ExComm talked on, John Kennedy repeatedly overruled advisers who favored diplomatic give-and-take. Early on, Stevenson had upbraided the president for being unwilling to resolve the crisis by trading away American overseas nuclear bases. When Kennedy found that Stevenson's other proposal—to invite Khrushchev to an emergency summit—had made it into a speech draft, he personally took it out. Proposing talks, he thought, would show that the U.S. government was in a "state of panic."[42]

Kennedy also overrode his secretary of state and his secretary of defense, both of whom thought Moscow would be more likely to yield if the United States were less demanding. For McNamara, insisting that all the missiles be withdrawn made it more likely that the U.S. forces would have to invade. Rusk also tried to chip away at his boss's resolve, suggesting that the Soviets might more easily agree to freeze construction of the missile bases than to dismantle them outright. Kennedy disagreed. The United States, he believed, had to get the missiles out, and Khrushchev should hear no hint that compromise was acceptable.[43]

After several days of thinking their way through different options, Kennedy and his advisers settled on a blockade of Cuba, not a military strike, as their opening gambit. They were guided in this choice by the same calculus that had inspired them a year earlier as they considered how to keep the Berlin crisis from escalating into nuclear war. They wanted the Soviets to take the risk of military confrontation seriously, but they also wanted to give them every opportunity to come to their senses before hostilities actually broke out. In almost the same words that he and his colleagues had earlier used about Berlin, Rusk described the blockade as "a brief pause for the people on the other side to have another thought before we get into an utterly crashing crisis." Khrushchev and the Politburo, he believed, had misjudged the likely American response to their actions. The United States now had to get them to "revise their judgment quick and fast."[44]

The decision to try to sober the Soviets up by imposing a blockade has often been read as a step toward diplomacy. But only a tiny minority of the ExComm—Stevenson (who was absent for most of the discussion), Ted Sorenson (the president's speechwriter), and McNamara—saw it this way. The majority, including both John and Robert Kennedy, treated the blockade as laying the foundations for a military strike. Like his colleagues, the president hoped that other governments, in the hemisphere and elsewhere, would give U.S. policy a legal blessing. But if they did not, he told senators before his speech, he would ignore them and proceed "illegally." He would not let multilateral consultations keep the United States from striking Cuba if necessary. "We're going to do it anyway."[45]

THE BLOCKADE ALLOWED Kennedy to delay a decision to attack. During this pause, his advisers told him, they had to "keep the heat on."[46] The days that followed were dominated by a series of dramatic confrontations that put Moscow under increasing pressure. On the high seas off Cuba, Soviet ships hesitated before challenging the U.S. blockade, and on October 24 a few of them (presumably those that had missiles or other sensitive items aboard) actually began turning back. On October 25, in the UN Security Council, a helpless Soviet diplomat squirmed in humiliation at the aerial photos presented by Ambassador Stevenson. That same day Nikita Khrushchev met with his senior party colleagues to argue that the crisis had become too dangerous. On Friday the 26th, he dictated a long, highly personal message to Kennedy (a letter, as Maxwell Taylor read it, "of a man either drunk or distraught, or both"). In it, Khrushchev hinted that the missiles could be removed in exchange for a U.S. pledge not to invade Cuba. On Saturday, Robert Kennedy received Soviet ambassador Anatoly Dobrynin at the Justice Department to deliver an urgent warning of "drastic consequences" unless Khrushchev's commitment was firmed up "by the next day." The Soviet leader accepted the deal in an open radio broadcast on Sunday morning, October 28.[47]

For the United States, this was a near-total victory. Khrushchev had folded in the face of American counterpressure. As early as the very first

ExComm meeting, Rusk had explained why this might happen: "We don't really live under fear of his nuclear weapons to the extent that he has to live under fear of ours." The Soviet leader knew that the largest massing of U.S. military forces since the Korean War was taking place in South Florida. By word and deed, Kennedy had made it, in Paul Nitze's words, "unmistakably clear" that he would strike or invade Cuba—or both.[48]

In the run-up to this victory, however, one member of the ExComm had grown increasingly anxious about American strategy, and that was John Kennedy himself. After offering on Friday to withdraw the missiles for a noninvasion pledge, Khrushchev had sent a second letter on Saturday demanding that the United States withdraw its missiles from Turkey. At this, it was the president, more than anyone else, who wavered. Throughout the crisis, almost all his advisers had ruled out concessions at the expense of American allies. Feelings on this point ran very high: Nitze considered Stevenson's readiness to trade away U.S. missiles in Europe "total appeasement." Lyndon Johnson warned that it would "dismantle the foreign policy of the United States." Yet the president believed the Soviet proposal could not simply be rejected. Of Khrushchev's gambit, the president said, with grudging admiration, "he's got us in a pretty good spot here."[49]

Kennedy was also unhappy with the countergambit that the ExComm concocted. In a celebrated moment of Cold War diplomacy, his advisers recommended that he ignore Khrushchev's tough new proposal and instead accept the softer terms of the earlier letter. They were proud of this move (dubbed the "Trollope ploy," since it echoed a plot twist by the nineteenth-century British novelist). The president, however, said it wouldn't work: "We might as well realize that." Khrushchev, he pointed out, had made his demand publicly and could hardly back down. Kennedy was gloomy. "We're not going to get these weapons out of Cuba, probably, anyway—but I mean, by negotiation. We're going to have to take our weapons out of Turkey."[50]

At this decisive moment of the crisis, Kennedy feared that the United States was driving too hard a bargain and that Khrushchev would not yield. Llewellyn Thompson, the senior Soviet expert present and the American who knew the Soviet leader best, told the president he was wrong. He and others argued that they were offering Khrushchev precisely the face-saving concession that he had asked for. There was no need to offer more. Even Robert Kennedy disagreed with his brother.

The ExComm had a good position, he said: "I don't think we should abandon it." Isolated but unconvinced, the president backed off—for the time being. He was willing to "try this thing. But [Khrushchev's] going to come back, I'm certain."[51]

John Kennedy now proposed to handle the Cuban missiles exactly as he had the Berlin crisis a year earlier—by looking for his escape hatch. On both occasions, the president delivered chest-thumping threats and put military muscle behind them. He observed the formal pieties of alliance commitments. He probed for Soviet flexibility by exchanging letters with Moscow. Yet in Berlin as in Cuba, he doubted that "normal diplomacy" could resolve the crisis fully. And in each case his solution was the same—open a secret channel and offer concessions that were not publicly acceptable. Gathering a handful of ExComm members in his office, the president authorized his brother to assure Ambassador Dobrynin that the Turkish missiles would be removed once Khrushchev took his own out of Cuba. The only condition was that there be no public reference to the deal.[52]

Kennedy's promise—kept secret for many years—was unnecessary to resolve the crisis. Khrushchev had already told his Politburo colleagues, before Dobrynin's report of his meeting with Robert Kennedy even arrived in Moscow, that the missiles had to come out. His position was simple and clear and, in its way, statesmanlike: he preferred humiliating retreat to calamitous defeat. Secret assurances about Turkish missiles did not matter to him. (If they really mattered as much as Kennedy thought, it is hard to see why Khrushchev agreed to keep the understanding secret.)[53]

John Kennedy had been sure military force would be needed to remove the Soviet missiles from Cuba. When muscular diplomacy began to do the job instead, he was unable—unwilling, it seemed—to recognize his own success. He was so sure that a satisfactory resolution of the crisis could be achieved only at a high price that he insisted on paying it even when others told him he was wrong.

Because the president's victory involved a concession that many of his closest advisers would have condemned had they known of it, a great effort went into controlling both the private and public record of the crisis. Robert Kennedy refused even to take possession of a letter from Khrushchev that alluded to the assurances about Turkey. He wanted no such document in the files and handed it right back to Dobrynin. The White House also made sure friendly journalists got a properly touched-up version of the crisis. Within days, *The Saturday Evening Post* published an authorized "inside" account of the ExComm's deliberations. In this corrected retelling, there had been no break in U-2 flights over Cuba, and only Stevenson had favored trading Turkish missiles for Cuban ones. ("Adlai wanted a Munich," one participant told the authors.)[54]

The *Post* story was highly fictionalized, but it captured the self-congratulatory mood of the president and his advisers. One ExComm member contrasted the administration's triumph with its poor performance at the Bay of Pigs. "This was different," he boasted. "We knew the facts, knew each other, and we thought it through, right to the end." Robert McNamara, the official whose role was perhaps most embellished by the *Post,* went even further in identifying a post-Cuba formula for statesmanship. "There is no longer any such thing as strategy," he declared, "only crisis management." The United States was so powerful that it didn't need the right military doctrines, just the right diplomatic technique.[55]

IN THE THIRTEEN MONTHS between the Cuban missile crisis and his death in November 1963, John Kennedy and his advisers redoubled their effort to wind down the Cold War. Victorious in history's most dangerous nuclear showdown, they wanted to reduce the risk of future confrontations. Their effort culminated in the first East-West arms control agreement, the Limited Test Ban Treaty outlawing nuclear explosions in the atmosphere, which was signed by U.S. and Soviet negotiators in July 1963.[56] The treaty's military significance was slight, but the president's rhetoric aimed to give it diplomatic momentum and historic meaning. In June, Kennedy had pushed negotiations forward with his famous "peace speech" at American University. In it he invoked the "basic common link" that united nations across the East-West divide: "We all inhabit this small planet; we all breathe the same air; we all cherish our children's future; and we are all mortal." Kennedy's goal, in his own ambitious words, was "not merely peace in our time, but peace for all time."[57]

While accommodation became the leitmotif of relations with America's main adversary, relations with friends moved in the opposite direction—just as they had after the 1961 Berlin crisis. Kennedy, Llewellyn Thompson told colleagues, "believed the United States could push its allies harder following the Cuban crisis." And push he did. He wanted the French to sign the test ban, even though they complained that it would constrain the development of their nuclear forces. He wanted the Germans to accept the downgrading of national reunification, even as a long-term goal. He wanted both of them to accept Britain into the European Common Market. He wanted all three allies to accept the primacy of the United States when it came to nuclear doctrine and decision making.[58]

Washington's relations with Paris and Bonn were riven by mutual suspicion and name-calling throughout the Kennedy administration, but in 1963 hostility reached a level not seen again until the Iraq War of 2003. The European leaders read U.S. policy as an attempt to deprive them of true foreign policy autonomy. In mid-January, De Gaulle announced that he would block Britain's effort to join Europe and signed a treaty with Germany creating—he hoped—an independent "axis" within the Western alliance.

Rusk was apoplectic. He saw the French president as a "devil with horns and a tail." Kennedy's view was still harsher. The French were trying "to run us out of Europe," he told his advisers. De Gaulle might even collude with the Soviets to achieve this goal. A turning point was at hand. The United States had been "generous" to its allies, the president said, but the time had come to "look out for ourselves."[59]

American policy makers demanded that the new treaty that De Gaulle and Adenauer had signed be revised so as to acknowledge the primacy of Germany's Atlantic ties; otherwise their new bloc would make it impossible to keep American forces in Europe. It might even spell "the end of Berlin." American diplomats lobbied the Bundestag to block ratification of the treaty unless it contained new language on NATO, and their efforts did not stop there. Believing that the aging Adenauer had outlived his usefulness, they consulted with the rising generation of Christian Democratic leaders about speeding up his retirement. On October 15, 1963, the only leader the Federal Republic had had since its founding finally stepped down.[60]

De Gaulle's duel with Washington lasted for years, climaxing with his demand in 1965 that NATO withdraw its headquarters from France. But the outlines of the clash were set in the Kennedy administration. Kennedy and his advisers saw little reason to listen to the French leader. In their view, he was "animated by anti-American prejudice," and there was nothing the United States could do about it. As Ball wrote to the president shortly after the test ban treaty was signed, "whenever the hand of friendship has been stretched across the sea, General De Gaulle has put a dead fish in it." European leaders, Ball believed, simply "lacked adequate vision" to accept a restructuring of their relations with the United States.[61]

When De Gaulle called the test ban treaty "another Yalta"—superpower collusion at the expense of lesser states—it was pure hyperbole. But he was right that Washington no longer regarded the Cold War as a joint enterprise. As Rusk grumbled to the Senate Foreign Relations Committee, it made no sense to negotiate "with our Allies looking over our shoulders." From Berlin to Cuba, one crisis after another had convinced the president and his advisers that successful decision making could not be shared. After Kennedy, no American president allowed his European colleagues to play more than an ornamental role in fashioning policy toward the Soviet Union.[62]

From this dominance, De Gaulle predicted a bad result. America, he regularly lectured the U.S. ambassador, was simply too powerful. Only the East-West military standoff placed real checks on the United States: "In every other form of power—industrial, commercial, agricultural, scientific, and financial—he saw the United States so far ahead of other nations, including the Soviet Union, that we would fall into error."[63]

WHEN JOHN KENNEDY was killed in November 1963, the United States had 16,000 advisers and trainers in South Vietnam. The president had given no major speech on the subject and had made no clear public commitment to keep the country from falling under Communist control. He had kept his options open. In Sorensen's words, Washington was "neither fully in nor fully out."[64]

Yet avoiding commitment was becoming harder. In the last months of Kennedy's life, South Vietnam consumed more of his time than any other foreign policy problem. The reason was the same one that frustrated him in Europe: the shortcomings of America's allies and clients. Fed up with the weak and unpopular rule of Ngo Dinh Diem and his family, Kennedy looked for ways to distance himself from them. He eventually cut back development assistance, publicly criticized the Saigon government, offered sanctuary in the U.S. embassy to Diem's leading Buddhist critic, asked the Pentagon to foster opposition to Diem in the South Vietnamese military, announced a target date for U.S. troop withdrawal, and deliberated endlessly with his advisers about whether to encourage a coup.[65]

American policy makers had long been critical of Diem. Even those who wanted to increase U.S. support for South Vietnam agreed that, because of him, the help might be wasted. In February 1963, Mike Forrestal, the new NSC staffer now covering Southeast Asia, advised the president that he and Averell Harriman planned to launch a "quiet campaign" to put pressure on Diem and his family. Forrestal's recent visit to Saigon had convinced him that while the war was going better, the country's out-of-touch leaders were losing the loyalty of the people. The United States would have to lean harder on Diem. Kennedy told Forrestal he was delighted with the analysis—the sort of thing, he said, that he never got from the professional bureaucrats.[66]

The administration's wish list for Diem was long and demanding. It wanted him to show the peasantry that the government put their welfare first. The United States wanted him to reach out to the non-Communist political opposition, especially Buddhist leaders, and to reverse the authoritarian measures pushed by his brother Nhu. American policy makers also wanted Diem to present himself more sympathetically to Western journalists, lest negative reporting from Saigon undermine support in Washington.[67]

In the summer of 1963, all these hopes were disappointed. When an elderly Buddhist monk burned himself on a busy street in June, Diem's sister-in-law laughed off the event as a "barbecue." She dismissed American journalists as "intoxicated by Communism," ridiculed the Kennedy administration's ceaseless urgings that Diem have more direct contact with the people, and blamed the United States for the country's political crisis. Madame Nhu was intentionally outrageous, but Diem said the same things in private. If Washington had lost confidence in him, he told the newly arrived ambassador, Henry Cabot Lodge, that was Washington's fault. Lodge's job was to "disintoxicate American opinion." For Diem, the desire for reform was proof of "American simple-mindedness."[68]

Steadily, the U.S. government wrote off Diem. Bundy, who had never set foot in Vietnam, said this was "the first time the world had been faced with collective madness in a ruling family since the days of the czars." Anticipating that the military would soon take over, General Paul Harkins, the U.S. commander in South Vietnam, wrote Maxwell Taylor that he thought a coup would be "easy" and involve "minimal violence." Diem's departure might, he thought, be a "blessing in disguise."[69]

It was no surprise, then, that in late August one of Lodge's first cables from his new post was a request for instructions about how to respond to two disgruntled South Vietnamese generals. Would the United States, they had asked, support a coup against Diem? The president, the secretary of state, the secretary of defense, the national security adviser, the chairman of the joint chiefs, and the director of the CIA were all out of town for the weekend when the cable arrived. Even so, Averell Harriman, now number three at the State Department, favored an immediate and positive response. He wanted to act, as Forrestal put it, "before the situation in Saigon freezes" again. In search of allies, Harriman intercepted George Ball, acting secretary of state while Rusk was away, at the end of his Saturday golf game. Ball was also eager to shake up Vietnamese politics. Diem, he had come to believe, "was a weak, third-rate bigot with little support." The United States would lose all "self-respect" by failing to oppose him.[70]

The cable that Harriman, Forrestal, and Roger Hilsman (head of State's Far Eastern bureau) drafted did not openly endorse a coup. But what it did demand—the ouster of his brother ("and his coterie")—amounted to the same thing. If Diem refused to take this step (and American officials assumed he would refuse), the cable declared that the United States would "no longer support" him. It directed Lodge to "make detailed plans as to how we might bring about Diem's replacement if this should become necessary." Ball and Harriman got their colleagues around town to approve the document by informing them that it reflected an administration consensus. And they got the president, relaxing on Cape Cod, to approve the cable by saying that his principal advisers were all in favor.[71]

To produce a quick, forward-leaning answer for Lodge, however, Ball and Harriman had cut too many corners and overridden too many doubts. When the senior officials who had been away for the weekend returned on Monday, there was an uproar. Discovering that few of his top advisers had even seen the document he had been told they all approved, Kennedy was furious. ("This shit has got to stop!" he barked at Forrestal.) At this point John McCone, the CIA director, explained the situation to an astonished Dwight Eisenhower. That the State Department was trying to run coups was no mere bureaucratic turf grab. Kennedy, McCone said, was surrounded by "liberals in his government who want to reform every country" in the world. The cable was called back.[72]

THE PRESIDENT AND his foreign policy team now commenced the full-dress discussion of Vietnam that they had not had before. They met frequently over the next several weeks, sometimes more than once a day. Participants compared the meetings to those of the ExComm during the Cuban missile crisis. They commissioned options papers and sent a series of senior officials to Saigon for quick assessments.

Yet the answers produced by careful and inclusive deliberation were hardly different from those in the cable to Lodge. The incident had generated, in Sorensen's view, "the deepest division over any issue during Kennedy's years in the White House." Robert Kennedy recalled that the president's advisers had "split in two." Endless meetings now restored their unity. Everyone, it turned out, wanted a fundamental change in the Saigon leadership; they all wanted Lodge to "wrestle with Diem" to force him to agree; and they all were ready to put much more pressure on him if he did not.[73]

There were, of course, some who wanted to push harder and faster to get rid of Diem. Ball and Harriman continued to argue this case. Ball claimed that the United States was already "beyond the point of no return." It was "no good" to rely on South Vietnamese generals to do America's work for it. Diem's family was an "evil influence," and to prevail against it, Washington had to "do the job right." Harriman believed that the war against the Communists was being lost. Only a quick, successful coup could save the United States from having to withdraw in defeat. Lodge, the Republican candidate for vice president in 1960, agreed with these two liberal Democrats. For him, a coup was "the only way in which the people in Vietnam can possibly get a change of government."[74]

Others worried that the American role was becoming too visible, that a coup might fail, and that a new government might be no more popular or effective. But these differences did not keep Kennedy and his advisers from dramatically turning the heat up on Diem. In press conferences and in personal appearances on all the TV network evening news programs, the president warned that the Saigon government was "out of touch with the people." He suspended aid programs that accounted for more than 60 percent of South Vietnam's imports. The White House also announced a 1965 target date for American withdrawal. The ambassador and his staff were instructed to increase their contacts with the opposition. In private conversations with South Vietnamese leaders, Americans conveyed their extreme frustration. Lodge let Diem know, just before the coup, that the United States would not condone "totalitarian" rule.[75]

Nothing better captured the administration's hardening view of Diem than McNamara and Taylor's visit to Saigon in early October 1963. The secretary of defense and the JCS chairman had been against throwing America's weight behind a coup, and both returned believing that there was "no solid evidence" that a coup could succeed. Two months earlier this judgment would have meant support for Diem. No longer. McNamara and Taylor now believed that if local actors could not produce a more effective government, then the United States itself would have to resolve the matter. They advised the president to "work with the Diem government but not support it." Pressure had to increase over the next two to four months, at which point more "drastic" action would be considered.[76]

Between August and November 1, when the South Vietnamese generals finally overthrew Diem, American policy makers moved ever closer, inch by inch, to outright support for his removal. (The slow pace did not bother the president. "I know from experience," he told Lodge, "that failure is more destructive than an appearance of indecision.") Yet even as the story reached its climax, Kennedy and his advisers imagined that they were still deliberating, still keeping their options open. They seemed not to understand that they had already made it perfectly clear to Diem's opponents where the United States stood. Right to the end, Washington's instructions to Lodge kept stressing skepticism about a coup's prospects and fear of being entrapped by Diem and Nhu. When they then learned that a coup was under way, many American officials reacted with surprise, even concern. The president's horror on hearing that the Ngo brothers had been killed showed how little Washington understood the impact of its own actions. "Kennedy," Taylor recalled, "leaped to his feet and rushed from the room with a look of shock and dismay on his face which I had never seen before."[77]

The killings aside, Washington was deeply satisfied by the result. Forrestal told his NSC colleagues it was "a well-executed coup, much better than anyone would have thought possible." Bundy was buoyed by evidence of popular support in Saigon: people throughout the capital "threw garlands of roses on the tanks and seemed genuinely pleased." Hilsman was still more effusive: "Singing bands of young people went marching about, cheering Americans as they had never been cheered before."[78]

As they reflected further, the president and his advisers recognized what they had not fully faced beforehand: that the coup was their own doing. Recording his thoughts, Kennedy acknowledged a "good deal of responsibility" for it. (Washington, he seemed to think, had actually "suggested" it.) Weighing the many factors that ended Diem's rule, Bundy concluded that the pressure of U.S. aid cuts had been decisive. And while all regretted that blood had been shed, some even found in the result a positive model for future policy. Ambassador Lodge felt the coup showed that the defects of Third-World partners need not handicap the United States. Those who did not measure up could be replaced. This had long been Galbraith's argument. Now that it had prevailed, he wrote to Harriman to commend him for "another great feather in your cap."[79]

Washington had seen South Vietnam's dysfunctional political system as the prime obstacle to military success against the Communists. Now, with new leaders in Saigon, what would become of the war effort? The president had said publicly that it was South Vietnam's struggle to win or lose, and he clearly hoped that the new junta would put more energy into the fight. But as they digested the results of the coup, some of Kennedy's advisers wondered whether military progress was possible without a larger American role. At the end of the year, one counterinsurgency specialist went so far as to suggest a full American take-over of the South Vietnamese armed forces. For Michael Forrestal, who had in a year on the job watched the steady deepening of American involvement, the idea could not be dismissed out of hand. Should the United States start running the war? The proposal was too drastic, Forrestal wrote to Bundy, but "the direction is right." The Kennedy administration practiced maximalism with an escape hatch. Even so, by the end of 1963, American policymakers seemed to be closing the hatch above them.[80]

SOON AFTER JOHN KENNEDY took office, the influential columnist Walter Lippmann voiced his disappointment with the president and his advisers. The junior officers of World War II, he thought, had brought too little change. They were turning out to be simply "the Eisenhower Administration thirty years younger."[81]

It was a serious misreading. Kennedy and his team left few Eisenhower policies unaltered. They carried out a huge military buildup, while also rethinking and revising the diplomacy that the buildup was supposed to support. They authorized more covert operations, offered more foreign assistance, had more disagreements with old allies, put more pressure on new clients, and deployed more forces abroad. They used more confrontational rhetoric—and more conciliatory rhetoric too. They were more ideological—and more cynical. They wanted to win the Cold War outright—and to end it in a tie. They were more ambitious—and more anxious about their ambition. They were, they did, and they wanted to do, more of everything.

Kennedy's strategy was virtually the opposite of Eisenhower's. A president preoccupied with stability over the long haul had been replaced by one committed to a burst of game-changing effort. American power surged in the early 1960s, and few others—whether friends or adversaries—were able to keep up. Yet the policy makers of the new administration did not fully understand the impact of what they had accomplished. They were committed both to boldness and to minimizing the risks of boldness. It is this combination that makes all conjecture about Kennedy's policies—that he would have become more aggressive, or that he would have become less—equally credible. He and his advisers wanted to make maximalism safe—to increase U.S. power and, at the same time, to discipline it as strictly as possible. At the end of the day, they found it hard to tell which impulse had been the key to their success.

The Berlin crisis of 1961, for all its tension, stayed within acceptable bounds because Kennedy made his warnings to Khrushchev more credible than he realized. By contrast, the secret talks that he hoped would prevent future crises produced nothing, other than ill will and suspicion within the Western alliance. The Cuban crisis of 1962 was an even more brilliant success, but its crucial ingredient was the atmosphere of extreme danger that Kennedy had created, not the hidden concession that he was willing to make. And when the leaders of South Vietnam were deposed and killed in 1963, American policy makers did not immediately grasp their own responsibility for the grisly result. Hadn't they agreed that they should, as always, keep their options open?

John Kennedy conducted a foreign policy based on the active use of unparalleled American power, managed with exquisite care but poorly understood. It would have been hard to think of a more challenging legacy for his successor.

5

"Mainly Violins, with Touches of Brass"

JOHNSON AGAINST HIS ADVISERS

Lyndon Johnson, Robert McNamara, and the Joint Chiefs of Staff

LYNDON JOHNSON was the first American president after World War II who did not believe that his predecessor's foreign policy was either already a failure or headed dangerously in the wrong direction. When he addressed a joint session of Congress on November 27, 1963, five days after John Kennedy's death, his theme was one of humble determination to carry on. "Let us continue," the new president urged the nation. Seeking popular acceptance, he made Kennedy's policies—and advisers—his own.[1]

Even as he emphasized continuity, however, Johnson was thinking about significant change. He was the first Cold War president to feel that his greatest challenges were on the home front rather than abroad. "Our real enemy," he liked to say, was the injustice of domestic poverty. He often contrasted grandiose international goals with more meaningful ones close to home. "This is the richest and most powerful country which ever occupied the globe," he observed in presenting the draft of the 1965 Voting Rights Act to Congress.

> The might of past empires is little compared to ours. But I do not want to be the President who built empires, or sought grandeur, or extended dominion. I want to be the President who educated young children to the wonders of their world. I want to be the President who helped to feed the hungry . . . . I want to be the President who helped the poor to find their own way and who protected the right of every citizen to vote in every election.[2]

For Johnson, the favorable international environment he inherited was a heaven-sent opportunity to pursue the creation of the Great Society. America's strong position—above all, the easing of the Cold War in Europe—enabled him to hope that providing for national security would demand less of his attention. It certainly seemed likely to cost less. The Pentagon budget had increased almost 10 percent under Kennedy. Johnson took office looking ahead to a 1.4 percent cut in the next fiscal year. Perhaps deeper ones would follow. "It was almost," he felt, "as if the world had provided a breathing space within which I could concentrate on domestic affairs."[3]

The foreign policy maxims that Johnson set forth at the start of his presidency were designed to support this refocused agenda. When he spoke at the State Department not long after Kennedy's funeral, his message was that national security did not depend on the balance of power alone. "America must be strong," the new president sermonized, "but America must be temperate and America must be just." The list of goals to which he proposed to "rededicate" his administration sounded all the notes of the best-intentioned liberalism. It began with "unswerving support of the United Nations" and ended with "reinforcement" of foreign aid. Johnson told his assembled diplomats that he had already communicated "to Mr. Khrushchev personally that the United States will go its part of the way in every effort to make peace more secure." Arms control was to play as large a policy role as the defense budget. And making democracy "effective and attractive" at home would be as important as fighting Communist subversion abroad.[4]

To this program of international accommodation, the new president added his own personal touches. As a professional politician, he often said his favorite passage of the Bible was Isaiah 1:18: "Come now, and let us reason together." He did not doubt his ability to ease conflict through direct human contact. "As long as I could take somebody into a room with me," he felt, "I could make him my friend." In this spirit, Johnson offered his State Department audience lessons learned from a long career of successful cajoling. Advancing American interests had to start with recognition "that the other man sees things in his own way." A good diplomat, he said, should always ask himself "how he would feel if he were in the other fellow's place." To be effective, the United States needed to "show patience and understanding of other systems as well as of our own."[5]

Lyndon Johnson began his tenure speaking the language of foreign policy restraint, of conciliation, and even retrenchment. How, then, did he end up leading the United States into its most disastrous—and divisive—overseas undertaking ever? The most maximalist enterprise of the Cold War was the work, it seems, of a president who was committed to limiting America's international role. Johnson wanted to remain faithful to "the woman I really loved—the Great Society," yet he found himself deeply and expensively involved "with that bitch of a war on the other side of the world." He had wanted to heal America's great racial, regional, and economic divides, but he launched policies that produced what one of his own closest advisers called the most severe governmental crisis since the Civil War. Sweeping plans gave way to a single intractable problem. As another aide put it, "No matter what we turned our hands and minds to, there was Vietnam."[6]

Countless attempts have been made to explain this strange transformation. Some see Johnson as unsure of himself in foreign affairs, unable to challenge the Kennedy legacy or defy Cold War conventional wisdom. Others argue that he was gripped by a visceral fear of the right-wing backlash that would follow defeat. One recent account treats his decisions as an example of national "hubris," overreaching spurred on by the boundless power of America in the mid-1960s.[7]

Johnson's own telling of his story confirms the scale of the ambitions that guided him as president. He was "determined to be a leader of war *and* a leader of peace," he said.

> I wanted both, I believed in both, and I believed America had the resources to provide for both. After all, our country was built by pioneers who had a rifle in one hand to kill their enemies and an ax in the other to build their homes and provide for their families.[8]

Over time Lyndon Johnson's presidency became the maximalist story he described—of both guns *and* butter, of the builder's ax *and* the soldier's rifle, of trying to do too much and failing at almost all of it. But it did not start out that way. Before the uncontrolled overreaching, there was the very deliberate underreaching. Making sense of where Johnson ended up depends on seeing clearly where he began: with a determined effort to resist the advisers who were taking him to war.

IN THE LONG HISTORY of American involvement in Vietnam, official Washington was sometimes guided by a too-rosy view of how the war was going. The first year and a half of Johnson's presidency was not one of those times. At the highest levels of the U.S. government, there was a strong consensus that the war was about to be lost. Soon after taking office, Johnson asked Robert McNamara to visit South Vietnam to make a firsthand assessment of where things stood in the wake of Diem's overthrow. The secretary of defense returned just before Christmas with a gloomy report. Unless current trends were quickly reversed—"in the next 2–3 months"—the result would be "a Communist-controlled state."[9]

The following March McNamara visited again—and came back even more alarmed. Forty percent of the country, he told the president, was now under Vietcong control. In more than half of the provinces, the Communists held more than half of the territory. Maxwell Taylor usually traveled with McNamara on these trips, and throughout 1964 he gave Johnson the same bad news. North Vietnam, he believed, was exploiting the confusion created by the murder of Diem to deliver "a coup de grace." By mid-fall, Taylor, who replaced Henry Cabot Lodge as ambassador in Saigon during the summer, urged Washington to face the fact that the insurgency was "succeeding, and that we Americans were playing a losing game."[10]

To this negative drumbeat, Johnson had a seemingly simple first response. "Win the war!" That was what he told McNamara, who said he got "quite a lecture" on the subject before his December 1963 trip to Vietnam. The president urged State Department staffers not to "go to bed any night without asking whether we have done everything that we could do that day to win the struggle there." Johnson also made sure his senior advisers understood what he expected of them. In Southeast Asia, he scolded, the United States "had spent too much time and energy trying to shape other countries in our own image." Security now had to take priority.[11]

> It was too much to expect young and underdeveloped countries to establish peace and order against well-trained and disciplined guerrillas, to create modern democratic political institutions, and to organize strong economies all at the same time. We could assist them with all three jobs, I said, but the main objective at present was to help them resist those using force against them.[12]

Such statements made Johnson seem ready from the very beginning for deeper military involvement in Vietnam. But his advisers soon learned otherwise. The new president wanted better results *without* deeper military involvement. The directive he issued within days of taking office, known as NSAM 273, put a strong emphasis on nonmilitary measures. It instructed U.S. officials to help the new South Vietnamese government build public support for itself. It told them to seek to "turn the tide not only of battle but of belief," and to work at improving economic growth (in particular, by getting more fertilizer to farmers in the Mekong Delta).[13]

The need to build popular unity in South Vietnam had been the main message of Johnson's own trip report to John Kennedy in 1961. Legitimate political leaders, he argued after his visit, had to reach out to the people. In March 1964 he returned to this theme, telling McNamara that he should use his upcoming visit to Saigon to bolster the new South Vietnamese leader. "Bob," he said, "I want to see about a thousand pictures of you with General Khanh, smiling and waving your arms and showing the people out there that this country is behind Khanh the whole way." Dutifully, the American visitors produced the pictures the president wanted: as Taylor recalled it, "Khanh on a platform in some town square with McNamara holding up his right hand, me his left in a posture befitting the victorious finale of a prize fight or of a party convention."[14]

The secretary of defense did not let the upbeat photos keep him from reminding the president that the war was going badly. Even so, on his return to Washington, he advised against increased military effort. The focus of U.S. policy, he said, should be on helping the Saigon government to perform better—by providing more training, more arms, and always more fertilizer (to be doubled in the year ahead and tripled in the year after that). McNamara had caught Johnson's preferences exactly: "do more of the same and do it more efficiently."[15]

The first year of Johnson's presidency brought a stronger emphasis on what was at the time called "pacification." This strategy for American involvement in Vietnam aimed to weaken the Vietcong by increasing the security of populated areas and winning popular support. Military success would be helped along by ambitious programs of economic development. As the new U.S. commander, General William Westmoreland, described it, the pacification campaign—code-named HOP TAC (Vietnamese for "cooperation")—was designed to expand from Saigon in concentric circles. As secure zones were created, civilian agencies of the government would be able to operate effectively. Villagers would enjoy a South Vietnamese version of the Great Society: new schools, wells, stores, and medical care. For Westmoreland, "The idea was to establish a standard of living perceptibly higher than the Viet Cong could provide." After his March trip, McNamara was a convert. "This so-called 'oil-spot' theory," he enthused to the president, "is excellent."[16]

At every stage of the Vietnam War, something like HOP TAC had ardent backers who considered it the only strategy that, if seriously implemented, might enable the United States to prevail. Among its many advantages, pacification reflected a sophisticated understanding of the political objectives that should guide a counterinsurgency campaign. Yet it never became the guiding principle of U.S. policy. The reason was simple. Policy makers tended to cast around for a new approach only when the enemy was on the brink of victory. At such moments, they wanted immediate results, not long-term promise. The idea of a spreading "oil-spot," or of winning "hearts and minds," was good, McNamara admitted, "but too slow." Westmoreland agreed: "We just didn't have time to do it that way."[17]

Not surprisingly, then, while the president talked grandly about economic development, his advisers pressed for urgent measures with a short-term payoff. In early 1964 the chiefs, with Ambassador Lodge's support, called for "bolder actions" against North Vietnam that would raise the costs of supporting the insurgency in the South. John McCone, the CIA director, dismissed the secretary of defense's recommendations—all that training, arms, and fertilizer—as "too little too late." Even McGeorge Bundy, who still had never visited Vietnam, started to talk about the need for American ground troops. He wanted to show, as he put it, that "this damn thing can be done."[18]

Urgency, however, was the last thing on Lyndon Johnson's mind. He was guided, as Maxwell Taylor saw it, by "the twin necessity of neither losing Vietnam nor expanding the war before the November 1964 elections." He liked pacification for precisely the reason that his advisers didn't. It offered the appearance of action while limiting its costs and risks, the appearance of commitment without the reality of confrontation. For the time being, that suited the president fine.[19]

SEEING HIS RESISTANCE, Johnson's senior civilian advisers—Bundy, Rusk, and McNamara—joined at the end of May in urging him to prepare to use force against North Vietnam. In a close-hold memo to the president, they presented an exquisitely gradual plan, built around slowly escalating warnings to Hanoi to call off the insurgency in the South. Successive UN resolutions to this effect were to be followed by multilateral armadas sailing "toward Southeast Asia," ready to strike if North Vietnam did not comply.

In their memo, Bundy and his colleagues, while maneuvering around the president's hesitations, urged him to authorize the expanded use of American military power. They assured the boss that their scheme would maximize the chance "of avoiding the actual use of force." Their hope, they said, was that "a pound of threat" might prove to be "worth an ounce of action." In the event that bombing raids actually had to be carried out, these "would be very carefully designed to have more deterrent than destructive impact, as far as possible."[20]

For all the tortured evasiveness of their proposal, Johnson's inner circle had crossed an important threshold. They favored escalation in Vietnam and had now said so on paper. The president was distraught. "I don't think it's worth fighting for," he admitted to Bundy, "and I don't think that we can get out. It's just the biggest damned mess that I ever saw." A few days later he received Walter Lippmann at the White House to hear the famous columnist warn against deeper involvement. Johnson was noncommittal, but after Lippmann left vented his frustrations in a long, rambling discussion with aides. George Ball summarized the president's political concerns that evening in a note to Rusk. "How," Johnson had asked aloud,

> could he maintain his posture as a man of peace in the face of the Southeast Asian crisis? How could he carry a united country with him if he were to embark on a course of action that might escalate under conditions where the rest of the world would regard us as wrong-headed?[21]

One argument that the president began to hear at this time from those urging action against North Vietnam was that nothing else could boost South Vietnamese confidence. Lodge said that General Khanh needed "a shot in the arm." Mike Forrestal of the NSC staff, back from a trip to the field in May, insisted that the only way for the United States to galvanize Saigon's "bickering" leadership was by taking the military offensive. "A bit of a shock is needed," he reported. Bundy, his boss, agreed. Washington had to provide "the tall American at every point of stress and strain."[22]

Johnson shared his advisers' view that the dysfunctions of South Vietnamese politics were a major obstacle to American success. But he drew exactly the opposite conclusion from their concern. Throughout 1964, the weakness of the Saigon government was the president's main argument against all proposals to escalate pressure on North Vietnam. For him, America's ally was too feeble and disorganized to withstand the retaliation that would surely follow. And Saigon's political turbulence seemed to bear him out. "[I want] no more of this coup shit!" Johnson declared. As he recalled later, "There was military rule, then civilian, then military again. First one man was in charge. Then there was a triumvirate. Then a council. General Khanh was in, and out, then in again."[23]

The South Vietnamese, the president believed, had "a strong impulse toward political suicide." Explaining why he would not authorize attacks on the North, he told General Earle Wheeler—Taylor's replacement as JCS chairman—that he was not about to "enter our fighter in a ten-round bout when he was in no shape to last the first round." The other senior official who focused most on the weaknesses of the Saigon regime was George Ball, who a year later became the most vocal in-house dissenter from the administration's Vietnam policy. In 1964, however, Ball was not a dissenter at all. He echoed the president's own doubts.[24]

Johnson did make one very famous and important exception to his foot-dragging on Vietnam. In early August 1964, after two torpedo boat attacks on U.S. naval vessels in the Gulf of Tonkin—one of them real, the other apparently imagined by those on the scene—the president ordered retaliatory raids on North Vietnam. He then sought passage of a congressional resolution (which his advisers had been preparing for months) authorizing him to use force to repel Communist aggression in Southeast Asia. Johnson clearly enjoyed the chance to demonstrate American power, and it gave him a solid bounce in the polls. "I didn't just screw Ho Chi Minh," he exulted. "I cut his pecker off!"[25]

The Gulf of Tonkin attacks and their aftermath did not, however, change the president's basic resistance to deeper involvement in Vietnam. He had repositioned himself only briefly—and reluctantly. After the first attack, in fact, he did not want to retaliate at all, and he overruled the recommendation of his new ambassador in Saigon, Maxwell Taylor. When that decision, and a meeting with congressional leaders, left Johnson feeling, as Bundy put it, "less firmly and effectively anti-Communist than he wanted to be," he changed course. But the reprisals he ordered were very limited—confined to the bases from which the North Vietnamese patrol boats operated and to the nearby oil storage facilities that supplied them.[26]

On the campaign trail, Johnson's rhetoric showed that he had not changed his reading of how Vietnam would play at the polls. He was still determined to be that year's peace candidate. And he wasn't subtle about painting his opponent, Barry Goldwater, as a reckless warmonger. The most famous political ad of 1964 opened with a little girl plucking petals from a daisy, followed by a nuclear explosion and the president's heartfelt, postideological voice-over: "We must love each other or we must die." Johnson claimed to be the only candidate who would "keep the United States out of the war in Vietnam." The Republicans were not his only target. In his first speech after the Democratic convention, he described his determination to resist a wider war—and took a subtle swipe at his own advisers.

> I've had advice to load our planes with bombs and drop them on certain areas that I think would enlarge the war and result in our committing a good many American boys to fighting a war that ought to be fought by the boys of Asia to help protect their own land.[27]

During the fall, the president rejected proposals for further attacks on North Vietnam. When, just days before the U.S. presidential election, the Vietcong staged a surprise attack on the Bien Hoa military airfield fourteen miles north of Saigon, wiping out most of a squadron of American planes, both the embassy and the commanders in the field again demanded retaliation. But again the president disagreed. As in August, he wanted to know whether the public would see inaction—his strong preference—as "a sign of weakness by the Administration." Once his pollster, Lou Harris, assured him that there was no such risk, Johnson ruled out a military response. He preferred to keep defying his advisers rather than remind the voters, in the run-up to Election Day, that the war was not going well.[28]

WITH THE 1964 presidential campaign over, and Johnson the winner in a historic landslide, his advisers assumed that he was at last ready for making decisions about the war. Many historians have assumed the same thing, and with some reason. Just before the election the president had appointed an interagency working group—chaired by McGeorge Bundy's brother, Bill, who oversaw Asia policy at the State Department—to develop a plan of action for Vietnam. Senior officials knew what they wanted to do and had long since spelled it out for the boss. The situation was desperate, and they saw only one way forward. Washington policy makers had "chosen war."[29]

Merely creating a group to devise a plan did not, however, mean that Lyndon Johnson was ready to accept it, and approving it did not mean he was ready to implement it. He told his aide Bill Moyers not to "assume that I am willing to go overboard on this—I ain't." Despite the urgings of his advisers, he did not settle quickly on a new course. The South Vietnamese government, he kept saying, was still too weak to help. Even after the massive bombing of an American officers' billet in the heart of Saigon on Christmas Eve 1964—which, in addition to U.S. military casualties, almost killed the legendary entertainer Bob Hope—the president vetoed retaliation. Through the entire first half of 1965, proposals to deepen American involvement in Vietnam—more forces in the South, more bombing of the North—led to endless haggling between the president, his civilian advisers, and his military commanders. Almost nine months passed after the election before a new policy emerged.[30]

Johnson's unwillingness to set a firm course in Vietnam led his advisers to seek new ways of overcoming his objections. To bring order to Saigon politics, Ambassador Taylor launched a series of angry encounters with South Vietnam's ruling generals that had few parallels in American diplomacy—and almost led to his expulsion. In December 1964 he called all the senior officers together for a steak dinner at Westmoreland's residence, to upbraid them for their endless feuding. Their "suicidal nonsense," Taylor warned, was putting United States support for South Vietnam at risk: "You people have broken a lot of dishes, and now we have to see how we can straighten out this mess." It was not an isolated encounter. The next time the generals in Saigon curtailed the authority of civilian officials, the ambassador summoned them again, for an even more heated dressing-down. "Do all of you understand English?" he barked. "I told you clearly at General Westmoreland's dinner we Americans were tired of coups."[31]

By his open hectoring, Taylor wanted to make it clear to the Saigon elite that General Nguyen Khanh, who had been the dominant figure in South Vietnamese politics since the Diem coup, was no longer "our boy." Khanh was soon sent into exile by his colleagues, the second leader in little more than a year to be ousted after losing American favor. But Saigon factionalism did not abate. From this, the ambassador concluded that there was no way "to translate into Vietnamese or French Ben Franklin's saying about hanging together or hanging separately." Sadly, Taylor told Washington that it was pointless to keep trying to stage-manage South Vietnamese politics. The United States, he wrote Johnson, cannot "change national characteristics [or] create leadership where it does not exist."[32]

While Taylor urged the president to pay less attention to the pathologies of South Vietnamese politics, McNamara and Bundy stressed the dire consequences of failing to act. On January 27 the two of them informed Johnson that in their view the entire policy was "on the brink of total collapse." In response, they proposed a strategy of what Bundy called "gradual and sustained reprisal." North Vietnam would be subjected to regular—and increasing—bombing until it lost its will to fight and stopped promoting war in the South.[33]

"Gradual and sustained reprisal" was the latest attempt by American policy makers to solve the problem of how to wage "limited war"—at the time, a hotly debated topic among defense thinkers both in and out of the government. Could the U.S. prevail in struggles in which it couldn't use its principal military, technological, and economic advantages? Bundy and McNamara's answer was that the enemy's will could in fact be broken if the United States kept increasing the pressure and made plain that there would be no letup. Their outlook was consistent with the strategic thinking of the time, which treated clearly communicated intentions as the key to military success.

In retrospect, American confidence that the Vietnamese Communists could be easily discouraged has come to seem both naïve (about their revolutionary determination) and arrogant (about the efficacy of U.S. power). But Johnson's advisers had a very practical reason to downplay the level of effort necessary to break North Vietnam's will: they had found that the president resisted all other arguments. They hoped to sway him by emphasizing measures that sounded, in Walt Rostow's approving words, "as limited and insanguinary as possible." In this spirit, Bill Bundy, who chaired the president's policy review, actually suggested that *low* levels of bombing might be more effective than *higher* ones. Lesser pressure, after all, would remind North Vietnamese leaders that greater punishment was possible in the future. This mounting fear, Bundy reasoned, would surely sap Communist morale. He used a revealing musical metaphor to describe the finely tuned and carefully orchestrated effort he had in mind. The bombing campaign he wanted the president to approve—"mainly violins, but with periodic touches of brass"—would be only as violent as absolutely necessary.[34]

THE DAY JOHNSON received McGeorge Bundy and Robert McNamara's memo about the looming "total collapse" of South Vietnam he was unhappy. An aide had "never seen [him] in as dejected a mood." But despair did not lead the president to accept the consensus of his advisers. For the next six months, in fact, he blocked the full implementation of their plan. Ho Chi Minh, Johnson announced (presciently), would not yield "to no airplanes." After the Vietcong raided an American outpost at Pleiku, in South Vietnam's jungle highlands, he did okay a round of air attacks on the North in February. Many of his advisers saw this decision as the watershed they had been waiting for (and the military gave the attacks a robust-sounding name, Operation Rolling Thunder). But the president did not approve follow-up strikes and refused suggestions to give a speech explaining the policy. What was intended to be a "sustained" campaign actually lapsed altogether (bad weather was a factor) for almost a month. When bombing resumed, it was at a leisurely once-a-week pace, and Johnson chose the number of North Vietnamese targets before each attack. "They can't even bomb an outhouse without my approval," he bragged.[35]

Through it all, the president was repeatedly and explicitly informed that the on-and-off bombing had no real effect. John McCone, the CIA director, told him that taking out "a bridge here and there" was pointless. General Westmoreland thought the high hopes for Rolling Thunder were "pie in the sky." Yet when the generals came to Johnson in April with a plan to put troops in South Vietnam, he continued to resist. He was willing, he said, to grant perhaps 5,000 of the 90,000 men that the chiefs had requested. Describing his offer as "another chip on the table," he berated them for inflexibility.

> It is just as if you went to a bank owned by Mr. McNamara and asked him for a loan of $90,000, and he told you that no he couldn't let you have that amount, but that he would loan you $5,000. What would you do? Let your business go into bankruptcy, or would you take the $5,000 and try to do something with it?[36]

In the end, Johnson accepted a small troop increase and even agreed that some units could have a combat role. But he continued to hope that nonmilitary measures would make intervention unnecessary. In a speech at Johns Hopkins on April 7, 1965, the president sketched a billion-dollar plan—modeled on the Tennessee Valley Authority—for peaceful economic development of the Mekong Delta. Bold schemes of this kind were, in Ambassador Taylor's words, "flogged to a new level of creativity by a president determined to get prompt results." More than sixty projects were proposed to the Saigon government, even though Taylor believed they actually harmed the cause they were intended to serve. South Vietnam—the struggling patient—was "in constant danger," he thought, "of being overfed, overphysicked, or constipated by the excessive zeal of his American physicians." For Taylor, development projects had no chance of working unless the problem of security was solved. "We should have learned from our frontier forebears that there is little use planting corn outside the stockade if there are still Indians around in the woods outside."[37]

Frustrated by Johnson's evasive, improvisational approach, General Westmoreland concluded that he would have to force the issue. "I made up my mind that . . . Washington had to face the task realistically." On June 7 he sent the Pentagon a plan for rescuing the desperate military situation. Arguing that only "extraordinary measures" could stave off collapse, he proposed to increase the number of American troops in South Vietnam to 175,000 by the end of the year, with another 100,000 to follow in 1966. As he later distilled his message, it was this: "no more niceties." The United States had to "take the war to the enemy."[38]

McNamara considered Westmoreland's June 7 cable the single most disturbing message he received in his entire tenure as secretary of defense. Even so, it produced no immediate change of course. Four days later, in fact, Johnson ended a National Security Council discussion of Vietnam with a short summary that, if anything, expressed still more intense resistance to a major U.S. commitment. "We must delay and deter the North Vietnamese and Viet Cong as much as we can, and as simply as we can," the president said, "*without going all out.*" For anyone who still did not understand his position, he added a further warning: sending more troops would only mean that "we get in deeper and it is harder to get out."[39]

IN MORE THAN A YEAR and a half as president, then, Lyndon Johnson had repeatedly ignored the advice of those who told him he had to do much more to avoid defeat in Vietnam. Sometimes he granted them a small part of what they proposed—some bombing here, some troops there, extra dollops of development aid to round out the strategy. But he resolutely avoided making major and irrevocable decisions.

In July 1965 this approach broke down. In May regular units from North Vietnam—well armed, well led, and twice as numerous as they had been in 1963—had launched an offensive that exceeded any of their previous operations in the South. Bloody, one-sided victories pushed South Vietnamese casualties to their highest level ever. Seeing the setbacks mount, McNamara picked up Westmoreland's June 7 cable and embraced its proposal for sharp increases. Another lightning trip to Vietnam confirmed the urgency of the moment. Without decisive action, the secretary told Johnson on his return, rapid defeat—so long anticipated—would finally be at hand.[40]

In this emergency atmosphere, the president opened a new phase of more intense deliberation about Vietnam than any he had ever held with his advisers. It began with long meetings of his national security team at the White House on July 21 and 22. Discussions continued at Camp David over the following weekend, then resumed at the White House on Monday, July 27. That evening Johnson met with the congressional leadership to review the options that a week of debate had generated. The next day, in a noon-hour television appearance, he spoke to the nation and announced his decision.

On the surface, everything about the president's July 1965 review of Vietnam suggested that he was ready to "go overboard" at last. He and his advisers were—like their predecessors at comparable moments of crisis in 1947, 1950, 1961, and 1962—focused on what most of them considered an acute challenge to American interests. In the course of discussions that, according to White House aide Jack Valenti, consumed "hundreds of hours," they settled on a large policy response—in this case, the "Americanization" of the war.[41]

But Johnson's role in this process was very different from that of his predecessors. He did not play the leader who goaded his subordinates to come up with more comprehensive, hard-hitting, and imaginative measures. That might have been his mode when he enthused about creating a TVA look-alike for the Mekong basin, but not now. In discussing deeper American involvement in the war, Johnson played the skeptic throughout. McNamara believed he was "tortured" by the decision before him. Ball was struck by his "agonizing reluctance." Even the question with which Johnson opened the discussion at the White House expressed resentment toward those who were urging him to act. "What I would like to know," he asked with faux innocence, "is what has happened in recent months that requires this kind of decision on my part."[42]

The president obviously knew the answer to his own question, but he told his advisers that he would not be rushed into a massive military commitment to South Vietnam. The recommendations before him, he observed to Valenti, "seem to be built on a pretty soft bottom." He would make no "snap judgments." He wanted to examine the plans "line by line, argument by argument"—to test their soundness.[43]

Johnson's doubts were particularly plain when he interrogated senior military officials about their plans. "Isn't this," he challenged the air force chief of staff, General John McConnell, "going off the diving board?" Of the secretary of the air force, Harold Brown (later secretary of defense under Jimmy Carter), he wanted to know, "Are we starting something that in two or three years we simply can't finish?" The president seemed especially wary of the argument that the United States had to redeem every pledge made to others, no matter how ill considered. "If you make a commitment to jump off a building and you find out how high it is," he cautioned Stanley Resor, the secretary of the army, "you may want to withdraw that commitment." And where, he wanted to know, were America's other allies? "Have we wrung every single soldier out of every country that we can? Who else can help us here? Are we the sole defenders in the world?"[44]

Beyond his own skeptical queries, Johnson also saw to it that these late-July meetings provided a forum for frontal opposition to the McNamara-Westmoreland buildup. George Ball, who had for months been sending the president long critiques of administration policy, now presented his views to the entire national security team. He described the Saigon regime for his colleagues as an "absurd travesty"—a "fiction" even. The United States, as Ball saw it, had to "[let] nature take its course"—accepting the take-over of South Vietnam by the North. Johnson made a further seat at the table for a trusted political adviser, Clark Clifford, who chaired the Foreign Intelligence Advisory Board but held no full-time government post. Clifford was shocked by what he heard. The generals' case, he told the president, was simply "ridiculous."[45]

Johnson wanted the meetings that started at the White House to continue into the weekend, and he invited Clifford to Camp David for an intimate Sunday-afternoon debate with McNamara and others. The result was dramatic. "I put more passion into what I was saying," Clifford later wrote, "than in any presentation I had ever made to a President." He launched the most heated attack on deeper involvement in Vietnam that Johnson had ever heard, predicting national "ruin" and "a huge catastrophe." "I hate this war," he declared. There was, he insisted, simply no need to wage it. The United States did not have to act as though it were going into "the last inning in the struggle against communism."[46]

By this late stage in a debate of such importance, most presidents would have made up their minds, and there is some evidence that Johnson already knew what he would decide when he had finished deliberating. Clifford suspected as much; as an old Washington insider, he knew the president's operating style well. Bundy, too, considered the "debate" partly for show, a way of making everyone feel consulted. All the same, Johnson seemed unusually troubled by the decision. He had spent his entire time as president dodging this issue. His sympathies had generally been with the critics. Their arguments had been his arguments. He also knew that some who had urged him to act had reservations about McNamara's plan. Bundy himself, on first reading the defense secretary's proposal for a massive buildup, had dismissed it as "rash to the point of folly."[47]

Just one day before his deliberations were to end, Johnson acted like a man who did not know what to do. Surprising his Camp David guests, he stood up from the meeting with Clifford and McNamara and disappeared. He spent the next two hours by himself, driving around the area and then pensively walking the grounds alone.[48]

LYNDON JOHNSON was a compulsively hands-on president. He used the process of consultation with his advisers to identify new options, to sharpen his feel for the political implications of a decision, and to fashion strategies most likely to command wide support. In late July 1965 such deliberations were his tool for weighing proposals, now pressed on him from all sides, to make a full military commitment to South Vietnam. Since becoming president, he had dodged this particular commitment many times. To judge by the questions he raised and the doubts he expressed, he would have liked to do so yet again. Endlessly talking the problem over was his way of finding out whether he had a choice.[49]

If so, the outcome disappointed him. A week of meetings had shown how hard it would be *not* to approve the buildup that McNamara and

Westmoreland had proposed. The president's senior advisers, doubtless recalling how often he had evaded past recommendations, now confronted him with a completely unhesitating case. They seemed unwilling to let Johnson think that there was any alternative. They knew what he could do when they equivocated.

To steel the president, Dean Rusk repeated, almost word for word, what he had told John Kennedy in their first discussion after missiles were discovered in Cuba three years earlier. Only the "integrity" of American security pledges, he said, kept peace in the world. "If the Communist world finds out that we will not pursue our commitments to the end, I don't know where they will stay their hand." Withdrawal from South Vietnam, he had written Johnson in a private note before the White House meetings, would lead to national "ruin"—and to "catastrophic war."[50]

McNamara's rhetoric was also uncharacteristically hot. Washington's leading policy rationalist—seen by many as an emotionless number-cruncher—warned the president that American "honor" was at stake. Defeat would reverberate on every single continent, even Europe. Both Rusk and McNamara endorsed the "domino theory," but their case for taking a stand in Vietnam did not rest merely on the regional consequences of defeat. The future of Southeast Asia was not their core concern. The secretary of defense and the secretary of state were warning Johnson that something far larger was at risk: the viability of the global order that the United States had created.[51]

The officials who favored the expanded American commitment in Vietnam—the likes of Rusk and McNamara—are sometimes seen as prisoners of inertia, unable to take stock and change course. The debate of July 1965 was not, however, between one side that proposed to get out gracefully and another that wanted to keep slogging mindlessly forward into the mire. It was, in fact, Rusk's and McNamara's *opponents* who were calling for more of the same. This surely weakened their case. The fiasco that the critics had predicted was right at hand, and everyone recognized it. McNamara, the generals, and the Pentagon civilians at least had a plan that they claimed might avert the worst. The dissenters, by contrast, had not put forward, in Johnson's words, a credible "alternative course." Their advice was to do almost nothing—and hope for the best. In his peroration, Clifford urged the president to "hold to our present course." The United States, he suggested, should be on the lookout for some undefined opportunity to disengage over the next six months.[52]

Ball's counsel was even more openly defeatist—"take our losses, let their government fall apart," he advised. He understood how little this appealed to Johnson. As he saw it, his boss was unable "to reconcile his vaunted Texas 'can-do' spirit with the shocking reality that America had painted itself into a corner with no way out except at substantial costs in terms of pride and prestige."[53]

Ball underestimated what the "can-do" impulse was capable of. American policy makers—including, finally, Johnson himself—were unwilling, as Harold Brown put it, to "strangle slowly." The president's advisers did not believe that they had yet given the Vietnam problem their best shot. For Maxwell Taylor, as for others, this was the decisive reason to do more. Asked later why he had not favored disengagement, he answered that "we had not exhausted our alternatives." The United States had hardly "made inroads into our vast resources. We could still try a number of things which might supply the new ingredient we were seeking." New approaches had to be tried, and a serious effort made, "before we thought of quitting."[54]

Perhaps the most important "new ingredient" that emerged from the discussions of July 1965 was the changed attitude of American policy makers toward South Vietnam. Johnson had long argued that the Saigon regime was too weak to hold its own in a wider war. Even Bundy worried that McNamara's plan was a "slippery slope toward total U.S. responsibility and corresponding fecklessness on the Vietnamese side."[55]

But the more the president's advisers thought about how to fend off disaster, the less they focused on helping the South Vietnamese to help themselves. They concluded that success would require them to push their little ally aside. Taylor, who wrote the president early in 1965 that there was no point in trying to change South Vietnam's "national characteristics," was one of the first to make this leap. By the end of July, his view was widely shared. In the White House discussions with the president, Henry Cabot Lodge, soon to return to Saigon for a second tour as ambassador, was one of many who expressed scorn for the South Vietnamese leadership. "There is no one who can do anything," he said. "We have to do what we think we ought to do regardless of what the Saigon government does."[56]

In July 1965 Johnson, McNamara, and other American policy makers believed they had to "wrest control of the war effort from the South Vietnamese." Like the authors of the Marshall Plan, they had concluded that the United States would succeed only if it could run the show. Clifford feared that this effort was bound to fail, but he had now seen, close up, how hard it was to shake the confidence underlying it. Those who advised the president to try to save South Vietnam, he felt, acted on "a misplaced belief that American power could not be successfully challenged, no matter what the circumstances, anywhere in the world."[57]

IN THE DECADES since Lyndon Johnson "Americanized" the Vietnam War in the middle of 1965, no reading of his motives has taken stronger hold among historians and other political observers than the idea that what really drove him was fear of a right-wing electoral backlash. He had to succeed, it seems, because the Korean War—and its harsh toll on the Truman administration—had shown the punishing price of failure. The president was unwilling to risk another round of anti-Communist hysteria at the Democratic Party's expense, even if it meant he had to take the country to war unnecessarily.[58]

Johnson left behind plenty of evidence to nourish this interpretation. His memorable description of right-wing nationalist sentiment as the "great beast" of American politics confirmed his anxiety. The voters, he had long worried, will "forgive you for everything except being weak." The political imperative of looking tough was still on his mind even after he left office. "I knew," he recalled,

> that if we let Communist aggression succeed in taking over South Vietnam, there would follow in this country an endless national debate—a mean and destructive debate—that would shatter my Presidency, kill my administration, and damage our democracy. I knew that Harry Truman and Dean Acheson had lost their effectiveness from the day that the Communists took over in China. I believed that the loss of China had played a large role in the rise of Joe McCarthy. And I knew that all these problems, taken together, were chickenshit compared with what might happen if we lost Vietnam.[59]

Johnson viewed his foreign policy choices in a stark partisan framework. Those who wanted to sway his decisions understood this. In February 1965 his new vice president, Hubert Humphrey, had sent him a confidential memo arguing against deeper involvement. The administration, he argued, was entering a "year of minimum political risk." An electoral landslide and a huge congressional majority made it possible to "face the Vietnam problem without being preoccupied with the political repercussions from the Republican right." Humphrey had little influence in foreign policy debate, but his intervention was telling. He knew the president would consider disengagement only if he thought he could manage the political risks involved.[60]

That Lyndon Johnson's decisions on Vietnam were driven by some sort of insecurity is almost beyond question. (Nothing else quite explains the bizarre response he once gave to reporters' questions about why the war was so important. "This is why," he answered, unzipping his pants and displaying his penis.) But political insecurity can take many forms, and it is a mistake to read Johnson's as primarily a fear of revived McCarthyism. Had he tried to disengage from Vietnam in 1965, he would have had to worry first about how to overcome the opposition around his own conference table. He knew the views of his senior advisers—McNamara above all, but also Rusk, Bundy, and Taylor. These men, on whom the president relied most, had urged him for more than a year to employ increased American military power to avert the collapse of South Vietnam. He knew how consistently he had ignored their advice—and how much more desperate the situation had become while he did so.[61]

Johnson clearly wished that his closest advisers were more receptive to the dissenting views of Clifford and Ball. But they considered the idea of letting South Vietnam fall to Communism repugnant. For them, the hope of achieving a negotiated settlement of the war was a fantasy. They treated American credibility as a meaningful strategic asset, not a slogan (and still less a metaphor for personal virility). Johnson had no reason to think that the recommendations these men gave him were anything other than their best judgment about how to wage the Cold War effectively.

We know, moreover, from Johnson himself how he imagined the political backlash that would follow withdrawal or defeat. After his resounding victory at the polls, the opposition movement he worried about most did not come from the Republican right. McCarthyism would now take a different form. "This time," he feared, "there would be Robert Kennedy out in front leading the fight against me,"

> telling everyone that I had betrayed John Kennedy's commitment to South Vietnam. That I had let a democracy fall into the hands of the

> Communists. That I was a coward. An unmanly man. A man without a spine. Oh, I could see it coming all right.[62]

No matter how lurid and overdrawn this picture was, Johnson was not wrong about his potential political vulnerability. As the military outlook in South Vietnam worsened in the first half of 1965, Robert Kennedy had in fact already spoken out against withdrawal. It would, he said in May, be "a repudiation of a commitment undertaken and confirmed by three administrations." Letting South Vietnam fall would "gravely—perhaps irreparably—weaken the democratic position in Asia."[63]

Over the next year, Kennedy changed his mind about the war, and some leading Democratic political figures did so well before he did. Eventually almost all of them turned against it. But in 1965 the mainstream liberal attitude toward South Vietnam was that a great deal was at stake in its struggle with the North. David Halberstam, whose book *The Making of a Quagmire* was published that same year, called it "one of only five or six nations in the world that is truly vital to U.S. interests." Drawing on his earlier reporting for *The New York Times,* Halberstam's book dismissed the idea of South Vietnamese neutrality. That was "out of the question," he wrote. Victory by the North would create a "drab, lifeless, and controlled society." He continued to believe that American policy had been hopelessly bungled for years, but that did not make pulling out the right course. Withdrawal, he argued,

> means that the United States' prestige will be lowered throughout the world, and it means that the pressure of Communism on the rest of Southeast Asia will intensify. Lastly, withdrawal means that throughout the world the enemies of the West will be encouraged to try insurgencies like the one in Vietnam.[64]

As much as Halberstam disparaged Washington policy, what he wrote in 1965 about disengaging from Vietnam left no daylight between him and Rusk or McNamara.

These were the views, then, of the president's most respected advisers, of his most feared liberal opponent, and of the best-known journalist writing on the problem at the country's most influential newspaper. As long as this was what Johnson heard from the center and the left, how much did it matter that he also worried about the power of political primitivism on the right? "Beasts" of all kinds kept Johnson from considering disengagement from Vietnam. The ones that scared him most were very close to home.

LYNDON JOHNSON had taken office wanting—at a minimum—"a breathing space" from costly foreign commitments. His decisions of July 1965 put an end to that idea. He had hoped to be a retrenchment president, but not because some large failure had made current policy seem unsustainable. Disaster in Korea and a runaway defense budget had made Eisenhower's retrenchment hard to argue with. Johnson, by contrast, wanted to retrench from success, when American power was at its peak. To have his way he fought a long rearguard action against his most senior and influential advisers.

To these advisers, the urge to retrench made no sense. In their view, current policy—or the still bolder, more activist policy they recommended—was completely sustainable. They saw no reason to curtail the global role of the United States or to shy away from large new challenges. The president yielded—in Jack Valenti's words—"reluctantly, stubbornly resisting all the way." But he did yield. He would now have to be "a leader of war *and* a leader of peace."[65]

It is easy to see Johnson's predicament as a freakish, one-of-a-kind story. The ambitious but insecure politician becomes president unexpectedly, inheriting a war that for many reasons he wants to ignore. He opposes deeper involvement so that he can be the peace candidate in an election he never dreamed he would contest. He lets the war deteriorate while trying to build the record of domestic achievement that will be his true claim to greatness. Finally, with disaster at hand, he can ignore it no longer. Maximalism replaces entrenchment.

For Walt Rostow, who—as McGeorge Bundy's eventual successor—came to play a large role advising Johnson on the war, this story was not the exception in American history. It was the rule. Like his twentieth-century wartime predecessors, Johnson had "waited until the military situation had degenerated to a point where the choice was narrowed to defeat or massive engagement." Delaying until it was almost too late, Rostow thought, was "typical of the national style." So was the gigantic effort that was about to unfold.[66]

6

“We Have Not Been Divided”

JOHNSON AT WAR

President Johnson

"THE AMERICANS," said Bui Diem, South Vietnam's ambassador to Washington during much of the war, "came in like bulldozers." And, of course, *with* bulldozers. Ambassador Diem marveled at the speed with which the United States began the buildup of 1965 and at its impact on his own country. Johnson and his advisers had abandoned the pretense that they were helping another government defend itself. America would now do the job alone. Plans sped forward to build new bases, longer runways, deepwater ports, a denser grid of highways and roads, supply depots, ammunition dumps, repair facilities, fuel distribution networks, field hospitals, modern communications systems, power generators, cold storage units, basketball courts, ice cream plants, and more.[1]

It was not easy to build fast enough to support the number of troops that the president had approved in July, and harder still to keep up with the increases he authorized after that. In September, Westmoreland revised his request for 175,000 men by the end of 1965; now he needed 210,000. A month later he told Washington the target for the end of 1966 should be 325,000 men, not the 275,000 approved in July. In November this goal ticked upward again, to 410,000. By February 1966, it had become 429,000—seven times the number of U.S. troops in South Vietnam just the previous summer. American troop strength eventually exceeded 500,000 but the upward spiral of requests was never again as steep, or the approvals as unhesitating, as they were in the half-year after July 1965.[2]

Some of Johnson's advisers were taken aback by Westmoreland's quick calls for more men. The president himself was unfazed. "Once he made his decision," Maxwell Taylor said of Johnson's impatient operating style in Vietnam, "he couldn't get going fast enough." Yes, the job was bound to be expensive, but after trying to dodge it for so long, he now wanted it done in a hurry. Others might think the war ahead had to be a protracted slog. Not Lyndon Johnson. He was, in Taylor's words, "the fellow with the black snake whip behind [the generals] saying, 'Let's get going now!' " The president summarized his outlook for Clark Clifford, claiming (perhaps in jest) to be quoting Lincoln: "You can't fertilize a field by farting through the fence."[3]

Every measure of the American military effort in Vietnam—from costs to casualties—surged upward after 1965. In three years, defense spending increased more than 50 percent. It rose as a share of GDP for the first time since Korea, from 7.4 percent in 1965 to 9.4 percent (of a much larger economy) in 1968. The increase in human costs was even sharper. In 1965 the number of American soldiers killed in action in Vietnam was 1,369—up almost ten times from the year before. In 1968, by far the bloodiest year of the war for the United States, the number rose to 14,589—one hundred times the level of 1964.[4]

Heavy casualties reflected the emphasis on ground operations, the "search and destroy" missions that chewed up troops. But aircraft losses soared too. The tonnage of bombs dropped on North Vietnam quadrupled in the two years after 1965, as did the number of sorties flown. In 1965 more than 375 U.S. planes were lost, more than one a day. In the next three years, the total jumped to almost 2,200. Roughly the same number of helicopters were also destroyed. (By comparison, only 27 planes—and 23 helicopters—were lost in combat during the Persian Gulf War of 1991.)[5]

For American commanders, these losses were an unavoidable consequence of their strategy for breaking the enemy's will. One of Westmoreland's deputies, General William DePuy, framed his goal in simple quantitative terms. "The solution in Vietnam," he said, "is more bombs, more shells, more napalm." Asked at a press conference how to beat back the insurgency, Westmoreland answered still more succinctly: "Firepower."[6]

Johnson heard the same advice from fighting men with even greater authority than the generals in the field. In July 1965, Dwight Eisenhower counseled the president not to hold anything back. "When you once appeal to force in an international situation involving military help for a nation, you have to go all out."[7]

THE VAST RESOURCES poured into Vietnam make it easy to see the war as the supreme example of American foreign policy's maximalist temptation. All the ingredients of hubris and overreaching were present, from the president's bullying personality to the immense power at America's disposal. Much opposition to the war was triggered by its sheer disproportion, by the huge costs in blood and treasure committed year after year to the defense of a small, poor, and distant country—and all, opponents claimed, for no good reason.

Yet this picture of the war is incomplete. Whenever Johnson discussed Vietnam with colleagues and advisers, he stressed his determination *not* to go "all out." His reasons were many: to avoid a nuclear confrontation with the Soviet Union or China; to avoid stirring hypernationalist sentiment at home; to keep the war from bringing down his ambitious domestic plans. It may seem absurd to treat the vast American effort in Vietnam, the only foreign policy problem to which the president gave serious and sustained attention, as a case of "limited war." But to Lyndon Johnson, the limits were fundamental. They shaped his conduct, and his concept, of the war from start to finish.

They also shaped the way he described it to the American people. Johnson wanted, in the words of one White House staffer, "to *sotto voce* the whole thing." He told his staff that he hoped to "avoid undue concern and excitement in the Congress and in domestic public opinion." Hence his claim that policy hadn't actually changed. The president described his cagey approach for winning support on Capitol Hill as a two-step process—presenting "the story now and the bill later."[8]

Johnson's strategy meant straddling, and often crossing, the line between savvy information management and outright dishonesty. In briefing congressional leaders, he informed them that the number of troops would be doubled by the end of 1965. (In fact, it was to be tripled.) His public announcement of new U.S. deployments to South Vietnam referred to an increase of 50,000 men. (This, when he had already okayed an increase of more than 200,000 men over the coming eighteen months.) None of these moves, he blandly assured the public, implied "any change in policy whatsoever." As for costs, the Pentagon advised the president that his decisions would require a $10 billion increase in spending in the first year alone. Yet he asked Congress for only a tiny fraction of this amount—$1.7 billion—as an emergency supplement to the budget. Next year, he promised, "the figures would be firmer."[9]

With a few notable exceptions, most of Johnson's advisers counseled against his disingenuous "*sotto voce*" approach. If the war were to go on longer than expected, they thought, the American people would need to understand it better, feel a stake in it, want it to succeed. McNamara went so far as to suggest that the president dramatize the importance of the war by proposing a tax increase. Johnson believed he could make maximalism workable by lying; McNamara, by admitting its cost. (Johnson prevailed.)[10]

It was the opponents of the policy—both George Ball and Clark Clifford—who were most firmly against explaining it honestly in public. Play the whole thing down, they urged Johnson. Ball and Clifford hoped a low-key approach would keep public opinion from identifying too closely with the war. Then, if things went badly, the president might quietly pursue a compromise peace, at acceptable political cost. Mike Mansfield also warned against overcommitment. "A quick stalemate," the Montana senator told Johnson, was the best the United States could hope for. "We cannot expect our people to support a war for three-to-five years."[11]

The failure to level with the country or with Congress eventually undermined the president's credibility. At first, however, events validated his approach. Johnson had been confident that he could "get our people to support us without having to be too provocative and warlike," and poll numbers bore him out. In August and September, Gallup and Harris found that the public approved of his actions by more than two to one. And Congress, while grumbling about how little information the administration had shared, quickly approved a supplemental appropriation for the defense budget.[12]

The president's *sotto voce* approach left him needing to build and sustain support for, as one journalist put it, a "strange, almost passionless war." Even at the time, many administration officials worried that they might be attempting the impossible. They were trying, Dean Rusk feared, "to do in cold blood what perhaps could only be done in hot blood." Gradualism, he thought, was at odds with "American impatience." Yet Rusk never disputed the reasons for waging the war in this way. He even claimed to find "a certain grandeur" in what he called "our record of restraint."

> We deliberately refrained from creating a war psychology in the United States. We did not try to stir up the anger of the American people over Vietnam, and we did not have military troops parading through the cities or put on big war bond drives. Neither did we send movie actors around the country whipping up enthusiasm for the

> war. We felt that in a nuclear world it was just too dangerous for an entire people to become too angry. There's too much power in the world, and it's too dangerous for great nations to get too mad.[13]

Fear of popular anger did not keep the president from becoming angry himself. Told by a briefer that it was often difficult for soldiers on "search-and-destroy" missions to locate the enemy, he exploded. They had to try harder. "Kill the goddamn bastards," he said, "kill 'em, kill 'em, kill 'em!" Johnson also found himself "emotionally drained" in speaking to military audiences. The pep talk he gave young officers during a quick flying visit to Vietnam in late 1966 turned into a series of half-shouted exhortations to "go out there and nail that coonskin to the wall!"[14]

These emotional moments were the exception. The president believed the war had to be waged within a framework of carefully calibrated restraints. Johnson and his advisers treated the careful selection of these limits as the key to success, and they debated them—almost daily—for the rest of his presidency.

UNTIL AFGHANISTAN DISLODGED IT, American involvement in Vietnam lived in the popular imagination—and even in the title of the most widely used textbook on the subject—as our "longest war." It is remembered as a grinding ordeal that undermined the nation's unity, its political institutions, its social fabric, its finances, its global standing, and its strategic confidence. The slow getting-in, followed by the slow getting-out, made it seem as though the United States had endured war for decades.

In fact, the true maximalist drama of Vietnam was extremely compressed. Within the long war was a short one in which American policy makers were ready, but only briefly, to do whatever was necessary to succeed. This short war—Lyndon Johnson's Vietnam War—lasted from the summer of 1965, started to unravel early in 1967, and was over in the winter of 1968. It began when the president was convinced that the United States had to do more, or face unacceptable international consequences. It ended when he was persuaded that the United States had to do less, or face unacceptable *domestic* consequences.

The first two years of this period were the only stretch of sustained high-level American optimism in the entire war. The president heard upbeat assessments from both military and civilian advisers. Maxwell

Taylor believed the Communists got "very much the worst of it" in this period. "Wastefully, expensively, but nonetheless indisputably," the NSC staff assured Johnson, "we are winning the war in the South . . . . We are grinding down the enemy by sheer weight and mass." Walt Rostow, who replaced Bundy as national security adviser in 1966, told Johnson the same thing. By mid-1967, he claimed, the war was no longer a stalemate.[15]

Two pivotal figures, however, did not share this optimism: the secretary of defense and the commander of U.S. forces in Vietnam. As the principal authors of American strategy, they were in a position to know. Both Robert McNamara and General William Westmoreland were loyal public spokesmen, but privately they told Johnson what few others would: that his policy could not succeed. Their dissents had a lasting impact on the conduct of the war. Taken together, they provide an answer to the greatest puzzle of Johnson's short war—why he did not change course when he had a chance.

McNamara's doubts appeared first. For him, Westmoreland's repeated calls for more troops were a disturbing sign that "things were slipping out of our control." The November 1965 request to build up to 410,000 men in the year ahead—just four months after the president had agreed to 275,000—was a particularly "shattering blow." What was the point of the detailed analysis that his Pentagon "whiz kids" had done if conditions could change so quickly? Unnerved, McNamara began to retreat from the brisk confidence he had expressed in July. "We have been too optimistic," he admitted to Johnson.[16]

Skepticism about the chances for early success in Vietnam was a theme of almost all McNamara's private reporting to the president. In January 1966, still just six months after the buildup began, he predicted that the most likely result one year down the road was "a military standoff at a much higher level" of fighting. By the early fall, after another inspection tour, he was no more hopeful. Defeat had been averted. But could the United States bring the war to a satisfactory conclusion within two years—that is, before Johnson faced reelection? "The prognosis," McNamara admitted, "is bad." Getting Hanoi to give up, he argued, "would require an effort which we could make but which would not be stomached either by our own people or by world opinion."[17]

Believing that success was going to take much longer than expected did not, at least initially, turn McNamara against the war. But it heightened his worry that the public would lose patience with the entire enterprise. To keep adding troops while ignoring the erosion of domestic support, he told the president, would be—he chose a strong term to get Johnson's attention—"suicide."[18]

McNamara's concern about politics on the home front made him a near-obsessive advocate of bombing "pauses"—the periodic halts that became a defining feature of American war diplomacy. Although presented as a way of probing Hanoi's interest in negotiation, their chief purpose was to show the American people the administration's honest desire for peace. Between 1965 and 1968 there were no fewer than sixteen such pauses, ranging in length from 24 hours to 214 days. All of them had the same negative result—a harsh rejection of American feelers by North Vietnam, plus a surge of men, weapons, and matériel into the South.[19]

Because he too worried about public support, Johnson was usually willing to go along with McNamara in suspending the bombing of North Vietnam. But he saw little value in the pauses. The first one, in mid-May 1965, he considered a "total failure." He particularly resented the North's readiness to exploit the lulls for military advantage. One pause, lasting five days, was timed to permit the delivery of a personal letter from the president to Ho Chi Minh in February 1967. According to Johnson, U.S pilots who monitored infiltration into South Vietnam from the air said the increased traffic on the trails during this pause made them look "like the New Jersey Turnpike."[20]

GENERAL WESTMORELAND's dissent was very different from McNamara's. He too worried about how long the American public would support an inconclusive war. But his concern took him in the opposite direction. He opposed any relaxation of pressure on the enemy, no matter how brief. Incessant pauses, he thought, conveyed the most damaging message to Hanoi. "The signals we were sending were the signals of our own distress."[21]

For Westmoreland, the only way to escape the administration's policy dilemmas was to intensify the war effort. When the entire U.S. national security team, including the president, assembled in Guam in March 1967 for a policy review, he tried to give Johnson the strongest possible jolt. Westmoreland wanted both more troops—670,000 men, up from the then-authorized ceiling of 470,000—and a more aggressive strategy, including ground operations in Laos and Cambodia, amphibious attacks on North Vietnam, and mining of its harbors. He called for mobilizing the reserves and gave his plan an annual price tag of $10 billion (by itself an increase over current-year military spending of 14 percent). Otherwise, he told the president—and this judgment gave the report its real impact—"the war could go on *indefinitely*."[22]

Around the conference table, Westmoreland later recalled, his forecast produced "looks of shock" and "disbelief." Understandably so. Apart from McNamara's warnings, Johnson had been assured that they were "indisputably" winning. Now his commanding general said they weren't. Worse, the general wanted more resources and a new strategy—or else the United States might have to keep fighting forever.[23]

Westmoreland's Guam proposal produced three months of wrangling within the administration—angry meetings, high-level maneuvering, a flood of papers—about how to wage the war in Vietnam. To head off escalation, McNamara sent Johnson the most emotional memos of his tenure at the Pentagon. The request for more men, he said, showed the war was "acquiring a momentum of its own that must be stopped." Sounding exactly like Clifford and Ball two years earlier, he forecast "a major national disaster" if Westmoreland's plan was adopted. The war, he told the president,

> is unpopular in this country. It is becoming increasingly unpopular as it escalates—causing more American casualties, more fear of its growing into a wider war, more privation of the domestic sector, and more distress at the amount of suffering being visited on the noncombatants in Vietnam. Most Americans do not know how we got where we are, and most . . . are convinced that somehow we should not have gotten this deeply in. All want the war ended and expect their President to end it. Successfully. Or else.[24]

At the same time that he described public defeatism, McNamara argued that adding troops would let loose popular demands for increasingly violent measures. Nuclear war with the Soviet Union or China was one possible result. Another was what he cryptically described as a "costly distortion in the American national consciousness."[25]

McNamara was ready to say whatever was necessary to convince Johnson not to listen to Westmoreland. Perhaps fearing that he only bolstered the case for increased effort by saying the war was going badly, the administration's leading pessimist suddenly turned optimist. Back from another Saigon visit in July 1967, McNamara informed the president that victory was now in sight. "For the first time," he said, "I feel that if we follow the same program we will win the war and end the fighting." Johnson seemed surprised—and surely grateful too, since he was now relieved of any need to consider a new strategy. To make sure there was no mistake, he asked McNamara to repeat his upbeat conclusion, wrote it down on the spot, and saved the copy.[26]

In the end, Johnson rejected almost everything Westmoreland asked for in Guam. He authorized a tiny fraction of the request for extra manpower and approved none of the increased pressures that the generals wanted to bring to bear against the North. Having granted countless requests for more resources since July 1965, the president had now turned down the most significant one. Clearly further proposals would also be rejected. In two years, America's investment in South Vietnam had reached its high-water mark.[27]

ALMOST HALF A CENTURY after the fact, there is no way to identify a strategy that might have succeeded in Vietnam. But it remains important to understand why Lyndon Johnson did not adjust policy when he had the opportunity and the incentive to do so. In 1967 the generals in the field and the bureaucrats back in Washington agreed that the Communist effort to conquer the South, so close to victory two years earlier, had been checked. Revolving-door Saigon politics had been replaced by relatively stable leadership. McNamara and Westmoreland urged the president not to see any of this as a real success. Existing strategy, they said, would not soon—would probably never—produce the outcome he and the American people wanted. Meanwhile it was getting steadily harder to give other foreign policy problems the attention they deserved. The Six-Day War in the Middle East, keeping NATO together in the wake of De Gaulle's partial pullout, starting arms control talks with Moscow—all these took second place to managing the war.

With defeat averted, victory distant, public patience fraying, and opportunity costs rising—Johnson had his one real chance to change course. That he did not seize it cannot be explained by a shortage of alternatives. Plans of all kinds—to escalate, to *de*-escalate, and even to do both at once—were put before the president. He embraced none of them. Why not?

Escalation would have been Johnson's least likely choice. He had turned down both the large package of escalatory measures that Westmoreland had presented at Guam in March 1967 and individual elements of the package that were proposed to him after that. The chiefs kept pressing him to relax the constraints that he had imposed on the conduct of the war, but the president had his usual blunt answer for them: "Bomb, bomb, bomb, that's all you know."[28]

Had Johnson wanted to pursue *de*-escalation of the war, a way of doing so was also available—by pursuing "pacification," the so-called "ink blot" strategy that emphasized village security and economic development. As a politician, he had long been drawn to its core claim, that popular support was the key to military success. In 1967 pacification's most important advocate was Robert "Blowtorch Bob" Komer, whom the president had sent to Saigon the year before to oversee what became known as "the other war." Komer offered Johnson a real alternative to Westmoreland's Guam proposals. The United States, he suggested, had a chance to turn more military tasks over to Vietnamese forces and to start drawing down its own troops as early as 1968.[29]

For an embattled president, it would be hard to think of a proposal with more potential appeal than this one. Pursuing Komer's idea would have served Johnson's domestic goals and helped him to find the time and energy for foreign policy problems other than the war. Some of the president's advisers actually came away from Guam believing that he had endorsed "pacification" as the new American strategy. But they were wrong. Although Komer's "other war" received regular lip service in 1967, it was not backed up by resources. It did not command the president's day-to-day interest. And it certainly did not embolden him to start pulling troops out of Vietnam.

Of all the policy alternatives available to him, the plan to which Johnson reacted most negatively—even violently—was one that combined escalation and de-escalation. In August 1966, General Victor Krulak, the deputy commandant of the Marine Corps, known as a brilliant military innovator, was invited to brief the president on his ideas for winning the war. Krulak used the occasion to present a full critique of existing strategy. He urged a serious commitment to "pacification" in the South, arguing that American lives were being needlessly lost in large-unit operations. At the same time, he pushed for a more aggressive effort against the North. Equipment and supplies had to be intercepted, he said, on the docks of Haiphong harbor, not when they were moving south through the jungle.[30]

Both politically and militarily, Krulak's proposal was the most sophisticated presentation about Vietnam ever made to Johnson. Each half of the plan could have helped him to deal with the risks created by the other. Fewer troops on the ground would have helped to limit the political costs of a bolder air campaign. More focused and effective pressures on the North would have protected a smaller force in the South. But the president did not want to explore this or, it seemed, any other option. He got to his feet, all but lifted the general from his chair (though nicknamed "Brute," Krulak was not a large man), and shoved him as quickly as possible out of the Oval Office. The idea was never raised again.[31]

One of Johnson's main motives was, of course, to avoid a direct conflict with the Soviet Union or China. His maximalist commitment to South Vietnam had to stop short of that. And yet risk aversion alone does not fully explain his stance. For he refused to hear that these risks might be diminishing, and he did not ask how to reduce them further. When the American buildup started, Mao Zedong had told the American journalist Edgar Snow that China would not intervene "beyond her borders." In 1966 and 1967 the intelligence community consistently told the president that Moscow and Beijing both had reasons of their own to avoid confrontation with the United States. Johnson paid no attention. His long-standing view was that the risk of a Korea-style clash with China was high, and he stuck to it. "I am not going to spit in China's face," he declared.[32]

Johnson's immobility had deeper sources. Two years earlier, when his closest advisers had pushed him to escalate, they had put aside their differences to leave him no way out. And finding no daylight between them, the president had done what they said. As Maxwell Taylor said, America had not exhausted its alternatives. Johnson agreed to let his advisers take their best shot.

In 1967 the situation was completely different. McNamara and Westmoreland both believed that existing policy was not succeeding, yet each preferred the status quo to what the other proposed. Each man put all his energy into demolishing the other's ideas. The president could not act without choosing between them.

In public, Johnson denied that these differences even existed. "We may have been wrong," he said, "but we have not been divided." This was easily the largest of all the untruths he told about the war. Johnson had been forced to stake his presidency on a risky and gigantic enterprise because he did not see a way to challenge his advisers' consensus. He had taken cover in it. But when they stopped agreeing, he had no idea what to do. Rather than use discord as a tool for finding a better policy, he ignored it. The opposing recommendations before him canceled each other out.[33]

IF JOHNSON WAS NOT going to change course, he needed a reinvigorated effort to justify the existing approach. This challenge too seemed to paralyze him. He opened his 1967 State of the Union address by announcing that the issue at stake in South Vietnam was "whether we have the staying power to fight a very costly war when the objective is limited and the danger to us is seemingly remote." He seemed even gloomier by the time he finished the speech. "I wish I could report to you that the conflict is almost over. This I cannot do. We face more cost, more loss, and more agony." The president concluded by calling for "patience . . . and I mean a great deal of patience."[34]

To such semidefeatist rhetoric, the public response was unsurprising. The idea that fighting in Vietnam had been a mistake all along gained more support in 1967 than in any year of the war. Overall approval of Johnson's performance, which had dropped from the 60-percentile range in 1965 to the 50s in 1966, descended into the 40s in 1967. Mainstream politicians distanced themselves from the war. By the end of 1966, Robert Kennedy, once a strong supporter, had already called for an end to bombing and pursuit of negotiations. In April 1967, Martin Luther King, Jr., gave a famous sermon calling the war "madness." In the academy, where antiwar sentiment had been strong for some time, hostility to Johnson reached new heights. Hans Morgenthau, the dean of international relations scholars, compared the president to Caesar. (The name-calling went both ways, of course. Johnson called his critics "those little shits on the campuses.")[35]

The almost effortless political dominance that the president had enjoyed in 1965 was undone by the off-year congressional elections of 1966. The Republicans picked up 47 seats in the House of Representatives and formed a de facto alliance with southern Democrats to challenge the Great Society. For Johnson, the problem of paying for the war now became inseparable from his domestic program. Facing a federal deficit that had already ballooned to three times the Treasury's forecast, he asked the new Congress in January 1967 to pass an emergency 6 percent surcharge on individual and corporate income taxes. In August, with the budget outlook seeming worse each month, he increased this to a still more controversial 10 percent. The Ways and Means Committee refused even to hold hearings on the measure.[36]

Despite the president's effort to enforce unity within the ranks of the administration, disagreements began to show. McNamara, having blocked Westmoreland's Guam proposals to do more in Vietnam, stopped making a secret of his preference for doing less. By August 1967, he was back to challenging the military's assessments of the war effort—and his public rhetoric became more heated. No bombing "short of annihilation," he told a Senate hearing, would break North Vietnam's will.[37]

At the end of October, McNamara seemed ready for a confrontation with the president himself. He told Johnson privately, but more emphatically than ever, that he considered administration policy "dangerous, costly in lives, and unsatisfactory to the American people." In a follow-on memo, he warned that a year hence—meaning, on Election Day 1968—the United States would be no closer to success. The public, McNamara insisted yet again, would not long support a stalemated effort. Only a radical change of direction could prevent disaster. He therefore proposed a set of measures designed to begin the process of extricating the United States from Vietnam: a cap on troop levels, a bombing halt, a scaling-back of military operations, and the beginning of negotiations.[38]

A president who prized unity, and who saw that support for the war was slipping away, could hardly retain a secretary of defense who privately called American policy dangerous and unlikely to succeed—and had started to say so publicly. Seizing an opportunity, Johnson announced that he would nominate McNamara as the new head of the World Bank. Suddenly the Cold War's most influential secretary of defense was on his way out, and as his departure neared, the physical and psychological toll of almost seven years at the Pentagon became increasingly apparent. The president exploited McNamara's exhaustion, deflecting attention from the departing secretary's renegade policy views to his shaky emotional state. Cruelly, Johnson let it be known that he "fear[ed] even for his survival." McNamara's behavior (including a farewell ceremony at which he was overcome with emotion and unable to speak) gave weight to this fear. His peculiar comment years later—that he didn't know whether he was fired or quit—left no doubt that he ended his tenure at the Pentagon in a daze.[39]

Johnson had ousted his best-known adviser without letting their disagreement erupt in public. But this success did nothing to ease the underlying policy problem that McNamara had urged the president to face. Could the United States stabilize South Vietnam before public opinion turned decisively against the war? Johnson now heard this concern everywhere he turned. On November 1, the very day that McNamara sent his final Vietnam memo, the president met to discuss the war with former senior officials and Establishment figures, a group that came to be known as the Wise Men. These graybeards—among them Dean Acheson, McGeorge Bundy, and even George Ball—cheered Johnson by urging him, unanimously, to stand firm in South Vietnam. Yet even they, unaware of McNamara's impending departure, highlighted the issue that had loomed largest in his dissent—how to sustain a policy whose support was collapsing.[40]

TO SUCCEED MCNAMARA, the president chose Clark Clifford, longtime Washington lawyer and Democratic fixer, widely considered (because he opposed bombing pauses) a "hawk" on the war. Few knew that he had been an outspoken in-house critic of the 1965 buildup, or that he had advocated bombing in order to speed American withdrawal. On that issue he was completely consistent. "I want to get out of Vietnam," he told Johnson.[41]

Clifford was confirmed on January 30, 1968—the day the Tet Offensive began in South Vietnam. American officials had known that a bold Communist move was in the works. Westmoreland had foreshadowed it on national television days before the first attacks. Still, the scale of the offensive was a surprise. Five of South Vietnam's six biggest cities—and 36 of its 44 provincial capitals—were simultaneously besieged. The U.S. embassy in Saigon was stormed (and briefly penetrated). Although fighting in almost all urban centers ended within days, the impression left on public opinion—that the huge American war effort had achieved far less than advertised—was a lasting one.[42]

Tet was a severe military defeat for the Vietcong but an even more severe blow for Johnson's policy. At the time and ever after, many explained its impact by contrasting the grim scenes Americans saw on television and the upbeat assessments they had heard from the administration. Virtually all senior policy makers—from the president on down—later expressed regret that they had not prepared the public for predictable shocks like Tet. The failure to do so early, they thought, shortened public patience later.[43]

Yet this was not the real reason Tet was so important. By the end of 1967, a near-majority of Americans had already concluded that the war was a mistake. They were rapidly becoming a majority and would surely have become one in 1968 even without shocks like Tet. The TV images of the offensive in February 1968 did not shake popular optimism. To the contrary, they reinforced popular *pessimism*—and made it ascendant in the country at large.[44]

Tet's impact, moreover, had at least as much to do with what came after it as with the offensive itself. The administration claimed that it had been a last-ditch effort, showing the enemy's desperation and weakness. Subsequent months, by far the bloodiest that American troops ever faced in Vietnam, told a different story. Combat deaths in the four months after the beginning of Tet exceeded 8,000—easily the highest for any comparable period in the entire war. (It took U.S. troops in Iraq five years, from March 2008 to March 2013, to reach even half this number.) Though casualties declined later in 1968, there was no sign of improvement during the spring. To the contrary, May's deaths—a staggering 2,415—represented the highest one-month total of the war. Small wonder, then, that the administration could not make its upbeat reading stick.[45]

The final turn in public opinion came quickly. In February 1968, at the peak of the offensive, many Americans who thought getting into Vietnam had been a mistake were still in favor of fighting on or even of fighting harder. By June they had changed their minds. Support for an increased war effort dropped from 53 percent to 35 percent. Those who wanted to get out rose from 28 percent to 49 percent. In just four months, an almost two-to-one majority in favor of fighting on had vanished, replaced by a three-to-two margin in favor of getting out.[46]

Public support for the war was further undermined by the administration's disorderly and dispirited debate about what to do next. The quick, high-level policy review that Johnson asked Clifford, as the incoming defense secretary, to chair was one of the strangest and most self-defeating examinations of a major national security problem ever conducted by the U.S. government. The only fully developed idea on the table was one that the president had already rejected a year earlier: Westmoreland's proposal, recycled from Guam, to bring in another 200,000 troops while expanding the war into Laos, Cambodia, and North Vietnam. The chance that Johnson would accept this plan now was so remote that Westmoreland later pretended he had not recommended it at all. He claimed that he had merely sketched steps to be taken if the United States wanted to "grasp the initiative."[47]

As implausible as the whole idea sounded, word spread quickly that the administration was considering a huge new deployment to South Vietnam. In every corner of the government, opposition mounted. At the Pentagon, the new secretary's civilian advisers lobbied daily against the idea. On Capitol Hill, three of the most influential and reliably hawkish members of the Senate—Richard Russell, John Stennis, and Henry "Scoop" Jackson—told Clifford that they would not support the call-up of reserves necessary to sustain a larger force. Rusk suggested that, with Congress still refusing to approve Johnson's 10 percent income tax surcharge, and the budget impasse unresolved, a troop increase was out of the question. A currency crisis added to the general alarm. Gold sales to prop up the dollar rose so sharply in March that the London gold market had to be closed.[48]

With Washington in turmoil, the outcome of Clifford's review was never in doubt. Reporting to the president in early March, he made only one clear recommendation—*not* to grant Westmoreland a large increase. Given the scale of the crisis at hand, this was an extraordinarily meager result. Clifford offered no suggestions for how to extricate the United States from the war; nor did he suggest extrication as a goal. American policy makers did not know what they wanted to do, but they were very clear on what they did not want. They did not want a new burst of effort any more than the public did.[49]

THE EARLY MONTHS of 1968 put senior members of the Johnson administration under a kind of stress rarely seen in official Washington. Rusk described the entire year as a "blur," survivable only on a regular diet of "aspirin, scotch, and four packs of Larks." Rostow felt the country—the whole world, even—was becoming "unhinged."[50]

As they tried to think about how to unwind their Vietnam commitment, members of the administration seemed to inhabit different universes. Westmoreland actually suggested that nuclear weapons might help to end the war. At the other end of the spectrum, Clifford's deputy, Paul Nitze, was so upset by the emptiness of his new boss's report to the president—by its unwillingness to think about disengagement—that he refused to testify in its favor to Congress. If ordered to do so, he said, he would resign.[51]

The government was losing its ability to formulate coherent policy, even to function normally. For his show of defiance, Nitze was disinvited from the regular Tuesday lunch meetings with the president on Vietnam. Westmoreland was firmly instructed to "desist" from further talk of nuclear weapons and, once his troop proposal was rejected, was removed as commander in Vietnam. Watching such developments, Clifford feared that the administration he had joined just weeks before "might come apart at its seams."[52]

No one's response to events was more unsteady or unpredictable than that of the president himself. Privately Johnson accepted the need to scale back the war. He had overruled Westmoreland's troop increase and encouraged Rusk to develop a plan for negotiations. But in public, he held to a harder line. On March 18, days after almost losing the New Hampshire primary, he gave his most bellicose speech of the year to the National Farmers Union in Minneapolis:

> Your president has come here to ask you people and all the other people of this nation to join us in a total national effort to win the war, to win the peace, and to complete the job that must be done here at home . . . . We will—make no mistake about it—win . . . — . . . We are not doing enough to win it the way we are doing it now.[53]

For Clifford, still new on the job, the president's call to arms was a shock. "My God," he asked himself, "after only eighteen days in office, am I in such fundamental disagreement with the man who appointed me?" Yet barely a week later Johnson's thinking had changed again. He treated his advisers to a long soliloquy on the hopelessness of his policy problem.

> How can we get this job done? We need more money—in an election year. We need more taxes—in an election year. We need more troops—in an election year. And we need cuts in the domestic budget—in an election year. And yet I cannot tell the people what they will get in Vietnam in return for these cuts.[54]

The president, Clifford was convinced, "understood the need for a dramatic change in policy." But he responded combatively when anyone else delivered this message. His late-March meeting with the Wise Men of the foreign policy establishment was typical. Most members of the group, who had been unanimously in favor of staying the course just months earlier, now called for getting out. Angry, Johnson demanded to know which of his advisers had "poisoned the well" against him. "The Establishment bastards," he groused after the meeting, had bailed out. His own political future had become clear to him. "I will go down the drain," he told Clifford.[55]

Throughout 1967, Johnson had hoped that staying the course might prove a viable approach. The winter of 1968 showed that it no longer was. After Tet, only 10 percent of the public supported existing policy in Vietnam (and by midyear it slipped further, to 8 percent). Democratic societies rarely express such a total rejection of the status quo. And when they do, the debate is pretty much over. Having repeatedly rejected proposals to do more, Johnson now had only one option left—to do less. In a nationwide address four days after his meeting with the Wise Men, he curtailed the bombing of North Vietnam, called again for peace talks, and announced that he would not stand for reelection.[56]

JOHNSON'S WITHDRAWAL was the end of the maximalist phase of policy that had started with John Kennedy's election in 1960. It began—haltingly and without strong or decisive leadership—America's second Cold War retrenchment. The president claimed that he had dropped out of the race to insulate all further decision making about the war from partisanship. When North Vietnam agreed to exploratory talks in Paris, he sent his negotiators off with a firm mandate to ignore the political calendar. "I want [the war] resolved," he lectured them, "but not because of the election. Don't yield anything on that impression."[57]

Yet many of Johnson's senior advisers rejected the idea that national security decisions should be free of partisanship, and his own views wavered. For the rest of the year, every decision about disengaging from Vietnam was also a decision about the election. "Domestic politics," Clifford felt, "was a legitimate and unavoidable part of a successful policy." He thought a complete halt to the bombing—at first, Johnson had merely confined it to North Vietnamese territory below the nineteenth parallel—was the only way to get Hanoi to negotiate seriously. Progress in the talks was also the only way to show voters that Democrats could end the war. "So what if a bombing halt helped Humphrey?" Clifford reasoned. "Continued bombing would help Nixon." Averell Harriman, who headed the U.S. delegation in Paris, was even more insistent that foreign policy be subordinated to partisan ends. Ending the war, he told colleagues, "paled in comparison to the necessity of keeping Nixon out of the White House."[58]

Between the opening of the talks and Election Day, the president's advisers kept urging him to announce a complete bombing halt. He kept resisting. The North Vietnamese had exploited his goodwill too often. Now he demanded a firm commitment not to increase infiltration and supplies into South Vietnam. When Harriman's team came up with vaguer formulas (based on "understandings" rather than commitments), Johnson scorned them. "The enemy," he fumed, "is using my own people as dupes." When Clifford presented a revised version of the same approach, the president dismissed it: "I don't agree with a word that you have said." And when Bill Bundy offered the same plan, Johnson took him aside for a private tongue-lashing: "I'm not having any part of it . . . and I don't ever want to hear about this again." The people pushing the idea, he complained, were trying to make him "the biggest boob of our time."[59]

Slowly, however, the president's resolve gave way. With the election barely a week off, Johnson declared himself ready for a bombing halt even without a firm commitment from Hanoi. For Maxwell Taylor, still nominally a White House adviser, the deal was an obvious "hoax" ("largely self-perpetrated," he admitted). The president claimed his goal was to put the war on a different course. "I don't think," he told Clifford, "I will have another opportunity."[60]

When American policy makers ratchet back a commitment, as they did in this case, there is usually an ally standing inconveniently between them and the exit. In Korea Eisenhower had faced this problem with Syngman Rhee, but the president of South Vietnam and his colleagues did not go half so easily. Clifford had seen the confrontation coming. In his early days at the Pentagon, he had warned Saigon's ambassador that Washington was rethinking the war:

> Tell your government we have run out of time for diplomatic niceties. We are sick to death of Thieu and Ky endlessly feuding while Americans die. Our people are sick and tired of this war, and our sup-

> port is limited. Your government is facing a clear decision either to broaden the government, clean up the corruption, and take measures to gain wide support among the people, or face the loss of American support . . . . Tell your leadership that Saigon's best friends in Washington are deeply worried as to whether or not the American public will continue its support of our efforts in Vietnam. It is not clear to me that your leaders now understand this. We are losing supporters every day.[61]

Despite such warnings, by late October Saigon had not budged from its insistence that the bombing should continue until Hanoi offered concessions. This was, of course, the same position that Johnson himself had taken until recently, but Clifford was indignant all the same. Saigon's reluctance to join formal negotiations, he huffed to the president, was "reprehensible and utterly without merit." The United States had to show its ally who was boss: "We must *force* them to Paris."[62]

Johnson remained uneasy. Some of his advisers suspected he didn't really want Humphrey to win. "I do not feel good about a quickie before the election," he pleaded with Clifford. The president proposed to give the South Vietnamese a little more time. But Thieu—with, it seems, some Republican encouragement—did not want to give the Democrats even a small victory. He kept refusing to announce any agreement on talks. "This latest message is thoroughly insulting," Clifford raged. "In fact it is horseshit!" At last Johnson relented. "We have to act," he agreed, "with or without Saigon."[63]

Speaking to the nation on October 31, and feeling that the South Vietnamese "had let me down," the president ordered a complete end to the bombing of the North. At the same time, he announced that the next session of the Paris talks would occur on November 6, the day after the U.S election. As for Saigon's role in the meetings, he lamely observed that its representatives were "free to participate" if they wanted to.[64]

The South Vietnamese government sent no delegation to Paris until December, and no agreement on a meeting of all delegations was reached until January. The first plenary session did not take place until January 25, 1969. Five days earlier, Richard Nixon had become president of the United States.[65]

7

Retrenchment and Vietnam

"GET GOING, TAKE RISKS, BE EXCITING"

Richard Nixon and Zhou Enlai

IN A NATIONWIDE ADDRESS about Vietnam a year after he was elected president, Richard Nixon ruminated on national character. "We Americans," he said, "are a do-it-yourself people. We are an impatient people. Instead of teaching someone else to do a job, we like to do it ourselves." He added a rueful observation: "This trait has carried over into our foreign policy." The United States, the new administration charged, had too long "led without listening, talked to our allies instead of with them, and informed them of new departures instead of deciding with them."[1]

Elected to lead a nation divided by war, Nixon had concluded that this do-everything, know-it-all approach to global security could not continue. For the second time since the start of the Cold War, Washington had to find a way to do less.

> America cannot—and will not—conceive all the plans, design all the programs, execute all the decisions and undertake all the defense of the free nations of the world. We will help where it makes a real difference and is considered in our interest.[2]

The United States would henceforth serve as "*a* weight—not *the* weight—in the scale."[3]

Every element of the Nixon administration's strategy reflected the new downsizing. Between 1969 and 1972, total military personnel dropped from 3.4 million to 2.3 million, the lowest level since before the Korean War. Half a million men were withdrawn from Vietnam; the U.S. troop presence in Japan and South Korea was cut by a third, in the Philippines by half. From its peak in 1969, the Pentagon budget began almost a decade of steady cuts. Announcing a new "doctrine," Nixon said that American allies would have to provide the manpower for their own defense. The United States would offer weapons and, when needed, a nuclear "umbrella," but it should not be expected to do the fighting. The goal of American nuclear strategy was also scaled back, from superiority to "sufficiency." Some planned weapons were shelved because, it was explained, they "thwarted vital domestic programs." And it was not just traditional diplomacy and national security strategy that felt the squeeze. Nixon devalued the dollar—twice.[4]

A more cost-conscious foreign policy was inevitable. Even so, it worried the new president. He confessed to his chief of staff, H. R. Haldeman, that the United States was in danger of going "down the drain as a great power." Everything Nixon knew of history, every political instinct he had, told him that the impact of a major setback like Vietnam would be extremely negative. Extraordinary exertion was needed to keep retrenchment from undermining American interests and influence. The president vowed to Haldeman that he would not let himself "fall into [the] dry rot of just managing the chaos better." He had to "get going, take risks, be exciting."[5]

What Nixon admired in great leaders—what he envied and sought to emulate—was their utter decisiveness. Only this, he thought, enabled them to rally a nation, or nations, to heroic effort. When polls showed that the public did not consider him "an activist president," he was despondent. He constantly exhorted his staff to see the enormity of the challenges before them and respond on the same scale. "Bold decisions make history," he lectured, "like Teddy Roosevelt charging up San Juan Hill, a small event but dramatic, and people took notice." Henry Kissinger, the Harvard professor whom Nixon had recruited to be his national security adviser, soon learned how often his new boss warned against half-measures. "You pay the same price for doing something halfway as for doing it completely," the president said. "So you might as well do it completely." No thought pops up more often in Nixon's memoirs, or on the tapes and transcripts of his Oval Office conversations, than the importance of being ready to "go for broke." His instinct was always, as Kissinger saw it, to "play for all the marbles."[6]

Going for broke was how Nixon expected to avoid going down the drain. Making bold strokes would keep withdrawal from Vietnam from becoming a disaster; they would preserve America's global standing while reducing its cost. Nixon always saw himself as just a brilliant initiative or two away from turning the tables on his opponents. This was as true of foreign policy—of dealing with North Vietnam or the Soviet Union or U.S. allies—as it was of domestic politics. America, he acknowledged, had "lost the leadership position we held at [the] end of World War II," but a few adroit moves could change all that. "[We] can regain it," he assured Haldeman, "if [we move] fast!" No problem was too big or too technical that daring and determination wouldn't help to solve it. When

Nixon took the United States off the gold standard and imposed wage and price controls in August 1971, he stressed the need to act boldly—"not timidly, not half-heartedly, and not in piecemeal fashion."[7]

Henry Kissinger shared much of Nixon's analysis. But he gave it, as those who write about him never tire of quipping, a different accent. Without disputing his boss's blustery, would-be-heroic talk, he doubted that—after "a decade of almost continuous decline"—the United States could recover all the ground it had lost. As a professor, he had long insisted that trying to do so was mistaken and unrealistic. Decisiveness alone was not going to restore lost dominance. For too long, Washington had been "living off capital." As Kissinger saw it, the new aim should be to "foster the initiative of others." Far from fearing the dilution of American leadership, he welcomed it. "Painful as it may be to admit," he had written just before leaving Harvard, "we could benefit from a counterweight that would discipline our occasional impetuosity and, by supplying historical perspective, modify our penchant for abstract and 'final' solutions."[8]

Only in a world that the United States stopped trying to dominate, Kissinger argued, would American diplomacy enjoy "a new period of creativity." In the future, its tools would be "maneuver, originality, and imagination." It was easy to parody the new national security adviser's ceaseless use of words like *nuance, maxim,* and *intangible,* but they were no mere stylistic tic. Fashioning a policy appropriate to the times, he believed, was "less a matter of expertise than philosophy." Not everyone in the new administration, it should be said, took to the smoke-and-mirrors style. For Haldeman, it was all "typical K gobbledygook."[9]

Nixon and Kissinger assumed responsibility for American foreign policy during its deepest crisis since the end of World War II. They agreed on the retrenchment strategy that would enable the United States to regain its balance. They also agreed on how to do it—secretly, and with little deference to others. The two of them imposed their own preferences as few American policy makers have ever done. Yet their approaches were not the same. Someone like Nixon, who aimed to "play for all the marbles," was bound to have his differences with someone who thought "ambiguity [was] the lifeblood of diplomacy." The policies they devised, those that were celebrated and those that are reviled to this day, were the product of these differences.[10]

NIXON WAS SURE he could end the Vietnam War quickly. It would be over in a year, he told an early cabinet meeting. The idea of inflicting a "knock-out blow" on the North appealed to him, and he ordered up a plan for such attacks, code-named "Duck Hook." To reinforce his military moves, he would get the Soviets to put pressure on Hanoi. If the Kremlin leadership wanted arms control agreements or increased trade, they would have to force North Vietnam to compromise. The president called this approach "linkage," and he explained it in brutal language to the Soviet ambassador. "You may think that you can break me," he snarled to Dobrynin. But if Moscow did not help, the war was bound to escalate. The United States was sick of "being diddled to death in Vietnam." On the home front, Nixon tried to increase his political maneuvering room by questioning his critics' patriotism. "The so-called best circles of America," he sneered in his commencement address at the Air Force Academy, despised the military. For them, love of country was "a backward fetish of the uneducated and the unsophisticated."[11]

This was strident rhetoric, but the new president did not actually want the confrontation and controversy that his strategies required. Nixon quickly backed away from all of them. Duck Hook was shelved first, lest aggressive military moves inflame the Congress, split the cabinet, and end his honeymoon with the public. Suppose key advisers or cabinet members resigned in protest? "I just wasn't ready for that," Nixon admitted. In place of escalation, he announced the first withdrawal of American troops—25,000 men—and an intensified effort, known as "Vietnamization," to train the South Vietnamese to take on the burden of the war themselves. Kissinger warned the president that the public would find withdrawals addictive—like "salted peanuts," he said. Nixon knew that once withdrawals started, there would be no turning back. It didn't stop him. At the end of the summer he announced another, even larger withdrawal—this time, 35,000 troops.[12]

The same goal—avoiding domestic controversy—led the administration to back away from linkage too. Though Kissinger insisted to Dobrynin on countless occasions that East-West relations were on hold until the Soviets helped end the war, he and Nixon clearly did not mean it. They were not willing to forgo the political benefits of détente just to see whether Moscow would pressure Hanoi. To the contrary, in the fall of 1969, the United States agreed to open talks on limiting strategic nuclear weapons. Nixon, in Kissinger's view, had backed down. The Soviets, he thought, had made skillful use of "reverse linkage"—exploiting the president's need for foreign policy progress while the war continued.[13]

Nixon backed away from confrontation even in his aggressive effort to win over the "silent majority." His November 3, 1969, speech to the nation was preceded by dark rumblings from the White House that it planned to give Hanoi an ultimatum. In the end, the speech contained little more than an appeal for patience and national unity. Domestic divisions, the president complained, were helping North Vietnam. The enemy, he said, believed that "all it has to do is to wait for our next concession, and our next concession after that one, until it gets everything it wants."[14]

Nixon believed his speech changed "the course of history," and there was no denying its effect on public opinion. An astounding 77 percent of Americans approved of his policy. Yet not even support of this magnitude altered the basic policy problem that the president faced in Vietnam. It did not free him from the expectations he had created when he started the process of withdrawal. As 1970 opened, the administration began to debate another round of cuts. This time it was Kissinger—the man who had pointed out the hazards of "salted peanuts"—who proposed a larger withdrawal (150,000 troops) than anyone else in the administration. Nixon backed him and—typically—even rationalized the decision to himself as a tough step that would increase pressure on Hanoi. How better to impress the North Vietnamese with his utter resoluteness than by keeping the home front quiet through continuing withdrawals?[15]

In more than a year in office, every choice Nixon had made was designed to sustain domestic support and pacify the opposition. He decided against new military pressures on North Vietnam, watered down his own policy of linkage in dealing with Moscow, and put American troop levels on an irreversible downward path. This was to be expected from a president who had embarked on retrenchment. But it could not fully satisfy one who thought the best way to solve problems was by "going for broke."

BEFORE LONG Nixon saw his opportunity. For years, American commanders in South Vietnam had complained about Washington's reluctance to clean out the North Vietnamese camps that operated just across the Cambodian border, not far from Saigon. General Creighton Abrams, Westmoreland's successor, thought it was "criminal" to give the enemy a sanctuary in which to "fatten up, re-indoctrinate, [and] get their supplies." Cambodia's own army was powerless to solve the problem. (Abrams felt it would have had trouble defeating "a wounded squad of Italian motorcyclists.") In the spring of 1970, political turmoil in Cambodia threatened to make things even worse. The entire country, it seemed, might fall under North Vietnamese control. All of Cambodia would then become a sanctuary for forces trying to bring down the Saigon regime.[16]

In the face of this increased danger, Nixon had the option of a limited response. That was the course urged on him by most of his advisers. But Abrams, perhaps knowing what the commander in chief thought of doing things halfway, argued that "partial measures will not suffice." The president agreed. He rejected a plan to limit the domestic uproar by using only South Vietnamese troops, even though he knew that sending American forces into Cambodia would have a "shattering effect" on public opinion. Both Melvin Laird, the secretary of defense, and William Rogers, the secretary of state, opposed the use of Americans. Much of the NSC staff was also against it (and several resigned in protest). Kissinger opined to Haldeman that the president was "moving too rashly without really thinking through the consequences." But Nixon sensed a chance to turn the war around. Perhaps, he wondered aloud to aides, this was also the moment to bomb Hanoi, or mine Haiphong harbor? At the Pentagon to review the operation, he started barking out orders to attack other enemy sanctuaries as well. "Make whatever plans are necessary, and then just do it. Knock them all out so that they can't be used against us again. Ever." Excited by his own decisiveness, he shouted, "Let's go blow the hell out of them."[17]

Actions of such scale and drama, Nixon hoped, would galvanize supporters. "You have to electrify people with bold decisions," he reminded his advisers. But opponents of the war were far more electrified. Preserving domestic calm had been Nixon's only real success to date. Now he began to reignite passions. Fearing a wider war, and stunned by the killing of students demonstrating against the invasion, Congress voted to prohibit the use of U.S. troops in future operations outside South Vietnam. This exercise of legislative power proved to be one of the rare restrictions on the war that had a significant military impact.[18]

The invasion of Cambodia had a payoff of sorts. It disrupted the North Vietnamese supply chain; American casualties went down; fears of a major military setback subsided. But these were all fleeting benefits, and the administration's actions acknowledged as much. In the aftermath of the invasion, it was Washington, not Hanoi, that rethought its negotiating position. Having long insisted that North Vietnamese forces withdraw from the South as part of any peace agreement, the president and his advisers now accepted the simpler idea of a cease-fire in place. They reassured each other that such a concession was possible because of their hard-won success in Cambodia. But Kissinger's private analysis for Nixon told a different story. The North Vietnamese, he admitted, might think things were going their way.

> They may well look at anti-war pressures in this country and calculate they can sit tight until progressive American withdrawals or political concessions undermine the GVN [the South Vietnamese government]. Time is on their side—the U.S. exodus from the South is irreversible and the GVN can never stand on its own.[19]

To get an adversary holding such views to negotiate seriously, Kissinger suggested, Washington might have to offer more concessions. It was with this in mind that the United States dropped its demand that North Vietnamese troops go home. Even so, more than two years passed—bringing yet another Communist offensive, and then yet another U.S. escalation in return—before Hanoi responded to this initiative with concessions of its own.[20]

Despite the costs of the Cambodia invasion, Nixon continued to think that a military breakthrough might produce a better outcome, and he kept looking for one. But Congress's restrictions on American troops meant that the next time the president decided to go for broke, South Vietnamese forces would have to conduct the operation alone. The result—the invasion of Laos in February 1971, designed to stop the flow of North Vietnamese men and matériel into the South—was a near disaster. Planned under heavy pressure from the White House despite military doubts, poorly executed, and aborted in midcourse, it showed that "Vietnamization" had not created an effective army.[21]

Publicly, Nixon and Kissinger always rejected any suggestion that these military gambles had not paid off. Privately, the president was not so sure. In May 1971, with the Cambodia controversy more than a year behind him but with Laos fresh in his mind, Nixon fretted about the consequences. "Trust," he told Haldeman, "is like a thin thread"—hard to mend once broken. Perhaps the Laos operation had "broken our thin thread with the American people as to the winding down of the war. . . . It's going to be very hard to put that together again."[22]

UNTIL THE SUMMER of 1971, the Nixon administration's effort to find a less costly, more sustainable new foreign policy was overshadowed by the president's military shocks in Vietnam. He had escalated the war, and revived public opposition, without weakening the enemy in any lasting way. Meanwhile, American forces continued to shrink.

Then came Henry Kissinger's dramatic visit to Beijing. Few initiatives in the history of U.S. foreign policy have had either its immediate surprise value or its long-term impact. It seemed to mark the regeneration of American diplomacy—even, as Kissinger later wrote, "a recasting of the Cold War international order." It provided new political cover for the administration's retreat from Vietnam, gave the Soviet Union stronger incentives to pursue détente with the United States, and created a cooperative foundation for Sino-American relations that has endured for decades. It gave both Nixon and Kissinger lifelong reputations as strategic sages and masters of realpolitik. (It even yielded a durable aphorism about policy innovation. "Only Nixon"—we still say this—"could go to China.")[23]

Through two terms, Dwight Eisenhower had hoped in vain for a comparably audacious move that would give his own foreign policy an inspiring public feel. From the moment the secret trip was arranged, Nixon saw it as a masterstroke. "Jesus, this is a hell of a move," he exclaimed. Welcoming Kissinger home from Beijing, he called it "the most significant foreign policy achievement in this century." En route to China in February 1972, the president relaxed all limits on rhetorical hyperbole. The trip, he felt, was "a voyage of philosophical discovery as uncertain, and in some respects as perilous, as the voyages of geographical discovery of a much earlier time." At the culmination of the visit, he toasted it as "the week that changed the world."[24]

Rapprochement with China was such a celebrated feat that Nixon and Kissinger never stopped vying for the credit. At the start of the administration, however, Kissinger had seen it as entirely Nixon's idea and repeatedly derided it. The president's 1967 *Foreign Affairs* article had said it was unwise to leave the world's largest country out of the international mainstream for too long. But the fanaticism of China's leaders, still in the throes of the Cultural Revolution, made reaching out to them seem far-fetched. After hearing Nixon explain his thinking, Kissinger called it a "flight of fancy." And when Haldeman reminded him that the president really did want to visit China during his first term, the man who forever after treated the initiative as his greatest achievement simply scoffed. "Fat chance," Kissinger replied. He later claimed that he and Nixon had come to the idea "independently." The president had a different take. When the Beijing trip went well, Nixon's reaction was completely proprietary. "I told you so," he exulted to Kissinger, "I told you so!" The written record clearly supports him. Kissinger's pre-1969 writings show no particular interest in China. He had, as an adviser in 1968 to presidential candidate Nelson Rockefeller, recommended a guarded effort to keep up with Nixon's own innovative stance. His formula: "contacts without illusions."[25]

Only after Chinese and Soviet border forces clashed in August 1969 did Kissinger change his mind. A war between two nuclear powers would be bad enough. One that America's global rival would surely win (perhaps installing a pro-Soviet government in the bargain) would be a disaster. Beijing's vulnerability—and Moscow's obsession with the rivalry—put the idea of Sino-American rapprochement in a new light. Offering China a lifeline might strengthen the balance of power. Kissinger saw a chance to play on Russian fears. "We're using the Chinese thaw," he explained to Haldeman, "to get the Russians shook."[26]

When he finally arrived in Beijing in July 1971, Kissinger was still thinking about each side's problems with the Soviets. "Reality has brought us together," he said in his opening remarks to Zhou Enlai, "and we believe that reality will shape our future." China, moreover, should not worry that the United States would ever side with the USSR against it. "We will never collude with other countries against the People's Republic of China, either with our allies or with some of our opponents." And there was more: "The U.S. will not take any major steps affecting your interests without discussing them with you and taking your views into account."[27]

Kissinger aimed to show the Chinese the concrete benefits of working with the United States. In May, as a goodwill offering two months before he arrived, he passed along word of a not-yet-public breakthrough in the Soviet-American strategic arms talks. In October, during his second visit, he alerted his hosts to a possible Taiwanese probe of the mainland's airspace, and he shared information on Soviet military facilities and capabilities. Such gestures reflected the thinking behind Kissinger's conversion to the new policy: help the weaker power against the stronger.[28]

In making the opening to China, Nixon and Kissinger had ignored the experts and bureaucrats, who preferred a gradual, step-by-step attempt to address long-standing bilateral problems between Beijing and Washington. (Kissinger derided these as "a shopping list of mutual irritations.") They had also ignored the moralists, who opposed dealing with blood-soaked totalitarians. By accepting "an ideological truce," the president and his national security adviser claimed to have shown what could be accomplished by a hard-boiled, quid pro quo approach to foreign policy. And look, they said, at the result: China had turned into a solid supporter of America's power and global presence. Kissinger and Nixon particularly enjoyed vexing their leftist critics by pointing out that even Chairman Mao was now on their side.[29]

For Nixon's political handlers, the breakthrough with China was a bonanza. It may well have saved his presidency. Despite Vietnam, Haldeman had long urged his White House colleagues to find means of portraying their boss as "Mr. Peace." Now they could point to an achievement that combined toughness and creativity of a kind that Washington had not seen in years. Kissinger found endless ways to capture this thought. He felt the China opening was "a breath of fresh air, a reminder of what America could accomplish as a world leader." It offered "a chance to raise the sights of the American people to a future of opportunity." It proved that "even in adversity, America still had the inner strength for great enterprises."[30]

PUBLICLY, THE CHINA opening was supposed to show that the United States could reclaim its pivotal role in the world (and, as the president had put it, "fast!"). But what had Nixon and Kissinger said to the Chinese in private? Behind closed doors the two of them presented a very different picture of the future of American policy. Its dominant theme was not revival but downsizing. In his first conversations with Zhou Enlai, Kissinger stressed that President Nixon rejected the foreign policy of his predecessors. The dominant position that the United States had acquired since World War II was, Kissinger said, "undesirable"—the result of a wrong-headed determination "to engage itself in every struggle at every point of the world at any point in time." Conservatives like Dulles had favored this approach, but Kissinger claimed that the "missionary tendencies" of American liberals had pushed it even further. Nixon was different. He would act "on the realities of the present and not on the dreams of the past."[31]

When it came to the specifics of retrenchment, Kissinger went far beyond merely affirming America's sincere desire to settle the Vietnam War, or promising to curtail its military presence on Taiwan. He told Zhou that across the region, the United States saw the political tide going against its friends—and accepted it. About Vietnam, Kissinger said, China need not fear that Washington would try to prop up its shaky client after withdrawing: "We are not proposing a treaty to stop history." He used other allies to make the same point. One of the first signals to China of an interest in exploring rapprochement had been the suspension of American naval patrols in the Taiwan Strait. (Kissinger has always described this decision as a strategic initiative, the acme of subtle diplomacy; in truth, the navy had proposed it as a budget measure.) His meetings with Zhou gave Kissinger an opportunity to explain how far the United States would go in breaking ties. Once Beijing and Washington reached an understanding, he pledged, "we will not stand in the way of basic evolution." Later in his visit, he expressed hope that the Taiwan problem would simply go away: "Maybe history can take care of events."[32]

Other Asian allies were discussed in the same fatalistic terms. America was reducing its presence in the region, Kissinger told Zhou, and this would ease frictions between China and the United States. It was "not a permanent feature of our foreign policy" to keep troops in South Korea. This problem too, he predicted, "will take care of itself." Japan raised a more acute concern, in Kissinger's view, since American policy there had been "extremely naïve" for many years. "We today regret," he confided during his October 1971 visit, "how we built up Japan economically." He endorsed the Chinese view that Japanese militarism was a threat. And he had a solution: if Japan rearmed, the best way to counter it would be an alliance between Washington and Beijing against Tokyo—what he labeled "the traditional relationship between China and the U.S."[33]

The Japanese bogey and its threat to China were favorite Kissinger props in arguing that Chinese leaders benefited from U.S. power. But the argument was not always as convincing to them as he liked to suggest. In a careful rebuttal, Zhou predicted that American allies would not survive. All of them, even the Japanese government, "will be chased off the stage of history by their own peoples." Unless the United States was prepared to accept this result, Nixon's endless talk about "a generation of peace" would prove unrealistic. "I don't think that will be possible," said Zhou.[34]

Kissinger responded to this challenge with more backpedaling. American commitments, he suggested, were flexible enough to make conflict between China and the United States unnecessary. About American allies, he assured Zhou, "we do not give them a veto over our policies, and we will not maintain them against the forces of history." And he added, somewhat lamely: "You could not respect us if we found this easy." China should recognize the awkwardness of the U.S. position and not push "beyond what is possible."[35]

In his 1967 *Foreign Affairs* article Nixon had proposed to reach out to China, but he put even more emphasis (today this part of his argument is usually forgotten) on rebuilding ties with traditional U.S. allies. In 1972, by contrast, to cement the new relationship with China, he and Kissinger talked ceaselessly about American disengagement. They told Mao and Zhou that because of domestic political factors, they could "do" more than they could "say" in giving Sino-American relations a solid base. In fact, the relationship they sought to create did not—with a few exceptions, such as intelligence sharing—involve "doing" much of anything at all. Concrete cooperation came slowly; full normalization was not anticipated until well into Nixon's second term. But there were no limits on what could be *said* in the secrecy of these initial meetings, and both sides laid it on thick.

Chinese hospitality reached its high point when Zhou praised the president (who swooned at the compliment) for having a "poetic turn of mind like Mao." For their part, Nixon and Kissinger claimed they wanted to give the relationship a "conceptual foundation." Although there was nothing especially conceptual about it, the underlying message—that "history" was likely to overwhelm American allies—came through loud and clear. The president put it still more starkly when he told Zhou that he had a "selfish reason" for encouraging the growth of Chinese power. "If China could become a second superpower," he urged, "the U.S. could reduce its own armaments." Nixon and Kissinger insisted that in private Chinese leaders talked up the importance of maintaining American power in Asia. What the two of them did not say was how much they themselves talked it down.[36]

Nixon knew that back home his conservative critics viewed the relationship with China as ideological capitulation. In his memoirs, he observed that if only these critics had seen the notes he jotted down for his last formal meeting with Zhou in Beijing, they would "at least have felt reassured that I had not approached the Chinese naively." In these notes, Nixon reminded himself to

> emphasize, in a very personal and direct way, my intense belief in our system and my belief that in peaceful competition it would prevail. I think we have gotten that across. I believe that it is essential not to let the assumption exist at all on their part that their system will eventually prevail because of its superiority.

The Chinese, the president wrote, should understand that "our system is not coming apart at the seams."[37]

Nixon's critics might well have been heartened to learn of such a spirited exchange between the Chinese prime minister and the leader of the Free World—had it occurred. But it didn't. When the president sat down with Zhou, he ignored his notes. For the rest of the trip, his resolve to be upbeat about America's bright future was simply forgotten.

THE OPENING TO China gave American foreign policy—and Nixon's presidency—a lift. But it could not prevent the escalation of the war in Vietnam once he and Kissinger returned from Beijing. How they responded did much to define the second prong of their new policy, détente with the Soviet Union.

North Vietnam had begun its preparations for a new offensive in the South as early as May 1971, while Kissinger was still getting ready for his trip to Beijing. The CIA estimated that Soviet military assistance to North Vietnam surged by 30 percent in 1971 (with deliveries of air defense equipment increasing tenfold). By the beginning of 1972, preparations for an all-out campaign were far advanced. But Nixon, who did not want to hold his meetings in China in an atmosphere of confrontation, preferred to ignore the buildup. In January, when General Abrams asked Washington for permission to bomb across the demilitarized zone between North and South, the White House turned him down. In March, with the president's trip over, Abrams repeated his request. The answer was still no. Had "the week that changed the world" made bombing unnecessary? Kissinger's deputy, General Alexander Haig, captured the White House's upbeat thinking: the new relationship with

China was expected to "substitute for more straightforward applications of national power."[38]

Once North Vietnamese units came across the border, of course, traditional forms of power were needed after all. As they had before the invasion of Cambodia, the soldiers and civilians of the Pentagon reassured the White House that Saigon could handle the extra challenge. A massive campaign against Hanoi was unnecessary. Nixon found such views absurd, even pathetic. Defeat, he warned, threatened not only his reelection but America's global influence. The whole point of being president would be put in doubt, he thought. "Suppose we are wrong?" he snapped at Laird. As always, Nixon discerned higher stakes than his advisers did. Once more he invoked "all the marbles." He had made "a basic decision to go all out to win the war now."[39]

With U.S. combat troops now reduced to a handful (fewer than 70,000 remained in April 1972), Nixon saw airpower as the only usable instrument for stopping the North Vietnamese offensive. And he used it with exceptional ferocity. All B-52s available worldwide were assembled for the campaign. Abrams summarized the result for Washington: "The level of violence, and the level of brutality, in this whole thing right now is on a scale not before achieved in the war in Vietnam." This was no mere revival of Johnson's on-again, off-again Rolling Thunder attacks, marveled General Bruce Palmer, the army vice chief of staff: "It was war." Nixon bragged to Kissinger that LBJ had lacked the will for an all-out contest, but "I have the will in spades," and "I intend to stop at nothing to bring the enemy to his knees."[40]

The president claimed that he was even ready to sacrifice his emergent détente with the Soviet Union. He would no longer "indulge the Soviet fiction that they could not be held responsible for what North Vietnam did." Linkage was now to get its final test. If Brezhnev and his colleagues wanted to hold a summit at the end of May, they had to help the United States end the war. Even Kissinger's late-April preparatory visit to Moscow had to be rethought. The trip could go forward, Nixon ruled, but the first and only item on its agenda had to be Vietnam. Arms control agreements, trade, the Middle East—everything else was on hold.[41]

This was not what Kissinger had in mind. Once inside the Kremlin, he discussed whatever he pleased. Explaining his conduct to the White House, he claimed that the Politburo needed a foretaste of how much the summit might accomplish. He rejected the president's own view of

Soviet policy: "I cannot share the theory on which Washington operates. I do not believe that Moscow is in direct collusion with Hanoi." On Kissinger's return, the North Vietnamese promptly downed several U.S. planes with their newly acquired, Soviet-manufactured SA-7 missiles; with this, his claim for Soviet innocence looked shaky at best. Relations between Nixon and his national security adviser had become extremely tense but the president's new military measures against North Vietnam also made their disagreement seem irrelevant. Announced on May 8, Nixon's actions included the mining of Haiphong harbor, through which most Soviet war matériel entered North Vietnam. With confrontation between East and West seemingly at a new peak, even Kissinger believed Brezhnev would cancel, or at least postpone, the summit.[42]

But he didn't. The Soviet leaders, it seemed, wanted their arms treaty, wanted their trade increases, wanted to keep up with the Chinese. So they protested for the record—and soldiered on. The trip was a go. Nixon and his inner circle could hardly believe their luck. "We are going to be able to have our mining and bombing," Kissinger rejoiced, "and have our summit too." As the presidential entourage took off for Moscow two weeks later, he was still more ebullient. It was "one of the great diplomatic coups of all times."[43]

From the Moscow summit on, Nixon and Kissinger never shook the feeling that, in going forward with the visit, the Soviet leadership had accepted an American-imposed humiliation. Sure, both sides benefited from détente, but at a moment of high tension the Soviets had admitted that they needed and wanted it more. To their own surprise, Nixon and Kissinger had stumbled on a formula for relations that was arguably even more advantageous to the United States than their original idea of linkage (which they had in any case never been able to make work). Washington no longer had to lecture Moscow that it wouldn't be allowed to enjoy the fruits of détente if it challenged American interests in the Third World. Now the United States would do what it had earlier accused the Soviets of wanting to do: show up for summits, sign arms agreements, and attack the other side's ally.

The Moscow summit of 1972 permanently shaped Nixon and Kissinger's sense of who had the upper hand in Soviet-American relations. It also gave them a lasting condescension toward the Soviet leaders themselves. Of Brezhnev and his Politburo colleagues, Kissinger observed that "philosophical discussions made them visibly nervous." The high-altitude repartee that made diplomacy with the Chinese so much fun was a nonstarter with counterparts who were "psychologically too insecure and insensitive to intangibles." For people like this, he observed with something approaching pity, "the 'spirit' of a document was a meaningless phrase." How much more satisfying to do business with those who understood the "nuances and interrelations" at the heart of foreign policy.

Nixon felt less intellectual contempt for the Soviet leaders than Kissinger did. It was a mistake, he thought, to see Brezhnev "either as a fool or simply an unintelligent brute." But the president was patronizing all the same. To him, the Kremlin elite were like American labor leaders—they had some raw feel for power, perhaps, but no finesse. Nixon mocked their "mushy sentimentality" and did not find them good company. "Six meals with this guy," he said of Brezhnev, were "enough to break anybody."[44]

Nixon and Kissinger were not far wrong about their Soviet hosts, but their personal feelings led them to misread the new superpower relationship. The idea that Moscow had, as Kissinger put it, "cut loose" from its "obstreperous ally"—the North Vietnamese—had no foundation. As for who needed the relationship more, the gratitude that the president and his aides felt for their visit to Moscow could hardly have been lost on the members of the Politburo. (Soviet officials enjoyed dealing with Kissinger so much, they gave him the nickname "pussycat"—in Russian, *kisa.*) Soviet-American détente gave Nixon a tool, in some ways even more powerful than the trip to China, with which to rebut his critics. The General Conference of the United Methodist Church had labeled the latest American attacks on North Vietnam a "crime against humanity." Ted Kennedy had called them "folly." Major newspapers saw national "dishonor" in them. And yet here was America's most powerful military rival—and Hanoi's patron—welcoming the president of the United States to Moscow for a week of pomp and treaty signings.

Brezhnev allowed Nixon to claim the peacemaker's mantle. Having once more "gone for broke" in Vietnam, he needed the help in Moscow. "The people want hope," Kissinger lectured Haldeman, "not just blood, sweat, and tears all the time."[45]

RETRENCHMENT, AMERICAN POLICY makers could now see, was going to be a success. Henry Kissinger described their mood after the Moscow summit as one of "optimism, even elation, untinged by excessive humility." (The last phrase was, as always, a reference to himself.) His sense of accomplishment was understandable. He had—in part by defying the president—made it possible to conduct a last-ditch military campaign in Vietnam without paying the slightest diplomatic or political price for it. This was a stunning rebound from two years earlier, when the invasion of Cambodia had torn the country apart. Kissinger was right about the change: "More of our future appeared to be subject to our control than in quite some time."[46]

He now saw a chance—and defying the president was again involved—to add a Vietnam settlement to his string of successes. The United States, he believed, was "in the best position ever" to conclude a satisfactory deal. Hanoi's Easter offensive had petered out. North Vietnam's leaders were surely unnerved by Washington's rapprochement with their two major allies, and they surely saw that Nixon's reelection was inevitable. Kissinger was convinced that Washington itself needed a quick settlement of the war. After the election, he expected more, not less, trouble between the administration and Congress.[47]

Kissinger read his adversaries shrewdly. In early October, just as he expected, North Vietnamese negotiators in Paris retreated on the biggest issue blocking agreement—the demand that the United States install a coalition government in place of President Thieu. With this concession in hand, Kissinger decided to "strike while the iron was hot." He envisioned a forced-march timetable to achieve a peace agreement by the end of the month, just days before the U.S. election. Without consulting Washington, he would wrap up most settlement details in a few marathon rounds of bargaining, bring the near-finished document home for quick blessing by Nixon, fly off at once to Saigon to get Thieu's approval, and arrive triumphantly in Hanoi a day later for a grand initialing of the agreement. A couple of negotiating all-nighters in Paris seemed to confirm that a deal was possible, and when Kissinger and his team returned to Washington, they were in a "near joyous" frame of mind. Haig's ebullient summary was typical. The North Vietnamese "have basically given up," he burbled to Haldeman. "They have no more hope and they're now going to try and establish friendship with us, which is what they say they want just like our China relationship."[48]

Yet if Kissinger had read his adversaries right, he grossly misjudged his own side. Neither Washington nor Saigon endorsed the quick deal he devised, and his around-the-world odyssey became a fiasco. By the time he returned to Washington, announcing that peace was "at hand," he had in fact already failed.[49]

The unraveling of Kissinger's "go for broke" diplomacy started with the president. Nixon welcomed him back from Paris with a celebratory steak dinner and joined in crowing over Hanoi's "capitulation." The president laughed that if Thieu rejected its terms, the United States would eventually "cram it down his throat." But—and here was the catch—he was unwilling to do so before the election. Nixon had made his view abundantly clear to Kissinger for months. He saw no electoral advantage in a settlement. "The American people," the president argued, "are no longer interested in a solution based on compromise, favor continued bombing and want to see the United States prevail after all these years." If Saigon could be persuaded to accept Kissinger's deal quickly, fine. But if not, Nixon would have no part of a "shotgun marriage."[50]

Kissinger knew, of course, that a shotgun marriage would be essential. When he and Thieu had met in August, the South Vietnamese leader rejected even small concessions designed to probe the North's flexibility. And again on October 4, days before the final Paris round, Thieu took the same position in a meeting with the visiting Haig. In tears, he said he and his colleagues were "solid [and] unified" against the U.S. approach.[51]

Despite these warning signs, Kissinger acted as though Thieu would have to fold—and as though Nixon would agree to squeeze him. Before his arrival in Saigon, he sent Thieu a half-mocking, half-bullying message certain to antagonize him: "Had we wanted to sell you out, there [would] have been many easier ways by which we could have accomplished this." Kissinger did not even bring a Vietnamese translation of the agreement to the meeting and refused to provide one when asked. (Unknown to him, the South Vietnamese already had a copy, the result of a chance capture of Vietcong documents by their military forces.) In urging Thieu to accept the deal, Kissinger brushed aside South Vietnam's security concerns. The key to a lasting peace, he said, was American psychology. Saigon should therefore take "a positive attitude"—so that "the American people could take pride" in ending the war. But Thieu, again in tears, still refused. Kissinger was enraged. "I'll never set foot in Saigon again," he said. "Not after this." He once more threatened to sign a separate peace with Hanoi—knowing, of course, that Nixon would not back him up.[52]

The collapse of Kissinger's preelection Vietnam peace offensive was the low point of his diplomatic career. He had played a game of chicken with both Thieu and Nixon and lost badly. It was, moreover, a completely unnecessary defeat. Kissinger had a clear alternative. Rather than try to stampede his own side, he had merely to praise the North Vietnamese compromise, promise to launch a careful study of its terms, and consult closely with his own government and allies—in short, stall until after the U.S. presidential election. Doing so would have produced a far easier endgame for the talks, in which he could have counted on Nixon's support.

The cost of Kissinger's failure went well beyond personal embarrassment. All the other parties to the peace talks—including his own boss—had new reasons to doubt his trustworthiness. Putting a settlement back together now required another brief, but extremely violent and politically costly, spasm of war.

IN THE ENTIRE HISTORY of American diplomacy, there have been few more peculiar episodes than the final phase of the Vietnam peace talks. The president and his national security adviser considered the deal they had in hand a brilliant achievement. Yet Saigon had balked. There followed a strange series of endgame confrontations—between the United States and its ally, between the United States and its adversary, between the president and his critics, and (arguably the iciest showdown of all) between Nixon and Kissinger themselves.

The prospect of another round of talks in Paris filled Kissinger, he acknowledged, with "impotent rage." He considered Thieu's objections to the October terms a mark of "insanity." To Saigon's representatives, he fumed that the Vietnamese were "a time-consuming race." In his view, their proposed "improvements" in the peace agreement were "preposterous." Yet he dutifully haggled his way through two rounds of overtime negotiations in Paris in November and December and even resolved about a dozen South Vietnamese concerns.[53]

As the talks dragged on, Nixon and Kissinger's defense of the advantages of the agreement that had (almost) been reached became steadily more exaggerated. The president assured the joint chiefs that his new relationships with China and the Soviet Union would make up for some of the limitations of the deal. "The settlement we are speaking about," he told them, "is not just the specific treaty itself. It is a series of interlocking understandings with other powers and reflects the strategic realities related to the conflict. It is these realities of power that count."

Linkage had never worked during the war, but was now counted on to keep the peace. Kissinger went further. The Soviets, he assured the South Vietnamese, had pledged to make "dramatic reductions" in their aid to the North. To the chiefs, he claimed that the one provision of the agreement that Saigon complained about more than any other—allowing North Vietnamese units to remain in South Vietnam—was in reality a severe problem for *Hanoi*. Its troops would be cut off from supplies and, he conjectured, might even be forced to withdraw. (This was absurd. Zhou Enlai, for one, knew better. Once the Americans were gone, he predicted, it will be "easy to deal with Nguyen Van Thieu.")[54]

Nixon and Kissinger's strained interpretations of the agreement did little to reassure the Saigon government. Nor did their claim that the most important thing was to project optimism. Nixon's letter to Thieu soon after the election suggested that he "take the political and psychological initiative by hailing the settlement." South Vietnam should not act "as if it had lost" when it had really won. As for Kissinger, he was not wrong when he lectured the South Vietnamese that their future depended on whether the agreement made Americans feel good. Yet he seemed to acknowledge that it didn't. "Your President," he berated Thieu's aides, "should thank our President for having accomplished a significant thing, so the American people can have some pride."[55]

With North Vietnamese diplomats, Kissinger struck a far more cordial tone. He looked forward to visiting Hanoi, he said, so he could "pay our respects to the heroic North Vietnamese people." He spoke feelingly about the burdens of war that they had borne. He even invited Le Duc Tho to give a course on Marxism-Leninism at Harvard. But empathy and bantering did not produce agreement. Judging the talks deadlocked, Kissinger broke them off on December 13, recommending that the president try military pressure instead. His words for Hanoi's diplomats were no longer so friendly. "They're just a bunch of shits. Tawdry, filthy shits."[56]

During the "Christmas Bombing" that followed, U.S. warplanes—including B-52 strategic bombers—pounded North Vietnam for twelve days. The campaign was preceded by the usual debate in the president's inner circle about how harsh the bombing should be. By now, all the participants knew their parts. Kissinger wondered whether a gradually intensifying campaign might be best. Haig warned against "incrementalism." And Nixon, of course, decided to "go for broke." He wanted relentless bombing with the most powerful aircraft available. As always, he saw the contest as a test of wills. Sending too-small planes, he feared, would "only make the enemy contemptuous."[57]

What made the Christmas Bombing unique, however, was not its destructiveness. American bombing during the Easter offensive, just months before, had also been brutal—and neither compared with the massive raids against German and Japanese cities during World War II. Although *The Washington Post* (and many others) questioned the president's "sanity," he had not gone mad. At this climactic moment, Nixon was, if anything, bored by Vietnam. Resigned to an unsatisfactory outcome, he took none of his usual relish in the challenge of rallying the nation behind a tough policy. There was "no option"—he had been saying this for weeks—"except to settle." When Kissinger urged a rousing prime-time television address to build support for the bombing, the president responded with a string of listless negative answers. "It simply isn't going to work," he argued. Endless exhortation, he added a few days later, "can wear very thin." Announcing a "resumption of the war with no end in sight and no hope, is simply going to be a loser." Again and again he shrugged off the idea of another speech: "We don't need public support."[58]

Nixon clearly enjoyed making his all-too-famous assistant the spokesman for his failed negotiation. (The White House staff loved the idea: "Let [Kissinger] do the briefing," they said.) More than this, the president's reluctance to speak out in defense of his own policy was a measure of how little he thought was actually at stake. Nixon, Kissinger claimed, "wanted the war over on almost any terms." Why did he not need to rally the country? Because the real purpose of the bombing was not to get a better agreement. It was simply to make a point, to show that the United States could punish those who did not cooperate. Kissinger described it accurately: a "massive, shocking step to impose our will on events and end the war quickly." When the bombing was over, both Hanoi and Saigon eventually agreed to go along.[59]

It was a costly success. The Christmas Bombing eliminated any remaining chance that the United States would be able to enforce the Paris agreements militarily. Public opinion on the president's use of force had shifted dramatically since the spring. Nixon's strong stand against the North Vietnamese invasion had enjoyed the support of 64 percent of the public. After the Christmas Bombing, a still larger number—71 percent—was against ever doing so again. The effort needed to revive Kissinger's peace agreement had finally used up the public's willingness to enforce it.

RICHARD NIXON UNDERSTOOD the advantages of maximalism. It was, for him, the only real strategy for political success. A lifetime of rough-and-tumble had taught him contempt for those who aimed only to "manage the chaos better." Timid half-measures, he thought, stirred up just as much opposition as bold strokes. They inflamed people without solving the problem at hand.

Yet Nixon's instinct, clearly right for other times, proved exactly wrong in an era of retrenchment. When cautious measures were not enough to wind down the Vietnam War in the way he wanted, he took more extreme steps. The costs surprised him. "Going for broke" provoked a far more intense reaction than halfway policies would have. Nixon thought presidents had to take the heat if they wanted to solve big problems. In Vietnam he got the heat but not the breakthroughs he expected. Of all his "electrifying" military moves, only the mining of Haiphong harbor paid off the way he had imagined. Cambodia, Laos, the Christmas Bombing—in every case, the halfway measures that he scorned would almost surely have served him better.

Nixon knew that retrenchment was unavoidable. During the four-year exit from Vietnam, his brief bursts of military power never once led him to suspend, or even slow down, the troop cuts he had announced. Going "all out" was his way of trying to limit the damage done by scaling back. The combination, the president sensed, had its problems. On the eve of the Christmas Bombing, he was reminded of a passage from Churchill, which in mid-December 1972 he described to his diary: "One can have a policy of audacity or one can follow a policy of caution, but it is disastrous to try to follow a policy of audacity and caution at the same time. It must be one or the other." To avoid the perils of pure retrenchment, Nixon had decided to try to do both.[60]

The effort to "take risks" and "be exciting" was not, of course, limited to military moves. In barely half the time it took them to get out of Vietnam, Nixon and Kissinger put in place the elements of détente with the Soviet Union and an opening to China. In the entire history of American foreign policy, the acclaim with which these diplomatic achievements were greeted has few parallels. They were treated as a kind of wizardry, as proof of genius. (Those responsible did not deny it.)

Nixon and Kissinger's diplomacy aimed to blunt the impact of retrenchment after Vietnam and to make future retrenchments unnecessary. By carving out "a more balanced and realistic American role in the world," they would avoid overcommitment and establish a policy that could last from one administration to another. This had been Dwight Eisenhower's hope when he first embarked on retrenchment, and it was perhaps bound to be disappointed the second time around as well. Just how disappointed, neither the president nor his celebrated adviser could yet imagine.[61]

8

Retrenchment and Détente

"A NIHILISTIC NIGHTMARE"

Gerald Ford and Leonid Brezhnev

HENRY KISSINGER SAW the start of Nixon's new term as a moment of "glittering promise." He told the president the administration's achievements to date were "the greatest revolution in foreign policy ever." November's overwhelming electoral victory offered a gigantic opportunity—a chance "to undertake negotiations of fundamental scope."[1]

Nixon was also excited—and equally ready to overstate. The United States, he proclaimed in his second inaugural address, aspired to build "a peace which can endure for generations to come." Americans had stopped doubting their role as global leader. They accepted its burdens "gladly," he claimed. "Only if we act greatly in meeting our responsibilities abroad will we remain a great Nation."Alexander Haig, soon to become the new White House chief of staff and after that the commander of NATO, thought the president looked forward to his second term as "a sort of Augustinian autumn in which he would reorganize the government, revitalize the republic, and confound and scatter the domestic enemies who had plagued and undermined him since the beginning of his public life."[2]

It was not to be, of course. Scarcely a year and a half later, Nixon resigned in the face of near-certain impeachment. A new president occupied the White House, and before long yet another. For years to come, critics and sympathizers alike put as much distance as they could between themselves and the disgraced former president.

Two events—Vietnam and Watergate—have cast a long shadow over our understanding of how American foreign policy unfolded in the 1970s. Both had a profound impact. The war energized those who believed American power had been too great and too brutally used. Watergate empowered those who believed that it had been too unaccountable, too concentrated in an "imperial presidency." The United States was certain to have a very different international role once these ideas took hold.

To combat them, Kissinger thought the administration had to "educate the American public in the complexity of the world we would have to manage." It had to "teach our people to face their permanent responsibility" in global affairs. He imagined himself in an ongoing struggle to persuade the country not to do too little. Yet the debate that dominated the decade ahead turned out to be completely different from what Kissinger expected. It was less and less about whether America was too strong, and more and more about whether it had become too weak.[3]

Those concerned about American weakness were not just imagining things. During the Nixon, Ford, and Carter administrations, the U.S. economy was in recession almost one-fourth of the time. It was battered by "energy crises," hitherto unknown except when the nation was at war, and by chronic inflation, which was three times higher in the 1970s than it had been in the 1960s. With the dollar's decline, American troops in Europe began to have trouble making ends meet.[4]

Because the Pentagon's budget was under pressure throughout the decade, the growth of Soviet military capabilities seemed even more dramatic than it was. Fear that the United States was losing ground unsettled policy makers, experts, and the public alike. Traditional allies questioned American leadership and staying power. From China, Washington's newest partner, came ever more pointed carping about U.S. firmness. At the end of the decade, Americans felt what was for many the greatest shock of all, their diplomats' fifteen-month captivity in Tehran. The hostage crisis seemed a national humiliation, but the reason for its impact predated the Iranian revolution. It confirmed a worry about America's position that had been growing for years.

The 1970s turned into one of the sourest, most frustrating, least successful periods of U.S. foreign policy. Like the 1950s, the decade began with an effort to put policy on a more sustainable footing. By the time it was over, new leaders had again persuaded the American people that retrenchment had gone too far.

THE YOM KIPPUR WAR of October 1973 was the first and most dangerous international test of Nixon's second term. It subjected Soviet-American relations to severe pressures, divided Washington from its major European allies, and created new tensions between the United States and the major states of the Middle East. In meeting these challenges, American policy showed none of the difficulties that would plague it later in the decade. It was activist, inventive, determined, and—at every stage of the crisis—extremely successful. If only for a moment, the "glittering promise" of January seemed fully realized.

To achieve this result, Washington put aside the cooperative assumptions of détente in the name of geopolitical advantage. When the military tide began to run against Israel at the start of the war, Kissinger—who had become secretary of state just days before Egypt's surprise attack—okayed a large resupply effort. But he did not want U.S. military planes to deliver the weapons and matériel, the better to avoid a competition with Moscow as to which side helped its client more. Private contractors, he thought, might be less provocative. Nixon overruled him. "Do it now!" he instructed. Adjusting quickly, Kissinger announced to colleagues that the U.S. goal was to "run the Soviets into the ground fast."[5]

This jockeying for advantage continued throughout the Yom Kippur War and beyond. Kissinger repeatedly assured Soviet officials that he and Nixon were deeply committed to cooperative problem solving. To show good faith, he visited Moscow in the middle of the war to hammer out a joint UN Security Council resolution calling for a cease-fire. There he found Brezhnev and Gromyko so relaxed and pliable in composing the text of the resolution that their discussion, in his view, barely counted as a "negotiation in the strict sense."

This welcome collaborative spirit did not keep the United States from trying to block any possible Soviet gains. When Kissinger thought Soviet forces might be preparing to help Egyptian units that were in danger of being surrounded by the Israeli army east of the Suez Canal, his response was extreme. Rather than merely issue a warning or demand a clarification, American policy makers chose to act, as Kissinger put it, "in a manner that shocked the Soviets into abandoning" any thought of military action. Their method: a nearly unprecedented worldwide alert of U.S. nuclear forces. It did not matter that the risk of Soviet intervention was almost entirely conjectural—based on a single, somewhat murky sentence in a letter from Brezhnev to Nixon. As Kissinger explained to colleagues, he did not want anyone to say the United States had "provoked this by being soft."[6]

Once a cease-fire was in place, American policy did even more to limit Soviet influence. The United States and the USSR agreed to serve as cochairs of a peace conference in Geneva in December 1973, but the occasion was almost entirely ceremonial. The diplomacy that really mattered was carried on in round after round of Kissinger's "shuttle" missions between Middle Eastern capitals. Here Soviet officials had no role. Moscow's own clients—both Egyptian president Anwar Sadat, who was clearly leaving the Soviet fold, and Syrian president Hafez Assad, who was not—clamored for Washington's diplomatic services. Their motives ranged from a desire to make use of Kissinger's new status as celebrity negotiator to recognition that only Washington could deliver meaningful agreements with Israel. Whatever the reasons, the result was the same. Out of a military crisis, the United States was building a stronger regional role for itself than ever. Kissinger wanted to edge the Soviets out but not to "rub in this fact." He was particularly eager not to personalize the contest. It was unwise, he told the Israelis, "to make the leader of another superpower look like an idiot." Making the other superpower look ineffectual and irrelevant was completely fine.[7]

Checking Soviet influence in the Middle East was not the only challenge for American policy. The war produced an embargo by Arab oil producers on exports to the United States and other Western countries, and an almost fourfold increase in oil prices between October and December 1973. For Kissinger, this display of monopoly power by the Organization of Petroleum Exporting Countries (OPEC) was "one of the pivotal events in the history of this century." Suddenly Americans were aware of a new kind of vulnerability—a threat to their economic confidence and well-being that was, for many, far more worrying than Soviet military might.[8]

How should the new challenge be managed? For a moment, but only that, Washington imagined that the answer was the same one it had come up with to contain the Soviet Union in the late 1940s—Western unity, spearheaded by the United States. Quickly, however, Kissinger discovered that America's principal allies "had no stomach for a concerted diplomacy." When U.S. officials proposed unified opposition to the Arab embargo, or other strategies of solidarity among energy-consuming countries, what they heard back were all the reasons that Europe could not act. "You only rely on the Arabs for about a tenth of your consumption. We are entirely dependent upon them," French president Georges Pompidou pleaded. Michel Jobert, the foreign minister, had a more basic problem with the U.S. approach: Europe, he told Kissinger, could not accept "American leadership." Even the Japanese wanted to go their own way.[9]

Nixon—sounding just like Kennedy ten years earlier—reminded the allies of how much they stood to lose by letting the United States down. They could not, he declared, "have it both ways. They cannot have the

United States' participation and cooperation on the security front and then proceed to have confrontation and even hostility on the economic and political front."[10]

With both the Europeans and the Japanese wilting, the administration made a familiar choice—the same one it had made in the 1940s too. It would, as Kissinger put it, "implement a strategy unilaterally." American officials, including both the secretary of state and the secretary of defense, began to make ominous statements about possible "countermeasures" against the oil producers. These were understood to include, at least as a last resort, military action.[11]

What really made Kissinger's unilateralism successful, however, was less the threat of force than his hyperactive approach to diplomacy. He quickly absorbed energy goals into his negotiating strategy. If Arab states Egypt and Syria wanted him to serve as a mediator between them and Israel, then they would have to serve as mediators between the United States and the oil producers—and get the latter to drop the embargo. Kissinger's shuttle diplomacy between Damascus and Tel Aviv was a marathon of intricate bargaining, but his message to Assad was very simple. As long as the embargo remained in place, there would be no agreement on a pullback of Israeli forces. The secretary admitted that this "linkage was audacious," but he insisted to colleagues that it reflected the uniqueness of American power. The Arabs, he boasted, "may have a monopoly on oil, but we have a monopoly on political progress."[12]

THE DIFFICULTIES THAT Kissinger faced in managing American Mideast policy in this period were immense. The war had unified Arab governments as never before. The successful use of the energy weapon had tipped the American economy into its longest recession since the end of World War II. The United States and its allies had not been so divided in their strategy toward the region since at least Suez. The Soviet Union was clamoring for a seat at the diplomatic high table. Meanwhile, domestic political turmoil limited Nixon's involvement in daily decision making and then, in the summer of 1974, drove him from office completely.

None of this slowed Kissinger down. He got the oil embargo lifted in March 1974. In April he got allied agreement on mechanisms for crisis energy coordination by the Western democracies. The Syrian-Israeli disengagement agreement was concluded in May. His cultivation of Sadat drew Egypt firmly into a Western orbit and established a decades-long

American monopoly over Arab-Israeli peace talks. And apart from private protests, Moscow seemed to accept its exclusion from anything but the most meaningless consultations. Kissinger's accomplishments gave him—for a secretary of state—unprecedented power and autonomy. It was hard to say he had not earned it.

Success in the Middle East also seemed to confirm that détente with the Soviet Union could be carried forward on terms highly favorable to the United States. Kissinger dismissed suggestions that Washington was "bound to be outmaneuvered" in its new relationship with Moscow. Experience had "convinced us of the opposite." The Soviet leaders' unconcealed anxiety about China, their slowing economy, their personal limitations and insecurity—didn't these factors make them prime candidates for manipulation by a skillful American diplomat?[13]

The secretary of state, of course, wanted to be the one who decided when, how, and to what end the Soviets were to be manipulated. But despite his successes, he soon lost the ability to make that judgment on his own. On one issue after another (the Middle East remained an exception), Congress began to question—and ultimately to dictate—his negotiating strategy. The first of these involved trade and human rights. Senator Henry Jackson and other members of Congress offered an amendment to the foreign trade bill that tied the opening of East-West economic relations to freer emigration, especially for Soviet Jews. Kissinger resented the challenge to his authority, found the goal relatively trivial, and argued that it would needlessly antagonize the Soviets. But Moscow's own behavior seemed to undercut him. Brezhnev and his colleagues had already backtracked once, rescinding an exit tax on emigrants just half a year after imposing it in 1972. And the number of people permitted to leave the Soviet Union had been increasing for several years, from a few hundred annually in the late 1960s to well over 30,000 in 1973.[14]

Were 30,000 emigrants the upper limit of Soviet flexibility? Kissinger said yes. He felt Jackson, in pushing for more, "was acting like a man who, having won once at roulette, organizes his yearly budget in anticipation of a recurrence." Yet the Soviets—this had to be maddening for the secretary of state—kept on backpedaling. In April 1974, Gromyko, amid much grumbling, agreed that perhaps 45,000 would be an acceptable annual level. Then in August, Dobrynin intimated that 55,000 might leave. He even accepted a plan for an exchange of letters in which Jackson and Kissinger would confirm this shared expectation. In return, Congress would grant the Soviet Union most-favored-nation

(MFN) status—what came to be called "normal trade relations"—for a trial period of eighteen months.[15]

Only when Jackson trumpeted this Soviet retreat as a "monumental accomplishment"—and claimed that the new numbers were a firm commitment—did the Kremlin's patience snap. Kissinger, arriving in Moscow days later, encountered a storm of outrage from Brezhnev and Gromyko. They did not meddle in American domestic affairs, they said. (The secretary of state did not disagree with them. "I wish I could say the same was true on our side," he replied.) The Soviet Union, Brezhnev vowed, would not tolerate American meddling. As for the eighteen-month trial offer, he pounded the table: "We cannot accept that 'gift.'" Gromyko handed Kissinger a letter denying that any emigration numbers had ever been agreed to; Soviet officials had merely been clarifying their procedures for the ignorant Americans. Anyway, the issue was now moot, said Gromyko. Interest in leaving the Soviet Union, it seemed, had suddenly dropped off.[16]

BESIEGED ON ALL SIDES, Kissinger tried to escape the situation by telling everyone something different. He insisted to Brezhnev that MFN would in fact be extended beyond the initial eighteen months. One reason to be confident was that the secretary of state himself planned to launch a public campaign to explain the benefits of détente. A debate between himself and Scoop Jackson, Kissinger claimed (he seemed to be making this up), had been scheduled but then postponed. A pity, he confided, because "I could have hurt him badly." Kissinger said he looked forward to taking on his critics. "I'll almost certainly win," he bragged. But to make this possible, Brezhnev had to do his bit—by wrapping up a new arms control treaty. "The best way," the secretary of state urged, "is if you and I are on the same side, and Jackson is on the other."[17]

Congress, Kissinger clearly hoped, would swallow whatever number of emigrants Moscow permitted as long as talks on arms control were going well. But he suggested the exact opposite in reporting on his meeting to Gerald Ford, who had replaced Nixon barely two months earlier. The Soviets, Kissinger told the new president, would make further concessions on emigration "to protect their relationship with you" and out of "fear of strengthening Jackson." He assured Ford (who after almost twenty-five years in Congress knew something of its workings) that he would discuss the issue with interested senators on his return to Washington. But when he testified before the Senate Finance Committee, he acted as though the Soviets had made no warnings at all. The United States, said the secretary, had "every right to expect" continuing increases in emigration. Even when an angry Gromyko set the record straight the next day by releasing his letter to Kissinger, the State Department spokesman pretended it didn't matter. All understandings between the administration and Congress on emigration were still in force.[18]

As in the Vietnam talks, Kissinger was gambling that someone else would back down and bail him out. Would it be the Soviets, as he told the Congress and the president, or would it be the Congress, as he told the Soviets? Neither the Kremlin nor Capitol Hill, it turned out, was willing to be manipulated further. Within two weeks, the deal collapsed. (Almost forty years passed before Congress revisited the issue and voted for permanent normal trade relations with Russia.)

What survived this fiasco was Kissinger's promise to Brezhnev to make a more vigorous public case for détente. In the ensuing year, he delivered a series of what his staff called "heartland" speeches. They were designed to persuade audiences in one American city after another—Milwaukee, Minneapolis, Pittsburgh, San Francisco, Dallas—that the administration's foreign policy was not a betrayal of democratic principle.[19]

Kissinger's "heartland" presentation typically included an acknowledgment that the United States had a "duty to defend freedom." But his bottom line was that American foreign policy could not make this duty paramount. If defending freedom was an important goal, so was preserving the peace, and so was avoiding a ruinously expensive arms race. Humanitarian purposes should be pursued, Kissinger said, "where we have the latitude." In criticizing other governments, Americans had to respect "the delicacy of the problem." Legislative pressure to protect human rights was "almost inevitably doomed to fail." Kissinger tried to seize the high ground from critics who considered détente weak and unworthy. In a world of nuclear weapons, he insisted, the ability to make pragmatic trade-offs was the true test of strong character; compromise was proof of moral fiber. "The issue is whether we have the courage to face complexity and the inner conviction to deal with ambiguity."[20]

These speeches were thoughtful and searching. In private, by contrast, Kissinger's view of those who pushed the issue of human rights was harsh, even bizarre. To Nixon, he ridiculed congressional interest in Soviet emigration. Even if the USSR put Jews in gas chambers, said the secretary of state who had escaped from Hitler's Germany, it would not be an American concern. ("Maybe," he granted, "a humanitarian concern.") To Gromyko, he mocked the human rights goals of European governments. Hadn't they learned from two world wars that the Soviet system could not be reshaped by external pressure? (The Kaiser, the Nazis, and Amnesty International, it appeared, were all committed to the same futile anti-Communism.) After Andrei Sakharov and other Moscow dissidents publicly appealed for support from abroad, Kissinger denounced them as irresponsible. "You know," he joked to George Kennan, "what would have happened to them under Stalin."[21]

The secretary of state's most outrageous statements were kept private, but the outlook that underpinned them came through clearly enough in public actions and gestures. When he blocked an Oval Office visit by Aleksandr Solzhenitsyn, the exiled Soviet writer and dissident, in the summer of 1975, others in the Ford White House began to wonder about the decision's impact. Donald Rumsfeld, the president's chief of staff, got a long memo on the subject from his young deputy, Richard Cheney. Détente, Cheney argued, didn't mean a relationship of "sweetness and light." In fact, he thought, meeting a prominent Soviet dissident offered "a nice counter-balance" to superpower summits. Three members of Ford's cabinet—including Secretary of Defense James Schlesinger, and Daniel Patrick Moyhihan, the newly appointed ambassador to the UN—seemed to agree, attending a dinner in Solzhenitsyn's honor given by the AFL-CIO.[22]

Kissinger was incensed to find himself isolated in this way. ("Listen," he hectored Moynihan, "how *could* you have gone to that dinner for Solzhenitsyn?") Yet the secretary of state did not change course. His handling of human rights issues became, if anything, more rigid and extreme. Shortly after the Solzhenitsyn furor, Ford had to attend a Europe-wide summit at which the so-called Helsinki Final Act was to be adopted. In later years it became clear that Moscow had made a major error in agreeing to the Final Act, which made "humanitarian" issues an accepted part of East-West diplomacy. But in 1975 both the meeting and the document were highly controversial. Many feared that they signaled Western acceptance of permanent Soviet control over Eastern Europe.[23]

To combat this impression, Ford's speechwriters thought it would be prudent—and good politics, too—to underscore that the United States did not recognize Moscow's absorption of the Baltic states during World War II. Kissinger would have none of it. Even a boilerplate statement of long-standing American policy was off limits if it was likely to offend

Moscow. "You will pay for this," he warned the White House staffers who had pushed the idea. "I tell you, heads will roll."[24]

THERE WAS A SECOND Jackson amendment that hampered Kissinger's effort to strengthen the new relationship with Moscow. When the Senate agreed to the arms control agreements of 1972, the senator from Washington had persuaded his colleagues to attach a requirement that no future treaty restrict U.S. nuclear forces to levels "inferior" to those of the Soviet Union. To this, Kissinger responded with exasperation. It was "strategically and politically illiterate," he insisted, to suggest that the administration had accepted inferiority. America's technological lead meant that it could increase the number of warheads on its long-range missiles more rapidly than the Soviets could. This was true enough. Yet from the moment in 1973 when Moscow began testing a new generation of so-called "heavy" missiles, it was also clear that the American edge that Kissinger touted could not last long. The Soviets would take the lead once they started putting more warheads on their (much) larger rockets.[25]

For the rest of the decade, the entire enterprise of Soviet-American arms control was defined by this asymmetry between the two sides' forces. The process became extraordinarily—even mind-numbingly—complex. Could the disparate strengths of the Soviet and American arsenals be limited in some way that would assure strategic parity? Which weapons would be restricted by a new agreement, and how? Could restrictions be made precise enough to prevent cheating, and could violations be detected? When Ford and Brezhnev met at Vladivostok in November 1974, they settled on a formula that seemed to meet Jackson's test of equality. Each side would be allowed to have up to 2,400 strategic "launchers," a cap that now included both missiles and bombers. The two leaders further agreed to make an equal number of launchers the heart of a ten-year treaty, to be completed as soon as possible.[26]

Ford was "euphoric" at this result. Kissinger argued that it provided for "essential equivalence" between Soviet and American nuclear forces and—just as important—that it met the standard Congress had established for a new agreement. He spent the remaining two years of Ford's presidency trying to turn the Vladivostok framework into a finished treaty. But he did not succeed. Within the administration, bureaucratic opposition mounted. Beyond it, former officials and members of Congress also raised objections. And as the 1976 elections approached, Ford himself was persuaded, reluctantly, to put the negotiations aside.[27]

Kissinger's most formidable opponents were his colleagues in Ford's own cabinet—first Secretary of Defense James Schlesinger, and then his successor, Donald Rumsfeld. Schlesinger was an economist who could go toe to toe with Kissinger on matters of nuclear strategy. For him, the enormous launching power—or "throw weight"—of the big Soviet missiles made it hard to speak of real equivalence between the two sides. His relentless criticism, Schlesinger admitted, "began to drive Henry wild." Ford himself suspected that the secretary of defense was behind leaks suggesting that the United States was making too many concessions to nail down a treaty.[28]

Rumsfeld, who had served in Congress with Ford and took over as defense secretary at the end of 1975, was less knowledgeable than Schlesinger, but he was a far more potent bureaucratic adversary. When Kissinger complained to the president that the Pentagon's incessant talk about the growth of Soviet military power was "creating a bad impression around the world," Rumsfeld had a simple defense of his department's position. "It's true," he said. As he saw it, Kissinger's desire to talk a good game internationally was making it harder to generate public support to stop the slide in U.S. military spending. Given his close relationship with Ford, Rumsfeld had no trouble making his case persuasive. He took Kissinger on in the Oval Office, right in front of the president. "We have been slipping since the '60s from superiority to equivalence," he argued. "And if we don't stop, we'll be behind."[29]

This challenge from within the administration was reinforced by a growing number of critics outside it. In the year after Vladivostok, former officials from both Democratic and Republican administrations expressed skepticism about its terms. A leading critic was Paul Nitze, who had not only served Truman, Kennedy, and Johnson but had been a member of the SALT negotiating team in Nixon's first term. In 1976 he and others formed the Committee on the Present Danger, to rally opposition to the proposed agreement.[30]

Many of these critics disliked Kissinger personally. (Privately, Nitze called him "a traitor to his country.") But their case was deeply technical too. The provisions of Vladivostok, Nitze wrote in *Foreign Affairs,* would leave Soviet missiles with a three-to-one "throw weight" advantage. Soviet negotiators, he said, never admitted that their goal was to achieve superiority over all other nuclear powers combined, but "watching the way they added things up and how they justified their position, this is what it boiled down to." Such criticisms shaped debate inside the government as well. When the outgoing CIA director, George Bush, approved a new intelligence estimate on Soviet nuclear policy at the end of 1976, it largely endorsed Nitze's views.[31]

Beneath all the technical details, the argument of Kissinger's critics was as much about retrenchment as it was about the Soviet-American nuclear balance. They thought the secretary of state—first with Nixon's support and now Ford's—had become so wedded to the process of arms control that he was indifferent to emergent American weakness. There were plausible technical answers to this charge, and Kissinger made them. But he also hurt his case with offhand rhetoric that was easy to distort. A reporter had asked him, at a 1974 press conference in Moscow, what would happen to the Soviet-American nuclear balance in the absence of an arms control agreement, to which Kissinger responded with a famous outburst that his critics never stopped using against him. "What in the name of God," he asked, "is strategic superiority? What is the significance of it, politically, militarily, operationally, at these levels of numbers? What do you do with it?"

Kissinger had a defensible case: it was not easy for the Soviet Union to achieve superiority in any usable sense. But he had come very close to saying that, since superiority was meaningless, the United States need not try to keep up. His critics had no trouble exploiting this concern.[32]

When Ronald Reagan challenged Ford for the Republican presidential nomination in 1976, his most inflammatory charge was the same one Schlesinger, Rumsfeld, Nitze, and others made: that the United States was letting itself fall behind the Soviet Union. "The evidence mounts," Reagan said again and again, "that we are Number Two in a world where it's dangerous, if not fatal, to be second best." He claimed that détente had become "a one-way street. We are making the concessions, we are giving them the things they want; we ask nothing in return."[33]

IN THE LATE 1950s, when Dwight Eisenhower sought to calm fears of a "missile gap," his efforts had been undercut by a string of crises—in Berlin, in the Middle East, in the Taiwan Strait, in Latin America. In the 1970s, a similar resurgence of Soviet-American competition in the Third World undermined Kissinger's claim to be running a successful foreign policy. North Vietnam, which had steadily strengthened its forces in the

South after the Paris agreement was signed in 1973, opened its long-anticipated offensive in January 1975. The chief of the Soviet general staff had visited Hanoi a month before to aid in the preparations, and Moscow's military aid surged. As South Vietnamese provincial capitals fell, and refugees fled from the oncoming Communist forces, Washington faced a painful question: would it—could it—do anything to prevent a Communist victory? The administration's answer produced another confrontation with Congress, for Kissinger the worst yet. It marked the start, in his words, of a "nihilistic nightmare."[34]

At first the secretary of state said he relished a scrap. He told his staff that his public stance on Vietnam would be aggressive. "We are going to say what we think the national interest is. And if we take a little heat from the Congress, we will take it." When the Pentagon drew up a list of legally permitted measures—from more reconnaissance flights over North Vietnam to sending an aircraft carrier briefly through the Gulf of Tonkin—Kissinger was for all of them. He urged Ford to press Congress to restore recently cut military aid for South Vietnam, then to seek a supplemental appropriation of more than $700 million. Only a strong stand would work, he argued. "It has been my experience that when we move timidly"—here he channeled Nixon again—"we lose. When we are bold, we are successful."[35]

Yet virtually no one answered Kissinger's call. The media uproar over possible military moves—even the largely meaningless ones being contemplated—was so strong that he quickly backtracked. Weeks passed with no congressional agreement to offer South Vietnam anything. Those who had once supported the war effort now felt a weary fatalism. Scoop Jackson himself—long Kissinger's most vocal critic for not standing up to the Soviet Union—rejected more aid. "There has to be a limit," he said. "There has to be a ceiling. There has to be an end."[36]

By April, although Ford kept asking for military assistance—and made his case before a joint session of Congress—the only real questions were how quickly the United States would evacuate its own people, and how many South Vietnamese it would take with it. New York senator Jacob Javits told Ford, "I will give you large sums for evacuation, but not one nickel for military aid." Senator Joe Biden of Delaware was less compassionate: "I will vote for any amount for getting the Americans out. I don't want it mixed with getting the Vietnamese out." Many in Congress shared this view. When the administration first asked for $500 million for refugee resettlement, the request was immediately rejected.[37]

As the collapse continued, Kissinger kept insisting, often vehemently, that the United States had to act. But he had trouble articulating the "national interest" that was at stake. It was hard to say exactly what "commitment" had been made to South Vietnam. Although Nixon had personally assured Thieu of American support, he had not done so publicly (and Jackson seized on this secrecy to explain his opposition to further aid). Writing Ford's speech to Congress, Kissinger proposed that he emphasize "credibility." Interviewed on television, he expressed a vaguer worry about "a general psychological climate that is created in the world as to who is advancing and who is withdrawing." As Saigon teetered, he stressed America's "underlying moral obligation" to save its friends.[38]

Whatever their melancholy force, these urgings won few converts. Just days before the end, Ford gave a speech at Tulane University in which he said the war was "finished as far as America is concerned." Kissinger, who had been kept in the dark about the president's intention, was stunned. But others, including many longtime supporters of the war, were ready to move on. For Dick Cheney, who was with the president for the Tulane speech, hearing him "say those words was welcome in a way it is hard to describe."[39]

Closing the book on the Vietnam War was not, at the very end, a contentious policy issue. Right and left were comfortable with it. The real issue, always contentious in periods of retrenchment, was what to do next. Kissinger insisted that the collapse of South Vietnam called for making a strong stand somewhere else. When he learned, scarcely two weeks after Saigon fell, that the American-owned cargo ship *Mayaguez* had been seized in international waters by the Cambodian navy, his response was eager. "Let's look ferocious!" he exclaimed. And when he sensed that Moscow was on the verge of a new success in southern Africa, Kissinger pushed for a covert confrontation. This was a region that had been largely left outside the rivalry of the Cold War. But when Portugal's dictatorship fell in 1974, the result was turmoil in its former colonies—Angola and Mozambique—and in neighboring territories like South-West Africa (now Namibia). These struggles, in which the Soviets, Chinese, and South Africans all had their favorites, now took on a meaning that Kissinger would never have accorded them before.[40]

As he had on other issues—from human rights to arms control—the secretary of state soon discovered that he did not have the rest of the U.S. government behind him. In Angola, the CIA had provided a printing press and walking-around money to one of the anti-Soviet groups early in 1975, and that might have been the end of it. Neither the State Department nor the intelligence community seemed impressed by the stakes. For Kissinger, this was wrongheaded. Moscow's clients were gaining the upper hand. If the United States stood by while Soviet involvement settled an African civil war, he argued, "we will pay for it for decades." Overruling his own assistant secretary for African affairs, he demanded action. By the end of July, Angola's neighbors had agreed to serve as staging areas for American aid, a counteroffensive was launched, and the United States had contributed its first planeload of arms.[41]

Here the competition escalated sharply, perhaps beyond the original expectations of either superpower. By air and sea, Soviet planes ferried thousands of Cuban troops into the Angolan war zone in the fall of 1975. Aided by Soviet military supplies, Moscow's clients were once more poised for victory. At Kissinger's urging, Ford responded by authorizing another $30 million of assistance—too little to turn the tide, since Soviet deliveries were far larger, but possibly enough to produce a stalemate and truce talks. (Again Kissinger was skeptical that a halfway strategy would achieve anything. There "are no rewards," he grumbled, "for losing with moderation.")[42]

Before any new American aid arrived, however, the entire story was leaked to *The New York Times,* and within a week Congress—even though many of its members had been briefed on the program for months—voted to prohibit any covert programs in Angola. Most senators, whatever their ideological stripe, felt that the United States should steer clear of deeper involvement in the region. The aid cutoff actually had the support of a majority of Republican senators present for the vote. They included liberals like Jacob Javits, moderates like Robert Taft, Jr., and some of the Senate's most conservative members, including Jesse Helms. The sponsors of the cutoff were two liberal Democrats, but Republican votes gave this landmark measure its two-to-one margin of victory. It was his own party—not come-home-America Democrats—that rebuffed the president.[43]

FOR KISSINGER, the Senate's action was simply incomprehensible. It proved, he raged to the president, that "Vietnam is not an aberration, but our normal attitude." Over the next weeks and months, his rhetoric grew steadily angrier. "It is time," he argued, "to stop dismantling our national institutions and undermining our national confidence." Alas, he saw little reason for hope. The country was clearly in a masochistic mood—of "self-doubt, division, irresolution."[44]

And this was only what Kissinger saw on the left. On the right, attacks on the administration's policies also mounted. Reagan began promising voters in the Republican primaries that if elected he would install a "new secretary of state." Ford's campaign managers let reporters know that they considered Kissinger a drag on the president's reelection chances. The word *détente* was officially dropped from use. At the summer nominating convention, the Ford camp decided not even to contest a platform plank on "Morality in Foreign Policy." It had been drafted by the Reagan camp for one purpose only: to humiliate, and repudiate, Henry Kissinger.[45]

The debate over his policies has always been, in Kissinger's version of the story, a contest between prudent centrism and America's irresponsible extremes. Ideologues of right and left, he claimed, were exploiting the nation's disorientation after Vietnam and Watergate. Meanwhile, he and the presidents he served sought—in a time of societal trauma—to hold a steady middle course, guided by the national interest.

The political wars that Kissinger complained about were real. He had enemies. In his latter years as secretary of state, liberals, conservatives, and neoconservatives tried to thwart him at every turn. Yet their opposition was not the main reason these struggles turned out so badly for him. Kissinger became isolated and vulnerable above all because he was at odds with those whose centrist credentials were at least as good as his. When he battled Schlesinger and Rumsfeld over arms control, the disagreement was neither ideological nor partisan. Schlesinger was a nonpartisan technocrat; Rumsfeld, a moderate midwestern Republican who had worked in the Nixon White House (where he was widely suspected of being soft on social issues and on Vietnam). Outside the government, the key critics of Kissinger's nuclear policies were not fringe figures but pillars of a bipartisan establishment. Paul Nitze had written NSC-68 for Dean Acheson while Kissinger was polishing his honors thesis at Harvard.

Nor did Kissinger keep the center with him when he rejected human rights as a significant foreign policy issue. Aleksandr Solzhenitsyn was snubbed by the Ford White House but was honored by the AFL-CIO, an organization that had for decades occupied the Cold War mainstream. It had recently sent millions of working-class Democrats over to Nixon when it chose not to endorse George McGovern for president. And as for standing up to the Soviets in the Third World, the administration's failure to get even a majority of Republican senators behind it on Angola was a telling defeat. There too Kissinger had lost the center.

So why did opposition to détente go mainstream in late 1974 and 1975? Vietnam and Watergate, the usual suspects, do not in fact provide the strongest answer to this question. Kissinger's virtuoso performances in the Middle East had shown that domestic political constraints could be overcome by creative diplomacy as long as it achieved widely shared American goals. His handling of other issues was, however, far less deft and far less purposeful. He was not able to negotiate an arms control treaty that the rest of the U.S. government would support. His efforts to play Capitol Hill and Moscow against each other on the subject of emigration and human rights blew up in his face. And when he wanted congressional funding for a covert action program in a region that had never been a major American national security concern—and for which he had no broadly convincing explanation other than providing a psychological counterpoint to the collapse of South Vietnam—almost no one supported him.

To prevail on these issues, Kissinger would have had to have a simpler, more coherent overall strategy toward the Soviet Union. It had to be shorn of "nuance," "ambiguity," and "complexity." Calling his critics "nihilists"—and claiming that commitment to ambiguity was courageous—won him no arguments. He simply looked angry and confused.

Kissinger—and even more, Nixon—had been acutely sensitive to the domestic political dimensions of getting out of Vietnam. While rejecting any end to the war that looked like defeat, they used accommodation with the major Communist powers to give their diplomacy a more hopeful and effective cast. One of Kissinger's deputies, William Hyland, described the connection well. "America needed a respite from failure," he wrote, "and détente provided it." Because it offered an alternative to demoralization and failure, a policy of skillful retrenchment had great appeal.[46]

But once the war was over, the politics of foreign policy changed. Détente began to be measured differently. Both Nixon and Kissinger—in the past so quick to sense the domestic resonance of their policies—were slow to understand what had happened. "I am carrying out the toughest policy" toward Russia, Kissinger growled, "that can be sustained over a long period." In his own mind, no one could be consistently tougher than he. But to his critics, the fact that he dismissed their approaches as not "sustainable" was all the proof they needed that he was satisfied with a low level of effort.[47]

Disagreement was sharpest on the issue of human rights. For Pat Moynihan, it was "the single greatest weapon we have left for the defense of liberty." Kissinger eventually acknowledged that diplomacy had to reflect national values, but he never treated these values as themselves a source of strength. Instead, they were a distraction and an indulgence, a costly American quirk that too often got in the way of other decisions. "I had to position our policy for a long haul," Kissinger later wrote to Moynihan in an attempt to smooth over their differences, " . . . while you were concerned with the immediate crisis." Almost the opposite turned out to be true. Kissinger was, as a secretary of state has to be, preoccupied with a large portfolio of immediate matters. In attending to them, he failed to put his policy on a secure long-term foundation. Thinking that his own approach was sustainable was perhaps his biggest mistake.[48]

WHEN JIMMY CARTER was elected president in 1976, he and his advisers had to choose between foreign policy continuity and the chance, after eight years of Henry Kissinger, to strike out in new directions. Carter made clear that he accepted much of existing policy. "I believe in détente with the Soviet Union," he said. "To me it means progress toward peace." And after the hyperactivism of the 1960s he had no problem with retrenchment. His inaugural address embraced a foreign policy of narrower horizons. "We have learned," the new president said, "that more is not necessarily better, that even our great Nation has its recognized limits, and that we can neither answer all questions nor solve all problems."[49]

All this was consistent with what Nixon, Ford, and Kissinger had bequeathed him. At the same time, Carter criticized what he called their "covert pessimism," "secret deals," and "manipulation." He demanded a more open policy, one more consistent with American values, less focused on the preoccupations of the Cold War—and less reactive. A new, less bipolar world was emerging, and the United States should not fear it. "We should help to shape it," he said. Throughout his time in office, Carter struggled to resolve this counterpoint between the policies he inherited and his desire to invigorate America's global role.[50]

Nothing the new president proposed marked a stronger policy departure than his approach to human rights. America's commitment to democratic principles, he said in his inaugural address, must be "absolute." He knew that pushing this cause would excite criticism from both right and left. Some argued that too much talk about human rights would jeopardize continuing rapprochement with the big Communist powers. Others warned that it would undermine right-wing authoritarian regimes friendly to the United States.

Neither concern deterred Carter. He added an ideological element to relations with both Moscow and Beijing. Within weeks of taking office, he had exchanged admiring letters with Andrei Sakharov, the Soviet dissident. (The wife of an American human rights lawyer got the new president's message through airport security in Moscow by hiding it in her bra.) As for the Chinese, Carter vowed not to "ass-kiss them the way Nixon and Kissinger did." He chose Leonard Woodcock, head of the United Auto Workers, to represent the United States in Beijing. Woodcock greeted his new staff with this declaration: "Never again shall we embarrass ourselves before a foreign nation the way Henry Kissinger did with the Chinese." Challenging other governments in this way evoked criticism, but in his diary Carter promised to be resolute: "I don't intend to modify my position."[51]

The new president wanted to overhaul other policies that he thought were underperforming. East-West arms control was a prime candidate, and he sent Secretary of State Cyrus Vance off to Moscow in the spring of 1977 with a proposal to cut strategic nuclear forces by as much as 25 percent, deeper than either side had ever discussed. The Soviet Union's "heavy missiles"—its most threatening weapons—were to be cut by half. In the Middle East, where Kissinger's time-consuming shuttle diplomacy had produced no major results since 1974, Carter wanted more "comprehensive" agreements. In Africa, he was similarly impatient with slow-moving British efforts to negotiate a transition to majority rule in Rhodesia (now Zimbabwe). "Continued hesitation and timidity," he thought, were getting nowhere. The United States would have to take over the process—"put together a clear concept of what we want, get as many people to join us as possible, ram it through, and then just take the consequences."[52]

This demanding, sometimes rigid approach was Carter's signature. In tackling a big problem, he would try to figure out what long-term solution made the most sense, then challenged others to accept it. He valued his role as path-breaker and seer. And if a problem, in addition to its practical importance, had a moral dimension as well, so much the better. Carter's spiritual side gave him—at least in his own opinion—a special feel for matters that involved America's national strengths, and its weaknesses too. Human rights evoked American strengths; overreliance on imported energy was an example of weakness. Energy, said Carter, was "the greatest challenge our country will face during our lifetimes." He tried to generate support for conservation, especially for lowering home thermostats, by delivering his first speech from the White House in a cardigan sweater. But a folksy style did not keep him from delivering hard-hitting messages. "I do not promise a quick way out of our Nation's problems," he said, "when the truth is that the only way out is an all-out effort."[53]

Many presidents have had Carter's yen for visible, history-changing macroinitiatives. Few have had his ability to sweat the details too. Large visions, he saw, needed careful implementation. In the middle of deadlocked talks between Menachem Begin and Anwar Sadat, it was Carter who rescued the agreement, fashioning compromise formulas that both sides could accept. He also found time to focus on small, inconspicuous initiatives that would only pay off in the long run. Early in his term the new president instructed the CIA to step up covert action programs that targeted the internal stability of the Soviet regime.[54]

Carter wanted to put foreign policy on a more promising activist course, and some of his efforts produced landmark results. The Panama Canal treaties that he made an early priority eliminated a potent anti-Yankee rallying cry in Latin American politics. The Camp David agreements that he mediated in 1978 quieted relations between Egypt and Israel for decades. Robert Gates, who served almost every president from Nixon to Obama, called Carter's encouragement of Moscow dissidents the most open challenge to Soviet legitimacy since World War II. With American support, Polish trade unionists and Afghan freedom fighters began to shake the Soviet empire.

CARTER'S ACHIEVEMENTS WERE significant. And yet far from reinvigorating American foreign policy, his administration was ultimately a time of deeper retrenchment. America's fortunes seemed to sag badly, and a confused president was widely considered to have made things worse. Carter was so burdened by a reputation for ineffectuality that, while flying to meet Leonid Brezhnev in Vienna in June 1979, he said he would not get off the plane with an umbrella, even though it was raining, for fear of reminding people of Neville Chamberlain. "I'd rather drown," he said, "than carry an umbrella."[55]

Bad luck played a part in this result. Carter inherited some of his biggest challenges; for others, he bore no real responsibility. He became president, as he complained early on, "in the middle of the worst economic slowdown of the last 40 years." The global rivalry between Moscow and Washington, which had already been getting sharper as the Ford administration ended, also took a political toll. "The Soviet star seemed to be ascending," recalled Gates, who was a junior NSC staffer at the time, "while the American one was falling." Halfway through his term, Carter was further blindsided by the Iranian revolution—an event foreseen by few experts, either in or out of government. By Election Day 1980, most of the U.S. embassy staff in Tehran had been held hostage for a full year. Some of the president's responses to these problems eventually bore fruit, but not, unfortunately for him, on his watch.[56]

Beyond bad luck, Carter's personal style undercut his efforts at leadership. Members of his own staff referred to him as "the nation's chief grammarian." In identifying large challenges to America's well-being and security, he often fastened on responses that seemed tiny and inconsequential. His famous "malaise" speech in July 1979 typified this habit. In it, he analyzed a crisis of morale that, he insisted, struck "at the very heart and soul and spirit of our national will." After this grand diagnosis, he offered annoying and trivial prescriptions. "Whenever you have a chance," he lectured the American public, "say something good about our country."[57]

Carter's biggest problem, however, was neither bad luck nor clumsy rhetoric. It was a persistent ambivalence in his approach to major foreign policy problems. He made voters, pundits, and sometimes his own advisers wonder whether he knew what he was doing. No issue highlighted this confusion more than his policy toward the Soviet Union. Although many of his initiatives—support for covert programs in the Soviet bloc, contact with dissidents, bold arms control proposals—showed a tough and skeptical outlook, his military policies seemed to carry a contrary message. In his very first days in office, Carter cut the Pentagon budget by $6 billion. He announced—without prior consultation—that American forces in South Korea would be reduced by half. Among weapons programs, the B-1 strategic bomber and the so-called neutron bomb were canceled. Although the president proposed to go ahead with the new MX missile, privately he called the decision to do so "nauseating." When pressed on defense spending, he shrugged the issue off. There was no popular support, he said, for increases.[58]

Even when Carter adopted a tougher and more coherent public line, it was unclear how seriously he meant it. At the Naval Academy in June 1978, he accused the Soviets of using détente as "a continuing aggressive struggle for political advantage and increased influence." Their aim, he said, was "to export a totalitarian and repressive form of government, resulting in a closed society." This was bruising, old-fashioned rhetoric, meant to convey concern about a rising tide of Soviet activism in the Third World. (That spring, Moscow had airlifted Cuban forces into another African civil war, this time in Ethiopia.) Leonid Brezhnev and his colleagues were taken aback by Carter's speech and called Ambassador Dobrynin home to show their displeasure. Zbigniew Brzezinski, the national security adviser, was thrilled. "They finally heard you," he reported to Carter. But getting the attention of Soviet leaders was exactly what the president did *not* want. The speech, he confessed to his diary, had been for domestic consumption. If, he wrote, the message was seen as "tough at home, and the Soviets consider it mild, that's perfect."[59]

Carter repeatedly confused his own closest aides as to his real views. "A big accident"—that was how Hamilton Jordan, the White House chief of staff, summed up the tough rhetoric of the Naval Academy speech. "Who the hell knows whether the president will not veer in some direction tomorrow or the day after tomorrow?" Harold Brown, the secretary of defense, found Carter's thinking about the Soviet Union "simplistic and naïve."[60]

The president made it hard to know what he was serious about. When Brzezinski sent him a memo in advance of the summit meeting with Brezhnev in Vienna in June 1979, Carter said he was "really peeved" by it. "Too *timid,*" he scrawled on the first page, and then again on the second. He was fed up with "lowest common denominator" approaches, he said, and instructed Brzezinski "to set maximum goals and work toward them." The key to good policy, he believed, wasn't to figure out what Moscow would accept. The point—the president scribbled this in the margins four times, with underlining for emphasis—was to figure out "what *we* want." Then, his little tirade having passed, he approved the entire memo.[61]

When Carter met Brezhnev, moreover, he settled for set-piece exchanges that Brzezinski himself described as "perfunctory." The summit "would be worthless," Brzezinski had told the president beforehand, unless the Soviet leaders understood that their activism in the Third World jeopardized arms control agreements, including the SALT II treaty that they had come to Vienna to sign. When the meetings were over, Brzezinski saw how little they had accomplished: "I doubt that any dent was made in Soviet thinking."[62]

THE SOVIET INVASION of Afghanistan in late December 1979 gave Carter an opportunity to put aside his ambivalence. Earlier, Washington had felt concern at Moscow's growing boldness; now it felt panic. Earlier, the U.S. aim had been to preserve a mixed relationship of competition and cooperation; now there was an urgent search for every conceivable way to push back against what was seen as a colossal outrage. The invasion triggered a Kennan-style "stone in the beehive" moment—around-the-clock meetings, cascading decisions, and fear of the new crisis around the corner if the United States did not deal firmly enough with the one at hand.

Carter's responses unfolded over weeks and even months, as he and his advisers called for new ideas, reviewed their options, and made their choices. First came the diplomatic protest via the hotline (the "sharpest" message he'd ever sent Brezhnev, Carter recorded). A week later the president asked the Senate to suspend action on the SALT II treaty, announced a cessation of grain exports to the Soviet Union, and called for a boycott of the 1980 Moscow Olympic games. Harold Brown, already scheduled to visit Beijing in January 1980, was quickly given a more robust brief, including approval of "nonlethal" military sales to China—an idea that the president had personally vetoed just a month earlier. In all, he approved twenty-six measures of this kind.[63]

Carter further authorized increased military supplies to the Afghan mujahideen, and he dispatched Brzezinski to Islamabad to discuss an assistance package that would ensure Pakistan's cooperation. In his 1980 State of the Union address, he announced a new "doctrine"—labeling the security of the Persian Gulf region a vital American interest and pledging military action to stop other states from threatening it. Even this did not exhaust the administration's responses. As the year went on, it sought to revive registration for the draft, asked Congress for an interim increase in the Pentagon budget, and completed a revision of U.S. nuclear strategy.[64]

Was retrenchment finally over? For once, electoral imperatives, congressional sentiment, bureaucratic politics, and the president's own thinking seemed to converge. "My opinion of the Russians," Carter announced, "has changed more dramatically in the last week than even the previous two and a half years." Critics ridiculed his statement, but the public seemed satisfied. The Gallup Poll's presidential-approval rating showed the biggest upward jump in its history, from 32 percent to 61 percent in a single month. To Brzezinski, the United States was at last ready to "concentrate our efforts on policies to preserve and maximize American power." He considered the president's initiatives, particularly closer cooperation with China and the new focus on the Persian Gulf, a "strategic revolution." The national security adviser had a catchy way of describing the new direction that Carter (and Mrs. Carter too) seemed to like. "Before you are a President Wilson," he counseled, "you have to be for a few years a President Truman."[65]

Carter's new strategy toward the Soviet Union positioned him as a stronger leader than in the past, and it might have saved him politically but for the Iranian hostage crisis. This challenge kept the president from shaking his reputation for weakness. So great was the burden that, long after he left the White House, whenever Carter was asked what he should have done differently in office, he pointed to the hostages. If only, he reflected wistfully, he had included an additional helicopter in the rescue attempt that he ordered in April 1980. With just one more helicopter, he thought, it might have been possible—even with mechanical difficulties—to carry out the entire operation.[66]

The hostage crisis kept voters from changing their minds about Carter. With the failure of the rescue mission, his poll numbers dropped back below 30 percent. But it was far from his only problem. For all his new resoluteness, the president had not abandoned the ambivalence that previously undercut his leadership. The Jimmy Carter who made policy after the "strategic revolution" of 1980 was strikingly similar to the one who had made policy before it. He remained reluctant to choose one direction over another. He wanted to be Wilson and Truman at the same time.

Carter's conflicting impulses surfaced even in his initial response to the Soviet invasion of Afghanistan. In February, having just announced the Olympic boycott, and with its prospects still uncertain, he explored the idea of sending a personal message to Brezhnev. He wanted the general secretary to know that the United States would consider a mere one-year postponement of the games if Soviet forces would only leave Afghanistan. Brzezinski and Vice President Walter Mondale were "appalled." An early signal of eagerness to compromise would confuse allies who had not yet decided whether to support the boycott. But Carter would not relent. "I feel a responsibility," he wrote, "even though we are rebuffed." He had heard rumors that the Politburo was divided, and he hoped to test the Soviet leaders' receptivity to a deal. (The effort was a flop: the Politburo was not divided enough to give the State Department's chosen emissary a visa.)[67]

Throughout 1980, even after the voters turned him out in November, Carter kept looking for opportunities to resume a less confrontational Soviet-American relationship. By itself, this was unexceptionable. Reagan, too, said he wanted better relations with Moscow. But for Reagan, that meant breaking with the policies of the 1970s. What Carter meant was not so clear. Which of the steps that he had taken after the Soviet invasion would last, and how long? His own staff had no idea. When the president told Brzezinski in the fall that the SALT treaty should be delinked from Afghanistan, it was not because he had decided on a more demanding approach to arms control or because the invasion had clearly failed. It was simply that the emotions aroused by the invasion had begun to subside.[68]

Carter privately confessed his ambivalence when, at the end of the administration, he approved a defense budget calling for sustained growth into the mid-1980s, just as Reagan did. But unlike Reagan, he felt the United States could not afford it. Resource constraints were going to hamper American efforts for years to come. For this reason, he told his diary, arms control agreements remained "absolutely imperative." Carter's real goal was not to put the 1970s behind him; it was to resume them. He wanted to "buy at least five or six years' time in getting along with the Soviets, at least on a shaky détente."[69]

PRESIDENTS RARELY CHANGE direction in office, even when problems mount. Jimmy Carter was an exception. Many of the measures for which Ronald Reagan was later known, and widely applauded, were in fact initiated by Carter. His foreign policy was an almost archaeological oddity—a species that becomes extinct even though it carries many of the same genes that help competitors to thrive and endure.

Knowing this, many of Carter's friends and supporters felt he had been unjustly treated. Mstislav Rostropovich, the great Soviet émigré cellist, expressed his views at a White House farewell dinner, comparing Carter to musical geniuses whose works were not immediately welcomed. Rostropovich's remarks consoled the president: "He said that history was going to treat my administration the same way they did Verdi, Puccini, and Beethoven."[70]

Yet what held Carter back was not that, like some of the great composers, he was too innovative. It was that he was not innovative enough. Presidents put aside previous policies and statements only with enormous difficulty. Even when circumstances call for something completely new, it is hard to go beyond a hesitant incrementalism. Carter came very close to putting his old ambivalence aside, and in a second term he might have gone further. But he stubbornly defended his past choices even as he tried to move on. And the more he did so, the less voters were likely to understand him, or to think that an ambivalent president would help the country deal with the problems it faced.

As Carter wrestled with his own views, the national debate about American foreign policy was changing. Republicans who had had their doubts about Nixon and Ford's policies, but kept quiet out of partisan loyalty, now expressed their opposition publicly. Before long, even the authors of détente demanded more robust alternatives. Henry Kissinger offered objections to Carter's SALT treaty that he would never have posed to his own. Al Haig resigned as NATO commander, letting it be known that he thought Washington was mismanaging relations with America's allies. Meanwhile all those who had been strong opponents of détente in the past—conservative Democrats and conservative Republicans alike—remained just as critical. The ranks of those prepared to defend administration policy steadily dwindled.[71]

America's second experience with retrenchment ended much the way the first one did. Détente in the 1970s evoked the same criticisms and dissatisfaction as Eisenhower's attempt to put foreign policy on a "sustainable" footing in the 1950s. Nixon had begun the process of pulling back from war and overcommitment. In the course of the decade, each new administration—reflecting different personalities, principles, and priorities—attempted to find its own way forward. Ford's policy was the pursuit of détente without Nixon; Carter's, the pursuit of détente without Kissinger. Yet all these different versions of retrenchment produced similar results. A strategy that was supposed to be sustainable over "the long pull" commanded strong support, ironically, only as an interim measure. When new problems and opportunities appeared, Americans demanded new responses to them. In 1960 this same choice—the desire to get America "moving again"—had had fundamental long-term consequences. In 1980 the same sort of maximalist transformation was about to begin again.

Part Three

1981 to the Present

9

"Outspend Them Forever"

REAGAN AND THE END OF THE COLD WAR

Ronald Reagan

LIKE MOST AMERICAN PRESIDENTS, Ronald Reagan came to office with little direct experience in the ways of international diplomacy. Communicating with Kremlin leaders posed a particular problem for him: how was he to get through to people who were likely hardened Communist ideologues? As it happened, the professional training of an earlier life came in handy. "I tried to use the old actor's technique of empathy," Reagan said, "to imagine the world as seen through another's eyes and try to help my audience see it through my eyes."[1]

Today eminent historians of American diplomacy and politics praise the fortieth president for empathy above all other attributes. His unique gift, one scholar has written, "was his willingness to reach out to a leadership he abhorred, men whose values he detested; to appreciate the concerns of his adversary; and to learn from experience."

Others find in Reagan qualities like "perceptiveness," "idealism," "emotional intelligence," and "optimism about himself." Though an old Cold Warrior, he was not, one historian concludes, "intimidated" by Cold War orthodoxy. He "deserves posterity's honor," another writes, for "knowing when to transcend and, finally, reject outdated and counterproductive ideas."[2]

The Reagan who entered the White House in 1981 was, to say the least, very different from the one historians now describe. He had won the presidency from Jimmy Carter by urging a much more competitive foreign policy. The goals Reagan set forth for dealing with the Soviet Union were especially crisp. "We win, and they lose," he once said to an aide. "What do you think of that?" In office, he did just as he said he would, sparing no expense to revive a nuclear arms race and mincing no words about America's main adversary. Reagan accused Soviet leaders of ruling an "evil empire," a phrase he later claimed was chosen "with malice aforethought." The president's words and deeds enabled opponents to portray him as a warmonger, an ideological fantasist, even a dimwit.[3]

Then, in the course of eight years as leader of the Free World, Reagan appeared to change his mind. The maximalism of his goals remained, but he discarded his old verbal belligerence. "I was talking about another time," the president told reporters, while enjoying an afternoon stroll in downtown Moscow in June 1988 with his new friend Mikhail Gorbachev, the leader of the Soviet Communist Party—"another era."[4]

The waning years of the Cold War were a disorienting time. Adjusting to surprises was a daily task. People changed their minds repeatedly, at different speeds, in different directions, and usually with very little patience for others who were trying to do the same thing. While Reagan was president, Henry Kissinger criticized his policies as destructive and utopian. Later, he praised them. He even contended—this was surely the highest praise of all—that they were a direct continuation of the strategies that he and Richard Nixon had devised when they were in charge of American foreign policy. Many conservatives, thrilled by how Reagan handled relations with Moscow in his first term, were horrified by the direction he took in his second; they now found themselves agreeing with Kissinger. *The Washington Times* actually compared the president to Neville Chamberlain. And it was not just on the right that opinions changed. Antinuclear activists, who had argued that Reagan was leading the world to war, later recognized him as one of their own—a visionary nuclear abolitionist before his time.[5]

The puzzle of the Reagan administration lies in explaining this historic turn from confrontation to conciliation. To reconcile the early Reagan and the late one, we need to understand which of his policies changed over time and which did not. Exactly which of his "outdated and counter-productive ideas" did the president cast aside, and when? Did he really conclude that hypercompetitive strategies were too costly and dangerous to succeed? Or did he think they *were* succeeding? Reagan obviously felt great enthusiasm for Gorbachev and wanted to support his reform program. But what tools did he rely on in offering this support? Empty rhetoric, unrealistic proposals, and starry-eyed expressions of hope? Meaningful concessions? Or continuing pressure?

The late 1980s were full of increasing personal warmth between Soviet and American leaders. But real meet-me-halfway accommodation was rare. "It's time for the Soviets to come up with a proposal of their own," the president liked to say. Or "We're in no hurry." He expected to get good results by keeping the heat on. The Ronald Reagan of our current historical imaginings was someone who liked to put himself in the other guy's shoes, who wanted to discover that there was just no good reason to keep fighting the Cold War. The Ronald Reagan who sat in the Oval Office had a different view. He did not like to give in.[6]

IN ITS FIRST YEAR, the Reagan administration brought a new maximalist edge to the East-West competition. For more than a decade, Washington policy makers had believed that neither the United States nor the Soviet Union could afford an arms race. Reagan's defense planners disagreed. They rejected one proposal after another for increasing the Pentagon budget, and all for the same reason: not big enough. The president made it known that he thought the Soviets were "on their keister," and he wanted to press them—hard. "I intended to let them know that we were going to spend whatever it took to stay ahead of them in the arms race." Within a month of taking office, he sent Congress a plan to increase military spending by almost 60 percent in just three years.[7]

Improving the balance of power was only one element of Reagan's strategy. Name-calling also had its place. The new president created a stir when he said at his very first press conference that Communists "reserve[d] unto themselves the right to commit any crime, to lie, to cheat" in pursuit of their aims. And he didn't exactly recant. "I wanted," he later said of his tough rhetoric, "to remind the Soviets we knew what they were up to."[8]

There were, to be sure, some elements of policy continuity in Reagan's approach. Because economic recovery was his top priority, the new president did not want foreign policy controversies to keep Congress from passing his tax cuts. He had picked Al Haig, the former Kissinger aide and Nixon chief of staff, to be his secretary of state; when Haig recommended that the United States abide by the terms of Jimmy Carter's unratified SALT II treaty, Reagan went along. In another bow to continuity, he agreed to begin Soviet-American negotiations on nuclear missiles in Europe, endorsing the two-track approach that NATO had adopted in 1979. To fulfill a campaign promise to the farm lobby, he even lifted Carter's post-Afghanistan grain embargo.[9]

Yet the new administration also demonstrated that existing policies could be made to serve very different ends. When Carter and his advisers proposed that the U.S. deploy new missiles in Europe as a counter to the Soviet SS-20s, they did so as a sop to NATO allies. The plan was part of an effort to win their support for the SALT II treaty. Under Reagan, the "Euromissiles" became a tool for developing a radical new strategy. The American goal in arms control talks was no longer to ensure "stability" or to ease Cold War tension through complicated, mutually offsetting compromises. The new administration saw arms control as a way of putting the Soviets on the defensive, of challenging them to abandon their most threatening weapons. The so-called zero option that Reagan proposed in November 1981 contained the seeds of his later nuclear abolitionism. In exchange for cancellation of the proposed American deployment in Europe, the Soviet Union would have to forfeit every single one of its roughly 500 intermediate-range missiles. The United States had never made such a one-sided arms control proposal.[10]

Some NATO governments had their own reason for liking the zero option, but it was not that the proposal demanded so much of Moscow. They hoped it might make the deployment of new American missiles unnecessary. Admittedly, no one could be sure that the allies would stand by the proposal once Moscow rejected it, and many American experts, both in and out of government, thought they obviously wouldn't. William Hyland, who had advised both Kissinger and Brzezinski on arms control (and was soon to become editor of *Foreign Affairs*), warned that the zero option would "end in disaster." West German chancellor Helmut Schmidt had the same fear. In the late 1970s, he had been among the first to sound the alarm about the Soviet SS-20s. Now he felt negotiations would have a year to show results. If a quick deal could not be worked out, support for deployments—and perhaps for the NATO alliance itself—would begin to collapse.[11]

Schmidt proved to be the first casualty of the "Euromissile" crisis. Just as he feared, his own Social Democrats refused to stick with the "two-track" decision if the United States would not agree to compromise. The chancellor's national security adviser, Egon Bahr, complained that American policy makers were risking world peace in their pursuit of "victory over evil." (He traced this dangerous messianism to the influence of "neo-conservatives.") The new government in Bonn publicly supported the zero option, but in private it too appealed for flexibility. When Schmidt's successor, the Christian Democratic leader Helmut Kohl, made his first visit to Washington, he told Reagan that to preserve his fragile majority, he needed real negotiations—"not a show." Margaret Thatcher offered the same advice.[12]

These appeals gained special force from an atmosphere of East-West tension that Europe had not felt in two decades. In one country after another, massive political demonstrations demanded that U.S. deployments be canceled. The Soviet buildup had sparked the Western response, and Moscow's bloodcurdling rhetoric had given rise to fears of war. Even so, it was American nuclear policy (and the European governments supporting it) that animated the protesters. In the United States, a "nuclear freeze" movement appeared, drawing crowds—more than a million in New York City—that rivaled Vietnam-era protests.[13]

As allied unity began to fray, American negotiators searched for a way out. Paul Nitze, whose long opposition to Kissinger gave him stature among the Reaganites, had been appointed to lead the talks on Euromissiles. In the summer of 1982, after quiet conversations with his Soviet counterpart, he came up with the so-called walk-in-the-woods formula. Nitze proposed to abandon zero and settle for equal numbers of missiles on both sides. But he could not get the president to go along. Reagan thought the Soviets would bargain more seriously after U.S. missiles were deployed at the end of 1983. Meanwhile, good nerves would be needed. In a famous face-to-face Situation Room exchange, the president told Nitze to explain to Russian negotiators that he worked for "one tough son of a bitch."[14]

As for the allies, the administration chose not to inform them that a compromise had even been broached. Too much information would only weaken their resolve and encourage them to call for more American concessions. Caspar Weinberger, the secretary of defense, had long since expressed his view of the Europeans. The alliance, he sniffed, needs "leadership, not compromise."[15]

REAGAN BELIEVED THAT in any negotiation, hanging tough was the key to success. One more split-the-difference agreement that left the Soviets with most of what they had would not put East-West relations on a new footing. Slowly, however, the president's advisers, especially Secretary of State George Shultz (who replaced Haig in 1982), persuaded him to make at least a show of flexibility. If the public and the Congress thought the United States was negotiating in good faith, they would be less likely to consider Reagan a reckless militarist. The allies would be more likely to go ahead with deployments on schedule. And the Soviets, with more reason to hope for an agreement, might restrain their own rhetoric.[16]

To nourish such hopes, the president began in early 1983 to emphasize that the zero option was "not a take-it-or-leave-it proposal." In February he let Shultz bring Anatoly Dobrynin, the Soviet ambassador, over to the White House for a friendly, unpublicized late-afternoon chat. More than two years into the administration, this was Reagan's first meeting with a Soviet official. It gave him a chance to extend assurances of American goodwill. In March the president went further still, announcing that—while zero remained a worthy goal—he was open to proposals that provided for equality between U.S. and Soviet missile forces. He knew that certain of his advisers were unhappy with such gestures, but that didn't deter Reagan. "Some of the NSC staff," he confided to his diary, were "too hard line."[17]

Efforts to document Reagan's emergence as a committed nuclear abolitionist often treat this first mini-thaw in his approach to East-West arms control as a kind of inflection point. A full two years before the advent of Gorbachev, it seemed, the president had already come to the conclusion that, having begun to rebuild Western strength, he could now probe for an achievable diplomatic payoff. His efforts produced no immediate result, but only because Soviet policy was so rigid. Three geriatric general secretaries ruled the Kremlin during Reagan's entire first term. From their hospital beds, they counted on Western unity to dissolve before the Euromissiles were actually deployed. With his Soviet counterparts disinclined (and perhaps unable) to bargain seriously, Reagan had no trouble explaining why he had failed to break the East-West impasse. "How am I supposed to get anyplace with the Russians," he liked to joke, "if they keep dying on me?"[18]

The small steps that the president took in 1983 to open channels of communication do help to anticipate his later policies, but they produced no real softening of the U.S. stance. To the contrary, they underscored how uncompromising Reagan's approach really was. His get-acquainted schmoozing session with Dobrynin was immediately followed by a new burst of anti-Communist rhetoric—the famous speech that referred to the Soviet Union as an "evil empire." A week after that came the unveiling of the Strategic Defense Initiative (SDI)—the speech in which Reagan offered up his plan to neutralize the Soviet nuclear deterrent by creating a "shield" against ballistic missiles. It would have been hard to imagine a less favorable atmosphere for honest give-and-take between Washington and Moscow.

Even the front-burner issue of the Euromissiles was handled in a way that had to raise Soviet doubts about American aims. Yes, Reagan claimed the zero option was no "take-it-or-leave-it" offer. Still, he refused to propose a specific agreement for anything other than zero. As deployments drew near and European publics grew more anxious at the seeming stalemate, Vice President George Bush was sent on a European tour to advertise a constructive-sounding invitation for a summit meeting with the new Soviet leader, Yuri Andropov. But the stated American goal for the meeting was exactly the same as before—to sign the zero option. When Andropov died early in 1984, the president rejected the suggestion that, as a goodwill gesture, he attend his funeral. He told his advisers, "I don't want to honor that prick."[19]

There is no doubt that Ronald Reagan hoped to create a new foundation for East-West relations, but he made no serious effort to achieve it through old-fashioned diplomatic compromise. Reagan wanted Soviet leaders to accept his ideas rather than try to split the difference between their ideas and his. Keeping American programs on track—above all, getting the Euromissiles into Europe—did more to achieve this goal than any number of back-channel feelers. The president gambled that Western governments would be able to maintain their support for the U.S. position despite intense public anxiety. Soviet policy makers gambled that NATO would not be able to hold its members together. When Reagan proved right, Moscow had little choice but to climb down from confrontation.

Mikhail Gorbachev himself acknowledged the impact of the Euromissile defeat. For understandable reasons, he never accepted the idea that American pressure had forced him to adopt perestroika and dismantle the Soviet system. But he did not deny what had produced new directions in Soviet foreign policy. The turning point, Gorbachev later admitted, was the lost battle with NATO over the nuclear balance in Europe.[20]

APART FROM DEEP nuclear arms reductions, nothing has defined Ronald Reagan's foreign policy legacy more than his support for peoples and movements trying to escape Communist rule. During his presidency, the United States offered significant assistance to anti-Soviet groups in Poland, Afghanistan, Nicaragua, Angola, Cambodia, and elsewhere. Robert Gates, who became deputy director of the CIA in the early 1980s, captured the practical meaning of what became known as the Reagan Doctrine in these words: "We would pass up no opportunity to challenge the Soviets and make life hard for them in the Third World until they [withdrew], or negotiate[d] a settlement satisfactory to us, or change[d] their behavior."[21]

This strand of Reagan's strategy arguably had an even more fundamental impact on American policy than did his approach to nuclear weapons. In Afghanistan, it helped to inflict a demoralizing defeat on the Soviet regime. It gave new prominence—with ideological and institutional implications that outlasted the Cold War—to the idea of "democracy promotion." And with its link to the so-called Iran-Contra affair, Reagan's "doctrine" even threatened to bring down his presidency.

Yet all this was for later. When the administration began, there was no such thing as the Reagan Doctrine, nor any real agreement on the individual initiatives that later comprised it. For three years, the guerrillas fighting the Soviet army in Afghanistan got no more aid—and little more attention—than the United States had provided under Carter. Doing too much, it was feared, could lead Moscow to retaliate against Pakistan. The right approach, Pakistani president Mohammad Zia ul-Haq told William Casey, Reagan's intelligence chief, was to "keep the pot boiling, but not boil[ing] over." The same wariness limited covert aid to the Solidarity trade unionists in Poland. Casey thought the AFL-CIO was doing a "first-rate" job helping Solidarity and worried that CIA activism might "screw it up." The administration's initial response to the imposition of martial law in Poland in December 1981 was so mild—the president suggested putting candles in windows—that Jimmy Carter claimed vindication. Reagan, Carter smirked, was "coming toward me all the time."[22]

Even in Central America, Reagan's first moves were cautious. He rejected the aggressive proposals of Al Haig, who saw Cuba as the real source of trouble in the region and proposed to confront Castro directly. For Haig, any approach that didn't "go to the source" was pure "limp-wristed, traditional, cookie-pushing bullshit." In March 1981 he told the president, "Give me the word, and I'll make that island a fucking parking lot."

Wild talk like this unnerved Reagan. He settled instead on relatively conventional steps—above all, increased assistance to friendly governments, like El Salvador, that faced Cuban- and Nicaraguan-backed insurgencies. It was not until the end of 1981 that he authorized a small covert training program for Nicaraguan rebel groups. (Haig considered the decision a complete "cop-out.") More than two and a half years passed before the president even mentioned the *contras,* as the rebels became known, in a major speech.[23]

How did this initial reticence become the full-throated global commitment to anti-Soviet freedom fighters with which Reagan began his second term? Part of the explanation was surely the president's growing personal conviction. Year by year his interest in exploiting Soviet vulnerability increased. When he made his famous prediction, speaking to the British Parliament in June 1982, that Marxism-Leninism would be left "on the ash-heap of history," he was expressing (as he acknowledged in the same sentence) a "hope for the long term." Two years later, when the president took up the same theme, this time in a speech to the Irish Parliament, his language was decidedly stronger. "All across the world today," he proclaimed, "in the shipyards of Gdansk, the hills of Nicaragua, the rice paddies of Kampuchea, the mountains of Afghanistan, the cry again is liberty."[24]

In the interim, the administration had discovered that pushing back against Soviet (and Cuban) influence in the Third World could be very popular. In October 1983, Reagan sent U.S. forces ashore on the Caribbean island of Grenada, ousting the pro-Castro New Jewel Movement just as it was descending into fratricidal anarchy. For policy makers who were uncertain about whether the public would support the use of force, the response to the intervention was a revelation. Shultz later called it "a shot heard round the world by usurpers and despots of every ideology." The American people seemed to like the idea that their government could quickly and cheaply unseat an unfriendly and violent regime. Grenadans were even more enthusiastic. When Reagan visited the island, Colin Powell, who accompanied him, was stunned by the "outburst of mass emotion" that his arrival produced. The president was welcomed as "the liberator, the Messiah, the savior."[25]

The Reagan Doctrine had its supporters in Congress too. Much of the impetus to boost support for the Afghan resistance above Carter levels actually came from Capitol Hill—in particular, from one insistent and flamboyant Texan member of the House of Representatives, later immortalized in a book and movie bearing his name, *Charlie Wilson's War*. Congressional pressure nudged the CIA forward; CIA pressure nudged the Pakistanis forward. By 1985, U.S. aid to the mujahideen was three times greater than it had been in 1983.[26]

FOR ALL THESE new shows of commitment, however, the emergence of the Reagan Doctrine as a global strategy had far less to do with success than with failure, and less to do with congressional support than with congressional opposition. In April 1984, *The Wall Street Journal* revealed that the CIA had lied to members of Congress about *contra* attacks in Nicaragua. In fact, the agency had mounted them by itself. The operation was almost comically minor, involving harbor mines designed more for noise than for destructive impact. Richard Nixon called the whole thing "Mickey Mouse." But the political blowback was violent. "I am pissed off," Barry Goldwater, the Senate Intelligence Committee chairman, wrote to Casey on learning that he had been deceived. Daniel Patrick Moynihan, the vice-chairman, resigned in protest. By the fall of 1984, Congress had banned further aid to the *contras*.[27]

With funding cut off, the administration needed a way to relegitimize its policy. Peter Rodman, Shultz's policy planning director, argued that covert action had to be put "on a higher moral plane." An unpromising question for public debate (were the *contras* really credible democrats?) had to be turned into a promising one (didn't opponents of Communist dictatorship deserve help?). A reframed debate, Rodman believed, might help "the glow of the popular cause (the Afghans) to rub off onto the unpopular one (the contras)." This was Reagan's tack in his February 1985 State of the Union address. "We must not break faith," he said, "with those who are risking their lives—on every continent, from Afghanistan to Nicaragua—to defy Soviet-supported aggression and secure rights which have been ours from birth."[28]

Two weeks later Shultz gave the argument another new twist in a speech to the Commonwealth Club of San Francisco. Yes, said the secretary of state, the administration wanted to support anti-Soviet "freedom fighters." But it saw them as just one part of a global trend that also included "advocates of peaceful democratic change in South Africa, Chile, the Republic of Korea, and the Philippines." The kind of help the United States should give, he admitted, "varies from case to case." Shultz reassured those who worried about getting drawn in to hopeless Third-World conflicts, with little chance of success: "The more we can lend appropriate help to others to protect themselves, the less need [there will] be for more direct American involvement to keep the peace." But the United States, Shultz insisted, could not stand aloof. It had a stake in the outcome. "The spread of democracy," he argued, "serves American interests."[29]

Reagan and Shultz were challenging their congressional opponents on *contra* aid by placing the issue in a global context. They dared the Congress to insist on one lone exception to this hopeful worldwide trend. Some scoffed at the president's Fourth of July rhetoric, but it produced an immediate surge of congressional interest in the other Reagan Doctrine conflicts. By the summer of 1985, the Senate voted to repeal the Clark Amendment, which had for ten years banned military aid to the insurgents in Angola; in the fall, the House agreed. Aid for the non-Communist opposition in Cambodia also won approval. Even on Nicaragua, the effort to globalize the debate had an impact. In April 1985, Congress reaffirmed the complete ban on *contra* aid that it had instituted the previous fall; in June, it made exceptions; in the summer of 1986, it authorized new funds.[30]

The president and his advisers did not use the term *Reagan Doctrine.* (Like the expression *Cold War,* it was coined by a journalist.) But they now *acted* as though they had an integrated strategy. In his memoirs, Robert Gates captured the increased effort of this period with the chapter title "Washington Pours It On." In March 1985, Reagan signed a directive declaring that the goal of American policy in Afghanistan was no longer to bog the Soviets down but to drive them out and win. Once Congress repealed its ban on aid to UNITA in Angola, the president authorized a covert program there as well.[31]

In both cases, a bureaucratic consensus took shape that the resistance fighters needed more and better weapons. Some experts, of course, wondered whether it made sense to give sophisticated weapons to barely trained Afghan and Angolan guerrillas. But spectacular early results stilled all doubts. The first time the Afghans used Stingers—the most advanced portable antiaircraft missiles in the U.S. inventory—against Soviet forces, they hit three of four targets. UNITA fighters had hit eight of ten. From then on, Gates recalled, "no one in the Reagan administration was prepared to ease up in challenging the Soviets in the Third World until they did change. No one."[32]

The Reagan administration's support for anti-Soviet insurgencies had some of the same negative effects that the Cold War and anti-Communist ideology often did on U.S. policy in the Third World. Washington frequently exaggerated the geopolitical stakes, sometimes entered into unsavory partnerships, and—by focusing so much on its rivalry with Moscow—probably paid less attention to other, very real problems facing developing countries. (The most famous example of unintended consequences: the fact that, in the course of building up the indigenous resistance to Soviet forces in Afghanistan, Americans ended up helping Osama bin Laden as well.)

Yet the Reagan Doctrine was also part of an extremely positive transformation of American Third-World policy—and in this transformation, anti-Communist ideology played a crucial role. Believing that global democratic trends offered a way to check Soviet influence, Reagan became more ready to withdraw support from dictators like General Augusto Pinochet in Chile and President Ferdinand Marcos in the Philippines. Escalating the Cold War ended up strengthening the role of democratic principle in American foreign policy. The president picked up this theme in his message to Congress in March 1986. Blocking Soviet expansionism was his principal focus, but he put it in a larger context. The American people, he declared, "oppose tyranny in whatever form, whether of the left or the right." This was not where Reagan had started out as president. In 1981 he had a far more traditional conservative affinity for right-wing dictators. A maximalist approach to the Cold War—and in particular the determination to rescue aid to the *contras*—had brought him to a new policy.[33]

By contrast, when Reagan's Third-World policy lost its ideological orientation, it seemed to lose its way completely. The administration's handling of Middle East issues was far less driven by the Cold War and far more confused and ineffective than policy in any other region. Lebanon was perhaps the most striking example. Between 1982 and 1984, the United States responded to civil war in that country first by intervening, then by redeploying its troops offshore, then by redeploying them back on land, and finally by pulling them out altogether.

Reagan's policy was equally directionless, and just as easily blown off course, in trying to balance Iraq and Iran. Despite the effort's pragmatic core, Washington policy makers misunderstood their relations with both countries. In 1983 and 1984, some imagined that Saddam Hussein was becoming a true ally; in 1985 and 1986, the president became foolishly convinced that he could build up "moderates" inside Iran. Other American initiatives in the region led nowhere, as Reagan himself acknowledged. "In 1988," he said ruefully, "the Middle East was as much a snake pit of problems as it was when I unpacked my bags in Washington in 1981."[34]

IN 1985, JUST AS THE United States began to "pour it on" in the Third World, Reagan faced, for the first time, a Soviet leader prepared to pursue new policies both at home and abroad. The president had long awaited this opportunity. Two years earlier he had written in his diary that he wanted the Soviets to "see there is a better world, if they'll show by deed that they want to get along with the Free World." In letters and speeches, through advisers, emissaries, and spokesmen, and sometimes even face to face, Reagan tried to tell Moscow that it had—as he reassured Andrei Gromyko in the Oval Office in 1984—"nothing to fear" from Washington. In November 1985 in Geneva, at his first meeting with Mikhail Gorbachev, he again insisted that America's aims were entirely peaceful. "Nuclear war," he reaffirmed, "cannot be won and must never be fought." This was Reagan's message in all five of the extraordinary summit meetings he had with Gorbachev—more than between any two Soviet and American leaders in the entire Cold War.[35]

To the president's expressions of goodwill, Soviet leaders responded with hostility and impatience. In 1983, after Reagan's first speech on SDI—in which he claimed high-tech defenses had the potential to "[change] the course of human history"—Yuri Andropov called the idea "insane." At Geneva, Gorbachev found himself unable to sit through one more rhapsodic description of how "Star Wars" would strengthen peace. Red-faced and angry, he blurted out, "Do you take us for idiots?"[36]

The president did not let the grousing get him down. He began his post-Geneva debrief for the national security team by endorsing Prime Minister Thatcher's view of Gorbachev: "Maggie was right. We can do business with this man." He saw great promise in the new Soviet leader—for reasons that often made little sense to others. He was especially heartened, for some reason, that in their meetings Gorbachev had not specifically endorsed the goal of "a one-world Communist state." Kenneth Adelman, who ran the U.S. arms control agency, was typical of other senior officials in seeing Reagan's enthusiasm as just another one of his "funny ideas."

Skepticism among his own experts had no more effect on the president than did Soviet intransigence. He sensed a chance to make a fundamental break with the strategic confrontation of the past. The extent of his aims was clear from his reaction to Gorbachev's splashy public proposal, made two months after Geneva, to abolish nuclear weapons by the year 2000. His close advisers wanted to dismiss the Soviet plan. Reagan did not. "Let's say we share their overall goals and now want to work out the details." About timing, he playfully asked Shultz, "Why wait until the end of the century?"[37]

The president's desire for an historic breakthrough gave Gorbachev an opportunity, as he put it to the Politburo, to "knock Reagan off balance." At their Reykjavik meeting in October 1986, the Soviet leader came armed with a proposal that he thought the Americans would be unable to refuse. It included not only the precise overall cuts—50 percent in five years—that the United States had been proposing but a further agreement to surrender the Soviet Union's long-standing advantage in "heavy" missiles. American negotiators (and even more, their critics) had recognized for more than a decade that only this concession would make the two sides' strategic forces truly equal. From Henry Kissinger on, they had been unable to get the Soviets to budge. Now the goal was in reach.[38]

Gorbachev was not, to be sure, offering this gigantic strategic retreat for free. He asked Reagan, with more than a little impatience, when the United States would finally "start making concessions of its own." Above all, he wanted tighter restrictions on SDI. Rather than negotiate this question, however, the Americans parried with an even grander proposal, calling for the elimination of all ballistic missiles within ten years. Reagan urged his new friend to appreciate the historic prospects before them. If the two of them agreed on this plan, they would be able to return to Iceland a decade hence to mark the occasion—and "give a tremendous party for the whole world." Gorbachev had no problem with this celebratory vision. He even topped it, offering a counterproposal that would eliminate nuclear weapons of all kinds.[39]

The Reykjavik summit became an almost manic exchange of ever more utopian ideas. But the dueling visions did not resolve the underlying disagreement. Reagan wanted testing of antimissile technology to continue while the superpowers dismantled their strategic forces. If, at the end of ten years, defenses seemed to be working, the United States would have to share whatever it had learned with the Soviet Union. Gorbachev derided the whole idea. "You are not willing to share with us oil well equipment, digitally-guided machine tools, or even milking machines," he countered. "Sharing SDI would provoke a second American revolution!" As for his own political situation, if he returned to Moscow with such an agreement, the Politburo would call him "a dummy and not a leader."[40]

Reagan's advisers were excited by this unprecedented opportunity: to bring home radical Soviet reductions in exchange for minor restrictions on SDI. Through diplomatic sleight-of-hand, Shultz hoped to give the Russians "the sleeves from our vest on SDI and make them think they got our overcoat." Even Richard Perle, the senior arms control official at the Pentagon, marveled at the "quite extraordinary leverage [we were getting] from a system that was a long way from being operational." But Reagan had not come to Reykjavik to play tricks, to find middle ground, or to squeeze out a few extra concessions. His answer to Gorbachev's question about when the United States would make concessions was now clear. It wouldn't make any, not unless the president got the entire scheme he had proposed. Frustrated and angry at the stalemate, he told Shultz, "Let's go, George . . . we're leaving."[41]

After the summit, Gorbachev told his Politburo colleagues that Reagan had revealed himself to be not only a "class enemy" of the Soviet Union but "a feeble-minded cave man." Fortunately his designs had been easy to see through. The United States, the Soviet leader complained to a group of visiting American legislators, "believes the Soviet Union is in a corner and can be squeezed." Washington was simply "waiting for us to drown."[42]

AS THE LAST two years of the Reagan administration began, the president and his advisers were afraid that he might be impeached as a result of the Iran-Contra affair. It had become known after the midterm elections of 1986 that Reagan, while publicly ruling out negotiations with terrorists, had sold arms to Iran to win the release of Americans held hostage in Lebanon. Worse yet, it emerged that members of the NSC staff had used some of the proceeds to get around congressional restrictions on aid to the *contras*.[43]

The resulting scandal was punctuated by the largest one-month drop ever in public approval of a president's performance, a raft of White House firings (including the chief of staff and the national security adviser), a blue-ribbon commission to establish what had happened, the appointment of a special prosecutor, televised congressional hearings, mass publication of executive branch documents and e-mails, and ultimately the trial and conviction of several middle-level officials. Reagan struggled, not totally successfully, to describe what he thought had been going on. Eventually the storm subsided. Yet the president's belated, passive-voice admission—"mistakes were made"—conveyed, at best, disengagement from the day-to-day business of his own administration. No one had ever accused Reagan of being a hands-on manager. Now the active phase of his presidency, such as it was, seemed over.[44]

With Iran-Contra at its peak, Reagan also faced increased criticism of the improvisational antinuclear ideas that had come to dominate his policy toward the Soviet Union. One line of attack on the president was led by Richard Nixon and Henry Kissinger, who now turned the tables on the man who had rallied opposition to their own policies a decade earlier. In a long, private White House discussion early in 1987, Nixon said he found Reagan's confidence in Gorbachev "somewhat disturbing." He was, in fact, so alarmed by what he heard that, for the first time since his resignation in 1974, he teamed up with Kissinger to challenge the administration's policy. Radical arms reduction schemes, the two of them claimed, courted "unimaginable perils." They stayed on the attack for the rest of Reagan's tenure. Writing in *The New York Times*, Nixon went so far as to claim that Gorbachev was "more aggressive, not less" than his predecessors. In his *Newsweek* column, Kissinger regularly mocked the administration for the "near-ecstasy" of its feelings for Gorbachev. The president's "irresponsible" denuclearization talk, he argued, was pushing the Atlantic alliance into crisis. In private, he was still more dismissive. When the INF treaty was finally wrapped up, Kissinger told Shultz that it "[undid] forty years of NATO."[45]

These criticisms paled, of course, in comparison to what more extreme conservatives said about Reagan. When Caspar Weinberger and key aides left the Pentagon in 1987, hard-liners saw their departure as the end of the administration's tough anti-Soviet line. Senator Jesse Helms warned the president not to "discard the people who brought him to the dance." Reagan, conservatives were convinced, believed arms control agreements were the only way to salvage his legacy. Gorbachev could relax; the United States would disarm unilaterally. William Safire, the conservative columnist, explained why the Soviets had become less critical of the president: "never murder a man who is committing suicide."[46]

The idea that the Reagan administration ended in a swoon of Soviet-American congeniality is not entirely a myth. American public enthusiasm for Gorbachev grew, especially after his trip to Washington in December 1987, and Reagan gave it strong personal encouragement. The atmosphere became especially friendly during the president's return visit to Moscow in June 1988. Reagan's famous never-mind about the "evil empire" speech—that he had said all those nasty things in "another time . . . another era"—was a gesture that Gorbachev and his advisers had long been angling for.[47]

Despite all the warmth, however, the substance of American policy hardly changed at all. In the year after his failed gamble at Reykjavik,

Gorbachev kept looking for ways to extract concessions from the United States. Looking ahead to the Washington summit, the highlight of which was to be the signing of the INF treaty, the Soviet leader asked whether Reagan might make the package a little easier to swallow by agreeing to token restrictions on SDI research. Then he pushed the idea that the treaty should apply only to Europe, so that the Soviet Union could keep its intermediate-range missiles in Asia. Later Gorbachev tried to deflect American demands that a shorter-range Soviet missile, not previously covered by the negotiations, would have to be dismantled as well. Throughout he insisted that the two sides had to reach at least tentative agreement on a follow-on treaty limiting long-range nuclear forces.[48]

Every single one of these issues was resolved in exactly the same way: the Soviets folded, and the Americans prevailed. The "euphoria" about which Kissinger kept fretting did not lead the United States—and least of all the president himself—to seek agreements through concession and compromise. If anything, American policy makers began to demand more. It was in the year between Reykjavik and Washington, for example, that Reagan made his famous speech in Berlin demanding that the Wall come down. Concurrently, Shultz began giving the Soviet leaders tutorials on why their economy was falling behind the rest of the world and how much they had to change their system in order to fix it. ("Psychological warfare," one State Department official called it.)[49]

That Reagan upped the ante at this time was, oddly, an expression of his high regard for Gorbachev. The Soviet leader seemed to recognize—and how could one not admire this?—that it was his responsibility to make all the significant concessions, on arms control and much more too. Moscow and Washington now began consulting closely on Afghanistan and other Third-World conflicts. To encourage Soviet withdrawal from Afghanistan, the United States had earlier indicated that it would stop supplying arms to the mujahideen once all Soviet forces pulled out. Just before the Washington summit, however, Reagan personally—and publicly—reneged on this understanding. "I don't think we could do anything of that kind," he told a TV interviewer. Gorbachev was "embarrassed and incensed" by the American reversal, but mere outrage did him no good. Not only did he come to Washington as scheduled to sign the INF treaty, but before leaving he offered yet another concession. Soviet military aid to Nicaragua, he promised, would be cut off. The president was ecstatic. The zero option and the Reagan Doctrine vindicated in a single visit! It was, he wrote in his diary, "the best summit we've ever had with the Soviet Union."[50]

AFTER GORBACHEV'S Washington visit, the tone of East-West relations grew steadily more cordial. And yet there was still almost no give in the substance of U.S. policy. Reagan, in fact, kept explaining why it was necessary to keep the pressure on. His speech before his return trip to Moscow in May 1988 was typical. "Some," he observed to an audience in Amherst, Massachusetts, "say the Soviet Union is reappraising its foreign policy these days to concentrate on internal reform.

> Well, clearly, there are signs of change. But if there is change, it's because the costs of aggression and the real moral difference between our systems were brought home to it. If we hope to see a more fundamental change, we must remain strong and firm.[51]

At the summit itself, Reagan barely departed from the story line he had developed in previous meetings. Gorbachev had clearly given up on reaching any new agreements. But he thought that perhaps the two sides might at least sign a document setting out basic principles of Soviet-American relations. Reassuring language about the importance of "peaceful co-existence" would, he seemed to feel, mollify the Politburo's unhappy conservatives. To the Americans, the text was abhorrent. It read like something Nixon and Brezhnev might have signed. Since re-creating détente was not Reagan's goal (no matter what Henry Kissinger later claimed), he disappointed his new friend once more.[52]

Nor did the president's usual good manners keep him from using the visit to retake the ideological offensive against Communism. Reagan had come to Moscow as a guest for the first superpower summit in the Soviet capital in fifteen years, and yet his meetings with Gorbachev were not the highlight of the visit at all. Far more attention was paid to the reception he gave for anti-Soviet dissidents at the American ambassador's residence, and to his speech at Moscow State University. Seeking to inspire the students, and to make clear what was wrong with the Soviet Union, he extolled principles like entrepreneurial freedom, the protections of the Bill of Rights, and local self-government.[53]

In Washington, Reagan had been a gracious host; in Moscow, an affable if provocative guest. His genuine liking for Gorbachev misled fellow conservatives as to the nature of his strategy, just as it has confused historians ever since. One person who was never fooled by the amiable manner was Gorbachev himself. Like Reagan, he considered Soviet-American relations intensely competitive. Unfortunately the cost of keeping up had ceased to be affordable. The United States was ready to keep running the arms race; under Gorbachev, the Soviet Union was not.

To describe how he had tried to transform Soviet-American relations, Reagan used to tell a joke in which one Red Army general said to another, "You know, I liked the arms race better when there was only one of us in it." The punch line was a surprisingly accurate echo of what was being said within the inner councils of the Soviet leadership. "We are stealing everything from the people," said the general secretary of the Soviet Communist Party to his colleagues, "and turning the country into a military camp." Seeing how little the United States was ready to compromise, Gorbachev made the case for a new direction both at home and abroad. Things could not go on as they were. "We have no choice," he told the Politburo in the months leading up to his Washington trip. "We are . . . at the end of our tether."[54]

Ronald Reagan was the most maximalist of modern American presidents. This was true not only of his goals but also of the tools he employed. His military spending outstripped any previous peacetime buildup. (John Kennedy, who set the previous record, increased the defense budget almost 10 percent in three years; the 1981–86 increase was 25 percent.) Reagan also re-escalated the ideological combat of the Cold War, turning Carter's pioneering interest in human rights into a far broader systemic challenge to Soviet Communism. He expanded the map of East-West competition in the Third World, bringing covert action out of the closet. The scale of the resources involved enabled the president and his advisers to do more than harass Moscow's unstable client regimes. The United States could actually hope to bring them down.[55]

It was this goal—to end the Cold War by winning it—that most set Reagan apart from his predecessors. No previous president had imagined the decisive outcome that he did. His fabled affability masked the reach of his ambition, but it did not alter his view of the conflict. To Reagan, empathy toward a political opponent did not mean forgetting about who came out on top or whose vision prevailed. The way he talked about empathy made that clear enough. Its purpose, after all, was to get others to see the issues at hand "through *my* eyes." Until they did so, he was not prepared to compromise America's competitive position. (Once they did, of course, compromise became less necessary.)

In preparing for his very first meeting with Gorbachev in 1985, Reagan had dictated a boiled-down summary of the message he wanted to convey. Failure to reach agreement, he said, would "leave no alternative except an arms race." Gorbachev should understand that there was "no way that we will allow them to win such a race." As he put it later, "We could outspend them forever."[56]

FROM THE BEGINNING of the Cold War, American policy makers, even those with maximalist inclinations, had accepted the idea that a permanent full-throttle competition with the Communist world was politically impossible. The country could not sustain a high level of effort indefinitely. That was one of the reasons Truman and his advisers thought the Marshall Plan needed a strict time limit, and that troop numbers in Korea needed a firm ceiling. High levels of risk and tension posed a similar problem. That was why John Kennedy was determined to resolve crises by making off-stage concessions.

Reagan was too experienced a politician to think that limits—whether of cost or risk—could be lightly ignored. By his second term, the defense buildup with which he began his first had flattened out. (Pentagon spending went up less than 1 percent between 1986 and 1989.) And even he sought to ease the tensions that had arisen in the course of the Euromissile standoff. All the same, there is no mistaking Reagan's willingness to push the envelope of public acceptance. He got approval for a buildup that Carter had considered completely unaffordable. He rode out fears of war that many who had managed American policy in previous administrations believed would tear Western societies—and the Western alliance—apart.[57]

We cannot know what made Reagan think he could manage the high risks and costs that went along with his policies. Even so, it is quite clear *how* he tried to limit them—not by empathy, but by rigidity. To win public support, he offered radical solutions. As he said at Westminster in 1982 (and not only then), "We must not hesitate to declare our ultimate objectives." Where others had made stability and mutual deterrence the watchwords of policy in the nuclear age, he proposed deep cuts and ultimately abolition. Where others had made coexistence the principle by which East and West would get along with each other, he proposed transformational democratic change. Others, especially the proponents of détente, had treated long-term sustainability—getting by—as the ultimate real-world test of good foreign policy. Reagan proposed success.

The process by which the president and his advisers turned this strategy into the everyday work of government was often an embarrassment. The administration lurched from crisis to crisis. That it avoided major direct military involvement was a virtual necessity; senior officials were too divided for the rigors of wartime. Yet the attempt to legitimize policy by attaching it to high purpose solved a problem that had eluded Reagan's predecessors. He simply did not feel the need to compromise. After eight years in office, he left the White House with higher levels of popular approval than any departing president in the second half of the twentieth century.

10

"No One Else Can Do This"

BUSH, CLINTON, AND THE RETRENCHMENT THAT WASN'T

George H. W. Bush and Bill Clinton

"THE COLD WAR IS OVER," Ronald Reagan said on the day he turned the presidency over to George H. W. Bush. George Shultz thought so too: "All over but the shouting." As the long conflict between the United States and the Soviet Union wound down, many of the key ingredients of America's global activism also seemed to disappear. One was a ready supply—particularly after the final Soviet collapse in 1991—of formidable enemies. That year Colin Powell, who was JCS chairman under Bush, told an interviewer in mock dismay, "I'm running out of demons. I'm running out of villains. I'm down to Castro and Kim Il Sung." In the ensuing decade, the United States faced a colorful cast of true international bad guys, but its foreign policy no longer revolved around the dangers created by one or two major hostile powers. Dick Cheney, Bush's defense secretary, summed up the situation: "The threats have become remote, so remote they are difficult to discern."[1]

In this new setting, American public opinion changed abruptly. When asked in February 1989 to identify the most important problems facing the country, only 10 percent of those polled chose international issues, down from 22 percent just two years earlier. By May—still six months before the fall of the Berlin Wall—the number had dropped to 6 percent. It did not rise above that level over the course of the next two presidential elections.[2]

With the public giving foreign policy lower priority, it commanded fewer resources. "We have more will than wallet," Bush lamented in his inaugural address. In the four years of his administration, defense spending dropped 15 percent. After eight years of Bill Clinton, it had fallen another 14 percent. The number of U.S. troops deployed overseas fell from 453,000 to 210,000 during their presidencies. (More than 80 percent of the decrease was made by Bush.) Other budgets were also cut. By 1995, Congress had reduced "foreign operations" spending—funds for the State Department, plus foreign aid—to its lowest level in twenty years. Thirty embassies and consulates were closed.[3]

Doubts about America's large international role were not limited to questions of cost. Presidents and their spokesmen found themselves under new pressure to justify foreign involvements. They often reached for economic rationales, but their explanations were not always successful. In the fall of 1990, as the nation debated its response to the invasion of Kuwait, Secretary of State James Baker made a much-derided claim that "jobs . . . jobs . . . jobs" were at risk if the United States did not act. The end of the Cold War had left policy makers in a conceptual vacuum. Bill Clinton regularly challenged aides to do better in expressing foreign policy goals. Whatever replaced "containment" should, he thought, fit on a bumper sticker.[4]

With the strategists of the national security priesthood having trouble enunciating new policies, others outside the priesthood seemed ready to challenge their authority. Officials who handled trade and finance had long occupied a second tier in the world of big-power diplomacy. Now a revised hierarchy seemed possible. Clinton's trade negotiator, Charlene Barshefsky, mused to *The New Yorker* that "globalization" was making military alliances obsolete. She felt trade agreements—of which the Clinton administration concluded more than three hundred—were the modern way to bring nations together in common cause. In 1999, *Time* magazine's famous "Committee to Save the World" cover—with its picture of Treasury secretary Robert Rubin; his deputy, Lawrence Summers; and Federal Reserve Board chairman Alan Greenspan—telegraphed the same idea. Economists were taking over from diplomats.[5]

A generational shift confirmed the feeling that American foreign policy had entered a new era. In the 1992 election, Bill Clinton defeated a man twenty-two years his senior, becoming the first president to be born after World War II and the only one since the start of the Cold War with no military record. Other baby boomers joined his administration. Not since John Kennedy had power passed so noticeably from one generation to the next. Henry Kissinger complained that national security decisions were now being made by people whose views were formed "in the trenches of the Vietnam protest movement." He claimed they were "suspicious of the role of power" in foreign policy and considered traditional American interests "outdated."[6]

These many transformations suggested that retrenchment after the Cold War would be more profound—materially, conceptually, even psychologically—than the scaling back that had followed the Korean and Vietnam Wars. In the early 1990s, it was hard to identify the geopolitical need for anything like the activist global role that the United States had established over many decades. The details of a new strategy were still unclear, but doing less seemed certain to be one of its central themes.

What happened was very different. Far from downsizing America's global role, the 1990s began with the largest U.S. combat operations since Vietnam—a military campaign cheered on by the public more enthusiastically than any war since 1945. In two terms as president, Bill Clinton deployed units of the armed forces in support of his policy no less than eighty-four times. By the end of the decade, defense spending was rising again. America, Clinton regularly boasted, was the "indispensable nation." European commentators began using a less favorable term: *hyperpower*. Even Kissinger seemed anxious about the global reaction to Washington's activism. Around the world, he wrote, many believed that the United States acted "arbitrarily, or inexplicably, or arrogantly."[7]

American foreign policy in the decade after the Cold War was the story of a widely anticipated pullback that didn't materialize. Even while spending a smaller share of GDP on national security, the United States enlarged its role in the world. Its alliances had been expected to atrophy; instead, they grew. And although a dangerous adversary had disappeared, policy makers' conceptions of their global responsibility expanded. Americans *felt* indispensable. What had happened to retrenchment?

IN 1989 THE NEW MAN in the White House did not really agree with Ronald Reagan that the Cold War was over. George Bush was the only president in the second half of the twentieth century elected to succeed someone of the same party. He took office convinced of the need for new directions. At home, Bush said he yearned for "greater tolerance," for a "kinder" and "gentler" America.[8]

Foreign policy was another matter altogether. The new president thought Reagan's diplomacy had overdone the gentleness thing. U.S. policy had been much too passive in responding to Soviet initiatives. In Europe, NATO was being weakened, and West Germany, one had to fear, was being lured into semineutralism. To protect its global position, the United States had to throw Moscow back on the defensive. "If we don't regain the lead," Bush fretted to his advisers, "things will fall apart."[9]

To blunt Gorbachev's initiatives, the new administration aimed to redefine Western goals in ambitious terms that Moscow could not easily accept. That meant going beyond arms control to demand liberalization in the Eastern bloc and a pullback of Soviet power. European publics needed to be reminded that the division of Europe was what had started the Cold War in the first place. James Baker, the new secretary of state, reported early on to the president that the entire issue of German reunification was rapidly "coming back." The only question was, who would "grab it first"? When Bush began to talk about the issue on his first European tour, at midyear, Soviet leaders took note—nervously. Why, Eduard Shevardnadze, the Soviet foreign minister, asked Hans-Dietrich Genscher, his West German counterpart, was the United States "fanning the flames against East Germany?"[10]

Having already staked out a position in favor of German unity, Washington did not have to improvise a new strategy when the entire edifice of Soviet control in Eastern Europe collapsed in the fall of 1989. The United States simply adopted a more radical version of the same approach. It had made political liberalization and the rollback of Soviet power the heart of its answer to Gorbachev. After the fall of the Wall, these themes became the core of an American campaign to redraw the map of Europe.

Support for German reunification placed the United States in opposition to the Soviet Union and almost all its own allies. François Mitterrand warned Bush that the revival of German power could become a casus belli. If mishandled, it would set Europe back to 1913. "We could lose everything," he said. Gorbachev's spokesman was angrily dismissive. Not a single European country wanted Germany reunified, he said. The issue was "not on the agenda." Margaret Thatcher considered Germany "by its very nature a destabilizing rather than a stabilizing force in Europe." She urged the United States to stall reunification for years. Until East Germany showed it could sustain a working democracy, Thatcher wanted unity off the table.[11]

How did Washington respond to these objections from Europe's most important leaders? The president and his colleagues listened respectfully, offering friendship and dialogue. But they were not moved by others' appeals and largely ignored them. When Bush received Thatcher's letter about East Germany, he deflected it with a cheery promise to "[put] our feet up at Camp David for a really good talk." Baker's public statements were also evasive. "Change," he told journalists, "is not necessarily destabilizing."[12]

Even when the administration tried to reassure nervous friends and allies, it kept the commitments it made to them only as long as it was convenient to do so. When the president and Gorbachev met in Malta in December 1989, the Soviet leader proposed that the issue of German unity be put aside indefinitely. "Let history decide," he pleaded. For his part, Bush was all goodwill and understanding. "I have conducted myself in ways not to complicate your life," he said. "That's why I have not jumped up and down on the Berlin Wall." He promised to "do nothing to recklessly try to speed up reunification." That was in December. In January the United States reversed course, deciding to "hit the accelerator" and achieve unity as quickly as possible. Gorbachev was not advised of the change.[13]

AMERICAN OFFICIALS had several reasons for preferring rapid unification. One was to head off possible chaos as East Germany's institutions dissolved. As East German citizens went to the polls in the winter of 1990, the Bush administration's rhetoric encouraged them to vote out leaders who favored gradualism. A second reason was to settle Germany's future before the pliable Gorbachev was replaced, as many thought he would be, by an old-style Soviet hard-liner.[14]

Yet the most important goal of rapid unification was, in American eyes, to reduce the influence of other governments. That was the motive behind the creation of the so-called Two Plus Four, an inclusive forum designed—or so Washington claimed—to give the two German states and all four World War II victors a hearing for their views. Two Plus Four was the most important U.S. initiative in the diplomacy of German unity, but its real aim was to keep other governments in line, monitor their thinking, block any initiatives of which the United States disapproved, and wrap up a deal quickly. The other victorious powers were to have no serious role.[15]

Bush made his approach clear when he met with Thatcher and Mitterrand in April 1990 to go over the agenda of the first Two Plus Four meeting. The president wanted to make sure that nothing significant was discussed. The group "should *not*," he argued,

> negotiate over Germany's right to remain a full-member of NATO; should *not* decide the fate of allied conventional or nuclear forces on the territory of the current FRG; should *not* agree on the future size of united Germany's armed forces; and should *not* replace the

> old four-power rights with new discriminatory limits on German sovereignty.[16]

Washington wanted the two German governments to work out the important details of unity on their own, without interference by others. At every step, the United States would act as Bonn's protector. The strategy, deception included, was a total success. Even today, German reunification remains associated with the Two Plus Four framework, whose very name made it sound like an instrument of diplomatic fair play. In fact, it did not resolve a single important issue.

Frustrated by American policy, other governments kept proposing alternative plans for European security. Both Gorbachev and Thatcher had the somewhat bizarre idea that after unification Germany should remain, indefinitely, a member of both NATO and the Warsaw Pact. The United States paid no attention to this suggestion and accepted no constraint on Germany's full membership in the Atlantic alliance. Nor, despite years of Russian claims to the contrary, did it promise not to add Eastern European members to NATO. American officials did draw up a list of measures to reassure Moscow that German unity would not threaten Russian security—all of them vague and relatively minor steps that the United States would have favored anyway. Even the pledge—adopted at NATO's London summit in June 1990—that the alliance would begin a process of (unspecified) change, was rammed through without the time-consuming consultative courtesies that are NATO's hallmark. The president's deadpan explanation: the issue was "too important . . . to review with the allies in the usual way."[17]

George Bush's view of reunification had a personal dimension. He said he had "a comfort level" about letting Germany regain its old boundaries. If others did not trust the Germans, that was their problem. Yet personal trust was not the true driver of American policy. Even without Europe's bloody memories, U.S. officials recognized that their ally's future direction was unpredictable and possibly dangerous. Chancellor Kohl had made that clear enough when, less than three weeks after the Wall came down, he gave a speech calling for reunification; he did not consult Americans or even his own foreign minister beforehand. Polls showing that 58 percent of Germans wanted to withdraw from both Cold War alliances deepened U.S. concern.[18]

The president and his advisers were just as determined to constrain

Germany's future options as any European leaders were. But others aimed to do so by saddling Germany with special restrictions and stalling until a better solution emerged. Bush warned Thatcher and Mitterrand that this approach was "a prescription for future instability." The Germans would resent second-class status and, inevitably, throw it off. Washington felt the best way to keep its potentially dangerous ally confined within NATO over the long run was to support its aims in the short. At bottom, the difference between European and American views was a matter of power. The United States was, as it had been in the early 1980s, the only power confident that it could manage an international upheaval, accept major changes in the status quo, and come out better off than it had been before.[19]

The unification of Germany at the end of the Cold War has for years been treated as a masterpiece of the diplomatic art—a brilliant improvisation that left Europe "whole, free, and at peace." It *was* a masterpiece—but not because the participants worked together harmoniously. They were deeply fearful and suspicious of one another, divided in their aims, and thoroughly confused about how to achieve them. American policy makers salvaged a successful outcome by transcending this discord. They steered the process to a positive conclusion by exploiting their partners' disarray and even by deceiving them. Had the United States deferred to its friends and allies, the results would have been far worse for all concerned.

EARLY ON THE MORNING of August 2, 1990, the Bush foreign policy team gathered at the White House to discuss a new and unexpected crisis. Hours earlier Iraqi forces had stormed across the border into neighboring Kuwait. For the first time in decades, a major issue of war and peace was not viewed in East-West terms, and the president and his advisers were not sure how to think about it. In a speech scheduled for later that day, Bush planned to say that, though the Cold War was over, the United States had to be able to "respond to threats in whatever corner of the globe they may occur." That morning he was much more tentative. As he later recalled, "I had no idea what our options were." An unfocused discussion ended without consensus.[20]

Brent Scowcroft, the president's national security adviser, left the meeting "appalled." What he had heard suggested "resignation to the invasion and even adaptation to a *fait accompli*." Huddling with his staff afterward about how to sharpen up the next session, he agreed to give what they called "the Churchill speech"—a spine-stiffener. When the National Security Council reconvened on August 3, Scowcroft explained what was at stake. Letting a dictator swallow up a friendly state in a vital region, he announced, "should not be a policy option." The costs to American credibility, regional stability, and energy security were too great. Bush agreed. The status quo, he told the group, was "intolerable." And he told the American people too: "This will not stand."[21]

Yet the hesitations that had produced a bad first meeting were not fully dispelled by the Churchillian rhetoric of the second. Senior officials, from the president on down, could not be sure that the public would support a strong military response to Saddam's invasion. They recalled the ways in which American power had misfired in the past. They knew that previous administrations had—above all, in Vietnam—failed to frame clear and achievable goals. Communication between civilians and the military had often been weak, and trust even weaker. Allies were ignored, and American forces had usually carried the entire burden of repelling aggression. Long and inconclusive conflict had demoralized the troops. Congress, when shown too little deference, became the president's enemy, as did the media. Public opinion often turned hostile.[22]

The president and his advisers became convinced that war was a necessity, but they knew that for many it was a very close call. Extraordinary effort would be needed to win over friendly governments, the American public, the Congress, even their own generals. No one's support could be taken for granted; everyone had to be courted. In the end, the campaign to marshal support for a tough and uncompromising policy shaped the way the war was waged and the way it was concluded. Bush's maximalism came with a very long to-do list attached.

From the start, the effort to work with other governments showed the doubts and suspicions to be overcome. Prince Bandar, the Saudi ambassador in Washington, told Cheney and Powell that he had heard American offers of help before. In 1979, he reminded them, Jimmy Carter promised to protect Saudi Arabia, dispatching planes that he then admitted were unarmed. Saudi suspicions were fully reciprocated. Scowcroft thought Arab leaders would "end up in a compromise with Saddam." "My worry," Bush said, "is the lack of Saudi will, and that they might bug out." The United States actually refused to send a high-level delegation to Riyadh for emergency consultations unless the Saudis agreed in advance to accept U.S troops. When Cheney arrived to seal the deal, he still doubted that the king would go through with it. The American ambassador warned him not to scare their hosts by talking about a too-large force, but Cheney paid no attention. He *wanted* to scare the Saudis, to make them see that urgent action was needed. Quickly King Fahd agreed. Explaining his decision to the princes who had assembled to meet the secretary of defense, he sighed, "The Kuwaitis waited, and now they are living in our hotels."[23]

DECIDING TO DEFEND Saudi Arabia—what became known as Operation Desert Shield—was the Bush administration's easy first step. But the president and his advisers were not in agreement about whether to go further and seek to retake Kuwait by force. The most significant critic of this goal was Colin Powell himself. The JCS chairman told his Pentagon colleagues that he was "opposed to dramatic action without the President having popular support." To Bush, he was still more negative. "Before we start talking about how many divisions, carriers, and fighter wings we need," he said, "we have to ask, to achieve what end?" Like the Saudis, Powell feared that the United States would deploy a massive force far from home only to change course when domestic opposition mounted. He didn't want to "leave tens of thousands of restless young Americans there, baking in the sun, under Islam's prohibitions, wondering which way their government would go." Better, Powell thought, to pressure Saddam with economic sanctions.[24]

Bush was unpersuaded. He was no more inclined to gamble on the success of sanctions than he had been to let German unity work itself out over the long term. The president and his civilian advisers listened to Powell's objections and to his pitch for sanctions as an alternative to force. Then they told him to start planning a military offensive. Even so, Powell did not let up. Throughout the fall of 1990, he tried again and again to undermine support for using force to drive Iraq from Kuwait. He lobbied Secretary of State Baker as a potential ally. He encouraged his predecessor, Admiral William Crowe, to push for sanctions in congressional testimony. He even told the president's air force briefers not to make a bombing campaign sound too attractive.[25]

Powell failed to keep George Bush, Sr., from attacking Iraq (as he later failed with Bush Jr.). But he did keep him from waging war on the cheap. When the decision was made at a White House meeting in October to prepare to push the Iraqis out of Kuwait, Powell announced that he needed half a million troops to do so—twice as many as were planned at that moment. Others gasped. Not the president. He preferred a cheaper, easier solution and kept asking Powell whether airpower alone might do the job. "A couple of bombs and they'll fold," he suggested. But Bush always backed down. A massive ground force was Powell's "price" for supporting the war, and the president was ready to pay it.[26]

Dick Cheney had his own disagreement with George Bush. The secretary of defense thought it was unnecessary—and too risky—to seek congressional approval for the war. But the president insisted on going the extra mile. His aim was not to gain legal authority to order American troops into battle (like most presidents, he felt he already had that), but to build political support. Throughout the fall, the administration's vote counters admitted that a resolution authorizing the use of force to liberate Kuwait would probably fail. Their assessment did not faze Bush. He assured aides that he was prepared to go to war no matter how the vote came out. He felt ready to defy Congress if it defied him. He did not feel he could ignore it.[27]

Cheney and the vote counters proved wrong about the congressional vote, but only barely. In both the House and Senate, a solid majority of Democrats were opposed. Many derided the idea of a "war for oil." Energy needs, Ted Kennedy said, did not justify spilling "a single drop of American blood." Pat Moynihan agreed there was no real need to act. "All that's happened is that one nasty little country invaded a littler but just as nasty country." In the Senate, the resolution authorizing the president to use force passed by just five votes—52 to 47. Only three Democrats outside the South voted yes; without them the measure would have failed. But congressional opponents of the war did not have the public with them. An ABC-*Washington Post* poll showed 66 percent approval of the president's policy. Once the bombing began on January 15, 1991, the number of those in favor immediately jumped another 18 points.[28]

BUSH HAD NOW checked every box on his to-do list. He had near-unanimous support in the UN Security Council, the approval of Congress, strong public backing, troops from thirty-four countries, and financial pledges so great that the war almost turned a profit. A unified administration was behind him. The president also waited through last-minute rounds of diplomacy, by Baker and then by Soviet emissaries to Baghdad. Most impressive, Bush managed to mobilize a global coalition without really limiting American freedom of action. "It was important," he judged, "to reach out to the rest of the world, but even more important to keep the strings of control tightly in our hands."[29]

The only thing that the administration's careful preparations did not anticipate was exactly what it got when the ground war began on February 24: a sudden, smashing victory. Reports from the front suggested that the bulk of Iraq's elite Republican Guard units had been destroyed, dispersed, or captured. In Washington, officials could not identify any unmet U.S. objectives. Mowing down enemy units as they streamed north from Kuwait would only generate embarrassing film footage. (Bush himself felt it would not be "chivalrous.") A mere "hundred hours" after the start of the invasion, Powell—at the president's direction—told his commanders to stand down.[30]

Why the United States wrapped up this massive enterprise so quickly has long been the most contentious question about the war. Administration officials have always had a clear and simple answer. The coalition had just one agreed aim, they said, and that was to liberate Kuwait. Moving the goalposts would jeopardize international support. Encouraging domestic upheaval in Iraq might cause it to break up, adding to the region's turmoil. In any case, policy makers thought, defeat had surely weakened Saddam. He was likely to lose power even without continuing military pressure.

So the president and his advisers said and thought at the time. Still, their deliberations remain a puzzle. For they were deeply uneasy about the future of the region if Saddam held on. Bush himself had brooded on the key unresolved question. "I don't see how it will work with Saddam in power," he wrote in his diary just before the war began, "and I am very, very wary." The United States had not said publicly, nor decided privately, that the Iraqi leader had to go. "Yet in many ways," the president continued, "it's the only answer in order to get a new start for Iraq in the family of nations."[31]

Administration policy makers knew that their huge military victory gave them an opportunity to dictate more favorable peace terms. When Baker cautioned against demanding that Iraq leave its tanks behind in Kuwait—because the UN had not called for it—Bush simply waved the concern aside. Having won big, the United States faced "a new ballgame," he said, "and *we were not bound by our earlier demands*." Other officials also believed it would be possible to enlarge their goals. The American ambassador to the UN, Thomas Pickering, came up with a plan, which had strong backing across the administration, for a demilitarized zone in southern Iraq. Allied forces would patrol it, to keep Saddam on the defensive. Pickering was confident he could get Security Council support.[32]

The public's rally-round-the-flag response to Desert Storm also gave Bush a chance to seek Saddam's ouster. As U.S. forces rolled into Kuwait, polls found that 92 percent of Americans wanted to keep fighting until Iraq withdrew from Kuwait. Fully 75 percent were ready to do so until Saddam was deposed. And 53 percent said they would be disappointed if he were even alive when the war ended. Victory had a similar effect internationally. American prestige was at an all-time high. Far from warning against an escalation of war aims, Saudi officials actually endorsed a more demanding approach. When he arrived in Riyadh for consultations after the cease-fire, Baker was greeted, to his surprise, with proposals to support the Shi'ite and Kurdish insurrections against Saddam's rule that were just then beginning.[33]

Merely driving Saddam from Kuwait, then, was *not* the coalition's only goal. It wanted to make Iraq take responsibility for the war and the damage done to its neighbor, and to keep it from being a threat in the future. To achieve these additional goals, the international community eventually ended up imposing an elaborate set of constraints on the Iraqi government. These included reparations payments, control of oil exports, limits on the size and capability of its army, and inspections to guarantee that it was no longer trying to develop weapons of mass destruction. The United States began to garrison troops in Saudi Arabia and to keep a larger military presence in the Gulf.[34]

All these additional measures were the direct result of the Bush administration's decision to wind down the war without first driving out Saddam. It took this step in large measure out of deference to the president's professional military advisers. Powell had been against retaking Kuwait from the beginning. If the job had to be done, he wanted the campaign to be very big—and very brief. The same thinking guided General Norman Schwarzkopf, the commander of Desert Storm, in all his end-of-war choices. Meeting on March 2 with the Iraqi chief of staff to formalize a truce, Schwarzkopf underscored the speed with which his forces planned to withdraw. He reassured the Iraqis—as though the United States had to convince them of its goodwill, rather than the other way around—that soon there would "not be one single coalition force member in the recognized borders of Iraq." He would send units home "as rapidly as we can get them out." Schwarzkopf opposed Pickering's plan to patrol a demilitarized zone inside Iraq because, he told Baker, it would delay the U.S. withdrawal. Getting the fighting over with, and the boys home, as soon as possible was the American high command's supreme goal.[35]

Even the military's rush for the exits cannot, however, fully explain why the United States ended the war the way it did. For more than six months, the president had kept Powell and the generals committed to a strategy that they did not like, and he certainly could have kept doing it if he had wanted. Something in Bush's own thinking made him too want to wrap up the war quickly. Uneasiness about the entire venture—and in particular about keeping the public behind it—had guided him and his team from the beginning. It bothered him at the end of the war as well.

From August to February, from the invasion to the cease-fire, every decision that American policy makers took reflected intense uncertainty about public support. It was the reason they described what was at stake in such exaggerated and unconvincing ways (from Baker's "jobs . . . jobs . . . jobs" remarks to Bush's own comparisons between Saddam and Hitler). It was why the president felt he needed to have the buy-in of the UN and Congress, to have other governments contributing troops and money, to have all his senior generals on board. Anxiety about public opinion (and how it would respond if the killing seemed excessive) was on his mind when he decided to call the fighting off. Finally, it was a source of worry when he realized that a decisive result had eluded him. Failing to bring down Saddam meant the struggle against him would drag on, and that the public would remember it differently. "It hasn't been a clean end," he wrote in his diary, contrasting it with the Japanese defeat in 1945. "There is no battleship Missouri surrender. This is what's missing to make this akin to WWII, to separate Kuwait from Korea and Vietnam."[36]

BARELY HALFWAY THROUGH his presidency, George Bush had now handled two huge international crises in very different ways. In 1990 he oversaw a German settlement whose every detail the United States insisted on resolving on the most favorable possible terms; he did not want a good result to depend on unforeseeable future developments. In 1991, by contrast, Bush ended up with a victory in the Persian Gulf War that left many fundamental issues completely undecided.

The difference between these two cases was enormous, but they had a common thread. At a moment of unchallenged American preeminence, the president and his advisers were still feeling their way, trying to figure out what sort of foreign policy would enjoy public backing. For all its victories, the administration was unsure whether the United States would play an active role in Europe even a few years down the road. The president was so uneasy about maintaining political support for combat operations in Iraq that he and his team measured their duration in *hours.*

The worry—shared by Washington policy makers in every decade of the Cold War and since then too—that America's global role would be undermined by popular indifference never had a more palpable impact than it did in the latter half of Bush's term. Once the Gulf War was over, the president recoiled at anything suggesting the need for increased American commitment. The downsizing of policy was particularly controversial in connection with the slow-motion breakup of Yugoslavia and the Soviet Union in 1991. Here were two multiethnic states, long ruled by Communist parties whose political monopoly had clearly become unsustainable. Each was eventually brought down by challengers to its central government, in revolutions much like the ones that had brought down the Soviet bloc two years earlier.

In 1989 the collapse of Communist Party rule in Eastern Europe had had full American support. Now, however, the United States tried to stand aloof. The administration went so far as to criticize those who were challenging the old order. Visiting Belgrade in June 1991, Secretary Baker warned separatist leaders that Washington was not with them. He was known to believe, in a widely quoted phrase, that the United States had "no dog in that fight."[37]

Bush took a similar stance against Ukrainian independence when he visited Kiev in early August. He condemned what he called "suicidal nationalism based on ethnic hatred." Two weeks later, when Soviet hardliners launched a coup against Gorbachev, the president's hesitant response bordered painfully on acceptance. "I think at this point," he told reporters, "what we do is simply watch the situation unfold." ("You've got to be careful," Scowcroft had counseled him. Of the plotters trying to oust Mikhail Gorbachev, he said, "We may have to deal with these guys.")[38]

The president's advisers did not directly challenge his shrinking conception of America's role. They knew he had his reasons and his political needs. The country was slowly coming out of recession; Bush was running for reelection and feared seeming too focused on foreign policy; the defense budget had surged in the 1980s and was ripe for cutbacks; the public was sick of providing security for others and wanted a peace dividend.

All these impulses came together in the president's extraordinary State of the Union address in January 1992. In it, he admitted that he had sometimes greeted the end of the Cold War too coolly. "I didn't always show the joy that was in my heart," Bush confessed. He wanted to leave no doubt that domestic needs now took unquestioned priority. "There's a mood among us," he acknowledged. "People are worried. There's been talk of decline." Fortunately, the country's Cold War sacrifices were over. "Now we can look homeward even more and move to set right what needs to be set right."[39]

This was Bush's most important policy speech of the year, perhaps of his entire presidency, and the near-total absence of any reflection on America's future global role was stunning. In the president's confusion, others saw opportunity. Richard Nixon charged that the administration's aid to Russia was too modest. ("The stakes are high, and we are playing as if it were a penny-ante game.") Bill Clinton put forward an assistance plan designed to make Bush's ideas look timid and unimaginative.[40]

Still broader efforts to sketch out a more robust U.S. strategy came from within the administration itself. Of these, the most famous, and most important, was the one developed at the Pentagon. In Secretary Cheney's view, the transition from war to peace—the necessary and inevitable dismantling of military capabilities after conflict—was "something America has always done badly before." In the final year of the administration, the secretary of defense and his team produced a succession of statements outlining what was intended to be a more successful approach. Some of these documents were public and unclassified; others were secret. But all of them sounded the same notes. Vital U.S. interests could be jeopardized even in a world in which America faced no real peer competitor. Coalitions and multilateral institutions could not be counted on to solve major security problems unless Washington led the way. To limit conflict in the post–Cold War world, the United States had to remain the principal source of global security.[41]

Like Bush himself, Dick Cheney acknowledged that uncertainty about public support was a major question mark for future American strategy. In congressional testimony of February 1992, just days after the president's State of the Union, he suggested ways of responding to this uncertainty. Future military operations had to be quick and decisive because the interests at stake were bound to be "less immediate" than in the past. When not directly threatened, Cheney explained, the American people weren't going to put up with long, drawn-out campaigns. The need for quick results would make technological superiority increasingly important.[42]

Later in the year, an early draft of one of these Pentagon planning documents was leaked to *The New York Times*, provoking charges that Cheney and his team were trying to define national security policy on their own. The criticism was true enough. The Defense Department planners did see a void of strategic thought and aimed to fill it with their own ideas. But their concern about the administration's seeming drift was widespread in Washington at the time. Across departments and agencies, across the branches of government, and across the political spectrum, the same question was being asked: had the president and his advisers, fresh from victories in Europe and the Middle East, given up thinking about what came next?

Even the State Department seemed to have its doubts. When it came time for the outgoing secretary of state to deliver a parting policy assessment to the incoming Clinton team, Lawrence Eagleburger—the career diplomat who had succeeded Baker—described a role for the United States that was, like Cheney's, significantly larger than the one the Bush administration had drifted toward by the end. "For better or worse," Eagleburger wrote, "people and governments still look to us to make sense of the changes swirling around them and show some initiative and purpose. No one else can do this."[43]

DURING THE 1992 CAMPAIGN, Bill Clinton criticized the Bush administration for standing by while the breakup of Yugoslavia turned into genocide. By the time he became president, only the struggle for Bosnia—the most diverse of the former Yugoslav republics—was still unresolved. There Bosnian Serb militias—who received military support from the government of Serbia proper—were gaining a bloody upper hand over the country's Croat and Muslim communities. Violence on this scale, Clinton told his very first NSC meeting, could not simply be left to the Europeans. The United States had to get involved, or "nothing will happen."

All the same, Clinton had not been president a hundred days before deciding to back down. He and his advisers had wanted to end the UN arms embargo to the Bosnian Muslims and to threaten the Bosnian Serbs with bombing attacks if they did not cease their campaign of ethnic cleansing. On an early trip to Europe, however, Secretary of State Warren Christopher discovered that the allies would not buy the new approach.

Having encountered opposition, Clinton's team was not prepared to make Bosnia the "manhood test [that breaks] NATO." Reluctantly, they scaled back their goals. The administration decided to settle for "containing" the spread of violence.[44]

To Clinton early in his first term, this helplessness seemed to typify post–Cold War policy making. The new president complained that the United States had "traded in one big problem for a whole bunch of little ones." Ethnic strife in the Balkans and Rwanda, collapsing political order in Somalia and Haiti, North Korea's effort to acquire nuclear weapons, Iraq's assassination plot against former president Bush, Mexico's failing currency—these issues might not have quite the impact on national or global security that Cold War crises did. "But they sure don't feel little," Clinton said, "when they're blowing up in your face."[45]

The new administration saw few openings to use American power constructively. When U.S. peacekeepers in Somalia were attacked, and eighteen of them killed, in October 1993, the president canceled the mission. A week later in Haiti, a rock-throwing mob kept an American naval vessel from landing to start up a new assistance program. As for Bosnia, Colin Powell, who stayed on as JCS chairman under Clinton, explained all the reasons not to intervene to his new colleagues. To this, Madeleine Albright had a famous retort. "What are you saving this superb military for, Colin," she asked, "if we can't use it?" Albright's comment was widely circulated, and it won her a small rhetorical victory. But it did not change the policy. For the time being, the United States remained a bystander in the Balkan wars.[46]

It took Clinton and his advisers more than two years to shake off their hesitation. Scaling back their goals, they slowly realized, did not make them any more attainable. Nor did it make failure less damaging. Eventually the Balkans became the proving ground for a new approach. In the spring of 1995, after a new upsurge in the fighting—and the shocking execution of eight thousand Muslim men and boys at Srebrenica—American policy makers stopped seeing Bosnia as a second-tier problem in which second-best results were acceptable. It was no longer merely a "humanitarian" issue. NATO looked weak, and that, the president told his advisers, was "doing enormous damage to the United States and to our standing in the world." As though to prove Clinton's point, Jacques Chirac, the newly elected French president, joked that "the position of leader of the Free World is vacant."[47]

But how to respond? If Bosnia was a major problem that had to be solved, the president said, "We have to seize control of [it]." Clinton and his advisers decided that the only way to end the disagreements among the allies was to stop listening to them. American policy makers would settle on a course of action and then send senior officials to Europe—to report their decision, not to consult. Allied acquiescence was expected. The United States, national security adviser Anthony Lake believed, was the "big dog" of NATO. If Washington set a firm enough example, the smaller dogs would surely fall in line.[48]

To its newly decisive style, the administration added more ambitious substance. "Containing" Balkan instability was now discarded as an acceptable goal. The United States had to envision a better outcome than merely keeping genocide at manageable levels. American planners were told to put aside incremental ideas and to work backward from a desirable end-state. The contrast between European policy and that of the United States was striking. In mid-1995, the French—themselves appalled by the failure of their peacekeeping effort—were prepared to deploy thousands of new troops to Bosnia to defend peacekeeping units that were already in place. Their mission, however, was not to forge a new strategy. It was only to shore up the old one.

The U.S. approach to the Balkans was far more muscular. It began with a call for diplomacy, but Washington told both its allies and the warring parties that if negotiations did not produce a peaceful solution, it would turn quickly to military coercion. The two steps turned out to be almost simultaneous. Even before U.S. proposals were fully laid out and the parties had a chance to react to them, a new outrage—the Sarajevo "marketplace bombing" of August 1995—produced calls for action. The Bosnian foreign minister, Mohammad Sacirbey (known as Mo), phoned Washington immediately. "No more fucking around with the UN!" he screamed over the line to an American official. "You people have to bring in NATO airstrikes *now*!" Screaming was no longer necessary. Washington was eager to be involved. More than sixty planes from U.S. bases in Italy and a carrier in the Adriatic began attacking Serb positions around Sarajevo.[49]

NATO's bombing produced what all previous policy had failed to achieve—a true peace conference, held (in a nod to the role of airpower) at Wright-Patterson Air Force Base, near Dayton, Ohio, in November 1995. In preparing for the talks, Richard Holbrooke, who led the U.S. team, argued for an escalation of U.S. aims. Military power had created a chance for a breakthrough, but the moment would pass. Another fragile cease-fire was not the right goal. To Holbrooke, the warring parties had to be charmed, bullied, threatened, bribed, wheedled, compelled by whatever means to accept what Washington saw as the only real solution—a single, multiethnic Bosnian state. Anything not nailed down at Dayton, Holbrooke knew, would never be agreed at all. He summarized his all-or-nothing strategy: "Better a high benchmark than a weak compromise."[50]

In the end, Dayton fell short of its ultimate aim. Holbrooke achieved only a peaceful divided state, not a peaceful united one. Yet it was a remarkable achievement. The United States had mobilized and used military power where its allies had only dithered. It had brought a bloody ethnic war to a close through focused, purposeful diplomacy. It punctured the idea that there was nothing to be done about barbarism and disorder. To gain relief from sanctions and from renewed bombing, the Serbs had been forced to back down. To get NATO peacekeepers on the scene, the Bosnian Muslims had accepted what they said they would not—"an unjust peace."[51]

Dayton's greatest impact, however, was felt beyond the Balkans. The United States was reinvigorated as a global force. The Europeans, Christopher told the president, "grumbled that we dominated Dayton, but they really know that it would not have gotten done otherwise." The French foreign minister, Hervé de Charette, put it more simply: "America is back."[52]

HOLBROOKE'S SUCCESS IN BOSNIA—a belated pivot from passivity to activism—might easily have proved an isolated Clinton victory. Instead, it was a turning point. Over the rest of the decade, the president and his advisers were now ready to brandish military power when they thought it could be useful. In internal debates and public declarations, the phrase "diplomacy backed by force" gained what Strobe Talbott, the deputy secretary of state, called a "talismanic quality." Clinton remained a thoughtful evangelist of globalization, of the idea that economic and technological change was leading the world in a peaceful direction. Even so, American policy makers had seen how easily this process could spin out of control. "Progress spreads quickly in our global neighborhood," the president said, but "problems can too." From Bosnia, he and his team learned that they—and, as they saw it, only they—had an answer to these problems. The United States—not the Europeans, not the UN—could keep the enemies of progress at bay. In the year after Dayton, while running for reelection, Clinton began describing America as "indispensable." Earlier this would have been a rhetorical flourish. Success in Bosnia made it a conviction.[53]

The idea that American power made globalization work, that it resolved conflicts and brought out history's hopeful possibilities, was expressed in policy toward every major region and problem. Early in the administration, Clinton had backed away from confrontation with China over human rights and put the full weight of relations on trade. He and his advisers treated Chinese accession to the World Trade Organization as a historic milestone. For the United States and China, the president said, expanding trade amounted to a "declaration of interdependence."[54]

Yet it was also the Clinton administration that, after Dayton, used military might to warn China not to put cooperation at risk. In March 1996, Beijing's effort to intimidate Taiwan—including by military exercises and missile firings—had provoked a minipanic on the island. Its economic boom was suddenly threatened by bank runs, capital flight, and a collapsing stock market. In response, the United States moved two aircraft carriers into position near the Taiwan Strait and warned Chinese officials that further action would have "grave consequences."[55]

This show of force—gunboat diplomacy, really—was as confrontational as any American action against China since Eisenhower. It would have been virtually unthinkable under any president since Nixon. Beijing, explained William Perry, the secretary of defense, had to be reminded who was the "premier military power in the Western Pacific." A month later, in Tokyo Bay, Clinton conveyed the message personally. Aboard one of the carriers that had taken part in the operation, he told cheering sailors that they had given the world "another example of America's power and America's character." The navy had helped to "calm a rising storm."[56]

Policy toward Russia rested on a similar mix of aims and ideas. No president had ever been more deeply committed to friendly relations with Russia than Bill Clinton was. Old enmity left no imprint on his thinking; reconciliation between former adversaries inspired him. He routinely told his advisers to come up with more resources to ease Russia's bumpy transition to a market economy. This hopeful outlook did not, however, stop Clinton from advancing another policy—the enlargement of NATO—that most Russians found hostile and provocative. How, they asked, could the United States deny that enlargement had an anti-Russian purpose? (American critics, from Brent Scowcroft to

George Kennan, raised the same question.) Wasn't it to check Russian influence that many prospective members, especially Poland, wanted to join NATO in the first place? Again and again, in the mid-1990s, Boris Yeltsin appealed to Clinton not to go ahead with this plan.[57]

The answer was always no. American policy makers believed that only an enlarged alliance would give the post–Cold War world structure and stability. The Balkans had already shown what happened when old antipathies had free rein—and when the United States did not meet its responsibilities. To the president and his advisers, NATO enlargement was the only safe way forward for Europe. Rather than leave the wreckage of the old Soviet bloc untended, they would gradually integrate its members into an American-led system of strategic cooperation.[58]

Clinton, to be sure, tried to help Yeltsin, just as Bush had tried to make it easier for Gorbachev to accept German unity. The United States invited Russia into the world's key "clubs"—the G-8, the World Trade Organization, Asian-Pacific summits. Russian troops were asked to join NATO peacekeepers in Bosnia. The alliance created a special forum for regular consultations with Russia. But one item was never on this list: anything implying that NATO's new members had second-class status. American policy makers did not want Eastern Europe to become a gray area of geopolitical uncertainty. Here the Clinton team's outlook was the same as the Bush administration's had been when it pushed German unity. It believed American power had to be used to solve problems when there was a chance to do so, rather than let them fester. The administration knew that to the Russians all this was so much "spinach"—an unappetizing dish the Americans (convincing no one) insisted was good for them. Though Clinton kept saying he "felt their pain," he never offered to change course. The United States was ready to proceed with enlargement, as Albright put it, "with or without [Russian] agreement."[59]

TWO PROBLEMS PREOCCUPIED American policy makers more than any others in 1998—Iraq, and a then-obscure terrorist organization known as al Qaeda. The administration feared that Saddam Hussein might, by defying the international controls imposed on Iraq after the war of 1991, be able to resume development of weapons of mass destruction. Al Qaeda became a top-tier worry for the United States when two American embassies in East Africa were bombed. For Clinton and his advisers, Iraq and terrorism were, of course, two separate problems. But as the year went on, they began to talk about them in very similar terms. And they responded to them in a similar way—with force. By the end of 1998, the administration's foreign policy team concluded that to deal with each problem it needed a new, more robust, more ambitious—and probably more militarized—strategy.

Iraq surfaced first. Saddam Hussein had long resented the UN weapons inspectors who monitored Iraq's compliance with its international obligations. In 1997 he launched an intensified campaign to oust them. Bill Clinton did not spare the hyperbole in public statements about this confrontation. Globalization's positive trends, he said after a briefing at the Pentagon in February 1998, were jeopardized by the "reckless acts of outlaw nations and an unholy axis of terrorists, drug traffickers, and organized international criminals." The threat posed by this "axis," he warned, would be even more dangerous if its members acquired weapons of mass destruction. In Clinton's portrayal, Saddam Hussein was a harbinger of challenges that the United States was likely to face in the century ahead—"a rogue state with weapons of mass destruction, ready to use them or provide them" to others.[60]

The confrontation with Iraq ebbed and flowed in the course of 1998, as Saddam probed the unity—and patience—of the major powers. When UN inspectors were finally forced out in mid-December, the United States (joined by Britain) retaliated with four days of bombing against military targets. Saddam, Clinton warned, was a threat to "the security of the world," and he confirmed an escalation of American aims. The "best way to end that threat once and for all," he said, "is with a new Iraqi government."[61]

Like Saddam, al Qaeda had preoccupied American intelligence and counterterrorism specialists long before 1998. (Its leader, Osama bin Laden, was indicted in a U.S. federal court for plotting to kill U.S. soldiers in Yemen six years earlier.) But in August two truck-bomb attacks on U.S. embassies in Kenya and Tanzania forced top policy makers to focus on the problem much more closely. The attacks killed more than two hundred people, including twelve Americans. In retaliation, the president ordered cruise missile strikes on a pharmaceutical factory in Sudan and on remote camps in Afghanistan—claiming (at least in the Sudanese case, with very fragmentary evidence) that these facilities had supported al Qaeda's operations and expanded its capabilities.[62]

As American policy makers thought through these new challenges, and as they offered public explanations of what was at stake in each case, they kept underscoring the similarities between them. In February, Clinton had spoken of the "unholy axis" of rogue states, terrorists, and transnational criminals, and he labeled Iraq a prominent part of it. America, he said after the August attacks, faced a "long, ongoing struggle between freedom and fanaticism, between the rule of law and terrorism." It could not opt out of the struggle. Ignoring Saddam now would only make him more dangerous in the future. "Mark my words," said the president, "he will develop weapons of mass destruction. He will deploy them, and he will use them."

For Clinton, al Qaeda posed the same sort of challenge. It had made the United States a target "precisely because we are leaders; because we act to advance peace, democracy, and basic human values; because we're the most open society on Earth; and because . . . we take an uncompromising stand against terrorism." Announcing the U.S.-U.K. attacks on Iraq in December, the president returned to these same themes. "In the century we're leaving," he said,

> America has often made the difference between chaos and community, fear and hope. Now, in a new century, we'll have a remarkable opportunity to shape a future more peaceful than the past, but only if we stand strong against the enemies of peace.[63]

From 1998 on Clinton and his advisers felt they were losing ground in their handling of both these problems. The United States and Britain—stymied by French, Russian, and Chinese foot-dragging—dealt with Iraq largely alone. In responding to terrorist attacks, the administration learned how difficult it was to find the right return address for military retaliation. American intelligence had failed to penetrate al Qaeda and knew little of its leadership. Lacking good information, senior officials more than once called off planned strikes on Bin Laden and his entourage.[64]

These frustrations produced a push within the administration for new policies. The president's team told him they needed more people, more money, more ideas, more commitment. George Tenet, still somewhat new in his job as CIA director, told Clinton in November that he needed a major increase in funding to head off an attack by al Qaeda on American territory. "We are at war," he told his own staff, exhorting them to spare no resources in expanding the agency's reach and knowledge. On December 18, he began writing a series of personal letters to the president, hoping that direct correspondence out of normal channels would better convey his alarm. Bin Laden, Tenet warned, might hit the United States at any time.[65]

American policy toward Saddam Hussein was changing too. When he announced the conclusion of the brief bombing campaign against Iraq on December 19, Clinton reiterated that the United States was committed to the goal of regime change. "So long as Saddam remains in power," the president said, "he will remain a threat to his people, his region, and the world." Sandy Berger, the national security adviser, charged the NSC staff with developing viable options to promote the Iraqi leader's ouster. The president's senior advisers, Berger told his staff, had concluded that they "could not keep playing cat-and-mouse games with Saddam." A more effective strategy had to be found.[66]

IN 1999 THE Clinton administration again went to war against Slobodan Milosevic—this time over Kosovo, Serbia's restive, Muslim-majority province. Their second "humanitarian intervention" showed how much more confident the president and his advisers had become in exercising American power. They felt they now knew what made Milosevic tick and would not be deflected by sham negotiations. The point of talking to him about Kosovo was simply to show others that talking was pointless. As one official said of the multilateral conference at Rambouillet, outside Paris, in February—a seeming failure—its real goal was to "get the war started with the Europeans locked in." To the Kosovar delegation Madeleine Albright explained how "diplomacy-backed-by-force" worked. "If you say yes and the Serbs say no," she promised them, "NATO will strike and go on striking until the Serb forces are out and NATO can go in."[67]

Milosevic had a chance to slow the momentum for war in an eleventh-hour bargaining session with Richard Holbrooke in late March 1999. But although he showed a little unexpected flexibility, it was too late. A leader with genocide on his record was not, Washington thought, entitled to the benefit of the doubt. Bombing commenced immediately, without even a pro forma round of further discussion within NATO. The United States was not looking to diplomacy to provide incremental improvement, nor to get another pause in the violence between Serbs and Kosovars. It wanted to remake the status quo in a way that only military action could accomplish.

Despite predictions of a short war, however, airpower failed to produce a quick success. Days passed, then weeks. The administration was criticized for providing an inadequate rationale for war, for failing to anticipate the vigor of Serb resistance, and for creating its own humanitarian crisis. (Of this last charge, there was no doubt. NATO's bombing led almost a million Kosovar Albanians to flee in panic.)[68]

Despite all the criticism, American policy hardened. As Clinton told his colleagues, "It's my war, and we're going to see it through to the end." Issues on which the United States had once been ready to compromise (such as whether all Serb forces had to leave Kosovo proper) became nonnegotiable. Allied suggestions for a bombing pause were ignored. Senior policy makers who had had doubts about the war now began to favor a ground invasion to break the impasse. "Failure," they told the media, "was not an option." When German chancellor Gerhard Schröder announced publicly that his government would block the use of NATO ground troops, the administration countered—also publicly—that his objections would have no effect. Only Milosevic's abrupt and essentially unconditional surrender in June saved the Clinton administration from having to roll over its ally's dissent.[69]

The United States and its allies had gone to war over Kosovo despite opposition from other major powers. Lacking a UN mandate, the bombing campaign generated the most vitriolic, anti-American rhetoric from Russian officials in many years. Chinese hostility was intensified by NATO's mistaken attack on the PRC's embassy in Belgrade, which killed three Chinese staffers. Yet the administration also saw how quickly such opposition subsided. While the war was still on, the Russians agreed to participate in a joint European-American mediation effort led by U.S. deputy secretary of state Strobe Talbott. When the fighting was over, both Moscow and Beijing joined in a UN Security Council resolution endorsing the terms that NATO had forced Milosevic to accept. Normally sticklers on issues of sovereignty, they accepted Washington's key demand, that Serbia cede control of Kosovo, even though it was universally acknowledged to be part of Serbia. The Russians actually sent peacekeepers, who served under a U.S. commander.[70]

From Kosovo, American officials also learned how easily damage to multilateral institutions could be repaired. Kofi Annan, the UN secretary general, quickly came to Washington's aid. NATO's campaign, he volunteered, had been "illegal," but its worthy goals made it "legitimate." Annan elaborated a new humanitarian principle, the "responsibility to protect," which envisioned international intervention against governments that abused their own people. Nothing better captured the Clinton administration's evolving view of international institutions than this denouement to the Kosovo war. The United States had done exactly what it wanted, launching a military campaign against another member of the United Nations without the support of the Security Council. It then won a multilateral seal of approval when the fighting stopped.[71]

This was a stupendous result, but even so Washington was not fully satisfied. Believing the Balkans to be unstable as long as Milosevic was around, the United States focused on what the war had not achieved: regime change. America's goal, said Albright, was to have its old foe "out of power, out of Serbia, and in the custody of the war crimes tribunal." There was a surge of U.S. assistance—covert and overt; technical, financial, and organizational—to Serbian opposition groups. Only when Milosevic fell in October 2000, after mass demonstrations against election fraud, did the Clinton administration feel the crises of the Yugoslav breakup might at last be over.[72]

AT THE END of the 1990s, it was hard to remember how many people had thought, when the decade began, that America's international role was declining. With the Cold War over, domestic support for an ambitious foreign policy seemed to be dropping off. Even those who favored continuing global leadership knew it would have to rest on a weaker material base.

Americans got their peace dividend after the Cold War. Defense spending fell from 5.5 percent of GDP in 1989 to 3.1 percent in 2001, and the number of troops abroad was cut by more than half. Yet retrenchment after success turned out to be very different from a pullback made necessary by failure. The United States felt none of the angry self-doubt that had followed the war in Vietnam, nor the sense, which followed Korea, that foreign policy had overheated into near-disaster. Victory in the Cold War did not discredit American strategy or American goals; it vindicated them. What followed was more of a breather than a real retrenchment, a stutter-step pause to take stock of the new world that was then emerging.

To this situation, the real parallel was the drift and ambivalence of American foreign policy right after World War II. In the wake of a huge victory, policy makers (like the public) did not reject international involvement so much as fail to see what it would be about, what an activist policy should try to achieve, and how. Within a couple of years after 1945, these questions were clarified. Critics of American policy became less likely to say that the country was doing too much, and more likely to say that it was too passive in the face of new threats.[73]

The same thing happened again in the 1990s. The Clinton administration's steady revival of an activist U.S. role was based on policy premises that were identical to those on which the policy makers of the Truman administration began to wage the Cold War. Their actions presumed that other governments were not really able to provide for their own security, and even less able to meet the requirements of true international leadership. The outlook of leaders elsewhere was too parochial for them to envision long-term solutions; their power was too slight to push them through. If someone was going to assure stability and progress in the postwar world—whether it was the world that followed World War II or the one that followed the Cold War—it would have to be the United States. Madeleine Albright explained the reason: "We see further than other countries into the future."[74]

In the revival of American activism in the 1990s, the absence of a single galvanizing threat did not prove decisive. As it had during the Cold War, the United States took a strong interest in problems that had once been considered only marginally significant. And it did so for the same reason—to protect its overall ability to lead. "Credibility" was as powerful a factor in Washington thinking during the Balkan crises of the 1990s as it had been in Vietnam in the 1960s.

By the time the Kosovo war ended, the Clinton administration had cemented a global perception of itself as arbiter of conflicts large and small. Political leaders from Pakistan and India, Ireland and Northern Ireland, Armenia and Azerbaijan, Israel and Palestine, Ecuador and Peru, Ethiopia and Eritrea, North Korea and South Korea, Russia and its neighbors—all these and others were regularly on the phone to, or across the table from, the president of the United States or his senior representatives. They sought diplomatic mediation, political support, military assistance, economic favors, approval of domestic reforms, even personal understanding.

For Clinton, one of these twilight efforts dwarfed the rest: the attempt to broker a peace between Israelis and Palestinians. It was his highest foreign policy priority, leading him to marathon negotiations at Camp David in July 2000 and to continuing detailed engagement even after the presidential elections that November. But Israeli-Palestinian peace was far from the only case of direct personal involvement by the president. In the final phase of his tenure, he orchestrated the pullback of Pakistan's forces after bloody clashes with India, kibitzed the continuing implementation of the Good Friday agreement in Northern Ireland, and but for the mushrooming Israeli-Palestinian process would probably have visited North Korea in December 2000 for a final bit of peacemaking.[75]

THE GLOBAL HYPERACTIVITY of the late Clinton administration capped what seemed in many ways the most successful two decades of American foreign policy in the nation's history. Even so, the president felt he had not convinced the public that a robust global role was both necessary and worth the cost. In December 2000 he devoted one of his last major speeches, a long address at the University of Nebraska, to a restatement of the case—a piece of advocacy that he had been going over in his mind, he said, for eight years.

Of all the Washington policy makers who had ever come to the "heartland" to defend their version of the national interest, few had had as easy a brief as Clinton. He did not, like Kissinger, have to argue for distasteful accommodation with adversaries or, like Reagan, for tension-filled competition with them. The world he described required neither compromise of principle nor existential danger. The United States, the president said, was at a unique "moment of prosperity, military and political power, social progress, and prestige." He put the point more baldly still: "Nobody in the world benefits from stability more than we do . . . . Nobody makes more money out of it. Just think about pure naked self-interest. Nobody."

And yet, despite American power, this incomparable status quo might not last. Globalization was a train with "more than one possible destination," Clinton argued. "If we want America to stay on the right track, if we want other people to be on that track and have the chance to enjoy peace and prosperity, we have no choice but to try to lead the train."

International leadership, as the president of the United States imagined it, had many elements: resisting protectionism, thwarting terrorism, promoting ethnic reconciliation, developing new energy technologies, paying UN dues, using force when needed. "We can do some things, because we've maintained a strong military, [that] nobody else can do." However long this list of responsibilities looked, Clinton insisted that

America's global role was a bargain. "Our annual global budget—for everything from diminishing the nuclear threat to preventing conflict to advancing democracy to fighting AIDS—is no more than what Americans spend each year on dietary supplements." ("In my case," he granted, "with mixed results.")[76]

The president also touched on a question to which the administration, as it drew to a close, had paid increased attention: anti-Americanism. At the State Department, Albright and Talbott presided over the periodic midafternoon seminar to elicit ideas on what came to be called the "hegemon problem." Everyone knew that the ubiquitous global activity of the United States stirred up hostility. But what was to be done about it? These discussions invariably ended with a kind of weary fatalism. A bristling global envy seemed the flip side of success, an unavoidable by-product of all that America stood for and had accomplished.[77]

Diplomats and midlevel policy makers might be satisfied with this conclusion. As a politician, Clinton was not. Americans, he used to say to his advisers, had to be sure to put an attractive and legitimate face on their role. "We're not going to be cock of the roost forever, you know." To his Nebraska audience, the outgoing president made the warning considerably sharper. "When we walk away from our responsibilities," he said, "people resent us. They resent our prosperity; they resent our power; and, in the end, when a whole lot of people resent you, sooner or later they find some way to manifest it."[78]

II

"Things Related and Not"

BUSH AND SEPTEMBER II

Donald Rumsfeld, George W. Bush, Dick Cheney, and General Peter Pace

OF ALL THE "stone in the beehive" moments in the history of American foreign policy—those sudden challenges that demand both an urgent response and a rethinking of long-term strategy—few can compare with September 11, 2001. In one stunning move, an enemy most Americans had never heard of exploited a vulnerability few had ever thought about. Who imagined that nineteen religious fanatics would be able to kill thousands of people by crashing hijacked airplanes into some of the world's best-known office buildings? After this astonishing feat, what might other terrorists do for an encore? And what, if anything, could be done to stop them? The popular response to the attack was shock, fear, and outrage—George W. Bush called it "bloodlust." These emotions remained a part of the national mood for years to come.[1]

The impact on policy was greater still. Decisions made in the aftermath of 9/11 led to the largest increases in U.S. defense spending since the Korean War, easily exceeding the Kennedy-Johnson or Reagan buildups. They produced the most significant reshaping of American national security institutions, especially of intelligence agencies, in decades. For the first time since World War II, the United States was simultaneously engaged in two large and protracted military campaigns. Almost every element of the response to terrorism, from visa policy and prisoner interrogation to counterinsurgency doctrine and the education of Muslim girls, became a subject of vigorous debate—inside the government, among outside experts, and in the public media.

The struggle against a new and little understood adversary posed conceptual as well as practical challenges. For Condoleezza Rice, President Bush's national security adviser, the United States now faced a world in which the "forces of order" were pitted against the "forces of chaos." To deal with it, Henry Kissinger claimed statesmen had to rethink precepts that had guided them since the seventeenth century. Senior officials and policy makers weren't sure how to deal with the revolutionary problems before them. Conventional wisdom could not be counted on to produce good answers. "Old doctrines," Vice President Dick Cheney insisted, "do not apply."[2]

Along with dangers, this disturbing new world also presented opportunities. Rice was not alone in calling for large policy initiatives like those of the early Cold War. Donald Rumsfeld, Bush's surprise choice to run the Pentagon for a second time, had the same thought. American statesmen, he said, had been able to "refashion much of the world" in the late 1940s because no one wanted to relive the horrors of the war just past. Rumsfeld hoped the 9/11 attacks might help push through measures on the grand scale needed. "It is easier" to do such things, he explained, "if there's an event."[3]

September 11 was that event. It produced the fourth big wave of American foreign policy maximalism since the late 1940s. The moment was marked by a surge of national unity and an outpouring of international support for the United States. And yet neither lasted long. Abroad, the Bush administration's effort to "refashion much of the world" generated the sharpest spike of anti-Americanism and the angriest disagreements with close allies in a generation. At home, it led to the strongest antiwar sentiment, including the most acute ill will between the president and Congress, in almost *two* generations. A seemingly unprecedented moment was turning into a familiar story after all. A bold but unsuccessful policy had fallen back to earth.

INCOMING AMERICAN PRESIDENTS typically disparage the foreign policy performance of their predecessors, whether for doing too much or for doing too little. George W. Bush went this familiar pattern one better, criticizing the Clinton administration's record twice, first for doing too much and then for doing too little.

The too-much theme preceded 9/11. Bush's inaugural address made obligatory nods to international duty. ("If our country does not lead the cause of freedom," he said, "it will not be led.") Still, the speech suggested little interest in large global aims. "Sometimes in life," the new president reflected, "we're called to do great things." But was the dawn of the twenty-first century one of those times? For Bush, a self-described "compassionate conservative," life's lesser chores offered a noble alternative to big projects. "Every day," he said, "we are called to do small things with great love." No president, it seems safe to say, had ever quoted Mother Teresa in his inaugural address.[4]

Doing less abroad had been one of Bush's themes as a candidate. He repeatedly complained of America's role in distant conflicts that involved no major national interest. These "vague, aimless, and endless deployments" had weakened the armed forces. Before any new foreign operations, he promised to pose one clarifying question: "When do we leave?" Rumsfeld was even harsher in describing the policies (and the worldwide network of military bases) that the administration had inherited. The United States, he believed, "had wasted billions of dollars, and we had been sitting in place across the globe for close to sixty years."[5]

This blunt talk was in tune with both public opinion and fiscal reality. Americans told pollsters in 2000 that foreign affairs were twentieth on their list of policy concerns. A pre-inaugural issue of *The New York Times Magazine* captured the new administration's mood. "Downsizing Foreign Policy," the cover proclaimed. In the spring of 2001, having made lower taxes his top political goal, the president cut the Pentagon's proposed spending increase in half. That summer the White House said deeper cutbacks—perhaps shrinking the army by two divisions—might be ahead.[6]

While many early moves by the Bush team were seen as unilateral, they were marked as much by disengagement as by self-assertion. The new administration scaled back efforts to promote an Israeli-Palestinian settlement, discouraged reconciliation talks between the Koreas, and reversed Clinton's support for both the Kyoto Protocol on greenhouse gas emissions and the International Criminal Court. Bush told Russian president Vladimir Putin in June 2001 that the United States planned to pull out of the thirty-year-old ABM (Anti-Ballistic Missile) treaty.[7]

As it rejected multilateral constraints on itself, the administration also signaled that it would not push its own norms on others. The new president lacked Clinton's zest for selling American institutions as a global model. "I just don't think it's the role of the United States," he had said in debating Al Gore, "to walk into a country and say, 'We do it this way, so should you.'" Bush repeated the point in his inaugural. The United States should show "purpose without arrogance," he suggested. Democracy promotion had lost its privileged place among U.S. policy goals.[8]

Terrorism was another problem that the Bush administration treated less urgently than its predecessor had. When George Tenet, whom the new president had kept on to run the CIA, asked the White House to grant his agency increased counterterrorism authority, he was told to recall the proposal at once. There was to be a broad review of terrorism policy, but with no time pressure. Bush's own interest in the subject seemed limited. While on vacation in August 2001, he expressed annoyance at the title of an item in his daily intelligence report: "Bin Laden Determined to Strike Inside US." "All right," the president told his CIA briefer, "you've covered your ass now." Rice assured her boss that the NSC staff was fashioning a strategy to "damage" al Qaeda over three to five years. It was hard for Tenet and his colleagues to object to this leisurely approach. "Something catastrophic was about to happen," they thought—but they didn't know where or when, or what to do about it.[9]

Seeing that foreign policy was not Bush's priority, his senior advisers adjusted. Dick Cheney wanted to make homeland defense his first project, but the president asked him to focus on California's energy brownouts instead. Rumsfeld knew his own big goal of shaking up the Pentagon would move slowly. "The reality," he admitted, "is that no one is going to be making any dramatic changes in anything, because that's just not how Washington works." Overhauling the armed forces depended on what the budget would permit, and money was tight. "We need every nickel," Rumsfeld gamely declared in a speech on September 10. Colin Powell wasn't fighting the president's priorities either. In a *Time* magazine cover story, also from September 10, the secretary of state claimed to be relaxed about the new team's policy disagreements. "It's not for me to be frustrated," Powell said. "That's not an option. 'Do it my way or else I walk'—it's not my style."[10]

THE BUSH ADMINISTRATION was deeply unprepared for the crisis that engulfed it on September 11, 2001. Unlike some of his maximalist predecessors (Kennedy and Reagan in particular), the president had not sought the White House so as to launch a new phase of international activism. He had not come to office with a theory of the case, had not selected his advisers to implement that theory, and had barely begun to work with them (or they with each other). He was far from developing a purposeful and coherent foreign policy or even an understood style of decision making. Some of this tentativeness disappeared at once in the heat of crisis; much of it plagued the administration for years.

That the president's advisers would favor an extremely large response to the 9/11 attacks was not in doubt. Past policy makers had believed that the United States, when challenged, had to push back quickly and hard, lest the enemy become more aggressive. That was what Bush's advisers recommended too. It was time, Cheney said, to "go on the offense." The president agreed. "We were going to find out who did this," he resolved, "and kick their ass." He told his generals to "take all constraints off your planning." They should be ready to "unleash holy hell."[11]

But where and how? Although al Qaeda's home base in Afghanistan was the obvious place to strike, some members of the Bush team considered it an inadequate target. The United States had absorbed an immense blow and needed a counterpunch big and quick enough to even the score. On the morning that the Pentagon was hit, Rumsfeld sketched a huge, almost indiscriminate response that he told aides had to be considered. "Go massive. Sweep it all up. Things related and not." These measures had to be implemented right away, he felt. Despite public shock, support for strong action was certain to fall off rapidly. Two days later, at the first full NSC meeting after the attacks, Rumsfeld complained that there just wasn't enough to destroy in Afghanistan. The United States would not be able to inflict "the kind of pain that was likely to change behavior throughout the terrorists' network, especially by the state supporters." Striking Iraq, he observed—now *that* would send a powerful message to sponsors of terrorism.[12]

Sending the right message was an immediate concern of policy makers as they reeled under the impact of 9/11. They wanted to prove that America's power was undiminished, that it could still punish enemies, solve problems, and maintain geopolitical order. Richard Armitage, Powell's number two, thought the "shock wave" generated by a quick success in Afghanistan would disrupt terrorist activity worldwide. Paul Wolfowitz, Rumsfeld's deputy, doubted it. How could victory in such an inconsequential place matter so much? And a "shock wave" that fell short, he pointed out, might actually encourage state sponsors of terrorism. Rumsfeld himself suggested that the United States strike where it was least expected—"preferably someplace like South America or Southeast Asia," he thought—just to show that it could.[13]

In the aftermath of al Qaeda's attacks, the urge for a maximalist strategy was a kind of strategic reflex. The instinctive desire to "go massive" reflected a fear that America might lose the psychological advantage to its enemies. Victory over the Taliban looked too slight to be satisfying. It was easy to brush this hyperactivist impulse aside, particularly its vaguest and most unfocused versions. (Rumsfeld's idea of lashing out somewhere in South America was not seriously considered.) But in deciding to strike Afghanistan first, Bush also acknowledged its limitations as a target. The president knew it was pointless to put "a million-dollar missile on a five-dollar tent." He vowed not to use America's vast power and technological superiority just to "pound sand." If the United States was going to act against terrorists, it should not settle for mere "retaliation." Tit-for-tat punishment that failed to change things was now seen as the Clinton administration's characteristic error. Bush wanted a full uprooting.[14]

Less than a month after the 9/11 attacks, the United States launched an operation to unseat al Qaeda and the Taliban. The effort was marked by its speed, stealth, agility—and very small scale. The CIA's covert operators and the military's Special Operations units reactivated ties with Afghan groups that had resisted, and ultimately defeated, the Soviets in the 1980s. As in that earlier struggle, Americans and their new allies relied on both traditional tools and the latest technology—small arms and supersophisticated communications, backpacks full of dollars, the support of intelligence services in nearby countries (this time including Russia), and plenty of horses and mules. Rumsfeld joked about ordering the "first cavalry charges of the 21st century." No more than a few hundred U.S. military and intelligence personnel were needed for the first phase of this campaign, which lasted barely five weeks. By mid-November, Kabul was in friendly hands.[15]

Bush had chosen a narrow initial response to the 9/11 attacks, focused on those directly responsible. But the case for a larger, sweep-it-all-up strategy did not go away. Al Qaeda, he and his advisers feared, had other havens besides Afghanistan, other sponsors besides the Taliban, and other projects in train. The United States was likely to face future dangers even worse than what had just happened. Terrorists armed with box cutters had done immense damage. Suppose future attackers had weapons of mass destruction—chemical, biological, or even nuclear weapons? Formulated this way, the demand for a more far-reaching response did not seem vague, reflexive, and unfocused, but precise, programmatic, and carefully thought through. This time the president did not brush it aside.

WHERE DID THE FEAR that terrorists might get their hands on WMD come from? It was not part of Rumsfeld's initial case for going big. It had barely come up when Bush and his "war cabinet" first sat down to discuss their options. It was not mentioned at all in the president's speech to Congress on September 20. When a prominent group of "neoconservatives" outside government wrote Bush that same day, they didn't mention this danger either. Yet within weeks it became the administration's number-one concern.[16]

The anthrax-by-mail scares of late September, in which envelopes of deadly powder were received by congressional and news media offices, played a role in the shift. So did the early October intelligence report that a nuclear device had been smuggled into midtown Manhattan. On October 18, White House sensors indicated—also incorrectly, it turned out—that the president and his staff had been exposed to deadly botulinum toxin. Not since at least the Cuban missile crisis had senior officials of the U.S. government worked in a setting of such policy urgency and perceived personal danger. People became jittery and prone to exaggerate. "Time is *not* on our side," Cheney worried to colleagues. "Every day that al Qaeda and its supporters went without major defeat," he asserted, the threat to America increased.[17]

In this heated atmosphere, it seemed that even fragmentary intelligence reports—often mere rumors, gossip, or hearsay—had to be taken seriously. Discovering that Bin Laden had years earlier expressed an interest in acquiring WMD added to official concern. Documents seized by U.S. forces in Afghanistan showed that al Qaeda was already exploring biological weapons development in 1999. Captured videos from terrorist training camps recorded the experimental use of chemical weapons on dogs. And about many problems, of course, there was no information at all. That, one intelligence veteran recalled, was absolutely "terrifying."[18]

No matter how alarming these reports—or the lack of them—may have been, the crucial step in the evolution of American policy was not simply the worry that terrorists might get weapons of mass destruction. More significant was the assumption policy makers made about *how* terrorists would get them—not through their own efforts but from governments hostile to the United States. The day after the false report about nukes in Manhattan (which was not immediately made public), Rumsfeld sketched the scenario he most feared for *The New York Times.* "There is no question," he warned, "but that the chemical and biological and nuclear weapons are in the hands of countries that wish us ill, who have engaged in terrorist activities, who have fostered and sponsored terrorist networks." Rumsfeld insisted that he didn't know which states might help terrorists in this way. "But it does not take a genius to project out that [it] will occur." And it took no special insight to see that he was again zeroing in on Iraq.[19]

Many senior members of the Bush team, including the president himself, had entered the government in early 2001 seeing Saddam Hussein as a major threat to American interests. But pet projects are common when administrations change hands, and this particular view had had little impact. Policy makers showed no urgency—and reached no consensus—in developing a new policy toward Iraq. It was a problem that Bush thought the United States might be able to "manage." Even the attacks on the World Trade Center and the Pentagon did not immediately alter this judgment. When Rumsfeld mentioned Iraq as a prime target for quick American action, he explained that what he was really trying to do was send a message to others. In late September, he was still writing spur-of-the-moment notes to his cabinet colleagues suggesting, as he had even before 9/11, that the best way to deal with Saddam might be to offer him a luxury retirement in exchange for stepping down.[20]

What finally moved Iraq to center stage of national security policy was the conviction that it was the kind of state Rumsfeld had described to the *Times,* one that might help terrorists acquire WMD. It was only conjecture, of course. No one could show that such help had ever been given. But if it was a problem worth worrying about—and in the feverish debate that followed 9/11, many thought it was—it was easy to see Iraq as a very worrying candidate. It had had proven programs and stocks of WMD in the early 1990s. Of all the world's aspiring proliferators, it had been subject to the most intrusive international controls and had the richest history of defying them. Saddam's ouster of UN weapons inspectors in the late 1990s had convinced policy makers and intelligence analysts in the Clinton administration—and Bill Clinton himself—that he was up to no good. More recent developments seemed to strengthen the case. Iraq was the rare country, even in the Middle East, where the 9/11 attacks were publicly hailed. It had apparently become a refuge for al Qaeda fighters fleeing capture by U.S. forces in Afghanistan. It even seemed that one of Bin Laden's senior lieutenants, Abu Musab al-Zarqawi, had relocated to Iraq, bringing with him a team of specialists working on (or so it was reported) biological weapons.[21]

The Bush administration's thinking about how to respond to terrorism had, by mid-fall 2001, led it back to Saddam Hussein. The process was half strategic logic, half utter speculation. Yet 9/11 had given utter speculation new respectability. Many analysts, both in and out of government, argued that America had been attacked because of a failure to "connect the dots." To avoid new disaster, disparate data had to be assembled into a coherent whole. The fragments of information produced by American intelligence fit so neatly with Saddam Hussein's past behavior that there was little pressure for a searching and skeptical examination of the case. The CIA did not even prepare a full National Intelligence Estimate on the subject until the fall of 2002, when preparations for war were far advanced.[22]

Was there, amid the worst-case fascination with weapons of mass destruction, something else pushing the United States to war with Iraq? Did the shock of 9/11 create an urge, hard to articulate but still important, to seize the initiative against other adversaries and threats? The desire to display American power was certainly some policy makers' first reaction to the attacks. And it was hardly the first time American statesmen had responded to a very specific challenge by trying to address national security problems across the board. When South Korea was invaded, Dean Acheson saw an opportunity to change policy in Europe too; and he said that if there was a choice between doing too much or doing too little, the right answer had to be too much.

Many well-placed observers saw something similar at work after 9/11. Richard Haass, Colin Powell's planning director, felt that America's easy win against the Taliban had failed to "scratch the itch." Henry Kissinger agreed that a full response to al Qaeda's attacks had to go beyond a single, too-small war. Radical Islamists had tried to humiliate the United States; now "we need to humiliate *them.*" For that purpose, he later reflected, "Afghanistan wasn't enough."[23]

If this demand for a larger response was the "itch" guiding American policy, the president began to scratch it very early on. In late November 2001, with what then seemed like a quick victory in Afghanistan behind him, Bush pulled Rumsfeld aside after a White House meeting and instructed him to dust off the Pentagon's blueprints for military action against Iraq. ("Do it outside the normal channels," he suggested.) Within a week, the secretary of defense had discussed the outlines of a campaign with General Tommy Franks, commander of CENTCOM. Three days after Christmas, Franks visited the president's ranch in Texas to present a more developed plan. At the end of their meeting, Bush gave the order for a steady buildup of American forces around Iraq over the coming year. The United States was now firmly on track toward its second war since September 11.[24]

IN THE NEXT fifteen months the Bush administration's policy toward Iraq became the most emotional and controversial issue of international debate, arguably the most emotional and controversial such issue in decades. To foreign audiences in particular, the president's in-your-face nationalist rhetoric—above all, his claim that one was either with the United States or with the terrorists—bespoke a familiar American arrogance. He and his advisers seemed so sure of their own righteousness, so caught up in their new existential struggle, so wedded to an absolutist understanding of national security, that they didn't care what others thought and would not compromise to win them over. European leaders seemed to forget how frequently they had been irritated by the Clinton administration and all its preening "indispensable nation" talk. Bush came across as still more high-handed and insulting. In time, many Americans had the same reaction. Political rhetoric became more heated. In *The Washington Post,* Leon Fuerth, previously Gore's chief foreign policy aide, accused the president and his advisers of a "dangerous intoxication with American power."[25]

Bush and his team mishandled the politics of the Iraq war, but it was not because they were indifferent to domestic or international support. They knew it would be difficult to sustain a hard-edged strategy in the teeth of intense opposition, whether at home or abroad. And they set about winning support in much the same way that the first president Bush did in 1990—by checking off items one by one on a long to-do list. Three were especially important. Endorsements from Congress and the United Nations were to provide procedural legitimacy. A reformist vision for the Arab Middle East would evoke American values and promise large future benefits. Keeping the U.S. military footprint small would keep costs down.

Together, these initiatives were the Bush administration's answer to the problem of how to sustain a maximalist policy. Many of them were unproductive; some proved counterproductive; others backfired spectacularly. One item on the administration's to-do list, however, was hardly a problem at all: bipartisan support. When George Bush used his State of the Union address in January 2002 to sketch the next phase of the war on terrorism, the Democrats' foreign policy establishment was almost completely on board. For them, Saddam Hussein was a serious national security problem. Al Gore said Iraq was in "a virulent class by itself." Joe Biden, the senior Democrat on the Senate Foreign Relations Committee, thought regime change was the right answer; the only question was "how to do it, in my view, not if to do it." New York's new senator, Hillary Clinton, believed "the risk of not acting" had become too great. Her constituents, she pointed out, had been through "the fires of Hell" on September 11. Dick Gephardt, the House Democratic leader, saw the problem the same way. "September 11," he said, "was the ultimate wake-up call." (Even Nancy Pelosi agreed that Saddam possessed biological and chemical weapons.)[26]

Democrats did not support the president unconditionally, of course. Before going to war, they insisted that the United States observe international due process. That meant taking any plan of action to the UN Security Council for its approval. Bush heard the same message from many American allies, starting with British prime minister Tony Blair, who pressed the idea on him while visiting the United States in April 2002. It was well-intentioned advice, coming—in Blair's case—from one of the strongest advocates of military action against Saddam Hussein.[27]

The administration found it extremely difficult to follow the advice—to show respect for global opinion while jealously protecting American freedom of action. Bush and his team had not agreed among themselves as to why they were consulting the UN, and their confusion showed. Were they hoping to control Iraq without war, or merely to win a mandate for invading? Colin Powell urged the president to see the UN as a cheaper, safer alternative to war. At a long private dinner with Bush and Rice in August 2002, the secretary of state laid out the enormous costs of a military campaign and the long occupation likely to follow. For Powell, getting strict international monitoring of Iraq's WMD programs would have been enough to satisfy basic American goals. He predicted that Saddam, if diplomatically isolated and militarily threatened, would submit to very intrusive inspections. Assuming such arrangements could be worked out, he told Bush, the United States should "take yes for an answer." A virtually identical case—though more openly opposed to war—was made days later in *The Wall Street Journal* by Brent Scowcroft, national security adviser to (and close friend of) the first president Bush. He too stressed the advantages of proposing a tough inspection regime. If Saddam rejected it, said Scowcroft, war would have a legal justification that it otherwise lacked.[28]

FROM HIS VICE PRESIDENT, Bush heard a completely different view. Cheney was all for getting the UN to endorse regime change, but for him the idea that improved monitoring offered a long-term solution was "fanciful." At most, the UN should be asked to label Iraq an international outlaw; the United States would do the rest. A decade earlier, as secretary of defense under Bush 41, Cheney had argued that multilateral mechanisms had often failed to "gel" quickly enough to deal with real-world threats. The record since then, as he read it, backed him up. Even before they were expelled from Iraq in the late 1990s, UN inspectors had often failed to uncover its most dangerous WMD programs. In the face of Iraqi defiance (and what Cheney called a clever "game of cheat-and-retreat"), the Security Council had been constantly deadlocked. Given this history, why should anyone believe the UN could keep Saddam Hussein from eventually acquiring whatever weapons he wanted? Inspections provided only "false comfort." They might even divert attention from the real goal. That, argued Scooter Libby, Cheney's chief of staff, was to disarm Iraq, not simply to inspect it.[29]

Hearing these opposing views, the president appeared to rule in favor of Powell. The United States would take its case to the UN. But Bush had not accepted Powell's key recommendation—to be willing to "take yes for an answer." On this, in fact, he seemed to agree with Cheney. Back in April, the president had publicly stated his goal, and it wasn't one that could be achieved by inspections. He had made up his mind, he said. "Saddam needs to go." Bush insisted he would not "allow a nation like Iraq, run by Saddam Hussein, to develop weapons of mass destruction and then team up with terrorist organizations so they can blackmail the world. I'm not going to let that happen."

During the fall of 2002, UN diplomacy gripped international attention. A Security Council resolution demanded that Baghdad fulfill its obligations; international inspectors resumed monitoring after a four-year hiatus; the Iraqi government released a mountain of mostly old documents about its weapons programs. This was the visible part of the U.S. policy iceberg. To Bush, however, none of it suggested that diplomacy was creating a satisfactory alternative to war. After the Iraqi document dump, he told his colleagues that the game was over. Saddam was "finished." Below the water line, continuing American military preparations reflected the president's judgment that war was now inevitable. On November 26—more than two months before Colin Powell's famous presentation of the U.S. case to the Security Council—Bush gave the green light for the final buildup of American forces around Iraq. General Franks and his planners called it "the mother of all deployment orders." Once additional units were in place, the United States would be ready to invade.[30]

Taking its case to the UN had produced both the benefits predicted by Powell and then the costs predicted by Cheney. Washington could not simply pocket the former without paying the latter. A declaration that Iraq was in "material breach" of past resolutions had strengthened the American position. It was followed, however, by a protracted Security Council debate that gave opponents of the war their opening to mobilize against the United States. To critics, it mattered little that Bush was ready to consult international opinion if he would not also accept its verdict.

In February 2003, Jacques Chirac and Gerhard Schröder, the French and German leaders, declared publicly that they would block any endorsement of U.S. military action. "Nothing," they said, justified the use of force against Iraq. By this time, a wave of anti-American sentiment had swept Europe. To those who rode it, defiance of the world's leading power felt like a thrilling and creative act. Dominique Strauss-Kahn, former French finance minister (and future head of the IMF), called it "the birth of the European nation." American policy makers responded in kind, with Cheney telling the French ambassador that France was no longer either "a friend or an ally." The United States had gone to the UN in search of legitimacy. It emerged from the Security Council debate with far less international support than it had when the process began.[31]

THERE WAS A SECOND strand in the Bush administration's effort to show that military action against Iraq was part of a comprehensive, thought-out, even inspiring strategy. The president and his advisers reexamined American policies on a host of issues to make them more responsive to a global consensus. After backing away from overinvolvement in Israeli-Palestinian negotiations, Bush now gave the first-ever explicit U.S. endorsement of a two-state settlement. He proposed an innovative foreign aid bill—the Millennium Challenge Account—that linked increased assistance with improved governance. Within months of the 9/11 attacks, the United States began a new push for liberalized trade, known as the Doha Round. In early 2003 the president put forward the largest global health initiative of recent times—an African AIDS relief program with a price tag of $15 billion. None of these initiatives were simply triggered by September 11, but all were spurred by the administration's new foreign policy activism.[32]

The most sweeping policy change, and the one most closely related to 9/11, was what came to be called the "freedom agenda"—Bush's embrace of democracy as the antidote to extremism. His interest in political and social reform, in why Muslim societies produced terrorists in the first place, gained special momentum from the campaign in Afghanistan. Both the president and the first lady spoke frequently of how much the overthrow of the Taliban helped Afghan women and girls. Laura Bush delivered the weekly White House radio address after Kabul fell to pro-American forces. "The fight against terrorism," she said, "is also a fight for the rights and dignity of women." In the immediate aftermath of 9/11, it had been critics of American policy who explained terrorism as a by-product of backwardness and despair. Now, in an ideological reversal, Bush began to stress the importance of addressing "root causes." They offered a way of making historical sense of what had happened on September 11. Even more, he saw in the explanation a compelling new mission for the United States.[33]

The president set out this mission in his January 2002 State of the Union address—best known for using the term "axis of evil"—to describe the link between outlaw states like Iraq and terrorist organizations like al Qaeda. Bush warned about WMD in Iraq, but his broader message was to recast American counterterrorism strategy in ideological terms. The United States had to see the importance of "development and education and opportunity in the Islamic world." The goals of liberty and justice were, Bush reminded the Congress, "right and true and unchanging for all people everywhere." Although he had earlier portrayed terrorists as neototalitarians who "hate our freedoms," the president had not claimed that democratic reform might overcome that hatred. Now, sketching a large reformist agenda for the Arab Middle East, he began to. "We have a greater objective," Bush claimed, "than eliminating threats and containing resentment."[34]

The White House considered this vision of a modernized Middle East such a blockbuster that Condoleezza Rice personally alerted the Saudi ambassador to what the president was going to say. Friends needed a heads-up when the United States was about to challenge them. Yet in a total surprise for the White House, the reformist themes of the speech got no attention at all. Media reaction focused almost exclusively on the "axis of evil" phrase, widely interpreted as a harbinger of war. That was news; an expression of hope for democracy was just filler.[35]

Bush was "stunned." But he and his spokesmen kept at it. Giving her first major speech as national security adviser, Rice emphasized that America aimed "not merely to leave the world safer but to leave it better." The two transformational goals were inseparable. Giving American ideals a combative edge, Rice said that the United States sought "a new balance of power that favored freedom." Progress would not always be peaceful. "Truly evil regimes," she insisted, "will never be reformed." They had to be "confronted, not coddled." Rice wanted America's friends (the Saudis seemed still on her mind) to see that they would not be coddled either.

> Nations must decide which side they are on in the fault line that divides civilization from terror. They must decide whether to embrace the paradigm of progress: democracy and freedom and human rights, and clean limited government. Together with others, we can help people and nations make positive choices as they seek a better future, and we can deter those who want to take away a better future for others.[36]

Critics later charged that the Bush administration took up the cause of democracy only when WMD were not found in Iraq. In fact, the president had paired the two themes from the beginning, treating them as complementary halves of the same policy. Modern political institutions would prevent the emergence of regimes determined to challenge the United States. In the run-up to war, Bush liked to remind listeners that the U.S. troops preparing to oust Saddam Hussein were part of a "humanitarian army" ready and able to improve the lives of Iraq's people. The president of the United States did not ratchet up his emphasis on democratic "nation-building" because no WMD were found. He did so because the invasion and its aftermath confounded his reformist expectations. They failed to show America's commitment to creating a modern Middle East. And they did so for one very important reason: the Pentagon had designed the war with a different set of priorities.[37]

THE BUSH ADMINISTRATION hoped that reformist goals would position it solidly on the side of progress. For many, they conveyed a different message—that the United States was on a crusade to impose its own political preferences. Even the British warned that the democracy talk came across as "Americanization." (German attitudes were captured by the newspaper headline "Bush Threatens More Freedom.") But of all the means the president and his advisers employed to build support for maximalist policies after 9/11, none had a deeper or more paradoxical impact than the effort to make them less expensive.[38]

Donald Rumsfeld was in charge of keeping the war costs down, and he took to the task with relish. He wanted to show that the use of modern military power was affordable. The Gulf War of 1991, he thought, had been an example of mindless Pentagon excess. Rumsfeld liked to cite the fact that 80 percent of the munitions that the United States sent to the front the last time around had returned home in their original packing material. For him, Colin Powell's brand of overpreparedness was not politically viable. If war required such vast effort and expense, who would be for it?

In preparing for a new invasion, Rumsfeld was plainly influenced by Cheney's postmortem on the experience of 1991. Back when he was secretary of defense to the first president Bush, Cheney had said that future military campaigns had to involve minimal casualties; they had to be quick; and they had to be cheap. The operation against Saddam, as Rumsfeld began to envision it, would show how much better small, light, fast-moving forces were at achieving these goals than their clumsy predecessors. Throughout 2002 he demanded that army planners shrink the invasion they had in mind. Fewer troops, deployed rapidly, would take the enemy by surprise, get the fighting over with fast, and incur minimal losses.[39]

In General Tommy Franks, who was to command the campaign against Iraq, Rumsfeld found a fellow scourge of Pentagon traditionalism. Franks picked up the secretary's small-is-beautiful lingo and used it with Texan gusto. He liked to brag that commanders of old—he singled out Eisenhower and Alexander the Great—had to aim at a force ratio of three to one in their favor; he, by contrast, could prevail even when the ratio was six to one in the *other* guy's favor. "Speed kills" was Franks's motto. With no more than an army division and a brigade of Marines—perhaps 20,000 men—he claimed he could make Iraq "implode."[40]

Rumsfeld loved such big talk. It helped him prod the hidebound planners to modernize their ideas. But he also knew the secretary of defense could push the military establishment only so far. Senior generals were cautious and stubborn—and well connected enough to rally supporters beyond the Pentagon. To overcome resistance to his minimalist concepts, Rumsfeld fudged. He accepted a plan for an invasion force of up to 250,000 troops—with the proviso, however, that it would be fully deployed only if unexpectedly stiff Iraqi resistance materialized, and only if he explicitly okayed it. To confuse the enemy, the operation would begin from what the planners called a "running start," with fewer than 100,000 U.S. troops already in place and the rest still in transit to the war zone. Then, if things went well, the orders bringing the extra units to Iraq could be canceled (an option known as "off-ramps"). With colleagues, Rumsfeld was open about his views. He said he was not going to be "stampeded" into approving the big force. Using the "off-ramps" became his recurrent theme throughout the invasion.[41]

As for how many troops would stay in Iraq after victory, and for how long, Rumsfeld's thinking was even more cost-conscious. Why, he often asked (as if there were no answer to his question), would it take a bigger force to occupy a country than to conquer it in the first place? The secretary envisioned a brisk drawdown to 30,000 troops or so once the fighting was over. Franks was in a bigger hurry still. He told his commanders to be ready to "take as many risks" leaving Iraq as they had in fighting their way in. The United States, he predicted, would be gone in a year.[42]

THE PENTAGON'S hit-and-run strategy shaped the entire confrontation between Iraq and the United States—from prelude to aftermath. Because it aimed to surprise the Iraqis, the administration actually encouraged Saddam to doubt that it would invade. As a result, the Iraqi leader felt little pressure to consider stepping down, much less fleeing for his life. American policy makers considered Saddam's exile the one thing that might prevent war. Long afterward Rumsfeld observed that more effort should have gone into ousting him short of war. But the failure to do so was no mere oversight. Forcing Saddam out would have required a completely different military strategy, one in which an overwhelming threat, patiently developed, was more important than surprise.[43]

A second result of the "running start" strategy was that U.S. forces gained possession of Baghdad before they were able to control it, much less to govern the entire country. Quick and brilliantly executed tank runs into the capital were followed by a breakdown of order. In addition to well-publicized targets like the National Museum, looters cleaned out government offices, telephone switching centers, power stations, and more. Bush was incredulous. He had not challenged Rumsfeld or Franks on troop numbers. Now he was seeing what it meant to topple Saddam with the smallest possible force. Where was his humanitarian army? "What the hell is happening?" he asked.[44]

The answer was simple. The world's most modern and powerful armed forces had been asked to depose Saddam Hussein, not to keep the peace once he was gone. They had no interest in the latter job and had not come equipped to do it. General James Mattis, an old-style Marine tough guy (his nickname was "Chaos"), had led the lightning maneuvers into Baghdad. He expressed a military view of the smaller tasks that followed combat. "We didn't come to Iraq," Mattis snorted, "to shoot some fellow making off with a rug." There was no glory—neither prestige nor promotions—in mopping-up operations. As Franks saw it, winding down the operation was "three star work." When a war ends, one of his planners observed, what remains is mere logistics. You just "pack everything up and send it back to Fort Stewart in Georgia." The tedium of reconstruction—from sewer repairs to street patrols—was for civil engineers and constables, not for warriors.[45]

Rumsfeld shrugged off the unexpected disorder. "Stuff happens," he said. Though he later apologized for the remark, it nicely captured his outlook. If things didn't go as planned, the United States could walk away, leaving others to cope with the consequences. A close aide to Rumsfeld expressed the same view even more baldly. Americans did not have to make sure the country was in good condition before handing it off. That was the Iraqis' job, he said. "We don't owe these people a thing."[46]

The early mishandling of the occupation had a lasting impact on U.S. policy. It altered assumptions about how long American forces should stay in Iraq, what they would do there, and who would take over when they left. Bush and his advisers had never reached consensus about how and when to constitute a post-Saddam regime, but the failure to maintain order ruled out some options that might have been considered. The first casualty, in fact, was the Pentagon's own preferred scenario—a quick transfer of power to Iraqi exile groups. Who would take such a risk in a country that suddenly looked so unstable?[47]

A second premise of Rumsfeld's approach, that America's friends would help to manage Iraq, was also in jeopardy as soon as the occupation began to look like a serious military challenge. Administration officials had hoped to persuade the Italians and the Portuguese, among other NATO allies, to take on large responsibilities—peacekeeping, police training, and so forth. Even the recalcitrant French, some imagined, might sign up. But once the vaunted armed forces of the United States started to have trouble maintaining control, getting less committed allies to put their own troops in harm's way became almost impossible. If creating stability in postwar Iraq was a hard job, the United States would have to do it largely alone. The bill for maximalism was clearly going to be bigger than planned.[48]

THE AMERICAN OCCUPATION of Iraq never fully escaped its early confusion. For years the Bush administration remained divided on the basic elements of its strategy. To oversee the occupation, Washington sent L. Paul Bremer, a career diplomat who had been the State Department's counterterrorism coordinator more than fifteen years earlier and had run Henry Kissinger's consulting firm in retirement. Iraq's "chaotic power vacuum" convinced Bremer that Rumsfeld's quick-handoff timetable was a "reckless fantasy." His first decisions—to dissolve the army and bar senior Baath Party officials from top government jobs—made sense only if Washington had decided on a long stay and a systematic remaking of Iraqi institutions. Bremer told Bush he foresaw "a marathon, not a sprint." Easily persuaded, the president endorsed the new, go-slow approach. "We will fend off the impatient," he promised Bremer.[49]

At the Pentagon, both civilian and military officials were unhappy with this change. They remained eager to leave Iraq quickly, but failed to create the conditions that would allow them to do so. While Washington argued, a real insurgency—made more formidable by raids on the army's now-unguarded ammunition depots—gained strength. Its heart was west of Baghdad in Anbar province, which invading U.S. forces had not even entered—another by-product of Rumsfeld's cost-conscious "off-ramps." The administration kept hoping that the insurgency's momentum would be broken by some symbolic event—the capture of Saddam in December 2003, perhaps, or the legal end of American control in June 2004. Time and again it was disappointed. In August 2004, Ayed Allawi, whom Washington had anointed as Iraq's first post-Saddam prime minister, wrote Bush to alert him to the mounting danger. The insurgent threat, Allawi warned, was "much greater now than it was a year ago." The country was "grossly unstable."[50]

John Negroponte, who took over as ambassador in Baghdad in the fall of 2004, seconded the new prime minister's judgment. "Iraq," he told Bush, "is a post-conflict failed state." Whatever the Iraqi people thought of the ouster of Saddam, they now blamed America "for not delivering better services, more security, and a swifter reduction of forces." Negroponte thought creating a viable political system might take five years. When Bremer had made the same forecast a year earlier, Bush had accepted it. But the president's patience was wearing thin. To Negroponte his answer was, "We don't have that much time."[51]

At the close of 2004, American forces in Iraq were still as large as they had been during the invasion. Their job, however, was incomparably larger, and the mismatch made it almost impossible for them to succeed. The strain showed in military operations, which became increasingly brutal. By the end of the battle of Fallujah in December 2004, the United States had turned up to 80 percent of the city's population into refugees; up to 20 percent of homes were destroyed. One American officer expressed a harsh and beleaguered view of Iraqis: "Why show them mercy, you know what I mean?" Having too few troops, American commanders had also come to rely on massive preventive roundups of suspected insurgents. These overwhelmed a prison system that was already both overcrowded and understaffed, and turned its facilities into what American officers called "terrorist universities." From all this, the abuses at Abu Ghraib were a completely predictable result.[52]

Despite deterioration in Iraq, Bush and his advisers hoped that the foreign policy of his second term might revolve less around the war than it had in his first. Their effort was a vigorous one. The president devoted his entire inaugural address in January 2005 to the issue of global democratic progress; he gave democracy promotion extra credibility by making it a priority of American assistance programs. Seeking to build on his path-breaking expansion of HIV/AIDS treatment, he launched a new effort against malaria. Condoleezza Rice succeeded Powell as secretary of state and enjoyed a first year of small but notable negotiating successes—in July 2005, a framework agreement with India on civil nuclear cooperation; in September, North Korea's declaration that it would roll back its nuclear program; in November, around-the-clock talks with Israelis and Palestinians that reopened a border crossing in Gaza. Achievements like these, Rice thought, had reestablished the "primacy of diplomacy in U.S. foreign policy." An aide explained that this phrase meant "we're sorry for Iraq."[53]

CONDITIONS IN IRAQ did not become any less horrifying because the administration wanted to change the subject. American officials saw they were floundering. Yet they seemed unable to set a different course. In the fall of 2005, another new American ambassador, Zalmay Khalilzad, assembled an advisory group (including both insiders and nongovernment experts) to help him understand the military outlook. The experts told him that current strategy—to "stand up" Iraqi security forces so that American troops could "stand down"—was not working. In its place, they recommended the same approach that had been so often proposed, but never adopted, during the Vietnam War—a counterinsurgency strategy designed to win the people's loyalty by protecting them.

In and out of government, military strategists began to argue for the same approach. Rice gave the idea greater currency by endorsing it in a congressional hearing in October 2005. American strategy, she claimed, was to "clear" areas held by insurgents, "hold" them against recapture, and "build" the infrastructure of economic and political renewal. But neither she nor other policy makers were ready to launch the bruising debate that would be needed to challenge the secretary of defense and his commanders. When Rumsfeld sent Bush an angry note about Rice's statements, the discussion died.[54]

The war in Iraq has often been compared to the war in Vietnam, and the administration's inability to fix a failing strategy was a crucial common feature. But there were enormous differences too. In Iraq, U.S. military commanders consistently rejected proposals for more troops or expanded operations. Not even the most dramatic terrorist act of the war, the bombing of the Golden Dome mosque in Samarra in February 2006, shook their view. American forces were moving steadily toward a training role—and eventually toward the exits. The generals were determined to stick with that plan. Although the Samarra bombing raised the prospect of civil war, General George Casey, the U.S. commander in Iraq between 2004 and 2007, opposed a strong policy response. Iraqi forces had to be kept "on the path to self-reliance." Accelerating the transition, he argued, would "[bolster] the confidence of all Iraqis in their government, the Iraqi Security Forces, and the Coalition." On this the secretary of defense and his commanders were in total agreement. Rumsfeld urged Bush to see that only Iraqis could save their country. The United States could not. "We have to take our hand off the bicycle seat."[55]

Rumsfeld was right that the United States had too few troops in Iraq to control the bicycle by itself. In two of the largest offensives of the war, Operations Together Forward and Together Forward II in the summer of 2006, American units were unable to hold territory after clearing it. Bush had been patient with his commanders, especially in public. "Absolutely," he insisted. "We're winning." But defeat was now a clear possibility, and the president began to rethink. In an August videoconference he spoke to Casey more bluntly than ever before. "We must succeed," he said. "We will commit the resources." Counting on the Iraqis to "stand up" was not the only option. "If they can't do it," the president said, "we will." The United States should be ready to retake control. "If the bicycle teeters," Bush instructed Casey, "put [our] hand back on."[56]

PUBLIC SUPPORT FOR the war in Iraq unraveled in 2006. Polls showed the American people disapproving of the policy by a two-to-one margin. Privately, Mitch McConnell, the Senate Republican leader, appealed to Bush to start pulling out troops. "Your unpopularity," he told the president, "is going to cost us control of the congress." Jack Keane, recently the army vice chief of staff, believed the entire enterprise was "going over a cliff." The bipartisan Iraq Study Group, chaired by former secretary of state James Baker and former House Foreign Affairs Committee chairman Lee Hamilton, began preparing a plan for dignified disengagement.[57]

For the Pentagon, of course, the idea of disengagement was entirely welcome. Getting out had long been the nominal goal of policy, and the effort was—at least as measured by casualties—paying off. By 2006 American commanders kept their troops as much as possible on large bases while training Iraqis to take over the fight. The result was a significant reduction in combat losses. In the first nine months of the year, despite a tripling of insurgent attacks, U.S. fatalities dropped 17 percent. This positive trend, commanders thought, justified their plan to reduce troop levels by one-third in 2007. But while the United States scaled back, Iraq was coming apart. American combat deaths averaged sixty per month; in December 2006, the number of Iraqis killed in sectarian violence was three thousand. Worst of all, Washington saw that key elements of the Iraqi government were actually abetting the violence. ("The militias are not a threat to the Iraqi state," *The New Republic* declared, "they *are* the Iraqi state.")[58]

This appalling situation pushed Bush to make what he called "the toughest and most unpopular decision of my presidency." Embracing ideas on which his most senior advisers had been unable to agree, he chose a plan that, beyond the White House staff, enjoyed strong support only among a small group of reform-minded military intellectuals. Its key features were an increase of 30,000 troops, a shake-up at the Pentagon, and a new counterinsurgency strategy. U.S. soldiers would have to reenter Baghdad neighborhoods, and show that they could protect the people against sectarian violence.[59]

With the struggle so far advanced, the risks of a major policy departure were obvious. Even ardent boosters admitted that the new mission was likely to increase American casualties. Bringing in more troops, the chiefs warned Bush, might "break the force." Fierce bipartisan opposition in Congress was also certain. Senator Chuck Hagel, a fellow Republican, said Bush's decision would be "the most dangerous foreign policy blunder in this country since Vietnam." Harry Reid, the Democratic leader in the Senate, called the war "lost." Even Henry Kissinger said publicly that it was no longer winnable. In this increasingly frantic atmosphere, the Baker-Hamilton group's plan for withdrawal (its euphemism was "redeployment") seemed to many the only prudent course—and the only way to restore a foreign policy consensus.[60]

Yet George Bush was uninterested in consensus. He seemed ready to roll the dice again. He was prepared, moreover, to take his chances with two kinds of support that presidents often rely on in announcing big decisions. Bush would have liked to be able to claim the backing of his own generals and of the Iraqi government. But the chiefs were against the plan and everyone knew it. Although the president met with them to hear their concerns (and even claimed to share them), he did not let the generals water down his plan. "What I want to hear from you," Bush lectured them, "is how we're going to win, not how we're going to leave."[61]

Under duress, the Pentagon leadership eventually yielded to the president. Those officials most wedded to the old policy (above all, Secretary Rumsfeld and General Casey) were removed from their posts. Those who remained in place were humbled. Rather than buy military support by compromising in ways that might lead to failure, Bush installed new commanders who were committed to helping him succeed. Six years into his presidency, this was arguably the first occasion on which the president understood what he had to do to make sure that a controversial decision was effectively implemented. One White House adviser summed up the new attitude: "If you're going to be a bear, be a grizzly."[62]

TO JUSTIFY AN INCREASED and risky military effort, any president also likes to claim he is helping a worthy ally solve its problems. Unfortunately for Bush, he was just as much at odds with the Baghdad government as he was with the chiefs. His advisers told him that Iraq's Shi'ite leadership opposed reconciliation with Sunnis. When Steve Hadley, Condi Rice's replacement as national security adviser, visited Iraq in October 2006, he came back skeptical. "Do we and Prime Minister Maliki," he wondered to Bush, "share the same vision for Iraq?" To Rice, the answer was clearly no. Although a year earlier she had publicly embraced a strategy of "clear, hold, and build," she now argued against deeper U.S. involvement. "If they want to have a civil war," she said of Iraqis, "we're going to have to let them." Adding troops would only make it easier for America's partners to avoid doing the right thing.[63]

When Bush finally presented the "surge" in a nationwide TV address in January 2007, he called it an "aggressive" new Iraqi plan that needed U.S. help to succeed. The opposite was closer to the truth. It was a new American plan that Washington wanted the Iraqi government to accept. The president pressed Maliki for hard pledges that he would at last begin to work with the Sunnis. But Bush and his advisers remained skeptical that he would follow through. After a one-on-one session with Maliki in Jordan, the president disparaged the prime minister. (Months later, he was still dubious. "Maliki," he told an NSC meeting, "may not be our guy.") Despite his doubts, Bush rejected the idea that the "surge" should depend—either at the outset or as it proceeded—on whether the Iraqis were keeping their promises.[64]

Bush confronted the same dilemma that many of his predecessors faced in dealing with a weak or unreliable client or ally. He had to decide whether the client's limitations were a reason to offer more help or less. Less, Rice urged. So did Rumsfeld. "Go minimalist," he advised in a final memo to Bush after his ouster.

To the president, proposals to scale back America's commitment were hard to understand. "We'll just let them kill each other," he asked Rice incredulously, "and we'll stand by and try to pick up the pieces?" When Maliki and Casey proposed cutting the number of extra troops in half, they got the same response. "I'm building a plan to win this thing. We're not going to shortchange it." Other presidents had made the same call Bush did. When Lyndon Johnson pushed the South Vietnamese aside in 1965, he too had concluded that only the United States was in a position to achieve results. But few American leaders had ever made this choice so late in the game, with the outlook so bleak. At the end of 2006, most experts and foreign policy heavyweights, not to mention the public, the Congress, and many of the president's own advisers, had written Iraq off. Rice was particularly withering. "This is your last card," she warned Bush. "It had better work."[65]

In 1968, Lyndon Johnson had reached a moment of comparable hopelessness in Vietnam, with casualties spiking, domestic support sinking, and the "Establishment bastards" bailing out. His outlook at that point was completely different from Bush's. He had pretty much given up. Johnson was entitled to think, rightly or wrongly, that the United States had given Vietnam its best shot. To keep the war from consuming his presidency, he had tried for more than a year and a half to stay out of it. Once in, however, he demanded a massive expenditure of resources, human and otherwise. When he finally decided to pull back, his policy had many critics. No one could say he had not tried.

Bush traveled a different path to his decision on the surge. He had never doubted the need to invade Iraq. Then after invading he hesitated. For almost four years he had accepted a less-than-maximum effort. The surge was his belated effort to succeed. Until he took his best shot, he could not get out.

FROM ONE PRESIDENCY to another, maximalism that crashes and burns always looks basically the same. Harry Truman in 1950 and then in 1953, Lyndon Johnson in 1965 and then in 1968, George Bush in 2003 and then in 2006—all three transformations tell a story of power and authority brought low, a painful reversal of national fortune in which presidents seem helpless to correct their mistakes.

Could the Bush administration have avoided this fate? Like its predecessors, it has often been criticized for arrogance and overreaching, even "hubris." Part of the indictment is unquestionably true. The president and his advisers had endured an attack that took them completely by surprise. Yet 9/11, no matter how shattering the experience, left the elements of national power basically untouched. The United States was challenged by terrorism without really being weakened by it. American policy makers emerged from the attack with enormous determination—spoiling for a fight, confident of the resources at their command, and certain that the rightness of their cause would enable them to prevail. Very little kept them from overdoing it.[66]

Even so hubris tells only part of the Bush administration's story. Just as important as its overconfidence was its lack of confidence. The president and his advisers did fear another attack at almost any moment and from almost any direction, they did want an international endorsement of their actions, they did worry about the war costing too much, and they did feel they had to present a progressive and ideologically compelling case for what they were doing.

The Bush administration handled all these matters badly. The president embraced maximalism without finding a way to make it work. He failed to unite overconfidence and lack of confidence in an effective policy. Again and again he provoked opposition when he sought support. If Washington wanted UN approval, it had to be willing either to act very quickly once it had the Security Council's initial endorsement, or to let the process play out much longer. If it wanted to depose Saddam and withdraw right away, it needed a larger force—one so credible that it might not have had to invade at all and so effective that it could maintain order once it did. If it wanted to install a legitimate Iraqi government, it needed a more transparent and participatory process for selecting it, and a military strategy that would enable it to succeed. Some of these measures would have increased public and international support; others would have, at least temporarily, undermined it. Had the president and his advisers fashioned a policy that could be over and done with as soon as possible, public support would have mattered far less. Success would have carried its own validation.

In his second term, George W. Bush sought to stabilize America's global position after the costly decisions of his first. A "kinder, gentler" approach to diplomacy, less pugnacious rhetoric, more deference to allies, a larger role for policy professionals—in the end, all these made only a marginal contribution to restoring American influence. As Iraq fragmented and the war came to seem hopeless, the United States was even more isolated than it had been three years earlier. The administration managed to right itself only in a final initiative that had, ironically, all the earmarks—and then some—of its earlier style. The surge of troops in 2007 was the product of a deeply divided administration, and of opaque and secretive decision making. In opting for more troops and a new strategy, Bush defied a political consensus that gave him little chance of success. The decision, made in near-total disregard of public opinion, sparked one of history's rare congressional votes demanding that the United States cut back a foreign military operation. (The president eventually vetoed it.) The surge was Bush's last burst of maximalism and—this probably explained his utter determination—the only one that could be said to have succeeded.

12

"No Wiggle Room"

OBAMA AND RETRENCHMENT

Barack Obama

ALMOST ALL PRESIDENTS take office determined to be different from their predecessors, but surely few have ever considered a change of direction more important than Barack Obama in 2009. Had it not been for early opposition to George Bush's foreign policy (Obama, unlike his rivals, had no awkward Iraq votes to explain away), he might not have won the presidency at all. Two wars, he saw, had drained national confidence and resources. The global economic crisis that coincided with the change of administrations further strengthened the case for change. Without new policies, American power seemed poised for steady, possibly steep decline. And if all this were not reason enough to chart a new course, there were the outgoing president's poll numbers. On the eve of the 2008 election, Bush's approval rating was just 22 percent, one of the lowest of any president since World War II. "People [are] tired of us," Condi Rice admitted to her boss as they prepared to leave Washington.[1]

Being different from Bush meant two separate things for Obama. There was, first, the obvious need to scale back America's international exposure. The public seemed to agree that retrenchment was a practical necessity. As the White House changed hands, 79 percent of Republicans—and the same percentage of Democrats—told pollsters that the United States "should pay less attention to problems overseas and concentrate on problems here at home." Had John McCain been elected in 2008, even he would have tried to distinguish himself from the forty-third president—fashioning a less costly global role, bringing troops home, cutting spending, and putting greater emphasis on domestic issues.[2]

Being different from Bush had a second, more activist meaning for the new president—restoring a positive global image for the United States; showing greater respect for the interests, traditions, and outlook of others; embracing a new agenda of foreign policy goals. In 2009 most of these ideas were not particularly divisive, either. Visionary rhetoric had been Obama's political signature as a candidate; when it came to controversial proposals he was far more cautious. Was the abolition of nuclear weapons, to take just one example, a radical concept? Establishment senior statesmen like George Shultz, Henry Kissinger, and Sam Nunn had been pushing it for years. As for Obama's oft-repeated readiness to negotiate directly with America's biggest enemies—stretching out a hand, he suggested, to those who would "unclench [their] fist"—he was careful about what this might mean in practice. The president envisioned hints, probes, and goodwill gestures—not a radically different diplomacy.

In selecting his national security team, Obama strengthened his centrist credentials by keeping Robert Gates on as secretary of defense. As national security adviser, he picked retired general James Jones, a former commander of NATO and known to have been on John McCain's short list for the job. Making Hillary Clinton secretary of state further signaled inclusiveness and reconciliation.

As he took office in January 2009, Barack Obama seemed well positioned to combine "hope and change" with a prudent downsizing of America's international role—and to wrap it in a spirit of national unity. Foreign policy might prove one more element of the "post-partisanship" he had championed in the campaign. Yet retrenchment can take many forms, and what one policy maker considers prudent another will call excessive and dangerous; yet another will find it completely insufficient to the needs of the moment. Would the new team alter policy only at the margin or more fundamentally? Neither the campaign nor the polls could answer this question. The senior officials Obama had assembled to advise him clearly favored a relatively gradual recalibration—some sort of revised Clintonism, perhaps, with "indispensable" American leadership as its watchword. The operating principles of the most recent Democratic administration were an obvious model for them. Even so, not everyone agreed. What gave the first year of the Obama administration its unexpected drama was the emergence of one especially influential dissenter—the president himself.

THE NEW ADMINISTRATION'S early decisions showed the strength of its initial consensus. Iraq, once the most divisive of political issues, no longer stirred much controversy. The Bush administration's plan had been to withdraw combat units over the course of eighteen months. Candidate Obama had proposed sixteen; President Obama announced that he would go with eighteen. With that, Iraq ceased to be a top-tier foreign policy problem.[3]

Afghanistan showed a similar convergence. George Bush had not disposed of a request for 30,000 more troops from the U.S. commander in Afghanistan. Right after Inauguration Day, the new president ordered up a quick policy review to map the way forward. Obama, who had run as a supporter of the "good war" in Afghanistan—unlike the "bad" one in Iraq—was considered certain to approve the request. He actually okayed the bulk of the increase before the group doing the policy review even finished its report. Only then did its members—including Richard Holbrooke, who had managed to get the Afghanistan portfolio at State; and General David Petraeus, who stayed on as commander of CENTCOM—give Obama their recommendations. To succeed in Afghanistan, the group advised, the United States needed both a larger force and a new approach—a "fully-resourced counter-insurgency strategy."[4]

Two years after the Iraq "surge," then, the new president's appointees read its lessons the same way that Pentagon generals did. Both groups dismissed the "minimalist" option of simply targeting al Qaeda and other terrorist fighters, favoring instead a "long-term commitment to assisting the Afghan people." Obama himself spoke at the unveiling of the strategy in March. He described what it would take to break the hold of extremist groups. Security was crucial, but so were improvements in Afghan agriculture, protection of women's rights, and the rule of law. (That Holbrooke also wanted a settlement with the Taliban did not by itself position him against the overall strategy or the troop buildup. More military punch, Holbrooke knew from the Balkans, would give the United States the leverage it needed for serious diplomacy.)[5]

In this first review, the administration had not addressed the cost of "nation-building" in Afghanistan nor fully sized up the Afghan government. It was unclear how large an American military presence would be needed for a successful "counter-insurgency" campaign. Yet even as members of Obama's team came to grips with the magnitude—and likely duration—of the commitment they had made, their near-unanimity held.

Policy makers knew that the failings of the Hamid Karzai government undermined American prospects. Holbrooke, in particular, was aware that a weak and corrupt client was unlikely to build capable institutions if Washington kept stepping in to do the job by itself. "The more help they need," he argued, "the more dependent they get for their help, and then it's 'Ah, let the Americans do that.'" Holbrooke had seen such dependency develop in Vietnam and did not want to repeat the mistake. Doing so would doom both "nation-building" and "counter-insurgency." America's goal, he told Afghan officials, was "to strengthen your government, not to do it ourselves."[6]

As always, the temptation to take over the problem proved hard to resist. Obama had approved more than $4 billion in aid—a tripling of Bush's program—and Holbrooke saw the new burst of assistance as a lever for improving Afghan performance, both economically and politically. "They need the kind of soup-to-nuts agricultural support," he said, "that Roosevelt gave the farmers during the Great Depression—roads, markets, irrigation, seeds, fertilizer, educational materials."[7]

This grand vision, Holbrooke understood, would come to nothing unless the Kabul government became more effective. In the summer of 2009, he lectured President Karzai that when U.S. forces cleared an area of insurgents, the authorities had to be ready with a "quick-reaction administrative effort to bring to the districts health, schools, and above all justice." There had been almost no progress in developing such institutional capacity, but that didn't discourage Holbrooke. An aide explained how his boss dealt with America's confused and unsteady allies. It was, he said, like therapy for psychologically abused children: "You don't focus on the screaming and violence—you just hug them tighter."[8]

General Stanley McChrystal, whom Gates had installed as the U.S. commander in Afghanistan at the beginning of 2009 with orders to make counterinsurgency work, had his own summary of Holbrooke's vision. "Government in a box," he called it, with no apparent irony—"ready to roll in." But a few months in his new job made clear to McChrystal the weakness of Afghan institutions and the shaky security outlook in much of the country. The Afghan army and police were unable to hold off the Taliban on their own. Until they could do so, the United States had to be responsible for security. One thing was obvious: a "fully-resourced program of counter-insurgency" required a big jump in America's commitment. McChrystal prepared a report for Washington on his manpower needs. Despite the big troop increase approved in March, he now wanted another. The general set out a range of options: the 85,000-troop increase he wanted; the 40,000 he felt might enable him to hold things together; 10,000 merely to do more training.[9]

By late summer of 2009, then, Obama's advisers—both civilian and military—had weighed the economic, political, and military capabilities of the Afghan government. They measured them against the requirements of success, and saw that there was a big gap between the two. Americans, they agreed, would have to fill it.

WHEN OBAMA and his senior advisers took up McChrystal's proposal for more troops in the fall, it was a very senior group indeed that sat around the table in the Situation Room. With an average age of almost sixty-six, the core members of the national security team—the vice president, secretary of state, secretary of defense, national security adviser, CIA director, and director of national intelligence—were the oldest a new president had ever assembled. (At the start of the Clinton administration, the same officials averaged fifty-five years of age; under Bush 43, they were fifty-seven; under John Kennedy, barely fifty.) Starting after Labor Day and continuing beyond Thanksgiving, these very seasoned officials talked for almost three months about whether to send more troops to Afghanistan. Their review lasted as long as it did for one reason above all others: not since Lyndon Johnson in July 1965 had any president been so reluctant to accept what his principal foreign policy advisers told him.

Both the secretary of state and the secretary of defense favored a stronger force. Gates had told the president that the right goal in Afghanistan was "victory." Hillary Clinton argued that only more troops would produce the governance changes necessary for the Afghans to stand on their own. The United States just wasn't "fighting enough," she felt. Clinton cautioned Obama not to whittle down McChrystal's request. Doing so would waste "time, lives, and money," she said. "If we go half-hearted, we'll achieve nothing."[10]

General Petraeus made the same case, that the president not try to get by with fewer than 40,000 troops: "You've got one bite at this apple. It ought to be a decisive one." Jim Jones, the national security adviser, thought it wise to consult more with the Europeans but not to count on them for a lot of help: "We all know who's going to do the bulk of the work." Leon Panetta, the CIA director, had the most concise advice for the president: stop fighting the military's recommendation. "Do what they say." Among senior members of the foreign policy team, only Vice President Joe Biden was a consistent dissenter. He opposed ambitious counterinsurgency and nation-building schemes, favoring a stripped-down "counter-terrorism" strategy that aimed simply to defeat al Qaeda.[11]

In 1965 Lyndon Johnson discovered that when a president's top advisers unite in a strong chorus of this kind, they leave him few options. But Obama was more ready than Johnson to challenge the consensus. Even in the initial rollout of Afghanistan strategy back in March, he had worried about cost. At that time, he publicly ruled out an "open-ended commitment of infinite resources." Now he asked budget director Peter Orszag to put a price tag on McChrystal's plan for fighting the war. Almost $900 billion over the coming decade, Orszag reported. Armed with this number, Obama unloaded on his team.

> This is not what I'm looking for. I'm not doing ten years. I'm not doing a long-term nation-building effort. I'm not spending a trillion dollars . . . . That's not in the national interest.[12]

Having recently described the struggle against al Qaeda and the Taliban as a "war of necessity," the president could hardly pull the plug on the effort. But in meeting after meeting, in what amounted to a long, multipart scolding of his advisers, he kept coming back to the theme of affordability. The United States was not going to fight the Afghan war forever, and he would not approve a policy of "as much as it takes for as long as it takes." Instead, Obama announced, "I want an exit strategy." Even the increase he had approved in March would have to be rolled back—and soon. "I'm not going to make a commitment that leaves my successor with more troops than I inherited in Afghanistan." This much was nonnegotiable. "There cannot be any wiggle room."[13]

By the end of November, the president approved McChrystal's 40,000-troop figure, but with three caveats that transformed the decision. First, American forces would not do the job alone. Obama authorized 33,000 troops; NATO allies would have to provide the rest. Second, to get the increases over with as fast as possible, they had to start as soon as possible. The Pentagon's proposal to build up over eighteen months was too leisurely; the president tightened it to six. (His brisk explanation: "Faster in, faster out.")[14]

Obama's final condition—the most important one—had not come up at all in prior discussions and caught his advisers by surprise. One year after the extra soldiers were in place, the president said, they would start to come home. Here he took the three-part mantra of counterinsurgency—"clear, hold, and build"—and added his own fourth term: "transfer." For Obama, the aim of the entire enterprise was to turn things over to the Afghans and get out. That goal should shape operational decisions right away. American lives were not to be lost clearing territory that Afghan forces could not hold when U.S. troops began to leave.[15]

The president personally went over each part of his decision in a separate video conversation with McChrystal and the U.S. ambassador in Kabul, Karl Eikenberry. Yes, he had endorsed the consensus in March, but what he was endorsing now was not that: "This is *not* a nation-wide counter-insurgency strategy." He was not going to make an open-ended commitment that the United States couldn't afford to keep or launch an effort that would only make the Afghan government more dependent on outside help. "No way."[16]

Three months of talking had made clear that, before leaving Afghanistan, almost all of the president's advisers wanted to take their best shot at a good result. Obama agreed to let them do so. At the same time, he specified just how long that best shot could last. And he warned his team not to think that the issue could be reopened down the road. "In 2010 we will not be having a conversation of how to do more. I will not want to hear that we're doing fine, Mr. President, but we'd be better if we just do more." The one topic, the president said, that he would be willing to discuss again in the future was "how to draw down faster."[17]

THE TIME LIMIT on the Afghanistan surge was the emblematic foreign policy choice of Obama's first term. With it, he took a consensus in favor of incremental adjustments to America's global role and pushed it toward a more thorough-going transformation. For many of his advisers, what the president was doing was not easy to accept or even to absorb. Would the United States really decide that the job of creating a viable Afghanistan was too much for it? Would Obama really say, "The hell with it, we have to leave," just because there was a rising tide of insurgent attacks? While the president was still making up his mind, Holbrooke told journalists that giving up was "just not an acceptable course of action." He had many doubts about the entire strategy, especially its heavy military component. But American staying power should not be questioned. In a series of conversations with *The New Yorker,* Holbrooke voiced the themes of an old-style maximalism. "I still believe," he said, "in the possibility of the United States, with all its will and all its strength, and I don't just mean military, persevering against any challenge. I still believe in that."[18]

Others, in and out of government, shared Holbrooke's unease. The president's decision was widely seen as self-defeating and unsophisticated. Didn't it undercut American bargaining leverage and encourage the enemy to wait the United States out? Many predicted that Obama would have to back down. Pentagon officials—Gates among them—suggested that the decision had been misunderstood. What the president really meant, they explained, was that there would be another review one year after the surge forces were in place; conditions on the ground, rather than an arbitrary schedule, would dictate what happened next. Senior generals told journalists that they were confident Obama would not start to withdraw troops if doing so might lead to an unraveling. The stakes were too high. As Petraeus put it, "This is the kind of fight we're in for the rest of our lives, and probably our kids' lives."[19]

Yet all the evidence suggested that the president would stick to his guns. He had personally dictated the details of his decision in a six-page legal "terms sheet." He had put defense spending on a downward track. Within months he fired McChrystal for making disrespectful comments about him to a *Rolling Stone* reporter. Perhaps most important of all, he began to rely on a set of new tools designed to reduce the cost and risk of providing for national security.[20]

One of Obama's new tools, and for a time the most controversial, was the enhanced use of small unmanned aircraft—known as drones—to eliminate terrorist fighters and leaders of al Qaeda. The advantages of remote-control warfare appeared to impress the new president from the outset. Aides confirmed publicly that he had instructed them early on to make "aggressive" use of "targeted killing." Semiofficial estimates indicated that Obama had ordered almost ten times as many drone attacks as Bush had. Soon more "pilots" were being trained for drones than for conventional fighters and bombers. Critics questioned the legal and diplomatic soundness of the approach, but they did not convince the public. Polls confirmed its popularity. In February 2013, the Pentagon announced a special new medal for heroics in drone combat.[21]

The president's desire for "innovative, low-cost, and small-footprint approaches" pushed policy makers to develop an entire family of policy tools with which to implement them. Where drone strikes were unsuited for a particular target, they had their manned equivalent in quick and lethal assaults by Special Operations forces. Ever more aggressive communications intercepts, including the acquisition of cell-phone "metadata," helped to disrupt the operations of extremist groups and the transfer of money, technology, equipment, and expertise between them.

A parallel set of tools focused on nuclear proliferation. Supersecret programs of cyber warfare aimed to sabotage an adversary's advanced computers. A series of nuclear summits targeted the underworld of global supply chains for illicit sensitive materials. Enhanced collection and sharing of financial and commercial intelligence made economic sanctions a more effective instrument of policy. The success of these new tools, like that of drones, was reflected in larger budgets even as overall national security spending went down. "Background" briefings for the media trumpeted their achievements.[22]

"Small-footprint" tools did not, of course, have to be part of a downsized American strategy. Many of them originated in the maximalist atmosphere of the Bush administration. And for some of Obama's critics, his fascination with these tools showed the deep underlying continuity with the policies of his predecessor. The president, however, clearly saw them differently. Monitoring and countering security threats at a distance offered an alternative to risky, expensive, up-close-and-personal involvement. What seemed maximalism under George Bush could, in Obama's hands, become instruments of retrenchment.

The administration's Afghanistan policy made the shift particularly clear. When Richard Holbrooke introduced the term *AfPak* as a nickname for his State Department portfolio, he meant it as a shorthand encapsulation of a far-reaching strategy. The future of Afghanistan, he insisted, was inextricably linked to Pakistan's—to its byzantine politics, troubled history, divided society, and tangled identity. American policy had to take all these factors into account. Holbrooke told his staff that their job was nothing less than to "change Pakistan." And maybe not only Pakistan. Ultimately, he thought, the United States had to address that country's unresolved conflict with India too. All the pathologies of South Asia should be on the U.S. policy agenda.[23]

This was a gigantic prescription—*maximalist* is not too big a word for it. To carry it out, Holbrooke imagined a complex and ambitious diplomatic effort. (He was even making a bit of progress on it. Just before his sudden death in November 2010, he had brokered a small agreement to open up Indo-Pakistani trade.) But the enterprise Holbrooke had in mind was too complex and ambitious to persuade a president with other things on his mind. Obama wanted a strategy that allowed him to care less about Pakistan, not one that gave him a fascinating analysis of why he should care more. The president, one State Department official believed, was skeptical of any ideas that involved changing other societies. He aimed to do "as little wiring as possible." The new tools at his disposal gave him an alternative to messy, intricate diplomacy. They enabled him to hope for a clean escape.[24]

Holbrooke was not the only senior official to challenge Obama's approach to retrenchment. Others replayed his concerns. Admiral Dennis Blair, the director of national intelligence, spoke out publicly against overreliance on covert action. "Overt tools of national power," he argued, would produce better results than working in the shadows. In early 2011, the ambassador to Pakistan, Cameron Munter, advised Washington that drone attacks were undermining broader U.S. aims in the region. Admiral Mike Mullen, the JCS chairman, agreed; so did the secretary of state.[25]

Sometimes disagreement between a president and his advisers clarifies the premises of American policy even when it's perfectly clear who is going to win the argument and why. Holbrooke's ideas about active American engagement in South Asia were a perfect example. They reflected Bill Clinton's outlook more than Barack Obama's. Holbrooke and his colleagues had no more hope of winning over the president than George Kennan had had of persuading Harry Truman to negotiate the neutrality of Germany and Japan with the Soviet Union in 1949, or than George Ball had of persuading Lyndon Johnson to write off South Vietnam in 1965. There were important differences of style and temperament in all these disagreements, but the core issue was the scale of American ambition. Kennan and Ball envisioned a foreign policy too small for their presidents to accept. Holbrooke envisioned one that was much too large.

FOR ANY PRESIDENT engaged in retrenchment, policy success is not measured simply by how well the United States extricates itself from old involvements. How well are new challenges handled? How much do narrower horizons diminish America's influence? The Obama administration faced these questions most acutely in its response to three sets of problems. In East Asia, China's neighbors, among them several U.S. allies, asked how Washington intended to prevent domination of the region by a single power. In the Arab world, a wave of unprecedented political upheaval obliged American policy makers to take sides in the region's new civil wars. Finally, Iran's seeming march toward nuclear weapons threatened the most dangerous breach in decades of the nuclear nonproliferation regime. In all three of these cases, defending American interests clearly called for more involvement, not less. They posed uncomfortable policy choices for a president in pursuit of retrenchment.

Although China's rise threatened the biggest long-term transformation of the global order, in the short term it was the easiest of these problems to deal with. Late in 2009, talking to NSC staffers about America's relationship with China, Obama compared it to the pressure that a once-dominant basketball team feels when others start doing better. China's economic success meant the United States had to reconsider its style of play. "For years, we used to trounce them," he said, "so if they threw a few elbows around in the lane it didn't matter, we could ignore it. Now the game was much closer, and they were continuing to throw elbows around, but the referee wasn't calling any fouls."[26]

With the dynamics of international competition changing, the president wondered, perhaps the United States had to "find a way to push back, to start throwing around a few elbows ourselves." Obama's comments were prompted by trade disputes. But China's rapidly growing power, and the resulting anxiety of its neighbors, meant that his basketball metaphor was picked up in other areas of policy as well. At the beginning of the administration, he and his advisers had hoped that Washington and Beijing might operate as collaborative senior partners—an informal "G-2"—in global affairs. Soon enough, American policy makers concluded that their interest in shared leadership had been read as weakness by the Chinese. A successful policy, it seemed clear, called for closer U.S. attention to the balance of power—and more assertive diplomacy. "I need leverage!" the president told his advisers. The United States had to start using its elbows.[27]

The first step toward renewed competitiveness was simply showing up. Visiting Asia on her first foreign trip as secretary of state, Hillary Clinton heard her hosts chide Washington for "diplomatic absenteeism." The new administration made clear it would be a joiner again. In November 2009, Obama held a first annual meeting with leaders of the Association of Southeast Asian Nations (ASEAN). In the past, U.S. secretaries of state had found ASEAN's annual meetings of foreign ministers too distant, and too tedious, to attend regularly. Geopolitical symbolism now trumped jetlag and boredom. In June 2010, at the urging of regional leaders, Obama further agreed as well to take part in a new forum, the

East Asia Summit, so that China would not be the dominant participant. Washington also sought to give trade ties a sharper political edge. Having concluded a free trade agreement with South Korea, the United States began lobbying major Pacific trading partners to join the Trans-Pacific Partnership, a grouping that would not, at least at the outset, include China at all.[28]

East Asia's regional gatherings, normally sedate affairs, now became forums in which to air geopolitical disagreements. The most famous encounter—a verbal standoff between Hillary Clinton and the Chinese foreign minister, Yang Jiechi—took place at the July 2010 meeting of the ASEAN Regional Forum in Hanoi. It was almost surely the most dramatic moment in the organization's history. Clinton used her Hanoi speech to deliver a message about China's territorial claims in the South China Sea—and its increasing identification of these waters as a "core" Chinese interest. Freedom of navigation, she emphasized, was an American interest too, and she offered support for negotiations to develop a maritime code of conduct. Prompted by Washington in the run-up to the meeting, other delegations made similar statements. The Chinese foreign minister called Clinton's speech "an attack on China," and he responded with a fierce counterblast. "China is a big country," Yang warned his colleagues in Hanoi, "and other countries are small countries, and that is just a fact." China's neighbors, he stressed, should not go looking to the United States for support.[29]

Rebuilding American influence in Asia could not, of course, rest on talk and meetings alone. Hard power—real military elbows—would be needed too. When North Korea sank a South Korean ship in March 2010, tension between Seoul and Pyongyang had its parallel in tension between Beijing and Washington. After meeting with Chinese president Hu Jintao, Obama publicly criticized China's policy as one of "willful blindness"—an unusually sharp term. The United States now went further, backing up its ally with large naval exercises—in the face of Chinese protests.[30]

Deploying warships in support of a friend sent a strong message, but a credible American "pivot" to Asia called for still more. Didn't planned cuts in defense spending mean the United States would be less able to help friends and allies in the future? To reassure regional states, Obama promised that he would maintain a strong military presence in East Asia for the indefinite future. The Pentagon budget might go down, the president told the Australian parliament in 2011, but with one exception.

"Reductions in U.S. defense spending will not—I repeat, will not—come at the expense of the Asia Pacific." He further announced the creation of a small Marine base on Australia's north coast and the stationing of four small coastal vessels in Singapore. And despite expectations that the navy would cut the number of its carriers to ten, he kept it steady at eleven.[31]

Barack Obama was the first president since the end of the Cold War who had to worry that America might actually be overtaken by a rival. To retain influence in Asia, Washington policy makers acknowledged, the United States had to "step up its game." If the administration failed to deal effectively with China, one senior diplomat admitted to journalists, "in thirty years that's the only thing anyone will remember."[32]

Whatever followed it, the "pivot" of American policy was certainly a start. Kurt Campbell, the State Department's senior official for Asia, thought the United States had staked its claim to a "dominant role in the Asia-Pacific region for the next forty, thirty, fifty years." For Tom Donilon, Jones's replacement as national security adviser, giving more attention to Asia was "as big a strategic move as the United States had made in a long time." Hillary Clinton pronounced it one of "the most important diplomatic efforts of our time."[33]

The echoes of Nixon and Kissinger were more than rhetorical coincidence. The Obama administration's "rebalancing" to Asia played the same role in its retrenchment strategy that the China opening had played in American retrenchment at the end of the Vietnam War. It was meant as proof that the United States was not, as Nixon put it, going "down the drain as a great power." It provided an escape from the seeming futility of military ventures, oriented Washington toward the challenges of the future, and offered American leaders a warm welcome at a time when anti-Americanism was the rule elsewhere. Best of all for a retrenchment president, it seemed—for a while, at least—very easy to afford.

THE "ARAB SPRING" posed far more difficult choices for Obama and his advisers. The administration had hoped to shift attention and resources away from the Middle East. The huge demonstrations against Egyptian president Hosni Mubarak that rocked Cairo in January 2011—and similar upheavals across the region—put that goal at risk.

Washington found it hard to respond when Arab crowds appealed for

American support against friendly governments. The president said he wanted to be on "the right side of history," but many of his advisers were anxious about which side was which. "We are entering the unknown," one of them said. "This could be 1989 or it could be 1979." Said another: "I don't think that because a group of young people get on the street that we are obliged to be for them." Big, unruly crowds, policy makers worried, were more likely to bring the Ayatollah Khomeini to power than Vaclav Havel. Obama did eventually call for Mubarak to step down—but only after American spokesmen made many statements suggesting that the United States wanted him to stay.[34]

Turmoil in Libya deepened the administration's confusion. The armed uprising against Muammar Gadhafi's forty-year dictatorship showed that the Arab Spring had powerful, regionwide momentum. Yet it also made painfully clear that replacing autocrats with popular rule could be a bloody and violent process. Simply stating American preferences would not ensure a satisfactory outcome. Among Obama's advisers, Gadhafi's attempt to crush his opponents energized those who wanted to prevent genocide, or to promote democracy, or to display American leadership. Even more, however, it energized those who did not want to put costly new burdens on the U.S. military. Robert Gates, preparing to step down as defense secretary but never shy about stating his views, publicly warned that anyone recommending military intervention in the Middle East should "have his head examined." Easy measures would not settle a struggle as chaotic as what was unfolding in Libya. Gates argued that enforcement of a no-fly zone, the favorite proposal of the interventionists, would be a massive operation—and probably inconclusive.[35]

These internal divisions delayed American intervention, but only briefly. Pressure to reopen the issue came from too many different directions. Both the British and French governments kept urging a no-fly zone. In Congress, both John Kerry and John McCain supported the plan. Even the Arab League endorsed it. Within the administration, Hillary Clinton, earlier hesitant to commit herself, now backed the idea. With governments of the region calling for Western intervention to check Gadhafi's bloodbath, Clinton challenged the White House to explain why the United States was opposed.[36]

The growing chorus—two key European allies, key senators from both parties, the secretary of state, and on top of it all, Arab governments too—forced Obama to reconsider. To stay on the sidelines while the

Libyan dictator massacred his opponents would show, one of his advisers admitted, that America "isn't really a leader." The same anxiety had, a decade and a half earlier, pushed Bill Clinton to intervene in Bosnia.

Supporters of intervention had made a policy change unavoidable. They had not, however, persuaded the president that they had a workable plan. At a meeting hurriedly convened to discuss a no-fly zone, and a UN Security Council resolution endorsing it, Obama asked his national security team whether the measures they favored would actually stop Gadhafi's killing spree. To their embarrassed admission that it would not, the president responded testily. The meeting they proposed was "not worth having," he said. The president wanted to hear about solving the problem at an acceptable cost—not about trying nobly, only to fail. That would get the United States in deeper, exactly what Obama wanted to avoid. "I want more options," he said, adjourning the discussion.[37]

This quick back-and-forth between the president and his advisers over Libya yielded essentially the same result as their protracted back-and-forth over Afghanistan a year and a half earlier. Obama again approved the use of U.S. military might, but on strict conditions. He required an early hand-off to the British and the French—and he insisted that Arab states be part of the operation. After helping to get it started, American forces would be involved only when they had some unique capability that NATO allies lacked.

That turned out to be often. For months, U.S. planes did 75 percent of the refueling, supplied most of the reconnaissance, and flew more sorties than anyone else. It was American officials who picked up the phone to wheedle the governments of Qatar, Jordan, and the UAE to stay involved when they wanted to drop out. When European munitions ran low, or drones were needed, American equipment and supplies filled the gap. An NSC staffer memorably described this role as "leading from behind" (a phrase borrowed from Nelson Mandela). The president echoed the thought. "Real leadership," he explained, "creates the conditions and coalitions for others to step up as well."[38]

It was closer to the truth, however, to say that others had created these conditions. It was the United States, not its allies, that had been obliged to step up. The Obama administration acted only after a broad international coalition had formed and could no longer be ignored. What Washington added was the conviction that an intervention had to be big enough to produce a decisive result. American power made success possible. (The same thing had been true in Bosnia too.) Otherwise Hillary Clinton's description of what had happened was right. "We did not lead this," she admitted to European audiences. The administration—and above all, the president—had not wanted to lead at all, even from behind. It had been a real challenge just to catch up.[39]

IN 1995, SUCCESS in Bosnia had put the Clinton administration, after great hesitation, on a more activist foreign policy track for the rest of the decade. The Obama administration's involvement in Libya might easily have been the same sort of turning point. But, far from giving him a new direction, intervention against Gadhafi in Libya—and even more, the raid against Osama bin Laden six weeks later—appeared to strengthen the president's commitment to retrenchment. Success in the Balkans showed Clinton how the U.S. role in the world might be reinvigorated. Obama's successes showed how to continue the pullback of American power. His decisions became more purposeful and more confident. He was less likely to be challenged by his principal national security advisers, and less deferential to their views.

In July 2011, Obama announced that all the additional troops he had ordered to Afghanistan at the end of 2009, having now been in place for one year, would come home in the year ahead. The decision was a disappointment to those who hoped the military would be given more time to accomplish its mission. General Petraeus admitted to Congress that it was a more "aggressive" drawdown than he had wanted. He had made the case for a slower withdrawal in two face-to-face meetings with the president, appealing to him to keep the bulk of the troops in place at least through the end of the next fighting season.[40]

Obama was no longer swayed by these appeals. The surge in Afghanistan had never acquired the prestige of its predecessor in Iraq. Its costs—especially measured in increased American casualties—were higher; and its benefits, harder to demonstrate. For a president with other priorities, this was a too limited payoff. Obama stuck to the simple standard he had announced during the long policy review of 2009. He had said then that the United States could not afford a large and protracted involvement in Afghanistan, and that by the end of his term he wanted fewer U.S. troops there than when he took office. At subsequent decision points, the generals wanted a little flexibility, a little more time, a bit more money, just as the president had predicted they would. And just as he warned them in 2009, he did not relent. The United States, Obama clearly believed, had taken its best shot. It would no longer "try to make Afghanistan a perfect place."[41]

How little Libya had done to reorient U.S. policy was confirmed by the president's handling of Syria. The decision to topple Gadhafi, administration spokesmen suggested, had been relatively straightforward. The strategic stakes in Syria, they acknowledged, were far higher but the chance of a clean and successful intervention was far lower. The Assad regime was better armed and had more powerful international patrons. Russia and China, in particular, vetoed Security Council resolutions condemning the Syrian government's brutality against its own people. Above all, the opposition to Assad was poorly organized, and as time passed radical Islamists played a growing role in it.

The reasons to steer clear of Syria were obvious enough. But the case for involvement was also strong. The mounting death toll stimulated humanitarian concerns. The escalating clash between Sunni and Shi'a forces raised questions about regional stability. Reported chemical weapons use challenged international legal norms. The fact that the United States was still on the sidelines after more than two years of civil war clearly exacerbated many of the struggle's most negative features—the disorder of the opposition, the ineffectual efforts of American friends and allies, the growing influence of Iran.

For all this, Obama remained opposed to deeper involvement. He gave ground only gradually—and under extreme duress. In the fall of 2012, the people he had chosen to lead the top three foreign policy agencies of the U.S. government—Hillary Clinton at State, Leon Panetta at Defense, and David Petraeus at the CIA—sent him a plan to begin arming the Syrian opposition. The president rejected it. In late spring 2013, as the number of deaths in the Syrian civil war passed one hundred thousand, the clamor, at home and abroad, to do something seemed hard to resist. (Even Bill Clinton said Obama risked looking like a "fool" if he did nothing.) But the president's concession to the uproar was minimal. He agreed to supply small arms and ammunition, one small step up from humanitarian relief and non-lethal aid.[42]

When the Syrian government killed more than fourteen hundred civilians in a chemical weapons attack in late August, Obama's hands-off strategy faced its most severe test. Even so, he resisted calls to throw American support fully behind opponents of the Assad regime. If the United States took any military action at all, it would be only to show that chemical weapons were taboo—and that the president, having said use of such weapons crossed a "red line," really meant it. Obama's stance did risk deeper involvement (many opposed it for this reason) but with little chance of ending the war (for others, this was even more objectionable). The British parliament voted against a strike; the U.S. Congress seemed ready to do the same. Only a Russian proposal—to force Syria to surrender its chemical arsenal—saved Obama from a humiliating bipartisan rebuff.[43]

It did not save him from a storm of derision. *Time* called it "one of the most stunning and inexplicable displays of presidential incompetence . . . ever witnessed." The cover of *The New Republic* proclaimed, "Obama Has No Foreign Policy." Many wondered whether the damage to his presidency could be repaired. Obama had for more than two years hoped to influence a military struggle without bringing any military tools to bear. He had found it impossible to do. When he needed support, virtually no one was with him.[44]

The entire affair was vivid proof of how policy options can be narrowed by waiting. Yet whatever the prestige costs—and they were high—Syria was not a problem that Obama had ever believed he had to solve. He had wanted to keep his distance, and at that—in the most dismal fashion—he succeeded. Looking weak and foolish was perhaps an acceptable cost.

Iran was a different story. It had been a high priority from the beginning of his administration—and under Bush and Clinton too. For five years, and more, the United States had explored every avenue of pressure, from economic sanctions and cyber sabotage to multilateral diplomacy. In declaring that he would never, under any circumstances, allow Teheran to acquire nuclear weapons, Obama had threatened force in a way that he had never been willing to do with Syria. In letting Vice President Biden declare, in March 2013, that presidents "cannot and do not bluff," he further nailed his feet to the floor.[45]

The election of Hassan Rouhani as president of Iran—with a seeming mandate to find a compromise on the nuclear issue—showed, of course, that sometimes delay creates new options. At the end of 2013, Obama found himself with an unexpectedly promising opportunity. Iran was weaker; his own hand, stronger. An interim agreement in November 2013, which exchanged a freeze on further Iranian nuclear development for limited sanctions relief, was the first result.

As the two sides began talks on a longer-term deal, it was unclear how well American leverage would hold up. Did Iran believe that sanctions had passed their high-water mark? How seriously did it take the threat of a U.S. military strike? Joe Biden had been right to point out that bluffing is dangerous, but wrong that presidents don't do it. Retrenchment presidents, in fact, bluff all the time. Their strategy revolves around cutting costs and risks, and bluffing—at least when it works—is cheap. (As if to make exactly this point, a new history of Eisenhower's foreign policy was published shortly before Biden's speech under the title *Ike's Bluff*. Obama's challenge was the same faced by any president who presides over the pullback of American power—how to downsize foreign policy while retaining the ability to act decisively.

ALMOST EVERY IMPORTANT decision of Barack Obama's presidency has been shadowed by the issue of resource constraints. The president invoked this question at each step in the unwinding of America's post-9/11 wars. Quoting Eisenhower's 1961 farewell address, he called for "balance in and among national programs." For Obama, retrenchment had a moral urgency. "Over the last decade"—some version of these words appeared in many of his speeches—"we have spent a trillion dollars on war, at a time of rising debt and hard economic times. Now we must invest in America's greatest resource—our people . . . . America, it is time to focus on nation-building here at home."[46]

The Pentagon budget—given its size and the huge increases it had enjoyed after 9/11—was, of course, the biggest target of cost cutting from the beginning of the administration. In the first budget that he presented, for FY 2010, the president cut almost $40 billion per year. And demands for reduced defense spending only grew. When Leon Panetta replaced Robert Gates as secretary of defense in mid-2011, the White House instructed him to start planning on still bigger cuts—almost $50 billion more each year, for a total of $487 billion over the course of the decade.[47]

Even that number kept growing. Within months, the "sequestration" plan worked out by the administration and Congress, imposing mandatory across-the-board spending cuts in the absence of a long-term budget plan, provided for another $400 billion–plus cut in defense spending on top of those already projected. This cut was considered so huge that it could never be accepted. Then, in March 2013, it was accepted. The

Pentagon budget for FY 2014 recorded the largest single-year drop since the Korean War.[48]

Military spending offered the biggest potential savings at a time when resources were tight, but smaller projects that the president cared about were hardly spared. After his Cairo speech of 2009—an attempt to reach out to the Muslim world—spending for Middle East projects under the Agency for International Development (AID) surged almost 50 percent in a single year. Then fiscal reality set in. Two years later, when the time came for another speech, in which Obama aimed to express American enthusiasm and support for the Arab Spring, his advisers tried to come up with projects that would make his statements seem credible. One aide remarked that the search for funds was like the quack chemistry that tries to turn "copper into gold—and about as successful." American assistance budgets did not keep up with what policy makers saw as a pivotal historic moment. The president, officials said, found the result "deeply disappointing." But he did not act to reverse it.[49]

International spending across the U.S. government showed the same pattern. In late 2011, when top officials of the International Monetary Fund (IMF) sought to assemble a stabilization fund to deal with shocks from the banking crisis in the eurozone, they approached the organization's major shareholders, of which the United States had always been by far the largest. By June 2012 pledges were received from thirty-seven IMF members, totaling almost half a trillion dollars. China made up 10 percent of the full amount; Japan, at $60 billion, even more. Among other countries outside the European Union, Saudi Arabia and South Korea contributed $15 billion each; Brazil, India, Mexico, and Russia offered $10 billion each. The Obama administration, knowing that Congress was unlikely to appropriate any money at all, particularly in an election year, offered zero.[50]

American policy makers claimed not to be particularly chagrined by this result. They explained to journalists that the IMF's lending capacity was adequate and insisted that they would not have been inclined to contribute even if they had been able to raise the money. The United States, they pointed out, already did a lot to provide global public goods. It had cooperated with European banks since the crisis of 2008–9 to keep the international financial system afloat. The benefits of that ongoing effort dwarfed the relatively minor embarrassment of being unable to pony up funds when Brazil, Mexico, Saudi Arabia, and China were able to do so.[51]

The power and wealth of the United States had been so great for so long that even tight resources could not keep it from playing a central role in international affairs. This was as true of military and diplomatic problems as it was of global finance. Yet as budgetary challenges mounted, American officials began to acknowledge the changes ahead. In June 2013, Chuck Hagel, Obama's second-term choice as defense secretary, had insisted to an audience of defense experts in Singapore that it would be "unwise and shortsighted" to doubt U.S. staying power in East Asia. By August, an administration that used to point with pride to the president's decision to keep eleven aircraft carrier groups in operation began explaining that, without changes in the fiscal outlook, the real number might drop down to eight or nine.

Because the navy was at the heart of American strategy in Asia, a cut of this kind had real political implications. For the other branches of the U.S. military, the outlook was bleaker still. The air force grounded thirteen of its fighter squadrons (one third of the total), canceled combat training exercises, and prepared to shrink its fleet of cargo planes. The army suspended routine training for all units except those about to deploy. In August, Hagel gave a public preview of his office's in-house study of future options. Not surprisingly, the army was the biggest potential victim. Under one scenario, its "end-strength" would drop from 570,000 to 380,000—the lowest in more than sixty years. Across-the-board cuts were required. As army chief of staff General Ray Odierno summed it up, "The money is gone."[52]

All this, of course, described what austerity was likely to do to America's military muscle. But what about its mission? General Martin Dempsey, the JCS chairman, made clear that here, too, rethinking was inevitable. With less to spend, he often said, "we'll need to adjust our ambitions to match our abilities."[53]

BECAUSE RETRENCHMENT always raises doubts about the future of American power, Obama's foreign policy team had long and vehemently disputed the idea that the United States was losing its grip on global leadership. Their real goal, they insisted, was the exact opposite: to *strengthen* its international role. Benjamin Rhodes, author of many of the president's speeches, said the administration wanted "to get America another fifty years as leader." Tony Blinken, Biden's chief aide and then deputy national security adviser in Obama's second term, described the U.S.

policy puzzle as "figuring out, in a more complicated world, with new constraints, how to maximize our power, and that's what we've done."[54]

In a "more complicated" world, of course, the United States had to make adjustments. It had to lead, as Hillary Clinton put it, "in a new way." Having more participants in global affairs seemed a hurdle all by itself. As her planning director Jake Sullivan complained, the proliferation of new players "doesn't always mean that they'll do what we want, when we want, how we want." All the same, Washington policy makers claimed they saw an American opportunity. "No other nation," Clinton liked to say, "can bring disparate countries and people together around common goals." She argued that this coordinating or convening role was not necessarily a sign of declining U.S. influence. It was in keeping with "the world we're trying to build"—and with American traditions. The United States had consistently tried "to advance not just our own good, but the greater good." The country's readiness for global leadership, Clinton enthused, "is in our DNA." Of all those who shaped the Obama administration's international strategy, the secretary of state was most comfortable with the precepts of a traditional maximalism. "We do believe," she said, "there are no limits on what is possible or what can be achieved."[55]

This was how many of the most influential people around Obama described their aims and assumptions. Most of his second term picks for senior jobs—John Kerry, Susan Rice, Samantha Power—had long talked the same way. The president himself did not. To be sure, he dismissed the idea of American "decline." (Those who thought the United States was a fading power, he said in his 2012 State of the Union address, "[don't] know what they're talking about.") But rejecting decline did not mean rejecting retrenchment. From the moment he took office Obama was the member of his own administration most firmly and consistently committed to rethinking both the ends and means of American foreign policy. As he saw it, shifting resources from problems abroad to "nation-building" at home was necessary to assure the country's long-term well-being. When his advisers challenged the specifics of this or that pullback, the president told them their plans and ideas were simply too expensive.[56]

Obama put more emphasis than any other member of his team on downsizing American aims. "We must be humble," he said, "in our expectation that we can quickly resolve deep-rooted problems like poverty or sectarian hatred." At the UN in September 2013, he used the same thought to express what America took away from a decade of war in remote and unfamiliar locales—a "hard-earned humility." Even when Obama spoke of a unique U.S. leadership role—and this was not often—he said that it was unlikely to continue. Global disengagement by the United States, he told the General Assembly, would leave a vacuum "that no other nation is ready to fill." But, he warned, the American people would support costly and dangerous foreign involvements only if others did their part. "We cannot and should not bear that burden alone."[57]

Other presidents have expressed the same frustration with what others contribute to international order. John Kennedy told foreign officials he was sick of their criticism of the United States. Richard Nixon said others should not count on American support while always challenging American policies. But neither of them ever figured out how to get friends and allies to contribute more. Half a century later, the Obama administration had not solved the problem either. "The United States," Hillary Clinton observed, "bears a disproportionate amount of the burden for trying to maintain peace and security and prosperity across the globe." Was there some way to ease that burden by a better division of international responsibilities? Clinton was skeptical—and seemingly nostalgic for the influence of a time gone by. "I wish," she added regretfully, "there were a way we could tell a lot of countries what they should do."[58]

EPILOGUE

"If It's Worth Doing, It's Worth Overdoing"

PROFESSIONAL HISTORIANS have a special dislike for what they call presentism, the tendency to shape our view of the past so that it matches up usefully with whatever we want to believe about the present. History being so rich with opportunities for intellectual manipulation, their disapproval is understandable. Yet presentism is an unavoidable part of trying to learn from the past and of making its lessons relevant to our own experience. For help in thinking about contemporary problems, we need feel no guilt in scrutinizing historical events, personalities, and decisions for their similarities to (or for that matter, their suggestive differences from) those of today. We simply have to be ready to think hard, and honestly, about what those similarities and differences really mean. Readers are *supposed* to toggle back and forth between the preoccupations of the moment and the stories told in this book. That's why it was written.[1]

Over the entire period we have looked at, two things have almost always been true of American foreign policy. The United States has been the single most important factor in world affairs—a formidable economic engine, a military giant, an influential diplomatic broker, a source of ideas and innovation. By whatever measure, and for both better and worse, it has been a power like no other.

Yet no matter where we dip back into the history of the last six or seven decades, we also find American policy makers doubting that they have gotten things right. The ends and means of policy have usually seemed out of whack to them. Especially at the start of new administrations, recalibration—a serious effort to correct a predecessor's mistakes—

has been the rule. (The exceptions to this pattern are extremely revealing. Of all our presidents since World War II, only two—Lyndon Johnson and Gerald Ford—took office feeling a strong sense of obligation to continue the policies they inherited. Both of them were eventually driven from power, a fate they might well have avoided had they tried harder to change course.)

In their regular quest for a new direction, presidents and their advisers have usually drawn policy answers from one of two strategic schools. We could call these (with apologies for oversimplifying complex ideas) the school of "more" and the school of "less." Harry Truman, John Kennedy, Lyndon Johnson (after 1965), Ronald Reagan, and George W. Bush (after September 11) are clear members of the "more" school. Dwight Eisenhower, Richard Nixon, Gerald Ford, Jimmy Carter, and Barack Obama make up that of "less." George H. W. Bush and Bill Clinton are hybrid cases. Each began in one school and ended up in the other. (Bush went from "more" to "less"; Clinton, the reverse.)

Presidents of the "more" school generally practiced some version of what this book has called maximalism. Their watchword was, as Arthur Schlesinger, Jr., described the Kennedy administration's outlook, that "the world was plastic, and the future unlimited." (*The New Yorker* went further. It said of Kennedy's foreign policy, "He did not fear the weather, and did not trim his sails, but instead challenged the wind itself.") Maximalist presidents assumed that international problems were highly susceptible to the vigorous use of American power and indeed were very unlikely to be solved without it.[2]

Our presidents of "less," by contrast, have had to oversee retrenchment, or the curtailment of American power after a period of overextension. The political horizons of these presidents have been narrower, their anxiety greater, their sense of the moment captured by the first George Bush in his 1992 State of the Union address. "People are worried," he confided to the Congress. "There's been talk of decline."[3]

RETRENCHMENT AND DECLINE are the big issues of contemporary American foreign policy that "presentists" among us might hope to understand better by looking closely at the past. The three and a half cases of downsizing that we have reviewed in previous chapters do teach us a few things about the enterprise that are often forgotten.

To begin with, retrenchment is not nearly as difficult or controversial as we tend to think. Maximalist presidents who get into stalemated wars are rarely able to extricate themselves; they pay a heavy political price for their failure. But their successors—the presidents who come in to clean up the mess—typically enjoy very strong domestic support. For taking on this job, Dwight Eisenhower, Richard Nixon, and Barack Obama were all decisively reelected. Since World War II, only one president who initiated a process of retrenchment has failed to win a second term. That was our confusing half-case, George H.W. Bush, whose fretful talk of decline followed, oddly enough, a string of foreign policy victories. The American people, it seems, are grateful to leaders who wind down unsuccessful wars for them. A president who decides to downsize after success is another story. He gets voted out.

The second thing our historical examples suggest about retrenchment is that it's no mere cleanup job. Presidents who get the assignment tend to define it more expansively. They seek to reorient American foreign policy as a whole, to bring ends and means into better balance. Quite apart from the Korean War, Eisenhower thought the acute psychological burden of nuclear confrontation with the Soviet Union was too much for the public to bear for very long. He put forward one ambitious arms control proposal after another to ease the strain. To make himself more "exciting," Nixon also wanted to wrap himself in the mantle of peacemaker. (As Henry Kissinger lectured his White House colleagues, you can't just offer people "blood, sweat, and tears all the time.") Bush's "new world order" slogan was employed in much the same spirit, to explain how international problems might take care of themselves for a while, with less American effort. As the first Democrat to launch retrenchment, Barack Obama might have been expected to bring some new themes to the project. Yet set alongside the lofty, unrealized hopes of his Republican forerunners, even his heal-the-planet talk seems quite familiar. Downsizing calls for a side dish of compensatory inspiration.[4]

Retrenchment presidents are (at least in their own minds) big-picture reconceptualizers. Bringing the boys home from war gives them an opening to deal with the deeper problems that produced the unsuccessful war in the first place. Here they usually come up with the same solution. Eisenhower wanted to replace Truman's "emergency" policies with an approach that would be good for the "long haul." Nixon, prompted by Kissinger, thought America was naturally disposed to an "oscillating" foreign policy—back and forth between feckless crusades and dangerous isolation. Building a "stable structure of peace" seemed a better way to serve American interests. In his second inaugural address, Obama paid little attention to foreign policy, but he said enough to put himself squarely in the Eisenhower-Nixon camp. The United States, he declared, did not need "perpetual war" to protect itself. "Engagement can more durably lift suspicion and fear."[5]

Because they are reelected, retrenchment presidents have a chance to get the "long haul" off to a solid start. Defense spending is not the only index of retrenchment, but it is an important one, and history shows that the scaling back from a big surge of outlays usually takes longer than the surge itself. Truman's burst of spending lasted less than three years; Eisenhower then tightened up for almost eight. Kennedy and Johnson provided an eight-year boost for the Pentagon budget, the biggest chunk of it in the last three years; the downsizing that followed Vietnam went on for a decade and more. The new wave of spending that Reagan launched lasted six years; after it began to recede, it took nine years to bottom out. On historical evidence alone, Obama—and the rest of the world, for that matter—should probably expect the unwinding of the Bush administration's buildup to take a solid decade or more.[6] A strong aversion to large military operations may last considerably longer.

The past also allows us to see more clearly how retrenchments end: not necessarily in tears, but usually in a chorus of complaint. There should be no surprise in this. A policy that aims to establish a steady level of American effort over a long period of time is going to seem inadequate when some unexpected problem arises. We have seen how frustrated Eisenhower was by the charge that he wasn't doing enough to deal with the new challenges of the late 1950s. We also know how Kissinger responded to critics who said he had to try harder to counter Soviet policy. They didn't understand, he fulminated, that his policy was already the toughest that could be sustained over the long haul.

Given the political alignments of our own time, it is easy to think that sensible retrenchment policies end when they fall victim to extremist attacks, particularly from right-wing members of Congress. Our history shows a somewhat different pattern. Retrenchment does enlarge congressional influence, and it does push foreign policy debate in wild and unexpected directions. This is especially true within the party responsible for the earlier maximalist excess. Democrats had their "McGovernite" wing in the 1970s. Republicans do today. But what undoes entrenchment is losing the support of the center. Who exactly opposed Eisenhower's sensible "long haul" policies? Its congressional critics included

John Kennedy and countless other Democrats. Inside the administration, even some of the president's closest advisers worried that the old man had lost his touch. Stung by the criticism, Eisenhower fumed about the "military-industrial" complex. What he said about its influence in his farewell address has won him—deservedly—a large audience of admirers over the years. But his critics—those who wanted to get the country "moving again"—were a far broader group than he let on.

In the retrenchment of the 1970s, "long haul" strategies centered again on nuclear arms control and détente. The critics of these policies were once more an extremely diverse group, with a strong establishment base. Within the government, they included both of President Ford's defense secretaries, James Schlesinger and Donald Rumsfeld. Outside government, George Meany of the AFL-CIO and Paul Nitze of the Committee on the Present Danger were opponents. Inside the Congress, senators as different as "Scoop" Jackson, Dick Clark, Jesse Helms, and Jacob Javits all cast votes against one or another of Kissinger's policies. On the presidential campaign trail, both Jimmy Carter and Ronald Reagan made their political fortunes by doing so. Critiques of détente were potent in part because they spanned the political spectrum.

This record has a clear message for Barack Obama. Retrenchment was easy in your first term—it almost always is. It gets harder once the wars you were elected to conclude are over. When that happens, don't expect your problems with Congress, or with the media, or with foreign policy experts, to come mainly from Rand Paul, John Bolton, Fox News, or the Heritage Foundation. Watch out even more for your centrist supporters—for Bill and Hillary Clinton, *The New York Times*, and the Carnegie Endowment for International Peace. Remember that when Madeleine Albright challenged Colin Powell to use his "superb military" twenty years ago, retrenchment prevailed over re-engagement—but only briefly. Because he at first commanded the center, Powell won round one; because he then lost it, Albright won round two.

Remember too that retrenchment and decline are not the same thing. Critics will say that these are matters of choice, and that a president who downsizes our foreign policy is needlessly squandering American influence in the world. This is half right. The American people have never hesitated to support retrenchment in winding down an unsuccessful war. At first, the scaling back doesn't feel like a choice at all. It's recognized as an inevitable adjustment—a way of *avoiding* decline. But policy debates and popular perceptions can change quickly. Retrenchment can go from being seen as a strategy for averting decline to being seen as one that accelerates, accepts, and even embraces it.

The history of American foreign policy provides a final, gloomy lesson for retrenchment presidents. Just like the maximalists they scorn, they tend to overdo it. They become convinced that only they have the formula for successful national strategy. We have not had a president who both launched a retrenchment and then, when new challenges arose, found the means to fashion an effective response.

OUR LOOK BACK over many decades tells us where Americans turn when they are dissatisfied with retrenchment: back to maximalism. They become persuaded once more that American power is the crucial stabilizing factor of global politics; that international challenges require a large, unhesitating, and uncompromising foreign policy; and that relying too much on others will produce unsatisfactory results. That this outlook is costly, that it can lead policy makers to overplay their hand, that it can antagonize close friends and encourage adversaries to see the United States as more threatening than we want or intend—well, the history of American foreign policy doesn't leave much doubt about any of that. When a friend of mine got to the end of reading draft chapters of this book, he inquired whether he had drawn the right conclusion from the story it tells. Was it correct, he asked, to say that maximalism has led us—decade after decade—to mishandle the most important international problems of our time?

The question is a good one, and there is much in the history we have looked at that supports this conclusion. Even so, it's not the right answer. Maximalism has been an essential ingredient of American success as well as of failure. Policy makers were hardly wrong to fear that Western European societies might unravel politically and economically in the late 1940s. Nor were they wrong to think that Soviet power increased the danger that such an unraveling might play out in a way highly unfavorable to the United States. West Berlin *was* blockaded. South Korea *was* invaded.

The stakes for American policy were perhaps never again quite so dangerously high as they were in the early years of the Cold War, but countering the Soviet challenge remained a necessary national security priority for decades. The fact that the "missile gap" of the late 1950s and early 1960s was based on overhyped bad intelligence had no lasting significance for the competition between East and West. While the United States and its allies worried that Moscow was gaining a nuclear edge, Soviet contentiousness grew. But what happened when the West's fears eased? Soviet policy became more contentious still.

The same thing can be said about the late 1970s and early 1980s. We now know that Soviet Communism was beginning to crumble in those years. Yet at least for a while, Moscow's foreign policy became less accommodating, not more. As for the post–Cold War world, American policy makers confronted a series of new challenges—genocidal conflicts in the Balkans, nuclear proliferation, the growth of Islamist terror networks, the rapid transformation of what were once called "emerging markets" into significant powers. Our presidents and their advisers believed that their response to these challenges would determine whether the international system of the twenty-first century tended toward order or disorder, toward continuing progress or something dangerously retrograde.

The real issue that needs debate, then, is not whether the United States faced real threats, either during the Cold War or after. It did. But could perhaps just as much, or even more, have been achieved with a less ambitious, less confrontational strategy? Did maximalism contribute to a heightening of international tension without any real payoff, prolonging the Cold War and making its aftermath needlessly tumultuous?

A careful look at American policy since the Second World War suggests an answer that many will find awkward: the United States achieved a great deal precisely by being uncompromising and confrontational. The early "present at the creation" years were often a little rougher than we like to remember. To keep from being driven out of Berlin by Stalin in 1948, Harry Truman had to overrule his senior military advisers, brush off the views of his most thoughtful diplomats, and ignore the pleadings of allies. At the time, some of the most pro-American European leaders seemed to think the United States was so bellicose, it must actually want war. This was an incorrect reading that probably helped keep the peace.

In ensuing decades, one president after another took similarly rigid stances—John Kennedy, when he decided that Khrushchev had to pull all his missiles out of Cuba; Ronald Reagan, when he decided that Brezhnev (and then Gorbachev) had to dismantle all Soviet intermediate-range missiles; George H. W. Bush, when he decided that Saddam Hussein had to pull all his forces out of Kuwait; and Bill Clinton, when he decided that Slobodan Milosevic had to pull all his troops out of Kosovo. *All* is a very big word in American foreign policy.

What makes the maximalism of American negotiating positions especially striking is that no absolutely vital national interest was at stake in any of these cases. The United States could certainly have decided that it did not need to stamp out ethnic violence in the Balkans in the 1990s. (Colin Powell, after all, was against trying to do so.) Hoping that the states of the Middle East would learn to live with Saddam's conquest of Kuwait was not a completely absurd idea. (Again, this was Powell's position.) Nor was it absurd to think that our European allies would learn to live with some ambiguity about the nuclear balance. (In the early 1980s many people believed this.) As for the Soviet missiles in Cuba, what exactly was it about Khrushchev's desire to deploy them that American policy makers, with their own missile force right across the Soviet border in Turkey, could not understand? (As we have seen, Kennedy himself challenged his advisers on this very point.)

Where did all this rigidity lead? Under Bush and Clinton, it led to war. Under Reagan, the result was a period of sustained East-West tension in which, as under Truman, many other governments—and the aroused publics of many friendly countries—feared that the United States was needlessly risking war. And John Kennedy's demand that the Soviet Union withdraw every single nuclear weapon capable of hitting American territory was probably as close as the Cold War ever got to becoming World War III.

From West Berlin to Cuba, from Kuwait to Kosovo, the United States accepted these risks in order to prevent something that it could definitely have decided to tolerate. Its decision not to do so reflected many different impulses, from moralistic outrage and ideological posturing to domestic electioneering. Washington's motives were not the same in any two cases. Yet one theme united them all—a keen attention to American power and influence. Failing to act in any of these cases would make it harder, policy makers believed, for the United States to defend its interests in the future. They were determined to protect U.S. primacy, or what is now usually called American "leadership."

Today, for all the fear and opposition they created at the time, most of these decisions are remembered with respect and admiration—and for good reason. They kept American adversaries permanently under pressure and on the defensive, limited their influence, challenged their legitimacy, and tipped the balance of power in the right direction. Had Truman accepted a graceful exit from Berlin, had Kennedy found a way to live with missiles in Cuba, had Reagan backed away from his zero option, the Cold War would have unfolded very differently—and in all likelihood, not nearly so well. Had Bush decided not to retake Kuwait (or if he had listened more to his allies about the dangers of German reunification), had Clinton not acted to stop genocide in the Balkans, had they accepted a downsizing of America's international role, the post–Cold War world would have unfolded differently too.

SO AMERICAN GLOBAL LEADERSHIP has conferred important global benefits. But what of its side effects? Didn't the same maximalism that we're crediting with so many successes also play a decisive part in our foreign policy's great disasters—in Korea, Vietnam, and Iraq?

To this, there is again no honest answer other than yes. As Admiral Dennis Blair, Obama's first director of national intelligence, put it: "We're Americans. If it's worth doing, it's worth overdoing." George Tenet, who ran the CIA under Bill Clinton and George W. Bush, made the same joke. Inside the Beltway, he said, for every action "there is an unequal and opposite over-reaction."[7]

The historical record certainly bears them out. One after another, surges of ambitious policy have been carried along by hyperconfidence about what the United States would be able to accomplish. The purveyors of this confidence have often been blind or self-deluding—and of course, sometimes simply deceptive—about the costs involved. The dynamics of American politics (and bureaucratic politics) have also spurred maximalism. More reputations have been made by supporting big initiatives than by speaking up for measured little ones. Guilty consciences have played a part too. The presidents who had to decide how to respond to the North Korean invasion of 1950, to the North Vietnamese offensive of 1965, and to the 9/11 attacks of 2001, all knew that they had done too little to prepare for these challenges.

Personal, political, and social-psychological factors help to explain why American policy has so often leaned in the direction of overdoing things. Still, the history examined in this book suggests other, more strategic explanations. They have almost surely been more important, and they make it difficult to distinguish between productive maximalism and the counterproductive kind. From the very beginning of the Cold War, and long after it, our presidents and their advisers had a very baleful view of what other countries might be able to contribute to international order. It is not too much to say that the Cold War started because American policy makers believed Western Europe's political and economic "model" was broken. They were convinced that the nations of the Old World would not be able to hold themselves together, much less resist Soviet pressure, without the "guidance" of the United States. That others needed help in solving—or even understanding—their own problems was virtually the founding insight of American globalism. For Truman, Marshall, and Acheson, this was a given. They did not expect it to be a central principle of our foreign policy for all times, of course. And yet Washington has had occasion to relearn it in every decade since, and in every region of the world.

American diplomacy has been further pushed toward big solutions by a recurrent and related doubt that halfway measures would hold up. Acheson, as we have seen, was led to favor unification of Korea in 1950 because he could not believe that merely restoring the status quo ante—even with U.S. troops on the thirty-eighth parallel—would be a viable long-term solution. The American public and international community would lose interest, and the Communists would gain the upper hand. Policy makers go maximalist because they fear short attention spans. In 1990, George H. W. Bush and his advisers felt precisely this unease about living with Saddam Hussein's conquest of Kuwait, even with American troops on the Saudi border. And in 2003, George W. Bush and his advisers thought that trying to control Saddam's WMD programs through long-term international monitoring and sanctions was completely unrealistic.

Again and again, the United States has seen itself as willing to pursue fundamental solutions to problems, while others simply hoped for the best. It has been precisely this shared conviction that led many policy makers and political figures, at crucial junctures, to put aside their reservations about where American decisions were heading. We might recall that, just days before U.S. troops were attacked in Korea in November 1950, General Omar Bradley actually wrote out orders to Douglas MacArthur to pull back from the Chinese border. But he decided not to send them. Bradley too desired a full victory; settling for a partial one would only store up problems for the future.

This maximalist outlook lasted through the Cold War and long after. In our own time, many who doubted the wisdom of the war in Iraq—from Colin Powell to Joe Biden—put aside their reservations and offered their support. They gave different reasons for their decision, but at bottom they were probably thinking something very much like what General Bradley thought. Saddam Hussein had been too big a problem for too long: after 9/11, it was time to grasp the nettle.

How to enjoy the benefits of maximalism without going too far—this is the recurrent dilemma of American policy. Who wants to leave money on the table when a little extra effort can solve a problem for good? Even retrenchers feel this urge. (It was Richard Nixon, after all, who always wanted to go home with "all the marbles.") Maximalists usually give in to temptation while thinking that they won't. Johnson was determined not to be Truman; George W. Bush was determined not to be Johnson. And neither of them was. All maximalists overdo it in their own way, for their own seemingly good reasons.

THE FACT THAT America's maximalist inclinations have been strong for many decades does not, of course, mean that they are eternal. All the factors that supported them in the past—from the personal to the political to the strategic—have come under pressure in the past decade. National confidence and commitment have been undermined by military and economic setbacks. Resources are scarce. Politicians and policy makers feel fewer incentives to develop ambitious new initiatives. In the years ahead, caution rather than boldness may seem a better route to career advancement. In our future policy debates, risk aversion may trump all other motivations.

If these are durable changes in the thinking of Washington policy makers, the retrenchment under way in American policy may turn out to be different from those that we have looked at in this book. A long era of American global dominance will begin to wind down. Even so, there will continue to be pressures pushing policy in the opposite direction. For all the setbacks that the United States has experienced of late, some of the factors that fueled maximalist policies in the past remain very potent. Two will be particularly important. Presidents and their advisers still find it hard to believe that other states can provide real leadership in addressing big problems. And they find it equally hard to believe that hopelessly compromised international arrangements and agreements will produce durable solutions.

Like many of its predecessors, the Obama administration sincerely wants other governments to do better. It was Eisenhower who said to his cabinet in 1955 that European unity would allow the United States "to sit back and relax somewhat." And it was Nixon who told Zhou Enlai in

1972 that "if China could become a second superpower, the U.S. could reduce its own armaments." But what was true of their times is true again today. American policy makers remain frustrated and disappointed by the limited readiness of others to step up to greater responsibility. There has been no more telling recent sign of this outlook than the agreement on Iran's nuclear program that was reached in Geneva at the end of 2013. Washington had for years touted the advantages of the "P5+1" forum for negotiating with Teheran. All the same, it was American and Iranian diplomats, meeting in secret, who hammered out the terms of the deal. Barack Obama was not the first president who liked the look of a big, inclusive conference table. Nor was he the first who wanted the real work done elsewhere.[8]

That presidents of the United States and their advisers are frustrated by the poor results of multilateralism in solving first-order security problems should be obvious. But the difficulty extends far beyond security, to an agenda of very different issues. One example among many can illustrate the point: for high officials of the Obama administration, the 2009 Copenhagen conference on climate change was a sobering, even shocking event. Some of the large countries on which Americans were counting to play a constructive role showed they were ready to have the conference collapse in failure. The United States, they figured, would take the blame. Hillary Clinton came away from the proceedings complaining that she had seen no institution function so badly since her eighth-grade student council.[9]

Almost seven decades ago Harry Truman and his colleagues concluded that a satisfactory global order—secure, prosperous, and democratic—was not possible unless the United States somehow called the shots. For all the differences between Truman's times and ours—and they are fundamental—Washington policy makers have surprisingly similar views today. Their daily experience of international problem solving does not soften this outlook; it usually fortifies it. As long as the world works no better than it does, America will have many reasons to try to make up the difference between mediocre results and good ones—and to rescue what it can of our maximalist past.

ACKNOWLEDGMENTS

One peculiar feature of the American foreign policy process has done much to shape this book. The executive branch of the U.S. government periodically absorbs a wave of inexperienced outsiders from think tanks, universities, law firms, and business, and challenges them to try to apply their big ideas. When the political tide turns, the government sends these people back where they came from—or someplace nicer still—to reflect on what they have learned and figure out how to use it. No other country that I know of runs its foreign policy in quite this way. The drawbacks of the arrangement should be obvious (people are constantly reinventing the wheel); so are its advantages (even the wheel needs a fresh look from time to time). As a Washington in-and-outer myself, I have benefitted greatly from our unusual system. Its influence is on every page of *Maximalist*.

I incurred all the usual debts, and then some, in writing this book—and I want to acknowledge them here. Two institutions allowed me to think at length about problems of American foreign policy—Columbia University's School of International and Public Affairs and the Council on Foreign Relations. I am indebted to SIPA's outstanding deans—Lisa Anderson, John Coatsworth, Rob Lieberman, and Merit Janow—and to its outstanding students. Special thanks to the members of my seminar on The U.S. Role in World Affairs. They have been an excellent captive audience for many of this book's ideas.

In my time at CFR, two of the Council's presidents—Richard Haass and Les Gelb—and those who ran the studies department for them—Jim Lindsay, Gary Samore, and Lee Feinstein—have done much to enlarge and strengthen an extraordinary institution. I could not have written this book without the Council's talented research assistants—Rositsa Petrova, John Elliott, Conor Savoy, Sha Luo, and the unbelievably helpful Allison Nour.

My thanks to friends and colleagues who read and commented on the manuscript. David Epstein, Adam Garfinkle, Carl Gershman, Stuart Gottlieb, Richard Haass, Robert Jervis, Robert Kagan, Lewis Libby, James Lindsay, Michael McFaul, Ray Takeyh, Strobe Talbott, James Traub, and Andrew Weiss all gave me valuable feedback on one or more (often many more) chapters. Boundless gratitude to those who read it all. I hope the final product shows how much I benefitted from their help.

At Knopf, my superb editor, Andrew Miller, offered exactly the right combination of patience and prodding. Thanks also to Mark Chiusano, who oversaw the tumult of production. Legions of copy editors, proofreaders, jacket designers, and others have tried to improve my understanding of English usage and publishing aesthetics. Erinn Hartman has already brought exceptional energy to the work of marketing and publicity.

It was the Wylie Agency that steered me to Knopf in the first place—for this alone, many thanks. Andrew Wylie proposed the book over a long-ago lunch. At every step Sarah Chalfant offered the careful insights that made it a reality. I needed only the good sense to follow her advice.

The final paragraph of acknowledgments is where authors choke up a little—and apologize for being such a burden to their families. I like to think this book had a happier gestation. My parents, Molly and Steve Sestanovich, got me interested in the entire subject early on. In a string of diplomatic assignments abroad, they were the gold standard for showing America at its most likeable. My son, Ben, and my daughter, Clare, interrogated me about maximalism over many a dinner and on long car rides. It is one of fatherhood's bracing pleasures to discover how much you can learn from talking to your children. My wife, Ann Hulbert, is the most brilliant editor I know. When she passes along the bad news about a chapter that still needs work, it feels like one more way of being in love. My debt to her is great not because this book took a toll on family life, but because it didn't.

NOTES

PROLOGUE

1. Ted Sorensen, *Counselor: A Life at the Edge of History* (New York: HarperCollins, 2008), p. 329.
2. Barack Obama, State of the Union Address, January 25, 2011, http://www.whitehouse.gov/the-press-office/2011/01/25/remarks-president-barack-obama-state-union-address.
3. Marc Trachtenberg, *A Constructed Peace: The Making of the European Settlement, 1945–1963* (Princeton, N.J.: Princeton University Press, 1999), p. 377; *Foreign Relations of the United States, 1961–1963, Volume XIII, Western Europe and Canada*, doc. 145, pp. 419–22.
4. Nigel John Ashton, *Kennedy, Macmillan and the Cold War* (New York: Palgrave Macmillan, 2002), pp. 7–8. See also Warren Bass, *Support Any Friend: Kennedy's Middle East and the Making of the U.S.-Israel Alliance* (Oxford: Oxford University Press, 2003), pp. 169, 182.
5. Hillary Clinton, "Foreign Policy Address at the Council on Foreign Relations," July 15, 2009, U.S. Department of State, http://www.state.gov/secretary/rm/2009a/july/126071.htm.
6. Arvind Subramanian, *Eclipse: Living in the Shadow of China's Economic Dominance* (Washington, D.C.: PIIE Press, 2011), p. 18; George C. Herring, *From Colony to Superpower: U.S. Foreign Relations Since 1776* (Oxford: Oxford University Press, 2008), p. 659; "Briefing on Current Foreign Policy Problems," June 5, 1963, *Senate Foreign Relations Committee (Historical Series), Volume XV, 1963* (Washington, D.C.: GPO, 1987), p. 328; Martin Walker, *The Cold War: A History* (New York: Henry Holt, 1993), p. 192; W. W. Rostow, *The Diffusion of Power: An Essay in Recent History* (New York: Macmillan, 1972), p. 230.
7. Ralph Waldo Emerson, "Experience," in *Essays: Second Series* (Cambridge, Mass.: Houghton Mifflin, The Riverside Press, 1876), p. 79.
8. George F. Kennan, *Memoirs: 1925–1950* (New York: Bantam Books, 1967), p. 527.
9. Ronald Reagan, "Announcement for Presidential Candidacy," November 13, 1979, Miller Center Presidential Speech Archives.
10. Robert L. Beisner, *Dean Acheson: A Life in the Cold War* (New York: Oxford University Press, 2006), p. 446; Dean Acheson, *Present at the Creation: My Years in the State Department* (New York: W.W. Norton, 1969), pp. 526–28; Clark Clifford with Richard Holbrooke, *Council to the President: A Memoir* (New York: Random House, 1991), pp. 505–6.
11. George W. Ball, *The Past Has Another Pattern: Memoirs* (New York: W.W. Norton, 1982), p. 404.
12. Tim Weiner, *Legacy of Ashes: The History of the CIA* (New York: Doubleday, 2007), p. 600.

13. John Kenneth Galbraith to Averell Harriman, November 4, 1963, W. Averell Harriman Papers, Box 463, Manuscript Division, Library of Congress.
14. Colin Powell, *My American Journey* (New York: Ballantine Books, 1995), p. 561.
15. Herring, *From Colony to Superpower,* p. 779.

1: TRUMAN AT THE CREATION

1. Walter Isaacson and Evan Thomas, *The Wise Men: Six Friends and the World They Made* (New York: Simon & Schuster, 1986), p. 393.
2. Robert L. Beisner, *Dean Acheson: A Life in the Cold War* (New York: Oxford University Press, 2006), pp. 55, 59 (emphasis mine). Truman devoted the entire first volume of *Memoirs* to his first "Year of Decisions"—1945. The rest of his presidency was covered in the second volume.
3. Robert H. Ferrell, ed., *Off the Record: The Private Papers of Harry S. Truman* (New York: Harper & Row, 1980), pp. 218–19.
4. Harry S. Truman, "Special Message to the Congress on Greece and Turkey," March 12, 1947, *Public Papers of the Presidents,* http://www.presidency.ucsb.edu/ws/index.php?pid=12846&st=&st1.
5. Robert Murphy, *Diplomat Among Warriors* (New York: Doubleday, 1969), p. 307.
6. Greg Behrman, *The Most Noble Adventure: The Marshall Plan and the Time When America Helped Save Europe* (New York: Free Press, 2007), pp. 51, 136; Tony Judt, *Postwar: A History of Europe Since 1945* (New York: Penguin, 2005), pp. 28, 90.
7. Judt, *Postwar,* p. 111; Isaacson and Thomas, *Wise Men,* p. 393; Benn Steil, *The Battle of Bretton Woods: John Maynard Keynes, Harry Dexter White, and the Making of a New World Order* (Princeton, N.J.: Princeton University Press, 2013), p. 330; Steil, *Bretton Woods,* p. 308.
8. Judt, *Postwar,* p. 116.
9. Geir Lundestad, *The Rise and Decline of the American "Empire"* (New York: Oxford University Press, 2012), p. 103; Dean Acheson, *Present at the Creation: My Years in the State Department* (New York: W.W. Norton, 1969), p. 221; George F. Kennan, *Memoirs: 1925–1950* (New York: Bantam Books, 1967), p. 598.
10. *Foreign Relations of the United States, 1947, Volume II, Council of Foreign Ministers; Germany and Austria,* pp. 337–44, esp. 343–44; Kennan, *Memoirs: 1925–1950,* p. 347; Marc Trachtenberg, *A Constructed Peace: Making of the European Settlement, 1945–1963,* (Princeton, N.J.: Princeton University Press, 1999), pp. 61–63.
11. Isaacson and Thomas, *Wise Men,* pp. 338, 368.
12. Robert L. Beisner, *Dean Acheson: A Life in the Cold War,* p. 56; Acheson, *Present at the Creation,* p. 222; "Party Division in the Senate, 1789–Present," http://www.senate.gov/pagelayout/history/one_item_and_teasers/partydiv.htm; "Party Divisions of the House of Representatives," 1789–Present," http://artandhistory.house.gov/house_history/partyDiv.aspx.
13. George F. Kennan, "The Sources of Soviet Conduct," *Foreign Affairs* (July 1947); Kennan, *Memoirs: 1925–1950,* pp. 347, 369.
14. Kennan, *Memoirs: 1925–1950,* pp. 336, 369.
15. Ibid., p. 342; Acheson, *Present at the Creation,* p. 226; Behrman, *Most Noble Adventure,* p. 54.
16. Harry S. Truman, "Special Message to the Congress on Greece and Turkey: Truman Doctrine," March 12, 1947, *Public Papers of the Presidents,* http://www.presidency.ucsb

.edu/ws/index.php?pid=12846&st=&st1=; Isaacson and Thomas, *Wise Men,* p. 397; Charles A. Bohlen, *Witness to History: 1929–1969* (New York: W.W. Norton, 1973), p. 261.

17. George Marshall, "Fourth Meeting of the Council of Foreign Ministers: Report, April 28, 1947," Avalon Project, http://avalon.law.yale.edu/20th_century/decade23.asp; Beisner, *Dean Acheson,* p. 59; Harry S. Truman, *Memoirs* (New York: Doubleday, 1956), p. 2:105.
18. Behrman, *Most Noble Adventure,* pp. 64, 181; Kennan, *Memoirs: 1925–1950,* p. 355 (emphasis mine).
19. Kennan, *Memoirs: 1925–1950,* pp. 355, 358.
20. Ibid., p. 355; Behrman, *Most Noble Adventure,* p. 144; George C. Marshall, Remarks at Harvard University, June 5, 1947, U.S. State Department Press Release, June 4, 1947, George C. Marshall Foundation, http://www.marshallfoundation.org/library/index_documents.html; Acheson, *Present at the Creation,* pp. 231–32 (my emphasis); Murphy, *Diplomat Among Warriors,* p. 308.
21. John Lewis Gaddis, *Strategies of Containment: A Critical Appraisal of American National Security Policy During the Cold War* (New York: Oxford University Press, 2005), p. 28; Beisner, *Dean Acheson,* p. 59.
22. Acheson, *Present at the Creation,* p. 231; Hadley Arkes, *Bureaucracy, the Marshall Plan, and the National Interest* (Princeton, N.J.: Princeton University Press, 1973), pp. 44–47.
23. Isaacson and Thomas, *Wise Men,* p. 420; Paul H. Nitze, *From Hiroshima to Glasnost: At the Center of Decision—A Memoir* (New York: Grove Weidenfeld, 1989), p. 54.
24. Nitze, *From Hiroshima to Glasnost,* p. 55.
25. Kennan, Memorandum by the Director of the Policy Planning Staff, September 4, 1947, *Foreign Relations of the United States, 1947, Volume III, British Commonwealth; Europe, 1947,* pp. 397–402. Kennan was so pessimistic about Britain's prospects that he envisioned that it would cease to exist as an independent state, ceding control of its affairs to the United States and Canada.
26. Behrman, *Most Noble Adventure,* pp. 4, 139, 333, 321; see also William I. Hitchcock, "Marshall Plan and the Creation of the West," in Melvyn P. Leffler and Odd Arne Westad, eds., *Cambridge History of the Cold War,* vol. 1, *Origins* (New York: Cambridge University Press, 2010).
27. Behrman, *Most Noble Adventure,* pp. 163, 252, 334.
28. Joseph M. Jones, *Fifteen Weeks* (New York: Viking Press, 1955), pp. 263–64. Jones titled the epilogue to his book "Foreign Policy Unchained" and argued that given the enormous challenge it faced—"directing the deep restlessness of the mid-twentieth century"—the United States should aim to do more than it could realistically expect to achieve: "Forward projects and commitments of a true world leader should . . . always exceed the ability at any given moment to carry them out."
29. Acheson, *Present at the Creation,* p. 378.
30. Behrman, *Most Noble Adventure,* p.117; Marc Trachtenberg, *A Constructed Peace,* p. 64.
31. Beisner, *Dean Acheson,* p. 128.
32. Kennan, *Memoirs: 1925–1950,* pp. 421, 425.
33. Ibid., p. 430.
34. Acheson, *Present at the Creation,* p. 376; John Lewis Gaddis, *George F. Kennan: An American Life* (New York: Penguin Press, 2011), p. 310.
35. Kennan, *Memoirs: 1925–1950,* pp. 422–23; Isaacson and Thomas, *Wise Men,* pp. 450–51.
36. Kennan, *Memoirs: 1925–1950,* p. 429.
37. The military favored a retreat because it expected further Soviet pressure. The State

Department was more relaxed about staying because the diplomats did not expect a full blockade. Bohlen, *Witness to History*, p. 276; Avi Shlaim, *The United States and the Berlin Blockade, 1948–1949* (Berkeley: University of California Press, 1983), p. 136.

38. Trachtenberg, *Constructed Peace,* pp. 81, 82; Stanley Allen Renshon and Deborah Velch Larson, *Good Judgment in Foreign Policy: Theory and Application* (Lanham, Md.: Rowman & Littlefield, 2003), p. 137.
39. Omar N. Bradley, *A General's Life* (New York: Simon & Schuster, 1983), p. 481.
40. Acheson, *Present at the Creation,* p. 260; Melvyn P. Leffler, *A Preponderance of Power: National Security, the Truman Administration, and the Cold War* (Stanford, Calif.: Stanford University Press, 1992), p. 201; Judt, *Postwar,* pp. 98, 125; Trachtenberg, *Constructed Peace,* p. 84.
41. Leffler, *Preponderance of Power,* pp. 215–17; Isaacson and Thomas, *Wise Men,* p. 455; D. M. Giangreco and Robert E. Griffin, *Airbridge to Berlin: The Berlin Crisis of 1948, Its Origins and Aftermath,* reprinted by the Harry S. Truman Library and Museum, http://www.trumanlibrary.org/whistlestop/BERLIN_A/PAGE_3.HTM; Stewart Patrick, *The Best Laid Plans: The Origins of American Multilateralism and the Dawn of the Cold War* (Lanham, Md.: Rowman & Littlefield, 2009), p. 276.
42. *Foreign Relations of the United States, 1948, Volume II, Germany and Austria,* pp. 975, 979–80; Walter Millis, ed., *The Forrestal Diaries* (New York: Viking Press, 1951), pp. 489, 500.
43. Shlaim, *United States and Berlin Blockade,* p. 310; Isaacson and Thomas, *Wise Men,* pp. 459–60.
44. Shlaim, *United States and Berlin Blockade,* p. 387.
45. Beisner, *Dean Acheson,* pp. 142, 146.
46. Kennan, *Memoirs: 1925–1950,* pp. 489–90.
47. Ibid., pp. 469, 431.
48. Ibid., p. 448.
49. Beisner, *Dean Acheson,* p. 118; Gaddis, George F. Kennan, p. 330.
50. Acheson, *Present at the Creation,* pp. 376, 380.
51. Ibid., p. 338; Kennan, *Memoirs: 1925–1950,* p. 489.
52. Kennan, *Memoirs: 1925–1950,* p. 385; Henry A. Kissinger, *White House Years,* p. 62; Kissinger's comment makes it hard to understand his claim to have favored an Achesonian strategy.
53. Nitze, *From Hiroshima to Glasnost,* pp. 72–73.
54. Beisner, *Dean Acheson,* pp. 248–49; Acheson, *Present at the Creation,* p. 380.
55. Acheson, *Present at the Creation,* p. 238.

2: TRUMAN AT WAR

1. Robert L. Beisner, *Dean Acheson: A Life in the Cold War* (New York: Oxford University Press, 2006), p. 148.
2. See Walter Millis, ed., *The Forrestal Diaries* (New York: Viking Press, 1951), chap. 13; Omar N. Bradley, *A General's Life: An Autobiography by General of the Army Omar N. Bradley* (New York: Simon & Schuster, 1983), p. 513; Clay Blair, *The Forgotten War: America in Korea, 1950–1953* (New York: Times Books, 1987), p. 31.
3. Bradley, *General's Life,* pp. 470, 502, 503; Dean Acheson, *Present at the Creation: My Years in the State Department* (New York: W.W. Norton, 1969), pp. 467, 469.
4. Blair, *Forgotten War,* p. 4.

5. Bradley, *General's Life,* pp. 473–74; Blair, *Forgotten War,* p. 28.
6. Millis, *Forrestal Diaries,* pp. 370, 372–73; Marc Trachtenberg, *A Constructed Peace: Making of the European Settlement, 1945–1963* (Princeton, N.J.: Princeton University Press, 1999), p. 90.
7. Aaron L. Friedberg, *In the Shadow of the Garrison State: America's Anti-Statism and Its Cold War Strategy* (Princeton, N.J.: Princeton University Press, 2000), pp. 100–3; Warner R. Schilling, "Budget," in *Strategy, Politics, and Defense Budgets* (New York: Columbia University Press, 1962), pp. 44–46, 100, 198.
8. Millis, *Forrestal Diaries,* p. 498.
9. Bradley, *General's Life,* pp. 496–97; Millis, *Forrestal Diaries,* pp. 500, 503–5.
10. Millis, *Forrestal Diaries,* p. 502.
11. Ibid., pp. 536, 544; Robert J. Donovan, *Conflict and Crisis: The Presidency of Harry S. Truman, 1945–1948* (New York: W.W. Norton, 1977), p. 143.
12. Millis, *Forrestal Diaries,* pp. 544–55.
13. Bradley, *General's Life,* pp. 501–3, Acheson, *Present at the Creation,* p. 441.
14. Friedberg, *In the Shadow,* p. 105; Bradley, *General's Life,* pp. 501–3.
15. Bradley, *General's Life,* pp. 507, 513; Warner R. Schilling, "Executive Choice: Rationality and Politics," in *Strategy, Politics, and Defense Budgets* (New York: Columbia University Press, 1962), pp. 169–70.
16. Bradley, *General's Life,* pp. 506–13.
17. Acheson, *Present at the Creation,* pp. 348–49, 358; David E. Lilienthal, *The Journals of David E. Lilienthal: The Atomic Energy Years, 1945–1950* (New York: Harper & Row, 1964), pp. 620–33, esp. 632; Harry S. Truman, *Memoirs* (New York: Doubleday, 1956), p. 2:309; Robert R. Bowie and Richard H. Immerman, *Waging Peace: How Eisenhower Shaped an Enduring Cold War Strategy* (New York: Oxford University Press, 1998), p. 16.
18. NSC-68, *Foreign Relations of the United States, 1950, Volume I, National Security Affairs, Foreign Economic Policy,* p. 237; *Foreign Relations of the United States, 1950, Volume III, Western Europe,* p. 620. Bohlen differed with Paul Nitze on intelligence regarding Soviet military danger but not in reading European confidence.
19. NSC-68, *Foreign Relations of the United States, 1950, Volume I, National Security Affairs, Foreign Economic Policy,* pp. 254–55.
20. Ibid., pp. 255, 264, 279 (emphasis mine).
21. Ibid., pp. 241, 255; Patrick, *Best Laid Plans,* p. 226.
22. Paul H. Nitze, *From Hiroshima to Glasnost: At the Center of Decision—A Memoir* (New York: Grove Weidenfeld, 1989), p. 96; NSC-68, *Foreign Relations of the United States, 1950, Volume I, National Security Affairs, Foreign Economic Policy,* p. 285; Beisner, *Dean Acheson,* p. 242.
23. Acheson, *Present at the Creation,* pp. 373–74; Nitze, *From Hiroshima to Glasnost,* pp. 93–96; Beisner, *Dean Acheson,* pp. 238–41; Walter Isaacson and Evan Thomas, *The Wise Men: Six Friends and the World They Made* (New York: Simon & Schuster, 1986), pp. 498–503; Beisner, *Dean Acheson,* p. 246.
24. Nitze, *From Hiroshima to Glasnost,* pp. 121–22; *Foreign Relations of the United States, 1950, Volume IV, Central and Eastern Europe; The Soviet Union,* p. 687.
25. *Foreign Relations of the United States, 1950, Volume IV, Central and Eastern Europe; The Soviet Union,* p. 688; Trachtenberg, *Constructed Peace,* p. 107.
26. Tony Judt, *Postwar: A History of Europe Since 1945* (New York: Penguin, 2005), p. 151.
27. Bradley, *General's Life,* pp. 529–31; Truman, *Memoirs,* pp. 2:325–29; Blair, *Forgotten War,* pp. 40–44.
28. Blair, *Forgotten War,* pp. 40–44; *Foreign Relations of the United States, 1950, Volume VII,*

Korea, pp. 8, 30–31, 39–41; Melvyn P. Leffler, *A Preponderance of Power: National Security, the Truman Administration, and the Cold War* (Stanford, Calif.: Stanford University Press, 1993), p. 338; Beisner, *Dean Acheson,* p. 327.

29. Bradley, *General's Life,* p. 535; Truman, *Memoirs,* pp. 2:332–34, 337.
30. Acheson, *Present at the Creation,* p. 405; Truman, *Memoirs,* p. 2:421; Leffler, *Preponderance of Power,* p. 366–67; *Foreign Relations of the United States, 1950, Volume VII, Korea,* pp. 139–40.
31. Charles E. Bohlen, *Witness to History: 1929–1969* (New York: W.W. Norton, 1973), pp. 292–93; *Foreign Relations of the United States, 1950, Volume IV, Central and Eastern Europe; The Soviet Union,* pp. 1224–29.
32. Truman, *Memoirs,* pp. 2:333–37; Acheson, *Present at the Creation,* pp. 404–12; Leffler, *Preponderance of Power,* p. 366.
33. Acheson, *Present at the Creation,* pp. 414–15; Beisner, *Dean Acheson,* 349.
34. *Foreign Relations of the United States, 1950, Volume VII, Korea,* p. 345.
35. Leffler, *Preponderance of Power,* pp. 371, 373, 402; Acheson, *Present at the Creation,* p. 421; Friedberg, *In the Shadow,* p. 122; John Lewis Gaddis, *Strategies of Containment: A Critical Appraisal of American National Security Policy During the Cold War* (New York: Oxford University Press, 2005), pp. 110–11.
36. Acheson, *Present at the Creation,* pp. 436–37. "Both as wrong as can be" was written by Truman in longhand across the top of two defense department reports at the time, "one urging German rearmament, the other cooperation with Franco Spain"; see Robert H. Ferrell, *Harry S. Truman: A Life* (Columbia: University of Missouri Press, 1996), p. 357.
37. Ibid., pp. 438–40; also Beisner, *Dean Acheson,* p. 364; Trachtenberg, *Constructed Peace,* p. 108; Leffler, *Preponderance of Power,* pp. 371, 388.
38. Beisner, *Dean Acheson,* pp. 366–68; Trachtenberg, *Constructed Peace,* pp. 108–9, 111; Leffler, *Preponderance of Power,* p. 388.
39. Acheson, *Present at the Creation,* p. 425; George F. Kennan, *Memoirs, 1925–1950* (New York: Bantam Books, 1967), p. 527.
40. Leffler, *Preponderance of Power,* p. 403; Acheson, *Present at the Creation,* p. 516.
41. Acheson, *Present at the Creation,* pp. 405, 450–51 ; Robert D. Hormats, *The Price of Liberty: Paying for America's Wars* (New York: Times Books, 2007), p. 184
42. *Foreign Relations of the United States, 1950, Volume VII, Korea,* p. 503, 506, 949.
43. Ibid., pp. 506–7, 570.
44. Truman, *Memoirs,* p. 2:351.
45. *Foreign Relations of the United States, 1950, Volume VII, Korea,* pp. 712–21, esp. 716 for discussion of operations north of the thirty-eighth parallel and the direction to plan the occupation of North Korea; Beisner, *Dean Acheson,* p. 398.
46. Bradley, *General's Life,* pp. 544–47; Isaacson and Thomas, *Wise Men,* pp. 531–2; also Acheson, *Present at the Creation,* p. 447.
47. Nitze, *From Hiroshima to Glasnost,* p. 105.
48. Acheson, *Present at the Creation,* p. 467; Bradley, *General's Life,* pp. 566–68; Isaacson and Thomas, *Wise Men,* p. 537.
49. Bradley, *General's Life,* pp. 560–61.
50. Beisner, *Dean Acheson,* p. 399; Harry S. Truman, "Address in San Francisco at the War Memorial Opera House," October 17, 1950, Harry S. Truman Library and Museum, http://www.trumanlibrary.org/publicpapers/index.php?pid=899.
51. Bradley, *General's Life,* pp. 583–85, 587, 588; *Foreign Relations of the United States, 1950, Volume VII, Korea,* p. 1194.

52. Thomas Christenson, "Threats, Assurances, and the Last Chance for Peace: The Lessons of Mao's Korean War Telegrams," *International Security,* Vol. 17, No. 1 (Summer 1992), pp. 122–54.
53. Bradley, *General's Life,* p. 588.
54. Ibid., p. 596; Acheson, *Present at the Creation,* p. 467.
55. George F. Kennan, *Memoirs: 1950–1963* (New York: Pantheon, 1983), p. 33; Acheson, *Present at the Creation,* p. 477; Isaacson and Thomas, *Wise Men*, pp. 542–44.
56. Acheson, *Present at the Creation,* pp. 472, 478–79, 487; Harry S. Truman, News Conference, November 30, 1950, Harry S. Truman Library and Museum, http://trumanlibrary.org/publicpapers/viewpapers.php?pid=985; Truman, *Memoirs,* p. 2:396.
57. Vice President Alben Barkley burbled mindlessly that he found Attlee "even younger and more handsome than he had been five years ago." Congress was less impressed: twenty-four Republican senators greeted the prime minister's arrival by cosponsoring a resolution demanding that any agreement between him and the president be submitted for ratification. Acheson, *Present at the Creation,* pp. 475, 481; *Foreign Relations of the United States, 1950, Volume III, Western Europe,* p. 1778.
58. Acheson, *Present at the Creation,* p. 483; *Foreign Relations of the United States, 1950, Volume III, Western Europe*, pp. 1760–61, 1714; Kennan, *Memoirs: 1950–1963,* p. 30; see also Truman, *Memoirs,* pp. 2:396–414.
59. *Foreign Relations of the United States, 1950, Volume III, Western Europe*, pp. 1712, 1716, 1729, 1733.
60. Ibid., pp. 1732, 1734; Acheson, *Present at the Creation,* p. 483.
61. Acheson, *Present at the Creation,* p. 484.
62. Office of Management and Budget, "Historical Tables," *Budget of the U.S. Government, Fiscal Year 2005* (Washington, D.C.: GPO, 2004), pp. 45–52, http://www.whitehouse.gov/sites/default/files/omb/budget/fy2005/pdf/hist.pdf.
63. Bohlen, *Witness to History,* p. 303; Leffler, *Preponderance of Power*, pp. 382, 434, 470–72.
64. Acheson, *Present at the Creation*, pp. 526–28; Beisner, *Dean Acheson,* p. 446.
65. Kennan, *Memoirs: 1950–1963*, pp. 94–95.

3: "ENOUGH IS ENOUGH"

1. Dwight D. Eisenhower, *At Ease: Stories I Tell to Friends* (New York: Doubleday, 1967), pp. 368–69; Stephen A. Ambrose, *Eisenhower* (New York: Simon & Schuster, 1984), p. 2:235; Emmet John Hughes, *Ordeal of Power: A Political Memoir of the Eisenhower Years* (New York: Atheneum, 1963), p. 124.
2. John Foster Dulles, "Evolution of Foreign Policy," Address to the Council on Foreign Relations, January 12, 1954, in *Department of State Bulletin,* January 25, 1954.
3. Peter Baker, "Bush to Hillary Clinton: I'm Truman, You're Ike," *The Washington Post* "Trail" blog, September 21, 2007, http://blog.washingtonpost.com/44/2007/09/bush-clinton-will-be-democrati.html; David Rothkopf, *Running the World: The Inside Story of the National Security Council and the Architects of American Power* (New York: PublicAffairs, 2005), pp. 68–73.
4. Dwight D. Eisenhower, Inaugural Address, January 20, 1953, in *Public Papers of the Presidents,* http://www.presidency.ucsb.edu/ws/index.php?pid=9600&st=&st1; Dulles, "Evolution of Foreign Policy."
5. Hughes, *Ordeal of Power,* pp. 346, 358.

6. Sherman Adams, *Firsthand Report: The Story of the Eisenhower Administration* (Harper & Brothers, 1961), pp. 42–44; Dwight D. Eisenhower, "I Shall Go to Korea Speech," October 25, 1952, Eisenhower Presidential Library and Museum, www.eisenhower.archives.gov/research/online_documents/korean_war.html.
7. Dwight D. Eisenhower, *The White House Years: Mandate for Change, 1953–1956* (New York: Doubleday, 1963), p. 95.
8. Ambrose, *Eisenhower,* pp. 2:31, 35, 51.
9. Eisenhower, *Mandate for Change,* p. 181.
10. Ibid., p. 180; Ambrose, *Eisenhower,* p. 2:51.
11. Hughes, *Ordeal of Power*, pp. 124, 136; Eisenhower, *Mandate for Change*, pp. 182, 185–87; Adams, *Firsthand Report,* pp. 101–2; Ambrose, *Eisenhower,* pp. 2:103, 106.
12. Ambrose, *Eisenhower,* pp. 2:107–8; Dwight D. Eisenhower, Memo to Charles Erwin Wilson and Harold Edward Stassen, September 30, 1953, in *Papers of Dwight David Eisenhower,* ed. Louis Galambos and Daun van Ee (Baltimore: Johns Hopkins University Press, 1996), Vol. 14, Part III, Ch. 6.
13. Townsend Hoopes, *The Devil and John Foster Dulles* (Boston: Little, Brown, 1973), p. 137.
14. Joseph Alsop and Stewart Alsop, *The Reporter's Trade* (New York: Reynal, 1958), p. 93; Robert D. Hormats, *The Price of Liberty* (New York: Times Books, 2007), p. 195; Dulles, "Evolution of Foreign Policy"; Ambrose, *Eisenhower,* pp. 2:52, 434; Eisenhower, *Mandate for Change,* p. 454.
15. John Lewis Gaddis, *Strategies of Containment: A Critical Appraisal of Postwar National Security Policy* (New York: Oxford University Press, 2005), pp. 169, 171; Ambrose, *Eisenhower,* pp. 2:88, 90.
16. Gaddis, *Strategies of Containment,* p. 147; Dulles, "Evolution of Foreign Policy."
17. Robert A. Divine, *Eisenhower and the Cold War* (New York: Oxford University Press, 1981), p. 36; Ambrose, *Eisenhower,* p. 2:224; Eisenhower, *Mandate for Change*, pp. 451–52.
18. Dulles, "Evolution of Foreign Policy"; Robert R. Bowie and Richard H. Immerman, *Waging Peace: How Eisenhower Shaped an Enduring Cold War Strategy* (New York: Oxford University Press, 1998), p. 204.
19. Dwight D. Eisenhower, "Chance for Peace," address to the American Society of Newspaper Editors, April 16, 1953, *Public Papers of the Presidents,* http://www.presidency.ucsb.edu/ws/index.php?pid=9819&st=&st1; Dwight D. Eisenhower, "Peaceful Uses of Atomic Energy," address to the General Assembly of the United Nations, December 8, 1953, *Public Papers of the Presidents,* http://www.presidency.ucsb.edu/ws/index.php?pid=9774&st=&st1; Gaddis, *Strategies of Containment*, pp. 189–90; Divine, *Eisenhower and the Cold War,* pp. 117, 120.
20. Dwight D. Eisenhower, "Inaugural Address," January 20, 1953, *Public Papers of the Presidents,* www.presidency.ucsb.edu/ws/?pid=9600.
21. Eisenhower Inaugural Address, January 20, 1953; Ambrose, *Eisenhower,* p. 2:36.
22. *Foreign Relations of the United States, 1955–57, Volume XIX, National Security Policy,* p. 151.
23. Marc Trachtenberg, *A Constructed Peace: The Making of the European Settlement, 1945–1963* (Princeton, N.J.: Princeton University Press, 1999), p. 156; Eisenhower, *Mandate for Change,* p. 141.
24. Gaddis, *Strategies of Containment,* p. 128; Ambrose, *Eisenhower,* pp. 2:49–50.
25. Trachtenberg, *Constructed Peace,* pp. 110, 149; Eisenhower, *Mandate for Change,* pp. 398, 405.

26. Geoffrey Warner, "The United States and the Rearmament of West Germany," *International Affairs* 61, no. 2 (Spring 1985), n28.
27. Ibid., pp. 284–85; Eisenhower, *Mandate for Change*, p. 404.
28. Ambrose, *Eisenhower*, p. 2:217.
29. Michael B. Oren, *Power, Faith and Fantasy: America in the Middle East, 1776 to the Present* (New York: W.W. Norton, 2007), p. 512; John Lewis Gaddis, *We Now Know: Rethinking Cold War History* (New York: Oxford University Press, 1997), p. 169; Anthony Eden, *Full Circle: The Memoirs of Anthony Eden* (Boston: Houghton Mifflin, 1960), p. 284.
30. Ambrose, *Eisenhower*, p. 2:184; Eisenhower, *Mandate for Change*, pp. 350–51.
31. Eisenhower, *Mandate for Change*, pp. 352, 371; Ambrose, *Eisenhower*, pp. 2:176, 182; Hughes, *Ordeal of Power*, p. 208. Late in his presidential campaign, Eisenhower made a similar point, lamenting the disproportionate burden carried by American youth in Korea and calling the conflict "a job for Koreans . . . . If there must be a war there, let it be Asians against Asians, with our support on the side of freedom." See Divine, *Eisenhower and the Cold War*, pp. 17–18; Foreign Relations of the United States, 1952–54, Vol. XIII, Part 2, Indochina Doc. 808; Fredrik Logevall, *Embers of War: The Fall of an Empire and the Making of America's Vietnam* (New York: Random House, 2012), p. 593.
32. Eisenhower, *Mandate for Change*, p. 371; Ambrose, *Eisenhower*, pp. 2:208–9.
33. Ambrose, *Eisenhower*, pp. 2:194–97.
34. Ibid., pp. 2:235, 239.
35. Ibid., pp. 2:243–44.
36. Diane B. Kunz, *The Economic Diplomacy of the Suez Crisis* (Chapel Hill: University of North Carolina Press, 1991), pp. 68–69; Gaddis, *We Now Know*, pp. 170–72; "Telephone Call to Allen Dulles," *Foreign Relations of the United States, 1955–1957, Volume XV, Arab-Israeli Dispute, January 1–July 26, 1956*, p. 866.
37. Kunz, *Economic Diplomacy of the Suez Crisis*, pp. 64, 70–71; *Foreign Relations of the United States, 1955–1957, Volume XV, Arab-Israeli Dispute, January 1–July 26, 1956*, pp. 866–873; Townsend Hoopes, *The Devil and John Foster Dulles* (Boston: Little, Brown, 1973), p. 341; Henry Kissinger, *Diplomacy* (New York: Simon & Schuster, 1994), p. 529.
38. Dwight D. Eisenhower, *The White House Years: Waging Peace: 1956–1961* (New York: Doubleday, 1965), pp. 36–40; *Foreign Relations of the United States, 1955–57, Volume XVI, Suez Crisis, July 26–December 31, 1956*, p. 62; *Foreign Relations of the United States, 1955–57, Volume XXVII, Western Europe and Canada*, pp. 677–78.
39. Eisenhower, *Waging Peace*, pp. 40, 77, 665, 667.
40. Charles E. Bohlen, *Witness to History: 1929–1969* (New York: W.W. Norton, 1973), pp. 428–31.
41. Eisenhower, *Waging Peace*, p. 51; Murphy, *Diplomat Among Warriors* p. 388; Hughes, *Ordeal of Power*, p. 211.
42. Ambrose, *Eisenhower*, pp. 2:358, 365; Divine, *Eisenhower and the Cold War*, p. 85; Hughes, *Ordeal of Power*, p. 217.
43. Ambrose, *Eisenhower*, p. 2:361; Eisenhower, *Waging Peace*, p. 83; Kissinger, *Diplomacy*, p. 546; Hughes, *Ordeal of Power*, p. 209. Hughes claims that Nixon's statement was written for him by Dulles.
44. Adams, *Firsthand Report*,, p. 261; Ambrose, *Eisenhower*, p. 2:363.
45. Bohlen, *Witness to History*, p. 432; Ambrose, *Eisenhower*, p. 2:368.
46. Ambrose, *Eisenhower*, pp. 2:374, 380; Eisenhower, *Waging Peace*, pp. 193–94.
47. Ambrose, *Eisenhower*, pp. 2:382, 388; Eisenhower, *Waging Peace*, p.178; Adams, *Firsthand Report*,, pp. 273–76.

48. Eisenhower, *Waging Peace*, p. 270.
49. Ibid., pp. 272, 277; Ambrose, *Eisenhower*, p. 2:465.
50. Eisenhower, *Waging Peace*, p. 272; Robert Cutler, *No Time for Rest* (Boston: Little, Brown, 1965), p. 364; Ambrose, *Eisenhower*, p. 2:471.
51. Divine, *Eisenhower and the Cold War*, p. 101; Murphy, *Diplomat Among Warriors*, p. 400; Ambrose, *Eisenhower*, p. 2:473.
52. Murphy, *Diplomat Among Warriors*, pp. 404–6, 409; Wilbur Crane Eveland, *Ropes of Sand: America's Failure in the Middle East* (New York: W.W. Norton, 1980), pp. 297, 299–300, 304. A frequently quoted line of Eveland's memoir has it that when American troops landed in Beirut, they were "welcomed by bikini-clad bathing beauties and soda-pop hawkers," as though the entire operation were pure farce. Yet Eveland admits (pp. 293–94) that he was not even in Lebanon when the landing took place and that he got his reports from journalists who were also not on the scene. The rest of his account confirms the violence and disorder of Beirut as described by Murphy.
53. Eisenhower, *Waging Peace*, p. 271; Ambrose, *Eisenhower*, p. 2:474.
54. Eisenhower, *Waging Peace*, pp. 290–91; Murphy, *Diplomat Among Warriors*, pp. 410, 413.
55. Ambrose, *Eisenhower*, pp. 2:454–56; Hughes, *Ordeal of Power*, p. 248.
56. Ambrose, *Eisenhower*, pp. 2:434–35; Eisenhower, *Waging Peace*, pp. 220–23; Gaddis, *Strategies of Containment*, pp. 182–85; Hughes, *Ordeal of Power*, p. 253.
57. Ambrose, *Eisenhower*, pp. 2:433–35; Gaddis, *Strategies of Containment*, pp. 183–84; Eisenhower, *Waging Peace*, pp. 220–23; *Foreign Relations of the United States, 1955–1957, Volume XIX, National Security Policy*, doc. 170, pp. 702–4.
58. Ambrose, *Eisenhower*, p. 2:493; Hughes, *Ordeal of Power*, p. 230.
59. Dwight D. Eisenhower, "Security in the Free World," March 16, 1959, *Public Papers of the Presidents*, http://www.presidency.ucsb.edu/ws/index.php?pid=11682&st=&st1.
60. Ambrose, *Eisenhower*, p. 2:470.
61. Ibid., p. 397; Eisenhower, *Waging Peace*, p. 299; Eisenhower, "Security in the Free World."
62. Eisenhower, *Waging Peace*, pp. 299–300; Gaddis, *Strategies of Containment*, p. 168; Ambrose, *Eisenhower*, p. 2:484.
63. Evan Thomas, *Ike's Bluff: President Eisenhower's Secret Battle to Save the World* (Boston: Little, Brown, 2012), p. 325; Ambrose, *Eisenhower*, pp. 2:515–16.
64. Ambrose, *Eisenhower*, p. 2:517.
65. Ibid., pp. 2:445, 449, 459.
66. Ibid., pp. 2:542, 553; Eisenhower, *Waging Peace*, pp. 432, 468.
67. Ambrose, *Eisenhower*, pp. 2:455, 493.
68. Dwight D. Eisenhower to Harold Macmillan, March 18, 1960, *Papers of Dwight David Eisenhower, Volume XX, Part IX, Chapter 21*.
69. Eisenhower, *Waging Peace*, pp. 543–59; Bohlen, *Witness to History*, p. 469.
70. Trachtenberg, *Constructed Peace*, p. 246; Eisenhower, *Waging Peace*, p. 483; Ambrose, *Eisenhower*, p. 2:605.
71. Eisenhower, *Waging Peace*, p. 519; Richard M. Nixon, *Six Crises* (New York: Warner Books, 1979), pp. 215–17, 260, 270; Adams, *Firsthand Report*, p. 381.
72. Eisenhower, *Waging Peace*, pp. 516, 525, 537; Ambrose, *Eisenhower*, pp. 2:553, 558; Cutler, *No Time for Rest*, pp. 375–76.
73. Eisenhower, *Waging Peace*, pp. 521, 524–25.
74. Ibid., pp. 534–38; Tim Weiner, *Legacy of Ashes: The History of the CIA* (New York: Doubleday, 2007), pp. 171–72.
75. Eisenhower, *Waging Peace*, p. 539.

76. Ambrose, *Eisenhower,* p. 2:555.
77. Ibid., pp. 557, 584.
78. Ibid., p. 608.
79. See Leslie H. Gelb, "Ike Speech that Eclipses JFK," *Daily Beast,* January 17, 2011; and William Galston, "Why I Miss President Eisenhower," *New Republic,* January 20, 2011.
80. Dwight D. Eisenhower, "Farewell to the American People," radio and television address, January 17, 1961, *Public Papers of the Presidents,* http://www.presidency.ucsb.edu/ws/index.php?pid=12086&st=&st1.

4: "BOY COMMANDOS" OF THE NEW FRONTIER

1. Thomas G. Paterson, ed., *Kennedy's Quest for Victory: American Foreign Policy, 1961–1963* (New York: Oxford University Press, 1989), p. 19; W. W. Rostow, *Diffusion of Power: An Essay in Recent History* (New York: Macmillan, 1972), p. 215. As attorney general, Robert Kennedy was a full member of the national security team; he had been an officer in training when World War II ended. McNamara did not hold the record as youngest defense secretary for long: Donald Rumsfeld was only forty-three when he assumed the office in 1975.
2. Richard L. Lyons, "Kennedy Hits Nixon Experience," *The Washington Post,* August 25, 1960, p. A18; Warren Bass, *Support Any Friend: Kennedy's Middle East and the Making of the U.S.-Israel Alliance* (New York: Oxford University Press, 2003), p. 3.
3. Deborah Shapley, *Promise and Power: The Life and Times of Robert McNamara* (Boston: Little, Brown, 1993), p. 102; John F. Kennedy, *The Strategy of Peace* (New York: Harper & Brothers, 1960), pp. 4, 6.
4. Senator John F. Kennedy, "America's Stake in Vietnam," *Vital Speeches of the Day,* August 1, 1956, p. 619; Kennedy, *Strategy of Peace,* p. 7.
5. Theodore H. White quoted in Paterson, *Kennedy's Quest for Victory,* p. 19; Clark Clifford with Richard Holbrooke, *Counsel to the President: A Memoir* (New York: Random House, 1991), p. 334.
6. Shapley, *Promise and Power,* p. 103; David Halberstam, *The Best and the Brightest* (New York: Ballantine Books, 1993), p. 215; George W. Ball, *The Past Has Another Pattern: Memoirs* (New York: W.W. Norton, 1982), p. 167; Rostow, *Diffusion of Power,* p. 126; Tim Weiner, *Legacy of Ashes: The History of the CIA* (New York: Doubleday, 2007), p. 180.
7. Paterson, *Kennedy's Quest for Victory,* p. 313; Arthur Schlesinger, "A Biographer's Perspective," in Kenneth W. Thompson, ed., *The Kennedy Presidency: Seventeen Intimate Perspectives of John F. Kennedy* (Lanham, Md.: University Press of America, 1985), pp. 22–23; Paul Nitze, *From Hiroshima to Glasnost: At the Center of Decision—A Memoir* (New York: Grove Weidenfeld, 1989), pp. 251–52.
8. Charles O. Jones, ed., *Preparing to Be President: The Memos of Richard E. Neustadt* (Washington, D.C.: AEI Press, 2000), p. 63; Ball, *Past Has Another Pattern,* p. 168.
9. Walter Isaacson and Evan Thomas, *The Wise Men: Six Friends and the World They Made* (New York: Simon & Schuster, 1986), p. 616; John Lewis Gaddis, *Strategies of Containment: A Critical Appraisal of Postwar National Security Policy* (New York: Oxford University Press, 2005), p. 199; Rostow, *Diffusion of Power,* pp. 174–76.
10. Rostow, *Diffusion of Power,* pp. 296–302.
11. The media paid more attention to Kennedy's proposals for East-West negotiations. Thurston Clarke, *Ask Not: The Inauguration of John F. Kennedy and the Speech That*

Changed America (New York: Penguin, 2004), p. 198; Rostow, *Diffusion of Power,* pp. 209–210; Weiner, *Legacy of Ashes,* pp. 173–77; Kai Bird, *The Color of Truth: McGeorge Bundy and William Bundy, Brothers in Arms* (New York: Touchstone, 1998), pp. 194–97; Arthur M. Schlesinger Jr., *A Thousand Days: John F. Kennedy in the White House* (Boston: Houghton Mifflin, 1965), pp. 249–59; Paterson, *Kennedy's Quest for Victory,* pp. 130–32.

12. Marc Trachtenberg, *A Constructed Peace: The Making of the European Settlement, 1945–1963* (Princeton, N.J.: Princeton University Press, 1999), p. 283; *Foreign Relations of the United States, 1961–1963, Volume XIV, Berlin Crisis, 1961–1962,* doc. 26, pp. 71–75.
13. William Taubman, *Khrushchev: The Man and His Era* (New York: W.W. Norton, 2003), pp. 497–98. For the official memoranda of conversation, see *Foreign Relations of the United States, 1961–1963, Volume XIV, Berlin Crisis, 1961–1962,* doc. 32, pp. 87–98. For a relatively full narrative account, see Michael R. Beschloss, *The Crisis Years* (New York: Edward Burlingame Books, 1991), chaps. 8–9.
14. *Foreign Relations of the United States, 1961–1963, Volume V, Soviet Union,* pp. 206–25.
15. *Foreign Relations of the United States, 1961–1963, Volume XIV, Berlin Crisis, 1961–1962,* doc. 49, pp. 138–59; Trachtenberg, *Constructed Peace,* pp. 289, 304.
16. *Foreign Relations of the United States, 1961–1963, Volume XIV, Berlin Crisis, 1961–1962,* doc. 49, pp. 138–59.
17. Charles E. Bohlen, *Witness to History: 1929–1969* (New York: W.W. Norton, 1973), p. 486; John F. Kennedy, "On the Berlin Crisis," radio and television report to the American people, July 25, 1961, *Public Papers of the Presidents,* http://www.presidency.ucsb.edu/ws/index.php?pid=8259&st=&st1; John Lewis Gaddis, *We Now Know: Rethinking Cold War History* (New York: Oxford University Press, 1997), p. 147; Michael R. Beschloss, *Crisis Years,* pp. 257–61.
18. Kennedy, "On the Berlin Crisis."
19. *Foreign Relations of the United States, 1961–1963, Volume XIV, Berlin Crisis, 1961–1962,* doc. 147, pp. 359–60, 402–3.
20. Clarke, *Ask Not,* p. 129; John F. Kennedy, Inaugural Address, January 20, 1961, *Public Papers of the Presidents,* http://www.presidency.ucsb.edu/ws/index.php?pid=8032&st=&st1; *Foreign Relations of the United States, 1961–1963, Volume XIV, Berlin Crisis, 1961–1962,* doc. 100, pp. 312–16; doc. 122, pp. 359–60.
21. *Foreign Relations of the United States, 1961–1963, Volume XIV, Berlin Crisis, 1961–1962,* doc. 238, pp. 672–78.
22. Ibid., doc. 268, pp. 759–60; doc. 296, pp. 819–22; *Foreign Relations of the United States, 1961–1963, Volume XV, Berlin Crisis, 1962–1963,* doc. 1, pp. 1–3.
23. *Foreign Relations of the United States, 1961–1963, Volume XV, Berlin Crisis, 1962–1963,* doc. 49, pp. 142–45.
24. *Foreign Relations of the United States, 1961–1963, Volume XIII, Western Europe and Canada,* doc. 249, pp. 695–701.
25. Ibid., doc. 145, pp. 419–22; doc. 251, p. 704; doc. 252, pp. 705–7.
26. Rostow, *Diffusion of Power,* p. 230.
27. Ball, *Past Has Another Pattern,* p. 181.
28. See Bass, *Support Any Friend,* p. 65.
29. *Foreign Relations of the United States, 1961–1963, Volume I, Vietnam, 1961,* doc. 60, pp. 152–57.
30. Ibid.; General Maxwell D. Taylor, *Swords and Plowshares* (New York: Da Capo Press, 1972), p. 228; Gordon M. Goldstein, *Lessons in Disaster: McGeorge Bundy and the Path to War in Vietnam* (New York: Henry Holt, 2008), pp. 55–58; *Foreign Relations of the*

United States, 1961–1963, Volume XXIV, Laos Crisis, doc. 195, pp. 443–45; *Foreign Relations of the United States, 1961–1963, Volume I, Vietnam, 1961*, doc. 210, pp. 477–532.

31. *Foreign Relations of the United States, 1961–1963, Volume I, Vietnam, 1961*, doc. 232, pp. 572–73; doc. 204, p. 464; Andrew Preston, *The War Council: McGeorge Bundy, the NSC, and Vietnam* (Cambridge, Mass.: Harvard University Press, 2006), p. 96. In *Lessons in Disaster*, Gordon Goldstein suggests that Kennedy may have quietly urged McNamara, who had initially opposed the plan because the Taylor-Rostow troop number was too small, to oppose troops altogether. But JCS criticisms of the proposal seem a much more plausible explanation of McNamara's changed stance. Goldstein does not explain why McNamara failed to disclose Kennedy's behind-the-scenes maneuvering in his own memoirs, since it would be crucial evidence for a question that does interest him greatly: how Kennedy would have handled Vietnam had he lived. *Lessons In Disaster*, p. 64.
32. *Foreign Relations of the United States, 1961–1963, Volume I, Vietnam, 1961*, doc. 239, pp. 580–82; Goldstein, *Lessons in Disaster*, p. 62; Ball, *Past Has Another Pattern*, p. 366; Bird, *Color of Truth*, pp. 220–21.
33. Preston, *War Council*, pp. 87, 97, 99.
34. *Foreign Relations of the United States, 1961–1963, Volume I, Vietnam, 1961*, doc. 233, pp. 573–75; doc. 238, pp. 578–79; doc. 251, pp. 601–3; *Foreign Relations of the United States, 1961–1963, Volume VIII, National Security Policy*, doc. 69, pp. 238–42.
35. Preston, *War Council*, pp. 103–4.
36. Weiner, *Legacy of Ashes*, pp. 194–95; Aleksandr Fursenko and Timothy Naftali, *One Hell of a Gamble: Khrushchev, Castro, and Kennedy, 1958–1964* (New York: W.W. Norton, 1997), p. 214. Rusk glides over this moment in his memoirs, insisting that "we checked out every rumor that we could," but unfortunately "reconnaissance overflights and on-the-ground espionage within Cuba yielded little new information." Dean Rusk, *As I Saw It: A Secretary of State's Memoirs* (London: I.B. Tauris, 1991), pp. 230–31.
37. An invaluable document for understanding American policy during the crisis is Ernest May and Philip Zelikow, *The Kennedy Tapes: Inside the White House During the Cuban Missile Crisis* (New York: W.W. Norton, 2002); also important are Fursenko and Naftali, *One Hell of a Gamble*, and most recently, Michael Dobbs, *One Minute to Midnight: Kennedy, Khrushchev, and Castro on the Brink of Nuclear War* (New York: Knopf, 2008). See also Taylor, *Swords and Plowshares*, p. 266ff.
38. May and Zelikow, *Kennedy Tapes*, p. 111.
39. Ibid., pp. 36, 49, 50, 62.
40. Ibid., p. 43.
41. Ibid., pp. 84, 50, 60.
42. Ibid., pp. 140–41.
43. Ibid., pp. 140, 147.
44. Ibid., p. 171.
45. Ibid., pp. 125, 144, 170, 178.
46. Ibid., pp. 171, 305; Rusk made the same point—about getting the Soviet leaders to rethink—at the first meeting that the president called after the discovery of the missiles. Ibid., p. 38.
47. Taylor, *Swords and Plowshares*, p. 275; May and Zelikow, *Kennedy Tapes*, pp. 297–99, 389–91, 402; Fursenko and Naftali, *One Hell of a Gamble*, p. 263; Taubman, *Khrushchev*, pp. 568–69.
48. May and Zelikow, *Kennedy Tapes*, pp. 41, 198–99; Nitze, *From Here to Glasnost*, p. 237.
49. Nitze, *From Here to Glasnost*, p. 227; Robert A. Caro, *The Passage of Power* (New York: Knopf, 2012), p. 219: May and Zelikow, *Kennedy Tapes*, p. 308.

50. May and Zelikow, *Kennedy Tapes*, pp. 306, 308, 326, 348.
51. Ibid., pp. 348–49, 351.
52. Ibid., pp. 387–89.
53. Taubman, *Khrushchev*, pp. 573–75.
54. May and Zelikow, *Kennedy Tapes*, p. 412 and fn.; Stewart Alsop and Charles Bartlett, "In Time of Crisis," *Saturday Evening Post*, December 18, 1962, p. 20.
55. Alsop and Bartlett, "In Time of Crisis," p. 20; Coral Bell, *The Conventions of Crisis: A Study in Diplomatic Management* (Oxford: Oxford University Press, 1971), p. 2.
56. Britain was the third original party to the treaty, but its negotiators' role was distinctly subordinate to that of the Soviet and American participants.
57. Ted Sorensen, *Counselor: A Life at the Edge of History* (New York: HarperCollins, 2008), pp. 326–27; John F. Kennedy, Commencement Address at American University, June 10, 1963, *Public Papers of the Presidents*, http://www.presidency.ucsb.edu/ws/index.php?pid=9266&st=&st1; Melvyn P. Leffler, *For the Soul of Mankind: The United States, the Soviet Union, and the Cold War* (New York: Hill & Wang, 2007), p. 182. Kennedy, says Sorensen, wanted "a reexamination of the cold war, a reexamination of our relations with the Soviet Union, and a reexamination of what kind of peace we truly wanted." See Jeffrey D. Sachs, *To Move the World: JFK's Quest for Peace* (New York: Random House, 2013), pp. 70–90.
58. *Foreign Relations of the United States, 1961–1963, Volume XV, Berlin Crisis, 1962–1963*, doc. 146, pp. 406–407, fn. 2.
59. Trachtenberg, *Constructed Peace*, p. 338; Leffler, *For the Soul of Mankind*, pp. 179–80; Paterson, *Kennedy's Quest for Victory*, p. 30.
60. Trachtenberg, *Constructed Peace*, pp. 374–77.
61. *Foreign Relations of the United States, 1961–1963, Volume VII, Arms Control and Disarmament*, doc. 358, pp. 866–69; Trachtenberg, *Constructed Peace*, p. 393; Ball, *Past Has Another Pattern*, p. 222.
62. Trachtenberg, *Constructed Peace*, p. 391; *Senate Foreign Relations Committee Historical Series, Volume XV, 1963* (Washington, D.C., U.S. GPO, 1987), p. 356.
63. Bohlen, *Witness to History*, p. 511.
64. Sorensen, *Counselor*, p. 359.
65. Paterson, *Kennedy's Quest for Victory*, pp. 247–48; Preston, *War Council*, pp. 47–48; David Halberstam, *The Making of a Quagmire* (New York: Random House, 1965), p. 259.
66. *Foreign Relations of the United States, 1961–1963, Volume III, Vietnam, January–August 1963*, doc. 29, pp. 97–98; Preston, *War Council*, p. 116.
67. Schlesinger, *Thousand Days*, pp. 548–49; Halberstam, *Making of a Quagmire*, pp. 210–12; Mark Moyar, *Triumph Forsaken: The Vietnam War, 1954–1965* (New York: Cambridge University Press, 2006), p. 225.
68. *Foreign Relations of the United States, 1961–1963, Volume III, Vietnam, January–August 1963*, doc. 77, pp. 140–43; Arthur M. Schlesinger, Jr., *Robert Kennedy and His Times* (Boston: Houghton Mifflin, 2002), p. 707; *Foreign Relations of the United States, 1961–1963, Volume II, Vietnam, 1962*, doc. 322, p. 745; Paterson, *Kennedy's Quest for Victory*, p. 244; Moyar, *Triumph Forsaken*, p. 230.
69. Preston, *War Council*, p. 125; *Foreign Relations of the United States, 1961–1963, Volume III, Vietnam, January–August 1963*, doc. 270, pp. 606–10.
70. Paterson, *Kennedy's Quest for Victory*, p. 247; Ball, *Past Has Another Pattern*, pp. 371–74; Schlesinger, *Thousand Days*, p. 990; Preston, *War Council*, pp. 121–22.
71. *Foreign Relations of the United States, 1961–1963, Volume III, Vietnam, January–August*

1963, doc. 281, pp. 628–29; Preston, *War Council,* p. 122; Moyar, *Triumph Forsaken,* p. 237; Schlesinger, *Thousand Days,* p. 991; Goldstein, *Lessons in Disaster,* p. 78; Taylor, *Swords and Plowshares,* p. 292.

72. Goldstein, *Lessons in Disaster,* p. 94; Weiner, *Legacy of Ashes,* pp. 599–600; Preston, *War Council,* pp. 123, 125.
73. Sorensen, *Counselor,* p. 354; Schlesinger, *Robert Kennedy and His Times,* p. 714; *Foreign Relations of the United States, 1961–1963, Volume IV, Vietnam, August–December 1963,* doc. 93, pp. 185–90.
74. *Foreign Relations of the United States, 1961–1963, Volume IV, Vietnam, August–December 1963,* doc. 1, pp. 1–6; Ball, *Past Has Another Pattern,* p. 372; Weiner, *Legacy of Ashes,* p. 218; Schlesinger, *Thousand Days,* p. 984.
75. Paterson, *Kennedy's Quest for Victory,* pp. 247–48; Preston, *War Council,* p. 127; Moyar, *Triumph Forsaken,* p. 237; *Foreign Relations of the United States, 1961–1963, Volume IV, Vietnam, August–December 1963,* doc. 220; "Report of McNamara-Taylor Mission to South Vietnam," October 2, 1963, *The Pentagon Papers,* ed. Senator Mike Gravel (Boston: Beacon, 1971), pp. 2:751–66, https://www.mtholyoke.edu/acad/intrel/pentagon2/doc142.htm.
76. *Foreign Relations of the United States, 1961–1963, Volume IV, Vietnam, August–December 1963,* doc. 167, pp. 336–46.
77. Ibid., doc. 18, pp. 35–36; Taylor, *Swords and Plowshares,* p. 301; Preston, *War Council,* p. 127; Goldstein, *Lessons in Disaster,* p. 88; Bird, *Color of Truth,* p. 263.
78. *Foreign Relations of the United States, 1961–1963, Volume IV, Vietnam, August–December 1963,* p. 518; *Foreign Relations of the United States, 1961–1963, Volume I, Vietnam, 1961,* doc. 263, p. 518; doc. 288, pp. 555–56; Roger Hilsman, *To Move a Nation: The Politics of Foreign Policy in the Administration of John F. Kennedy* (New York: Doubleday, 1967), p. 521; Preston, *War Council,* p. 128.
79. Moyar, *Triumph Forsaken,* pp. 275–76; Weiner, *Legacy of Ashes,* p. 242; see also Kennedy's November 4, 1963 dictation regarding the coup against Diem in South Vietnam, available through the Miller Center: http://whitehousetapes.net/clip/john-kennedy-john-kennedy-jr-caroline-kennedy-jfks-memoir-dictation-assassination-diem.
80. Bird, *Color of Truth,* p. 265; John F. Kennedy, "Broadcast with Walter Cronkite Inaugurating CBS Television News Program," September 2, 1963, *Public Papers of the Presidents,* http://www.presidency.ucsb.edu/ws/index.php?pid=9388&st=&st1.
81. For Lippmann's views of Kennedy, see Ronald Steel, *Walter Lippmann and the American Century* (Boston: Little, Brown, 1980), chap. 40.

5: "MAINLY VIOLINS, WITH TOUCHES OF BRASS"

1. Lyndon B. Johnson, Address Before a Joint Session of the Congress, *Public Papers of the Presidents,* November 27, 1963, http://www.presidency.ucsb.edu/ws/index.php?pid=25988&st=&st1; see also Robert A. Caro's *The Passage of Power,* chapter 16, for a rich description of Johnson's speech and his emphasis on continuity between administrations.
2. Lyndon B. Johnson, Inaugural Address, January 20, 1965, *Public Papers of the Presidents,* http://www.presidency.ucsb.edu/ws/index.php?pid=26985&st=&st1; Lyndon B. Johnson, "The American Promise," special message to the Congress, *Public Papers of the Presidents,* March 15, 1965, http://www.presidency.ucsb.edu/ws/index.php?pid=26805&st=&st1.
3. Bureau of the Budget, *The Budget of the U.S. Government for the Fiscal Year Ending June*

30, 1965 (Washington, D.C.: GPO, 1965), p. 71; Doris Kearns Goodwin, *Lyndon Johnson and the American Dream* (New York: Harper & Row, 1976), p. 193.

4. Lyndon B. Johnson, Remarks to Employees of the State Department, December 5, 1963, *Public Papers of the Presidents,* http://www.presidency.ucsb.edu/ws/index.php?pid=26154&st=&st1.
5. Ibid.; Goodwin, *Johnson and the American Dream*, p. 194. For Isaiah, see LBJ Library Staff, "Religion and President Johnson," http://www.lbjlib.utexas.edu/johnson/archives.hom/faqs/Religion/religion_hm.asp.
6. Goodwin, *Johnson and the American Dream*, p. 251; Clark Clifford with Richard Holbrooke, *Counsel to the President: A Memoir* (New York: Random House, 1991), p. 506; Jack Valenti, *A Very Human President* (New York: W.W. Norton, 1975), p. 243.
7. See David Halberstam, *The Best and the Brightest* (New York: Random House, 1969); Leslie H. Gelb and Richard K. Betts, *The Irony of Vietnam: The System Worked* (Washington, D.C.: Brookings Institution Press, 1979); Campbell Craig and Fredrik Logevall, *America's Cold War: The Politics of Insecurity* (Cambridge, Mass.: Harvard University Press, 2009); and Peter Beinart, *The Icarus Syndrome: A History of American Hubris* (New York: HarperCollins, 2010).
8. Goodwin, *Johnson and the American Dream*, p. 283.
9. Robert McNamara to Lyndon Johnson, "Vietnam Situation," memorandum, December 21, 1963, *The Pentagon Papers,* ed. Senator Mike Gravel (Boston: Beacon, 1971), pp. 3:494–96, https://www.mtholyoke.edu/acad/intrel/pentagon3/doc156.htm; Robert S. McNamara with Brian VanDeMark, *In Retrospect* (New York: Random House, 1995), p. 105.
10. *Foreign Relations of the United States, 1964–1968, Volume I, Vietnam, 1964,* doc. 84, pp. 153–67; General Maxwell D. Taylor, *Swords and Plowshares* (New York: W.W. Norton, 1972) pp. 317, 326.
11. Johnson, Remarks to Employees of the State Department; McNamara, *In Retrospect*, pp. 102–3.
12. Lyndon Baines Johnson, *The Vantage Point: Perspectives of the Presidency, 1963–1969* (New York: Popular Library, 1971), p. 44.
13. National Security Action Memorandum 273, November 26, 1963, *Foreign Relations of the United States, 1961–1963, Volume IV, Vietnam, August–December 1963,* doc. 331, pp. 637–40.
14. McNamara, *In Retrospect,* p. 112; Taylor, *Swords and Plowshares,* p. 310.
15. *Foreign Relations of the United States, 1964–1968, Volume I, Vietnam, 1964,* doc. 84, pp. 153–167; George C. Herring, *America's Longest War: The United States and Vietnam, 1950–1975* (Boston: McGraw Hill, 2002), p. 138.
16. *Foreign Relations of the United States, 1964–1968, Volume I, Vietnam, 1964,* doc. 84, pp. 153–167; General William C. Westmoreland, *A Soldier Reports* (New York: Dell, 1980), p. 104.
17. Victor H. Krulak, *First to Fight: An Inside View of the U.S. Marine Corps* (Annapolis, Md.: U.S. Naval Institute, 1984), p. 186.
18. H. R. McMaster, *Dereliction of Duty: Lyndon Johnson, Robert McNamara, the Joint Chiefs of Staff, and the Lies That Led to Vietnam* (New York: HarperCollins, 1997), pp. 64, 202; *Foreign Relations of the United States, 1964–1968, Volume I, Vietnam, 1964,* doc. 84, pp. 153–67. McCone's observations were apparently crossed out of his and McNamara's trip report to the president.
19. Taylor, *Swords and Plowshares,* p. 309.

20. *Foreign Relations of the United States, 1964–1968, Volume I, Vietnam, 1964,* doc. 173, pp. 374–77.
21. Michael R. Beschloss, ed., *Taking Charge: The Johnson White House Tapes, 1963–1964* (New York: Simon & Schuster, 1997), pp. 370–73; *Foreign Relations of the United States, 1964–1968, Volume I, Vietnam, 1964,* doc. 185, pp. 400–4.
22. Andrew Preston, *War Council: McGeorge Bundy, the NSC, and Vietnam* (Cambridge, Mass.: Harvard University Press, 2006), pp. 145–46, 149.
23. Johnson, *Vantage Point,* p. 64; Halberstam, *Best and Brightest,* p. 352.
24. Ibid., Johnson, *Vantage Point,* p. 64; McNamara, *In Retrospect,* p. 155.
25. Halberstam, *Best and Brightest,* p. 414.
26. Taylor, *Swords and Plowshares,* pp. 318–19; Gordon M. Goldstein, *Lessons in Disaster: McGeorge Bundy and the Path to War in Vietnam* (New York: Times Books, 2008), pp. 133–34.
27. Julian E. Zelizer, *Arsenal of Democracy: The Politics of National Security—from World War II to the War on Terrorism* (New York: Basic Books, 2010), pp. 189–90; Ted Gittinger, ed., *The Johnson Years: A Vietnam Roundtable* (Austin: University of Texas Press, 1993), p. 41; McNamara, *In Retrospect,* pp. 146–47.
28. Taylor, *Swords and Plowshares,* pp. 323–24; McMaster, *Dereliction of Duty,* p. 174.
29. Kai Bird, *The Color of Truth: McGeorge Bundy and William Bundy: Brothers in Arms* (New York: Touchstone, 1998), p. 293; Frederik Logevall, *Choosing War: The Lost Chance for Peace and the Escalation of War in Vietnam* (Berkeley and Los Angeles: University of California Press, 1999), p. 111.
30. *Foreign Relations of the United States, 1964–1968, Volume III, June–December 1965,* doc. 11, p. 33; Taylor was particularly outraged on this occasion by the feebleness of the reasons he was given for inaction. Perhaps, the White House cable explained, the Communists had merely been "bragging" when they claimed credit for the attack? Taylor, *Swords and Plowshares,* pp. 332–33.
31. Taylor, *Swords and Plowshares,* pp. 330–31; McNamara, *In Retrospect,* pp. 163–64; McMaster, *Dereliction of Duty,* pp. 198–99.
32. Robert W. Komer, *Bureaucracy at War: U.S. Performance in the Vietnam Conflict* (Boulder, Colo.: Westview Press, 1986), p. 28; Taylor, *Swords and Plowshares,* p. 318; McNamara, *In Retrospect,* p. 166.
33. McMaster, *Dereliction of Duty,* p. 212; *Foreign Relations of the United States, 1964–1968, Volume III, January–June 1965,* doc. 84, pp. 174–85.
34. Stephen Peter Rosen, "Vietnam and the American Theory of Limited War," *International Security* 7, no. 2 (Autumn 1982), p. 91; Bird, *Color of Truth,* p. 294.
35. Gittinger, *Johnson Years,* p. 48; Bird, *Color of Truth,* pp. 306–8; Randall B. Woods, *LBJ: Architect of American Ambition* (New York: Free Press, 2006), p. 603; McMaster, *Dereliction of Duty,* pp. 234–38.
36. McMaster, *Dereliction of Duty,* pp. 230, 257, 270–71.
37. Taylor, *Swords and Plowshares,* pp. 339–40, 342; Lyndon B. Johnson, "Peace Without Conquest," address at Johns Hopkins University, April 7, 1965, *Public Papers of the Presidents,* http://www.presidency.ucsb.edu/ws/index.php?pid=26877&st=&st1.
38. Westmoreland, *Soldier Reports,* pp. 179, 180–81, 183; McMaster, *Dereliction of Duty,* p. 297.
39. McNamara, *In Retrospect,* p. 188; McMaster, *Dereliction of Duty,* p. 296; *Foreign Relations of the United States, 1964–1968, Volume II, Vietnam, January–June 1965,* doc. 347, pp. 757–59.

40. Mark Moyar, *Triumph Forsaken: The Vietnam War, 1954–1965* (New York: Cambridge University Press, 2006), p. 372; Halberstam, *The Best and the Brightest,* p. 582.
41. Valenti, *Very Human President,* p. 352.
42. McNamara, *In Retrospect,* p. 191; George W. Ball, *The Past Has Another Pattern: Memoirs* (New York: W.W. Norton, 1982), p. 399; Valenti, *Very Human President,* p. 326.
43. Johnson, *Vantage Point,* p. 147; Valenti, *Very Human President,* p. 341.
44. Valenti, *Very Human President,* pp. 326, 345, 346, 350.
45. *Foreign Relations of the United States, 1964–1968, Volume III, Vietnam, June–December 1965,* doc. 7, pp. 16–21; Clifford, *Counsel to the President,* p. 415; Ball, *Past Has Another Pattern,* p. 400.
46. Clifford, *Counsel to the President,* pp. 418–22.
47. Ibid., p. 416; Goldstein, *Lessons in Disaster,* pp. 214, 217; McNamara, *In Retrospect,* p. 194.
48. Clifford, *Counsel to the President,* p. 421.
49. David M. Barrett, *Uncertain Warriors: Lyndon Johnson and His Vietnam Advisers* (Lawrence: University Press of Kansas, 1993), p. 24.
50. Johnson, *Vantage Point,* p. 147; McNamara, *In Retrospect,* p. 195.
51. Clifford, *Counsel to the President,* p. 413.
52. Ibid., p. 420; Valenti, *Very Human President,* p. 329.
53. Ball, *Past Has Another Pattern,* p. 399; Valenti, *Very Human President,* p. 329.
54. Taylor, *Swords and Plowshares,* p. 327 (emphasis mine); Valenti, *Very Human President,* p. 346.
55. Bird, *Color of Truth,* p. 331.
56. Goldstein, *Lessons in Disaster,* p. 211.
57. Clifford, *Counsel to the President,* p. 411; Preston, *War Council,* p. 146.
58. See Peter Beinhart, *The Icarus Syndrome*; Fredrik Logevall and Campbell Craig, *America's Cold War*; Melvyn P. Leffler, *For the Soul of Mankind.*"
59. Goodwin, *Johnson and the American Dream*, pp. 252–53; Ball, *Past Has Another Pattern,* p. 494.
60. Gittinger, *Johnson Years,* app. 3, p. 157.
61. Beinart, *Icarus Syndrome*, p. 180.
62. Goodwin, *Johnson and the American Dream*, p. 253.
63. Michael Lind, *Vietnam: The Necessary War* (New York: Simon & Schuster, 1999), p. 197; Moyar, *Triumph Forsaken,* p. 391.
64. David Halberstam, *The Making of a Quagmire* (New York: McGraw Hill, 1965), p. 177; Henry Kissinger, *Diplomacy* (New York: Simon & Schuster 1994), p. 669.
65. Valenti, *Very Human President,* p. 353; Goodwin, *Johnson and the American Dream*, pp. 193, 283.
66. W. W. Rostow, *The Diffusion of Power: An Essay in Recent History* (New York: Macmillan, 1972), p. 529.

6: "WE HAVE NOT BEEN DIVIDED"

1. Neil Sheehan, *A Bright Shining Lie: John Paul Vann and America in Vietnam* (New York: Random House, 1988), pp. 621–23; George C. Herring, *America's Longest War: The United States and Vietnam, 1950–1975* (Boston: McGraw Hill, 2002), p. 165.
2. Robert H. McNamara with Brian VanDeMark, *In Retrospect* (New York: Random House, 1995), p. 213; Kai Bird, *The Color of Truth: McGeorge Bundy and William Bundy:*

Brothers in Arms (New York: Touchstone, 1998), p. 340; General William C. Westmoreland, *A Soldier Reports* (New York: Dell, 1980), p. 206.

3. Andrew F. Krepinevich, Jr., *Army and Vietnam* (Baltimore: Johns Hopkins University Press, 1986), p. 148; Clark Clifford with Richard Holbrooke, *Counsel to the President: A Memoir* (New York: Random House, 1991), p. 436.
4. Robert D. Hormats, *The Price of Liberty: Paying for America's Wars* (New York: Times Books, 2007), p. 215; Office of Management and Budget, "Historical Tables," *The Budget of the U.S. Government, Fiscal Year 2005,* pp. 47–48, http://www.whitehouse.gov/sites/default/files/omb/budget/fy2005/pdf/hist.pdf; Herring, *America's Longest War,* p. 267.
5. Chris Hobson, *Vietnam Air Losses: United States Air Force, Navy and Marine Corps Fixed-Wing Aircraft Losses in Southeast Asia 1961–1973* (Hinckley, U.K.: Midland, 2001), p. 286; Michael Clodfelter, *Warfare and Armed Conflicts: A Statistical Reference to Casualty and Other Figures, 1500–2000* (Jefferson, N.C.: McFarland, 2002), pp. 656, 659, 775–76; McNamara, *In Retrospect,* p. 244.
6. Herring, *America's Longest War,* p. 183; Krepinevich, *Army and Vietnam,* p. 197.
7. Mark Moyar, *Triumph Forsaken: The Vietnam War, 1954–1965* (New York: Cambridge University Press, 2006), p. 409.
8. H. R. McMaster, *Dereliction of Duty: Lyndon Johnson, Robert McNamara, the Joint Chiefs of Staff, and the Lies That Led to Vietnam* (New York: HarperCollins, 1997), p. 313; Herring, *America's Longest War,* p. 166; Lyndon B. Johnson, *The Vantage Point: Perspectives of the Presidency, 1963–1969* (New York: Popular Library, 1971), p. 150.
9. Lyndon B. Johnson, news conference, July 28, 1965, *Public Papers of the Presidents,* http://www.presidency.ucsb.edu/ws/index.php?pid=27116&st=&st1; Moyar, *Triumph Forsaken,* p. 416; Herring, *America's Longest War,* p. 166; McNamara, *In Retrospect,* p. 205; Hormats, *Price of Liberty,* p. 212; McMaster, *Dereliction of Duty,* p. 319–20.
10. Hormats, *Price of Liberty,* p. 212; Paul H. Nitze, *From Hiroshima to Glasnost: At the Center of Decision—A Memoir* (New York: Grove Weidenfeld, 1989), pp. 262–63; McNamara, *In Retrospect,* p. 205.
11. Clifford, *Counsel to President,* p. 422; Jack Valenti, *A Very Human President* (New York: W.W. Norton, 1975), p. 355.
12. Johnson, *Vantage Point,* 149; Hormats, *Price of Liberty,* 212; McNamara, *In Retrospect,* p. 208; Lyndon B. Johnson, "Special Message to the Congress Requesting Additional Appropriations for Military Needs in Vietnam," May 4, 1965, Public Papers of the Presidents, www.presidency.ucsb.edu/ws/?pid=26940.
13. Herring, *America's Longest War,* p. 169; Dean Rusk, *As I Saw It: A Secretary of State's Memoirs* (London: I.B. Tauris, 1991), pp. 498–500; McNamara, *In Retrospect,* p. 253.
14. Nitze, *From Hiroshima to Glasnost,* p. 264; Clifford, *Counsel to President,* p. 443, Johnson, *Vantage Point,* p. 363.
15. *Foreign Relations of the United States, 1964–1968, Volume V, Vietnam, 1967,* doc. 91, pp. 208–10; General Maxwell D. Taylor, *Swords and Plowshares* (New York: W.W. Norton, 1972), p. 382; W. W. Rostow, *The Diffusion of Power: An Essay in Recent History* (New York: Macmillan, 1972), p. 459.
16. McNamara, *In Retrospect,* pp. 213, 221, 225.
17. Ibid., pp. 236–37, 263; Sheehan, *Bright Shining Lie,* p. 681.
18. McNamara, *In Retrospect,* p. 223.
19. Clifford, *Counsel to President,* p. 433–34; Johnson, *Vantage Point,* p. 578.
20. Johnson, *Vantage Point,* pp. 233, 252–53, 578.
21. Westmoreland, *Soldier Reports,* p. 153.
22. Ibid., p. 281 (emphasis added); McNamara, *In Retrospect,* pp. 264–65.

23. Westmoreland, *Soldier Reports,* p. 280.
24. *Foreign Relations of the United States, 1964–1968, Volume V, Vietnam, 1967,* doc. 177, pp. 423–38; Randall B. Woods, *LBJ: Architect of American Ambition* (New York: Free Press, 2006), p. 800.
25. McNamara, *In Retrospect,* pp. 269–71, 274–77.
26. Clifford, *Counsel to President,* p. 447; McNamara, *In Retrospect,* pp. 269–71, 283.
27. Herring, *America's Longest War,* p. 217.
28. Ibid., p. 216.
29. Johnson, *Vantage Point,* p. 259; Westmoreland, *Soldier Reports,* p. 280–81.
30. Victor H. Krulak, *First to Fight: An Inside View of the U.S. Marine Corps* (Annapolis, Md.: U.S. Naval Institute, 1984), p. 202; Sheehan, *Bright Shining Lie,* p. 814.
31. Krulak, *First to Fight,* p. 202.
32. Moyar, *Triumph Forsaken,* p. 360; Herring, *America's Longest War,* p. 216.
33. McMaster, *Dereliction of Duty,* p. 137.
34. Lyndon B. Johnson, State of the Union Address, January 10, 1967, *Public Papers of the Presidents,* http://www.presidency.ucsb.edu/ws/index.php?pid=28338&st=&st1.
35. Rostow, *Diffusion of Power,* p. 479; Woods, *LBJ: Architect of Ambition,* p. 733; Clifford, *Counsel to President,* p. 417.
36. Hormats, *Price of Liberty,* pp. 218–220; Woods, *LBJ: Architect of Ambition,* p. 743.
37. McNamara, *In Retrospect,* p. 286.
38. Clifford, *Counsel to President,* p. 457; McNamara, *In Retrospect,* 307; *Foreign Relations of the United States, 1964–1968, Volume V, Vietnam, 1967,* doc. 375, pp. 943–50.
39. Clifford, *Counsel to President,* pp. 456–60; McNamara, *In Retrospect,* pp. 311–17.
40. Walter Isaacson and Evan Thomas, *The Wise Men: Six Friends and the World They Made* (New York: Simon & Schuster, 1986), pp. 676–81.
41. Clifford, *Counsel to President,* p. 437.
42. Westmoreland, *Soldier Reports,* p. 418; Herring, *America's Longest War,* pp. 225, 228; Clifford, *Counsel to President,* p. 472.
43. Johnson, *Vantage Point,* p. 384; Westmoreland, *Soldier Reports,* pp. 438–39.
44. Rostow, *Diffusion of Power,* p. 479.
45. Westmoreland, *Soldier Reports,* p. 463; Casualty figures drawn from Defense Casualty Analysis System, accessed online at http://aad.archives.gov/aad/fielded-search.jsp?dt=2513&cat=WR28&TF=F&b.
46. Rostow, *Diffusion of Power,* p. 481. An important, somewhat different view is put forward by Adam Garfinkle in *Telltale Hearts: The Origins and Impact of the Vietnam Antiwar Movement* (New York: St. Martin's Press, 1995), especially pp. 13–19. Garfinkle argues that public opinion was shaped by the confusion of the president and his advisers, rather than the other way around. There is no doubting the impact of Johnson's loss of conviction, his withdrawal from the presidential race, and the administration's deep divisions. Still, this view understates the public's growing disenchantment with the war over the previous two years, even as policy makers appealed for support.
47. Westmoreland, *Soldier Reports,* p. 463; Clifford, *Counsel to President,* pp. 492–95; Nitze, *From Hiroshima to Glasnost,* p. 273; McNamara, *In Retrospect,* pp. 264–65.
48. Clifford, *Counsel to President,* pp. 493–95, 498; Johnson, *Vantage Point,* p. 406–7; Hormats, *Price of Liberty,* p. 222; Eichengreen, *Exorbitant Privilege,* p. 58.
49. *Foreign Relations of the United States, 1964–1968, Volume VI, Vietnam, January–August 1968,* doc. 103, pp. 314–16.
50. Rusk, *As I Saw It,* p. 417; Rostow, *Diffusion of Power,* p. 522.
51. Westmoreland, *Soldier Reports,* p. 444; Nitze, *From Hiroshima to Glasnost,* p. 278.

52. Westmoreland, *Soldier Reports,* p. 445; Nitze, *From Hiroshima to Glasnost,* p. 278; Clifford, *Counsel to President,* p. 476.
53. Clifford, *Counsel to President,* p. 502; Lyndon B. Johnson, Remarks to the National Farmers Union Convention, Minneapolis, March 18, 1968, in *Public Papers of the Presidents,* http://www.presidency.ucsb.edu/ws/index.php?pid=28741&st=&st1=.
54. Clifford, *Counsel to President,* pp. 507, 516.
55. Woods, *LBJ: Architect of Ambition,* p. 834; Clifford, *Counsel to President,* pp. 515, 516, 518.
56. Rostow, *Diffusion of Power,* p. 481; Lyndon B. Johnson, "Address to the Nation Announcing Steps to Limit the War in Vietnam and Reporting His Decision Not to Seek Reelection," March 31, 1968, *Public Papers of the Presidents,* http://www.presidency.ucsb.edu/ws/index.php?pid=28772&st=&st1.
57. Woods, *LBJ: Architect of Ambition,* p. 855.
58. Clifford, *Counsel to President,* pp. 537, 581; Rudy Abramson, *Spanning the Century: The Life of W. Averell Harriman* (New York: William Morrow, 1992), p. 667. For Clifford and Harriman, a bombing halt was a second-best option. They would have preferred to withdraw from South Vietnam almost immediately—by the end of the year, if possible. Rusk considered their ideas "outright surrender." Rusk, *As I Saw It,* p. 490.
59. Clifford, *Counsel to President,* pp. 567–68; Bird, *Color of Truth,* p. 370; Woods, *LBJ: Architect of Ambition,* p. 860; Taylor, *Swords and Plowshares,* p. 396.
60. Clifford, *Counsel to President,* pp. 576, 591; Johnson, *Vantage Point,* p. 525; Taylor, *Swords and Plowshares,* p. 396.
61. Clifford, *Counsel to President,* p. 508.
62. Ibid., p. 587.
63. *Foreign Relations of the United States, 1964–1968, Volume VII, Vietnam, September 1968–January 1969,* doc. 150, pp. 437–41; Clifford, *Counsel to President,* 591.
64. Lyndon B. Johnson, "Address to the Nation Upon Announcing His Decision to Halt the Bombing of North Vietnam," October 31, 1968, *Public Papers of the Presidents,* http://www.presidency.ucsb.edu/ws/index.php?pid=29218&st=&st1; Johnson, *Vantage Point,* p. 524.
65. Johnson, *Vantage Point,* p. 529.

7: RETRENCHMENT AND VIETNAM

1. Richard Nixon, "On the War in Vietnam," address to the nation, November 3, 1969, *Public Papers of the Presidents,* http://www.presidency.ucsb.edu/ws/index.php?pid=2303&st=&st1; Richard Nixon, "On Foreign Policy for the 1970s," first annual report to Congress, February 18, 1970, *Public Papers of the Presidents,* http://www.presidency.ucsb.edu/ws/index.php?pid=2835&st=&st1.
2. Nixon, "On Foreign Policy for the 1970s."
3. Richard Nixon, "On Foreign Policy," second annual report to Congress, February 25, 1971, *Public Papers of the Presidents,* http://www.presidency.ucsb.edu/ws/index.php?pid=3324.
4. Tim Kane, "Global U.S. Troop Deployment, 1950–2005," Heritage Foundation, May 24, 2006, http://www.heritage.org/research/reports/2006/05/global-us-troop-deployment-1950-2005; Richard M. Nixon, *The Memoirs of Richard Nixon* (New York: Warner Books, 1978), p. 1:488; Henry Kissinger, *White House Years* (Boston: Little, Brown, 1979), pp. 223–25; Nixon, "On Foreign Policy for the 1970s"; Barry Eichengreen, *Exorbitant Privilege: The Rise and Fall of the Dollar and the Future of the International Mon-*

etary System (New York: Oxford University Press, 2011), p. 62; Office of the Under Secretary of Defense (Comptroller), "Table 6-8, Department of Defense BA by Title," *National Defense Budget Estimates for FY 2013,* March 2012. http://comptroller.defense.gov/defbudget/fy2013/FY13_Green_Book.pdf.

5. H. R. Haldeman, *The Haldeman Diaries: Inside the Nixon White House* (New York: G.P. Putnam's Sons, 1994), p. 73.
6. Ibid., pp. 330–31; Walter Isaacson, *Kissinger: A Biography* (New York: Simon & Schuster, 1992), p. 269; Henry Kissinger, *On China* (New York: Penguin Press, 2011), p. 215; Kissinger, *White House Years,* p. 303; *Foreign Relations of the United States, 1969–1976, Volume XXXIV, National Security Policy, 1969–1972,* doc. 69, pp. 253–54.
7. Haldeman, *Diaries,* p. 73; Richard Nixon, "The Challenge of Peace," address to the nation outlining a new economic policy, August 15, 1971, *Public Papers of the Presidents,* http://www.presidency.ucsb.edu/ws/index.php?pid=3115&st=&st1.
8. Henry Kissinger, *The Necessity for Choice* (New York: Harper & Bros., 1961), p. 6; *Foreign Relations of the United States, 1969–1976, Volume I, Foundations of Foreign Policy, 1969–1972,* doc. 4, pp. 21–48.
9. Kissinger, *White House Years,* pp. 66, 86; Haldeman, *Diaries,* p. 445.
10. Kissinger, *On China,* p. 356.
11. Raymond L. Garthoff, *Détente and Confrontation: American-Soviet Relations from Nixon to Reagan* (Washington, D.C.: Brookings Institution Press, 1994), p. 280; Kissinger, *White House Years,* p. 284; Nixon, *Memoirs,* pp. 1:428, 430, 503–4; Richard Nixon, Address at the Air Force Academy Commencement Exercises, Colorado Springs, Colo., June 4, 1969, *Public Papers of the Presidents,* www.presidency.ucsb.edu/ws/index.php?pid=2081&st=&st1.
12. Isaacson, *Kissinger,* pp. 238, 248; Nixon, *Memoirs,* pp. 1:484–85, 491.
13. Isaacson, *Kissinger,* p. 168; Kissinger, *White House Years,* p. 144.
14. Nixon, *Memoirs,* pp. 1:496–97; Nixon, "On the War in Vietnam."
15. Nixon, *Memoirs,* p. 1:506; Lewis Sorley, *A Better War: The Unexamined Victories and Final Tragedy of America's Last Years in Vietnam* (San Diego: Harcourt, 199), p. 169; Peter W. Rodman, *Presidential Command: Power, Leadership, and the Making of Foreign Policy from Richard Nixon to George W. Bush* (New York: Vintage Books, 2010), pp. 63–64; Nixon, *Memoirs,* pp. 1:500–1.
16. Sorley, *Better War,* pp. 56, 191.
17. Ibid., p. 117; Nixon, *Memoirs,* pp. 1:556, 562; Haldeman, *Diaries,* p. 154; Isaacson, *Kissinger,* pp. 265, 269.
18. Isaacson, *Kissinger,* p. 269; Stephen P. Randolph, *Powerful and Brutal Weapons: Nixon, Kissinger, and the Easter Offensive* (Cambridge, Mass.: Harvard University Press, 2007), p. 13.
19. Sorley, *Better War,* p. 213; *Foreign Relations of the United States, 1969–1976, Volume VI, Vietnam, January 1969–July 1970,* doc. 347, pp. 1133–39; Nixon, *Memoirs,* p. 1:475.
20. *Foreign Relations of the United States, 1969–1976, Volume VI, Vietnam, January 1969–July 1970,* doc. 347, p. 1134; Berman, *No Peace, No Honor,* p. 80.
21. Randolph, *Powerful and Brutal Weapons,* pp. 13–15.
22. Haldeman, *Diaries,* p. 292.
23. Kissinger, *On China,* p. 234.
24. Robert Dallek, *Nixon and Kissinger: Partners in Power* (New York: HarperCollins, 2007), pp. 267, 293; Nixon, *Memoirs,* p. 2:26; Richard Nixon, "Toasts of the President and Chairman Chang Ch'un-ch'iao at a Banquet in Shanghai," February 27, 1972, *Public Papers of the Presidents,* http://www.presidency.ucsb.edu/ws/index.php?pid=3755&st=&st1.

25. Alexander M. Haig, Jr., *Inner Circles: How America Changed the World* (New York: Warner Books, 1992), p. 257; Isaacson, *Kissinger*, p. 336; Margaret Macmillan, *Nixon and Mao: The Week That Changed the World* (New York: Random House, 2007), p. 201; *Foreign Relations of the United States, 1969–1976, Volume I, Foundations of Foreign Policy, 1969–1972*, doc. 4, pp. 21–48; Kissinger, *White House Years*, p. 1086; Jeremy Suri, *Henry Kissinger and the American Century* (Cambridge, Mass.: Harvard University Press, 2007), p. 182.
26. Haldeman, *Diaries*, p. 275.
27. *Foreign Relations of the United States, 1969–1976, Volume XVII, China, 1969–1972*, doc. 139, pp. 359–97.
28. *Foreign Relations of the United States, 1969–1976, Volume E–13, Documents on China, 1969–1972*, doc. 129, pp. 1–15.
29. Kissinger, *On China*, pp. 235, 270.
30. Dallek, *Nixon and Kissinger*, p. 246; Kissinger, *White House Years*, pp. 194, 716, 717.
31. *Foreign Relations of the United States, 1969–1976, Volume XVII, China, 1969–1972*, doc. 139, pp. 359–97.
32. Ibid., doc. 143, pp. 494–52.
33. Ibid., doc. 139, pp. 359–97; *Foreign Relations of the United States, 1969–1976, Volume XVII, China, 1969–1972*, doc. 164, pp. 524–58; *Foreign Relations of the United States, 1969–1976, Volume E-13, Documents on China, 1969–1972*, doc. 44, pp. 1–40.
34. *Foreign Relations of the United States, 1969–1976, Volume E-13, Documents on China, 1969–1972*, doc. 51, pp. 1–25.
35. Ibid.
36. Nixon, *Memoirs*, p. 2:43; Kissinger, *On China*, p. 235; *Foreign Relations of the United States, 1969–1976, Volume XVII, China, 1969–1972*, doc. 196, pp. 693–719.
37. Nixon, *Memoirs*, pp. 2:51–52.
38. Randolph, *Powerful and Brutal Weapons*, pp. 33–34, 50, 88–90.
39. Nixon, *Memoirs*, pp. 2:62–63; Kissinger, *White House Years*, p. 1184; Haldeman, *Diaries*, pp. 453, 455.
40. Sorley, *Better War*, pp. 327, 331; Nixon, *Memoirs*, pp. 2:85–86; Gideon Rose, *How Wars End* (New York: Simon and Schuster, 2010), p. 171.
41. Nixon, *Memoirs*, p. 2:64.
42. Kissinger, *White House Years*, p. 1160; Randolph, *Powerful and Brutal Weapons*, p. 150.
43. Nixon, *Memoirs*, pp. 2:87, 89.
44. Kissinger, *White House Years*, pp. 130, 1210; Nixon, *Memoirs*, pp. 2:91, 100; Dallek, *Nixon and Kissinger*, p. 494; Arkady Shevchenko, *Breaking with Moscow* (New York: Ballantine Books, 1985), p. 287.
45. Henry Kissinger, *Ending the Vietnam War: A History of America's Involvement in and Extrication from the Vietnam War* (New York: Simon & Schuster, 2003), p. 288; Kissinger, *White House Years*, p. 1201; Sorley, *Better War*, p. 339; Nixon, *Memoirs*, p. 2:84; Haldeman, *Diaries*, p. 452; Arkady Shevchenko, *Breaking with Moscow*, p. 287.
46. Kissinger, *White House Years*, pp. 1202, 1251.
47. Kissinger, *Ending the Vietnam War*, pp. 298–99.
48. Kissinger, *White House Years*, pp. 1329–59; Haldeman, *Diaries*, p. 517.
49. Kissinger, *White House Years*, p. 1394.
50. Ibid., pp. 1331, 1340, 1360, 1394; Isaacson, *Kissinger*, p. 454.
51. Kissinger, *White House Years*, p. 1339.
52. Ibid., pp. 1363, 1373, 1386; Randolph, *Powerful and Brutal Weapons*, p. 326; Larry Berman, *No Peace, No Honor: Nixon, Kissinger, and Betrayal in Vietnam* (New York: Touchstone, 2002), p. 169.

53. Kissinger, *White House Years,* p. 1327; Berman, *No Peace, No Honor,* p. 209; Dallek, *Nixon and Kissinger,* p. 426; Isaacson, *Kissinger,* p. 462.
54. Randolph, *Powerful and Brutal Weapons*, p. 332; Gideon Rose, *How Wars End: Why We Always Fight the Last Battle* (New York: Simon & Schuster, 2010), p. 353.
55. Kissinger, *White House Years*, p. 1411; Nixon, *Memoirs,* p. 2:195; Berman, *No Peace, No Honor,* p. 211.
56. Isaacson, *Kissinger*, p. 450; Nixon, *Memoirs,* p. 2:241; Kissinger, *White House Years,* p. 1442; Berman, *No Peace, No Honor,* p. 189.
57. Haig, *Inner Circles*, p. 309; Nixon, *Memoirs,* p. 2:242.
58. Nixon, *Memoirs,* pp. 2:229, 233, 237; Haldeman, *Diaries,* p. 549; Herring, *America's Longest War,* pp. 315–17.
59. Haldeman, *Diaries,* p. 549; Kissinger, *White House Years,* p. 1446, 1448.
60. Nixon, *Memoirs,* p. 2:244.
61. Nixon, "On Foreign Policy for the 1970s."

8: RETRENCHMENT AND DÉTENTE

1. Henry Kissinger, *Years of Upheaval* (Boston: Little, Brown, 1982), pp. 5, 6; Robert Dallek, *Nixon and Kissinger: Partners in Power* (New York: HarperCollins, 2007), p. 487.
2. Richard Nixon, Oath of Office and Second Inaugural Address, January 20, 1973, *Public Papers of the Presidents*, http://www.presidency.ucsb.edu/ws/index.php?pid=4141&st=&st1; Alexander M. Haig, Jr., with Charles McCarry, *Inner Circles: How America Changed the World* (New York: Warner, 1992), p. 298.
3. Kissinger, *Years of Upheaval,* p. 981; Henry Kissinger, *White House Years* (Boston: Little, Brown, 1979), p. 125.
4. For recessions, see "U.S. Business Cycle Expansions and Contractions," National Bureau of Economic Research, http://www.nber.org/cycles/cyclesmain.html; for inflation, see U.S. Department of Labor, Bureau of Labor Statistics, "Consumer Price Index: All Urban Consumers," ftp://ftp.bls.gov/pub/special.requests/cpi/cpiai.txt. See also Barry Eichengreen, *Exorbitant Privilege: The Rise and Fall of the Dollar and the Future of the International Monetary System* (New York: Oxford University Press, 2011), p. 65.
5. Walter Isaacson, *Kissinger: A Biography* (New York: Simon & Schuster, 1992), pp. 520–22; Kissinger, *Years of Upheaval,* p. 531.
6. Kissinger, *Years of Upheaval,* pp. 553, 584, 589.
7. Ibid., pp. 531, 576.
8. Ibid., p. 885.
9. Ibid., pp. 897, 910; Daniel Yergin, *The Prize: The Epic Quest for Oil, Money and Power* (New York: Simon and Schuster, 1991), pp. 628–29.
10. Richard Nixon, Question-and-Answer Session at the Executives' Club of Chicago, March 15, 1974, *Public Papers of the Presidents,* http://www.presidency.ucsb.edu/ws/index.php?pid=4386&st=&st1.
11. Kissinger, *Years of Upheaval,* pp. 874, 880, 891.
12. Ibid., pp. 881, 935.
13. Ibid., p. 985.
14. Ibid., p. 98.
15. Ibid., pp. 252–53, 987, 995; Isaacson, *Kissinger,* pp. 616–17, 619.
16. Isaacson, *Kissinger,* p. 618; Memorandum of Conversation, October 24, 1974 (morning),

pp. 4–6, from Box 1, October 24–27, 1974, Kissinger-Brezhnev Talks in Moscow (Folder 3), Gerald Ford Presidential Library.

17. Memorandum of Conversation, October 24, 1974 (evening), pp. 4–5, 9, from Box 1, October 24–27, 1974, Kissinger-Brezhnev Talks in Moscow (Folder 3), Gerald Ford Presidential Library.
18. Brent Scowcroft to the President, October 27, 1974, Gerald Ford Presidential Library; "Emigration Amendment to the Trade Reform Act of 1974," Finance Committee Hearing, 93rd Cong. (Washington, D.C.: U.S. GPO, December 3, 1974, p. 55; Christopher S. Wren, "Letter Published: In It, Gromyko Tells Kissinger a Linkage Is Ruled Out," *The New York Times,* December 18, 1974, p. 18.
19. Henry A. Kissinger, *American Foreign Policy* (New York: W.W. Norton , 1977), p. 203.
20. Ibid., pp. 205, 206, 208, 210, 211.
21. Mario Del Pero, *The Eccentric Realist: Henry Kissinger and the Shaping of American Foreign Policy* (Ithaca, N.Y.: Cornell University Press, 2006), p. 142; Adam Nagourney, "In Tapes, Nixon Rails About Jews and Blacks," *The New York Times,* December 10, 2010; audiotape at http://nixon.archives.gov/forresearchers/find/tapes/tape866/tape866.php (Conversation No. 16); *Foreign Relations of the United States, 1969–1976, Volume XXXIX, European Security,* Doc. 184, pp. 546–49.
22. James Mann, *Rise of the Vulcans: The History of Bush's War Cabinet* (New York: Penguin, 2004), p. 65; Sean Wilentz, *The Age of Reagan: A History, 1974–2008* (New York: HarperCollins, 2008), p. 57; Zelizer, *Arsenal of Democracy,* pp. 258–59.
23. Daniel Patrick Moynihan, *A Dangerous Place* (New York: Berkley, 1980), p. 96.
24. Isaacson, *Kissinger*, p. 661.
25. Del Pero, *Eccentric Realist,* pp. 123–24; Strobe Talbott, *Endgame: The Inside Story of SALT II* (New York: Harper & Row, 1979), pp. 24–25.
26. Ibid., p. 32.
27. Gerald R. Ford, *A Time to Heal* (New York: Harper & Row, 1979), p. 218; Kissinger, *Years of Upheaval,* p. 1016; Isaacson, *Kissinger,* p. 629.
28. Isaacson, *Kissinger,* p. 623; Ford, *A Time to Heal,* p. 320.
29. Donald Rumsfeld, *Known and Unknown: A Memoir* (New York: Sentinel, 2011), p. 228.
30. Strobe Talbott, *The Master of the Game: Paul Nitze and the Nuclear Peace* (New York: Knopf, 1988), pp. 146–47.
31. Ibid., p. 141; Robert M. Gates, *From the Shadows: The Ultimate Insider's Story of Five Presidents and How They Won the Cold War* (New York: Simon & Schuster, 1996), pp. 106–8; Paul H. Nitze, "Assuring Strategic Stability in an Era of Détente," *Foreign Affairs* 54, no. 2 (January 1976), pp. 215, 217–18.
32. Kissinger, *Years of Upheaval,* p. 1175.
33. Julian E. Zelizer, *Arsenal of Democracy: The Politics of National Security—from World War II to the War on Terrorism* (New York: Basic Books, 2010), p. 267; Ronald Reagan, "To Restore America, Ronald Reagan's Campaign Address," March 31, 1976, http://www.reagan.utexas.edu/archives/reference/3.31.76.html.
34. Henry Kissinger, *Years of Renewal: The Concluding Volume of His Memoirs* (New York: Touchstone, 1999), p. 481; Zelizer, *Arsenal of Democracy,* p. 263.
35. Kissinger, *Years of Renewal,* pp. 474–75, 484, 486.
36. Ibid., pp. 491–92.
37. Ford, *Time to Heal,* pp. 255, 257.
38. Kissinger, *Years of Renewal,* pp. 484, 491, 526; Isaacson, *Kissinger,* p. 648.
39. Dick Cheney, *In My Time: A Personal and Political Memoir* (New York: Threshold, 2011), p. 82.

40. Isaacson, *Kissinger,* p. 651.
41. Kissinger, *Years of Renewal,* p. 807; Gates, *From the Shadows,* pp. 66–67.
42. Gates, *From the Shadows,* p. 68; Kissinger, *Years of Renewal,* p. 813.
43. Gates, *From the Shadows,* p. 68; H.R. 9861 Bill Summary and Status, 94th Congress (1975–1976), Library of Congress—THOMAS.
44. Zelizer, *Arsenal of Democracy,* p. 263; Henry Kissinger, "The Permanent Challenge of Peace: U.S. Policy Toward the Soviet Union," speech delivered in San Francisco, February 3, 1976, *Department of State Bulletin,* February 23, 1976, p. 211.
45. William G. Hyland, *Mortal Rivals: Superpower Relations from Nixon to Reagan* (New York: Random House, 1987), p. 176; Zelizer, *Arsenal of Democracy,* p. 270.
46. Hyland, *Mortal Rivals,* p. 196.
47. Kissinger, *Years of Upheaval,* p. 1030.
48. Daniel P. Moynihan, "The Politics of Human Rights," *Commentary,* August 1977; Moynihan, *Dangerous Place,* p. 316.
49. Jimmy Carter, Inaugural Address, January 20, 1977, *Public Papers of the Presidents,* http://www.presidency.ucsb.edu/ws/index.php?pid=6575&st=&st1; Jimmy Carter, University of Notre Dame commencement address, May 22, 1977, *Public Papers of the Presidents,* http://www.presidency.ucsb.edu/ws/index.php?pid=7552.
50. Jimmy Carter, University of Notre Dame commencement address, May 22, 1977, *Public Papers of the Presidents,* http://www.presidency.ucsb.edu/ws/?pid=7552#axzz2h9MSLMq4.
51. Samuel Moyn, *The Last Utopia: Human Rights in History* (Cambridge, Mass.: Harvard University Press, 2010), pp. 155–56; James Mann, *About Face: A History of America's Curious Relationship with China from Nixon to Clinton* (New York: Vintage Books, 2000), pp. 78–79; Jimmy Carter, *White House Diary* (New York: Farrar, Straus & Giroux, 2010), p. 37.
52. Talbott, *Endgame,* p. 60; Carter, *White House Diary,* pp. 30, 39; Wilentz, *The Age of Reagan,* p. 110.
53. Julian E. Zelizer, *Jimmy Carter* (New York: Times Books, 2010), p. 61; Jimmy Carter, "On Energy and National Goals: 'Malaise Speech,'" address to the nation, July 15, 1979, *Public Papers of the Presidents,* http://www.presidency.ucsb.edu/ws/index.php?pid=32596&st=&st1.
54. Zbigniew Brzezinski, *Power and Principle: Memoirs of the National Security Adviser, 1977–1981* (New York: Farrar, Straus & Giroux, 1983), p. 521; Gates, *From the Shadows,* 142.
55. Talbott, *Endgame,* p. 7.
56. Jimmy Carter, "Remarks from the White House Library," report to the American people, February 2, 1977, *Public Papers of the Presidents,* http://www.presidency.ucsb.edu/ws/index.php?pid=7455&st=&st1; Gates, *From the Shadows,* p. 105.
57. Gates, *From the Shadows,* p. 73; Carter, "On Energy and National Goals."
58. Carter, *White House Diary,* p. 323.
59. Jimmy Carter, U.S. Naval Academy commencement address, June 7, 1978, *Public Papers of the Presidents,* http://www.presidency.ucsb.edu/ws/index.php?pid=30915&st=&st1; Zelizer, *Jimmy Carter,* p. 77; Carter, *White House Diary,* p. 199.
60. Brzezinski, *Power and Principle,* pp. 222, 518.
61. Carter, *White House Diary,* pp. 321–22.
62. Brzezinski, *Power and Principle,* pp. 340, 344.
63. Carter, *White House Diary,* p. 382; Mann, *About Face,* p. 111; Brzezinski, *Power and Principle,* pp. 431–32, 434.

64. Jimmy Carter, State of the Union Message, January 21, 1980, *Public Papers of the Presidents,* http://www.presidency.ucsb.edu/ws/index.php?pid=33062&st=&st1; Brzezinski, *Power and Principle,* p. 448; Zelizer, *Arsenal of Democracy,* pp. 292–93.
65. Zelizer, *Arsenal of Democracy,* p. 290; Wilentz, *Age of Reagan,* p. 117; Zelizer, *Jimmy Carter,* p. 104; Brzezinski, *Power and Principle,* pp. 193, 454, 432.
66. Carter, *White House Diary,* p. 530.
67. Zelizer, *Jimmy Carter,* p. 107; Brzezinski, *Power and Principle,* pp. 435, 436; Carter, *White House Diary,* p. 406.
68. Carter, *White House Diary,* p. 471.
69. Ibid., p. 496.
70. Ibid., p. 506.
71. Haig, *Inner Circles,* pp. 531–44.

9: "OUTSPEND THEM FOREVER"

1. Ronald Reagan, *An American Life* (New York: Threshold Editions, 1990), p. 595.
2. Melvyn P. Leffler, *For the Soul of Mankind: The United States, the Soviet Union, and the Cold War* (New York: Hill & Wang, 2007), p. 341; John Lewis Gaddis, *Strategies of Containment: A Critical Appraisal of Postwar National Security Policy* (New York: Oxford University Press, 1982), p. 376; Joseph S. Nye, Presidential Leadership and the Creation of the American Era (Princeton, N.J.: Princeton University Press, 2013), p. 55; Sean Wilentz, *The Age of Reagan: A History, 1974–2008* (New York: HarperCollins, 2008), p. 281; Leffler, *For the Soul of Mankind,* p. 341.
3. Richard Allen, "The Man Who Won the Cold War," *Hoover Digest* 1 (2000), http://www.hoover.org/publications/hoover-digest/article/7398; Steven F. Hayward, *The Age of Reagan: The Conservative Counterrevolution, 1980–1989* (New York: Crown Forum, 2009), p. 289.
4. Wilentz, *Age of Reagan,* p. 263.
5. Henry Kissinger, *Years of Renewal: The Concluding Volume of His Memoirs* (New York: Touchstone, 1999), p. 110; Wilentz, *Age of Reagan,* p. 261.
6. Reagan, *American Life,* p. 586; James Mann, *The Rebellion of Ronald Reagan: A History of the End of the Cold War* (New York: Viking, 2009), p. 260.
7. Colin Powell, *My American Journey* (New York: Ballantine Books, 1995), p. 249; Reagan, *American Life,* p. 267; White House, Office of the Press Secretary, *America's New Beginning: A Program for Economic Recovery,* February 18, 1981, p. 11.
8. Ronald Reagan, news conference, January 29, 1981, *Public Papers of the Presidents,* http://www.presidency.ucsb.edu/ws/index.php?pid=44101; Reagan, *American Life,* p. 569.
9. Leffler, *For the Soul of Mankind,* pp. 347–48.
10. Zbigniew Brzezinski, *Power and Principle: Memoirs of the National Security Adviser, 1977–1981* (New York: Farrar, Straus & Giroux, 1983), p. 435; Strobe Talbott, *Deadly Gambits,* p. 88.
11. George P. Shultz, *Turmoil and Triumph: My Years as Secretary of State* (New York: Charles Scribner's Sons, 1993), p. 348.
12. Jeffrey Herf, *War by Other Means: Soviet Power, West German Resistance, and the Battle of the Euromissiles* (New York: Free Press, 1991), p. 164; Margaret Thatcher, *Downing Street Years* (New York: HarperCollins, 1993), p. 587; see also Stephen Sestanovich, "American Maximalism," *The National Interest,* Spring 2005, pp. 13–23.
13. Herf, *War by Other Means,* p. 137.

14. Jay Winik, *On the Brink: The Dramatic, Behind-the-Scenes Saga of the Reagan Era and the Men and Women Who Won the Cold War* (New York: Simon & Schuster, 1996), p. 203.
15. Strobe Talbott, *Deadly Gambits* (New York: Vintage Books, 1985), p. 48.
16. Herf, *War by Other Means,* p. 137; Shultz, *Turmoil & Triumph,* pp. 160–65; Matlock, Reagan & Gorbachev, p. 64–66; Mann, *The Rebellion of Ronald Reagan,* p. 79.
17. Winik, *On the Brink*, p. 209; James Mann, *The Rebellion of Ronald Reagan: A History of the End of the Cold War* (New York: Viking, 2009), p. 85; Reagan, *American Life,* p. 572; Ronald Reagan, "Address to the Nation on Defense and National Security," March 23, 1983, *Public Papers of the Presidents,* www.presidency.ucsb.edu/ws/?pid=41093.
18. Reagan, *American Life,* p. 611; Ronald Reagan, "Address to the Nation on Defense and National Security," March 23, 1983, *Public Papers of the Presidents,* www.presidency.ucsb .edu/ws/?pid=41093.
19. Jack F. Matlock, *Reagan and Gorbachev: How the Cold War Ended* (New York: Random House, 2004), p. 87; Talbott, *Deadly Gambits,* p. 176.
20. Hans-Dietrich Genscher, *Rebuilding a House Divided: A Memoir of the Architect of Germany's Reunification* (New York: Broadway Books, 1998), p. 165.
21. Robert M. Gates, *From the Shadows: The Ultimate Insider's Story of Five Presidents and How They Won the Cold War* (New York: Simon & Schuster, 1996), p. 354.
22. Ibid., p. 237, 252; Gates, *From the Shadows,* p. 237; Steven F. Hayward, *The Age of Reagan: The Conservative Counterrevolution, 1980–1989* (New York: Crown Forum, 2009), p. 249.
23. Lou Cannon, *President Reagan: The Role of a Lifetime* (New York: Public Affairs, 1991), pp. 163, 299, 312; Peter W. Rodman, *More Precious Than Peace: Fighting and Winning the Cold War in the Third World* (New York: Scribner, 1994), p. 238; Reagan, *American Life,* p. 361.
24. Rodman, *More Precious Than Peace,* p. 265.
25. George P. Shultz, *Turmoil and Triumph: My Years as Secretary of State* (New York: Scribner, 1993), p. 340; Powell, *My American Journey,* p. 303.
26. George Crile, *Charlie Wilson's War* (New York: Grove Press, 2003); Gates, *From the Shadows,* p. 321.
27. Wilentz, *Age of Reagan*, p. 167; Cannon, *Role of a Lifetime*, p. 331; Hayward, *Age of Reagan,* p. 354.
28. Rodman, *More Precious Than Peace,* pp. 260, 271, 272.
29. George P. Shultz, "America and the Struggle for Freedom," address to the Commonwealth Club of California, San Francisco, February 22, 1985, *Department of State Bulletin,* Vol. 85, No. 2097, pp. 16–21.
30. Rodman, *More Precious Than Peace,* pp. 245, 270.
31. Ibid., p. 337.
32. Gates, *From the Shadows,* pp. 350, 428; Rodman, *More Precious Than Peace,* p. 339.
33. Ronald Reagan, "On Freedom, Regional Security, and Global Peace," message to Congress, March 14, 1986, *Public Papers of the Presidents,* http://www.presidency.ucsb.edu/ws/index.php?pid=36995&st=&st1.
34. For Lebanon, see Cannon, *President Reagan,* 15; Wilentz, *Age of Reagan,* pp. 158–59, 280; Reagan, *American Life,* p. 704.
35. Jack F. Matlock, *Reagan and Gorbachev: How the Cold War Ended* (New York: Random House, 2004), pp. ix, 165; Leffler, *For the Soul of Mankind,* p. 364.
36. Hayward, *Age of Reagan,* p. 295; Matlock, *Reagan and Gorbachev,* p. 162; Ronald Reagan, "On Defense and National Security," address to the nation, March 23, 1983, *Public Papers of the Presidents,* http://www.presidency.ucsb.edu/ws/index.php?pid=41093&st=&st1.

37. Max Kampelman, "Bombs Away," *The New York Times*, April 24, 2006; Reagan, *American Life,* pp. 641, 651; Paul Lettow, *Ronald Reagan and His Quest to Abolish Nuclear Weapons* (New York: Random House, 2005), p. 207; Shultz, *Turmoil and Triumph,* p. 700.
38. Jonathan Haslam, *Russia's Cold War: From the October Revolution to the Fall of the Wall* (New Haven, Conn.: Yale University Press, 2011), p. 356; Lettow, *Quest to Abolish Nuclear Weapons,* p. 220.
39. Ibid., pp. 221, 223.
40. Ibid., p. 225; Matlock, *Reagan and Gorbachev,* p. 222.
41. Lettow, *Quest to Abolish Nuclear Weapons,* pp. 208, 215 (original quote in Shultz, *Turmoil and Triumph,* p. 716); Wilentz, *Age of Reagan*, p. 257.
42. Matlock, *Reagan and Gorbachev,* pp. 237, 260; Leffler, *For the Soul of Mankind,* p. 375.
43. Cannon, *President Reagan*, p. 626.
44. Wilentz, *Age of Reagan*, p. 228.
45. Mann, *Rebellion of Reagan*, pp. 49–50, 275, 287; Henry A. Kissinger, "A New Era for NATO," *Newsweek*, October 12, 1987, p. 57; Shultz, *Turmoil and Triumph*, p. 988; Richard Nixon and Henry Kissinger, "A Real Peace," *National Review,* May 22, 1987, pp. 32–34.
46. Zelizer, *Arsenal of Democracy,* p. 351; William Safire, "Secrets of the Summit," *The New York Times,* December 6, 1987, http://www.nytimes.com/1987/12/06/opinion/essay-secrets-of-the-summit.html.
47. Mann, *Rebellion of Reagan*, pp. 304–6.
48. Matlock, *Reagan and Gorbachev,* p. 274; Mann, *Rebellion of Reagan,* pp. 239–41, 259–61.
49. Mann, *Rebellion of Reagan,* pp. 243–44.
50. Rodman, *More Precious Than Peace,* pp. 345, 346; Reagan, *American Life,* p. 701.
51. Ronald Reagan, Remarks to the World Affairs Council of Western Massachusetts in Springfield, April 21, 1988, http://www.presidency.ucsb.edu/ws/?pid=35716#axzz1ovsi6BZq.
52. Mann, *Rebellion of Reagan,* pp. 298–300.
53. Ronald Reagan, Remarks to Soviet Dissidents, Spaso House, Moscow, May 30, 1988, *Public Papers of the Presidents,* http://www.presidency.ucsb.edu/ws/index.php?pid=35894&st=&st1; Ronald Reagan, Remarks and a Question-and-Answer Session with the Students and Faculty, Moscow State University, May 31, 1988, *Public Papers of the Presidents,* http://www.presidency.ucsb.edu/ws/?pid=35897#axzz1ovsi6BZq.
54. Reagan, *American Life,* p. 587; Matlock, *Reagan and Gorbachev,* pp. 251, 254; Mann, *Rebellion of Reagan,* p. 245.
55. Mann, *Rebellion of Reagan,* p. 247; National Defense Budget Estimates for FY 2013 (DOD Green Book), Table 6–11: Department of Defense Outlays by Title, p. 155.
56. Matlock, *Reagan and Gorbachev,* p. 153; Reagan, *American Life,* pp. 267, 595.
57. Mann, *Rebellion of Reagan,* p. 247; National Defense Budget Estimates for FY 2013 (DOD Green Book), Table 6–11: Department of Defense Outlays by Title, p. 155.

10: "NO ONE ELSE CAN DO THIS"

1. Sean Wilentz, *The Age of Reagan: A History, 1974–2008* (New York: HarperCollins, 2008), p. 286; George P. Shultz, *Turmoil and Triumph: My Years as Secretary of State* (New York: Scribner, 1993), p. 1131; Melvyn P. Leffler and Jeffrey W. Legro, eds., *In Uncertain Times: American Foreign Policy After the Berlin Wall and 9/11* (Ithaca, N.Y.: Cornell University Press, 2011), p. 204; Dick Cheney, Statement Before the House Armed Services Com-

mittee in Connection with the FY 1993 Budget for the Department of Defense, February 6, 1992, p. 3, www.dtic.mil/cgi-bin/GetTRDoc?AD=ADA246700.

2. Steven Kull and I. M. Destler, *Misreading the Public: The Myth of a New Isolationism* (Washington, D.C.: Brookings Institution Press, 1999), pp. 22–23.
3. George H. W. Bush, Inaugural Address, January 20, 1989, *Public Papers of the Presidents,* http://www.presidency.ucsb.edu/ws/index.php?pid=16610&st=&st1; Tim Kane, "Global U.S. Troop Deployment, 1950–2005," Center for Data Analysis Report no. 06-02, Heritage Foundation; Kull and Destler, *Misreading the Public,* pp. 16–17; National Defense Budget Estimates for FY 2013 (DOD Green Book), Table 6–11: Department of Defense Outlays by Title, p. 155.
4. Derek Chollet and James Goldgeier, *America Between the Wars: The Misunderstood Years Between the Fall of the Berlin Wall and the Start of the War on Terror* (New York: Public Affairs, 2008), pp. 66–67; James A. Baker, *The Politics of Diplomacy: Revolution, War and Peace, 1989–1992* (New York: G.P. Putnam's Sons, 1995), pp. 335–36.
5. Elsa Walsh, "Negotiator," *The New Yorker,* March 18, 1996; George C. Herring, *From Colony to Superpower: U.S. Foreign Relations Since 1776* (New York: Oxford University Press, 2011), p. 937.
6. Henry Kissinger, "New World Disorder," *Newsweek,* May 31, 1999; see also "For U.S. Leadership, a Moment Missed," *The Washington Post,* May 12, 1995.
7. Herring, *From Colony to Superpower,* p. 936; Kissinger, "New World Disorder."
8. Bush, Inaugural Address.
9. George Bush and Brent Scowcroft, *A World Transformed* (New York: Vintage, 1999), p. 44.
10. Ibid., p. 100; Baker, *Politics of Diplomacy,* p. 159; Hans-Dietrich Genscher, *Rebuilding a House Divided: A Memoir by the Architect of Germany's Reunification* (New York: Broadway Books, 1998), p. 268.
11. Bush and Scowcroft, *World Transformed,* pp. 78, 201; Baker, *Politics of Diplomacy,* p. 166; Margaret Thatcher, *The Downing Street Years* (New York: Perennial, 1995), p. 791.
12. Thatcher, *Downing Street Years,* p. 793; Baker, *Politics of Diplomacy,* p. 167.
13. Melvyn P. Leffler, *For the Soul of Mankind: The United States, the Soviet Union, and the Cold War* (New York: Hill & Wang, 2007), p. 450; Bush and Scowcroft, *World Transformed,* p. 167; Philip Zelikow and Condoleezza Rice, *Germany Unified and Europe Transformed: A Study in Statecraft* (Cambridge, Mass.: Harvard University Press, 1995), p. 160.
14. Robert Zoellick, "Two Plus Four," *National Interest,* Fall 2000, p. 17; Mary Elise Sarotte, *1989: The Struggle to Create Post–Cold War Europe* (Princeton, N.J.: Princeton University Press, 2009), p. 200.
15. Baker, *Politics of Diplomacy,* p. 198–99; Bush and Scowcroft, *World Transformed,* pp. 234–35.
16. Sarotte, *1989,* p. 261 (emphasis mine).
17. Baker, *Politics of Diplomacy,* p. 170; Bush and Scowcroft, *World Transformed,* p. 293.
18. Bush and Scowcroft, *World Transformed,* pp. 188, 246.
19. Sarotte, *1989,* p. 261.
20. George Bush, Remarks at the Aspen Institute Symposium, Aspen, Colorado, August 2, 1990, *Public Papers of the Presidents,* http://www.presidency.ucsb.edu/ws/?pid=18731; Bush and Scowcroft, *World Transformed,* p. 314–15; Richard N. Haass, *War of Necessity, War of Choice: A Memoir of Two Iraq Wars* (New York: Simon & Schuster, 2009), p. 61.

21. Bush and Scowcroft, *World Transformed,* p. 317; Haass, *War of Necessity, War of Choice,* p. 62; Peter Rodman, *Presidential Command: Power, Leadership, and the Making of Foreign Policy from Richard Nixon to George W. Bush* (New York: Knopf, 2009), p. 197; Gideon Rose, *How Wars End: Why We Always Fight the Last Battle* (New York: Simon & Schuster, 2010), p. 205; George Bush, "On the Iraqi Invasion of Kuwait," remarks and an exchange with reporters, August 5, 1990, *Public Papers of the Presidents,* http://www.presidency.ucsb.edu/ws/index.php?pid=18741&st=&st1.
22. The thinking of Bush administration policy makers during this period is described in Richard Haass, *War of Necessity, War of Choice;* Michael Gordon and General Bernard Trainor, *The Generals' War;* James A. Baker, *The Politics of Diplomacy;* George H. W. Bush and Brent Scowcroft, *A World Transformed.*
23. Bush and Scowcroft, *World Transformed,* pp. 319, 328; Haass, *War of Necessity, War of Choice,* pp. 66–67; Dick Cheney, *In My Time: A Personal and Political Memoir* (New York: Threshold Editions, 2011), p. 191.
24. Rodman, *Presidential Command,* p. 197; Colin Powell, *My American Journey* (New York: Ballantine Books, 1995), pp. 451, 461–62.
25. Cheney, *In My Time,* p. 185; Powell, *My American Journey,* pp. 466–67; James Mann, *Rise of the Vulcans: The History of Bush's War Cabinet* (New York: Penguin Books, 2004), pp. 184–85; Michael R. Gordon and General Bernard E. Trainor, *The Generals' War: The Inside Story of the Conflict in the Gulf* (Boston: Little, Brown, 1995), p. 156.
26. Powell, *My American Journey,* pp. 463, 475; Haass, *War of Necessity, War of Choice,* pp. 96–97.
27. Cheney, *In My Time,* pp. 207–8; Haass, *War of Necessity, War of Choice,* pp. 95–96; Bush and Scowcroft, *World Transformed,* p. 357–59.
28. Julian E. Zelizer, *Arsenal of Democracy: The Politics of National Security—from World War II to the War on Terrorism* (New York: Basic Books, 2010), p. 370; Bush and Scowcroft, *World Transformed,* p. 445; Dominic Tierney, *How We Fight: Crusades, Quagmires, and the American Way of War* (New York: Little, Brown, 2010), p. 193; John Mueller, *Policy and Opinion in the Gulf War* (Chicago: University of Chicago Press, 1994), p. 237; Cheney, *In My Time,* p. 208.
29. Cheney, *In My Time,* p. 208; Bush and Scowcroft, *World Transformed,* p. 491; see also Baker, *Politics of Diplomacy,* chap. 19, and Haass, *War of Necessity, War of Choice,* chap. 3.
30. Powell, *My American Journey,* p. 509; Herring, *From Colony to Superpower,* p. 911.
31. Rose, *How Wars End,* pp. 221–22.
32. Bush and Scowcroft, *World Transformed,* pp. 481–82; Gordon and Trainor, *Generals' War,* pp. 450–51.
33. Mueller, *Policy and Opinion,* p. 267; Gordon and Trainor, *Generals' War,* p. 454.
34. Cheney, *In My Time,* p. 364–67; Gideon Rose, *How Wars End,* p. 241.
35. Gordon and Trainor, *Generals' War,* p. 447, 451.
36. Bush and Scowcroft, *World Transformed,* p. 487.
37. Thomas L. Friedman, "Baker Urges End to Yugoslav Rift," *The New York Times,* June 22, 1991.
38. George Bush, "On the Attempted Coup in the Soviet Union," remarks and an exchange with reporters, Kennebunkport, Maine, August 19, 1991, *Public Papers of the Presidents,* http://www.presidency.ucsb.edu/ws/index.php?pid=19911&st=&st1; Michael R. Beschloss and Strobe Talbott, *At the Highest Levels: The Inside Story of the End of the Cold War* (Boston: Little, Brown, 1993), p. 429.
39. George Bush, State of the Union Address, January 28, 1992, *Public Papers of the Presidents,* http://www.presidency.ucsb.edu/ws/index.php?pid=20544&st=&st1.

40. James Mann, *The Rebellion of Ronald Reagan: A History of the End of the Cold War* (New York: Viking, 2009), p. 337; Chollet and Goldgeier, *America Between the Wars,* pp. 118–19.
41. Dick Cheney, Statement Before the House Armed Services Committee in Connection With the FY 1993 Budget for the Department of Defense, February 6, 1992, p. 28, www.dtic.mil/cgi-bin/GetTRDoc?AD=ADA246700; Dick Cheney, "Defense Strategy for the 1990s: The Regional Defense Strategy," Department of Defense, January 1933, retrieved from the National Security Archive, George Washington University, http://www.gwu.edu/~nsarchiv/nukevault/ebb245/doc15.pdf. See also essays by Paul Wolfowitz and Eric Edelman in *In Uncertain Times,* eds. Melvyn P. Leffler and Jeffrey W. Legro (Ithaca: Cornell University Press, 2011).
42. Ibid., p. 27.
43. Derek Chollet and James Goldgeier, *America Between the Wars: From 11/9 to 9/11* (New York: PublicAffairs, 2008), p. 50.
44. Ivo H. Daalder, *Getting to Dayton: The Making of America's Bosnia Policy* (Washington, D.C.: Brookings Institution Press, 2000), pp. 9, 36.
45. Talbott, *Great Experiment,* p. 294.
46. Powell, *My American Journey,* p. 561; Madeleine Albright, *Madam Secretary* (New York: Miramax Books, 2003), p. 182.
47. Albright, *Madam Secretary,* p. 186; Ronald D. Asmus, *Opening NATO's Door: How the Alliance Remade Itself For a New Era* (New York: Columbia University Press, 2002).
48. Daalder, *Getting to Dayton,* p. 80; Peter Beinart, *The Icarus Syndrome: A History of American Hubris* (New York: HarperCollins, 2010), p. 284.
49. Talbott, *Great Experiment,* p. 306; Richard Holbrooke, *To End a War* (New York: Random House, 1998), pp. 91–92.
50. Holbrooke, *To End a War,* pp. 231–33.
51. Ibid., p. 311.
52. Chollet and Goldgeier, *America Between the Wars,* p. 131; Holbrooke, *To End a War,* p. 186.
53. Talbott, *Great Experiment,* pp. 280, 309; Chollet and Goldgeier, *America Between the Wars,* p. 337.
54. William J. Clinton, Remarks, University of Nebraska at Kearney, December 8, 2000, *Public Papers of the Presidents,* http://www.presidency.ucsb.edu/ws/index.php?pid=957&st=&st1.
55. Chollet and Goldgeier, *America Between the Wars,* p. 137.
56. James Mann, *About Face: A History of America's Curious Relationship with China from Nixon to Clinton* (New York: Vintage Books, 2000), pp. 336–38; William J. Clinton, Remarks to the Seventh Fleet Aboard the USS *Independence,* Yokosuka, Japan, April 17, 1996, *Public Papers of the Presidents,* http://www.presidency.ucsb.edu/ws/index.php?pid=52679&st=calm+a+rising+storm&st.
57. Strobe Talbott, *The Russia Hand: A Memoir of Presidential Diplomacy* (New York: Random House, 2007), pp. 100–101, 130–131, 136.
58. Ibid., p. 136; Asmus, *Opening NATO's Door,* pp. 26, 98.
59. Talbott, *Russia Hand,* 76, 174–176; Albright, *Madam Secretary,* p. 255.
60. William J. Clinton, Remarks at the Pentagon, Arlington, Virginia, February 17, 1998, *Public Papers of the Presidents,* http://www.presidency.ucsb.edu/ws/index.php?pid=55483&st=&st1.
61. Albright, *Madam Secretary,* p. 287; William J. Clinton, "Announcing Military Strikes on Iraq," address to the nation, December 16, 1998, *Public Papers of the Presidents,* http://www.presidency.ucsb.edu/ws/index.php?pid=55414&st=&st1.

62. George Tenet, *At the Center of the Storm: My Years at the CIA* (New York: HarperCollins, 2007), pp. 108–9, 114, 116–17.
63. William J. Clinton, "On Military Action Against Terrorist Sites in Afghanistan and Sudan," address to the nation, August 20, 1998, *Public Papers of the Presidents,* http://www.presidency.ucsb.edu/ws/index.php?pid=54799&st=&st1; Clinton, "Announcing Military Strikes on Iraq"; Chollett and Goldgeier, *America Between the Wars,* p. 179.
64. Tenet, *Center of the Storm,* p. 109.
65. Ibid., pp. 117, 118, 122.
66. William J. Clinton, "On Completion of Military Strikes in Iraq," address to the nation, December 19, 1998, *Public Papers of the Presidents,* http://www.presidency.ucsb.edu/ws/?pid=55436; Kenneth Pollack, *The Threatening Storm: The United States and Iraq: The Crisis, the Strategy, and the Prospects After Saddam* (New York: Random House, 2002), p. 95.
67. Ivo H. Daalder and Michael E. O'Hanlon, *Winning Ugly: NATO's War to Save Kosovo* (Washington, D.C.: Brookings Institution Press, 2000), p. 89; Albright, *Madam Secretary,* p. 403.
68. Albright, *Madam Secretary*, pp. 406.
69. Chollet and Goldgeier, *America Between the Wars,* p. 211; Daalder and O'Hanlon, *Winning Ugly*, pp. 138, 163.
70. Albright, *Madam Secretary,* p. 421, 424; Talbott, *Russia Hand,* p. 347.
71. James Traub, *The Best Intentions: Kofi Annan and the UN in the Era of American Power* (New York: Picador, 2006), pp. 108, 115.
72. Albright, *Madam Secretary,* p. 500–1; Michael McFaul, *Advancing Democracy Abroad: Why We Should and How We Can* (Lanham, Md.: Rowman & Littlefield, 2010), p. 180.
73. Figures taken from SIPRI military expenditure database http://www.sipri.org/research/armaments/milex/milex_database
74. Albright, *The Today Show* interview with Matt Lauer, February 19, 1998: http://secretary.state.gov/www/statements/1998/980219a.html
75. Albright, just back from her own Pyongyang trip in October, told the president that Kim Jong Il was ready to sign an agreement forswearing nuclear weapons and ballistic missiles. Albright, *Madam Secretary,* pp. 468–70; Talbott, *The Great Experiment,* p. 344.
76. Bill Clinton, Remarks at the University of Nebraska at Kearney, Nebraska, http://www.presidency.ucsb.edu/ws/index.php?pid=957#axzz2h9MSLMq4.
77. Asmus, *Opening NATO's Door,* p. 221.
78. Talbott, *The Great Experiment,* p. 330; Bill Clinton, Remarks at the University of Nebraska at Kearney, Nebraska, http://www.presidency.ucsb.edu/ws/index.php?pid=957#axzz2h9MSLMq4.

11: "THINGS RELATED AND NOT"

1. George W. Bush, *Decision Points* (New York: Random House, 2010), p. 148; John Mueller and Mark G. Stewart, "The Terrorism Delusion," *International Security* 37, no. 1 (Summer 2012), p. 108.
2. Condoleezza Rice, "On Terrorism and Foreign Policy," remarks at Paul H. Nitze School of Advanced International Studies, Johns Hopkins University, April 29, 2002, http://georgewbush-whitehouse.archives.gov/news/releases/2002/04/20020429-9.html; Dick Cheney, "Vice President Honors Veterans of Korean War," San Antonio, Texas, August 29, 2002, http://georgewbush-whitehouse.archives.gov/news/releases/2002/08/

20020829-5.html; see also Henry Kissinger's *Does America Need a Foreign Policy?*, 2002 edition.

3. Donald Rumsfeld, interview by *The New York Times,* U.S. Department of Defense, October 12, 2001, http://www.defense.gov/transcripts/transcript.aspx?transcriptid=2097.
4. George W. Bush, Inaugural Address, January 20, 2001, *Public Papers of the Presidents,* http://www.presidency.ucsb.edu/ws/index.php?pid=25853&st=&st1.
5. George W. Bush, "A Period of Consequences," remarks at the Citadel, South Carolina, September 23, 1999, http://www3.citadel.edu/pao/addresses/pres_bush.html; Donald Rumsfeld, *Known and Unknown: A Memoir* (New York: Sentinel, 2011), p. 303.
6. George C. Herring, *From Colony to Superpower: U.S. Foreign Relations Since 1776* (Oxford: Oxford University Press, 2008), p. 937; James Traub, *The Freedom Agenda: Why America Must Spread Democracy (Just Not the Way George Bush Did)* (New York: Farrar, Straus and Giroux, 2008), p. 102; Rumsfeld, *Known and Unknown,* p. 332; Michael R. Gordon and Bernard E. Trainor, *Cobra II: The Inside Story of the Invasion and Occupation of Iraq* (New York: Pantheon Books, 2006), p. 9.
7. Dick Cheney, *In My Time: A Personal and Political Memoir* (New York: Threshold Editions, 2011), p. 326; Elliott Abrams, *Tested by Zion: The Bush Administration and the Israeli-Palestinian Conflict* (New York: Cambridge University Press, 2013), p. 6.
8. Presidential Debate in Winston-Salem, North Carolina, October 11, 2000, *Public Papers of the Presidents,* http://www.presidency.ucsb.edu/ws/?pid=29419; Bush Inaugural Address; see also James Mann, *Rise of the Vulcans: The History of Bush's War Cabinet* (New York: Penguin Books, 2004), p. 257.
9. Wilentz, *The Age of Reagan: A History, 1974–2008* (New York: HarperCollins, 2008), p. 440; Condoleezza Rice, *No Higher Honor: A Memoir of My Years in Washington* (New York: Crown, 2011), p. 66; George Tenet, *At the Center of the Storm: My Years at the CIA* (New York: HarperCollins, 2007), p. 144.
10. Mann, *Rise of the Vulcans,* p. 290; "Odd Man Out," *Time* 158, no. 10 (September 10, 2001), p. 24; Donald Rumsfeld, "DOD Acquisition and Logistics Excellence Week Kickoff: Bureaucracy to Battlefield," U.S. Department of Defense, http://www.defense.gov/speeches/speech.aspx?speechid=430.
11. Cheney, *In My Time,* p. 333; Bush, *Decision Points*, p. 128; Douglas J. Feith, *War and Decision: Inside the Pentagon at the Dawn of the War on Terrorism* (New York: HarperCollins, 2008), p. 15; Rumsfeld, *Known and Unknown,* p. 359.
12. George Packer, *The Assassins' Gate: America in Iraq* (New York: Farrar, Straus, & Giroux, 2005), p. 40; Feith, *War and Decision,* p. 15.
13. Feith, *War and Decision,* pp. 49, 66; Mann, *Rise of the Vulcans,* p. 309.
14. Bush, *Decision Points,* p. 135; Feith, *War and Decision,* p. 12; General Tommy Franks, *American Soldier* (New York: HarperCollins, 2004), p. 280.
15. See Gary C. Schroen, *First In: An Insider's Account of How the CIA Spearheaded the War on Terror in Afghanistan* (New York: Presidio Press, 2005).
16. For the war cabinet meeting, see Rumsfeld, *Known and Unknown*, chap. 26; Bush, *Decision Points,* chap. 7; Cheney, *In My Time,* chap. 11; George W. Bush, "On the U.S. Response to the Terrorist Attacks of September 11," address before a joint session of Congress, September 20, 2001, *Public Papers of the Presidents,* http://www.presidency.ucsb.edu/ws/index.php?pid=64731&st=&st1; William Kristol et al., "Letter to President Bush on the War on Terrorism," September 20, 2001, Project for the New American Century, http://www.newamericancentury.org/Bushletter.htm.
17. Cheney, *In My Time,* pp. 341–44; Graham Allison, *Nuclear Terrorism: The Ultimate Preventable Catastrophe* (New York: Owl Books, 2004), p. 1.

18. "Forgotten Computer Reveals Thinking Behind Four Years of al Qaeda Doings," *The Wall Street Journal,* December 31, 2001, http://online.wsj.com/article/SB1009751714799020000.html?mg=id-wsj; Tenet, *Center of the Storm,* p. 342; and Franks, *American Soldier,* p. 403.
19. Secretary Rumsfeld Interview with the *New York Times*" October 12, 2001, US Dept of Defense Office of the Asst. Secretary of Defense (Public Affairs) http://www.defense.gov/transcripts/transcript.aspx?transcriptID=2097
20. For Bush's discussion of foreign policy priorities with Bill Clinton before Inauguration Day, see Strobe Talbott, The Great Experiment (New York: Simon & Schuster, 2008), p. 347; Bush, *Decision Points,* p. 229; Rumsfeld, *Known and Unknown,* pp. 346, 424.
21. Rice, *No Higher Honor,* p. 270; Cheney, *In My Time,* p. 368.
22. Michael J. Gerson, *Heroic Conservatism: Why Republicans Need to Embrace America's Ideals (And Why They Deserve to Fail If They Don't)* (New York: HarperCollins, 2007), p. 128; Tenet, *At the Center of the Storm,* pp. 342–3.
23. Richard N. Haass, *War of Necessity, War of Choice: A Memoir of Two Iraq Wars* (New York: Simon & Schuster, 2009), p. 235; Bob Woodward, *State of Denial: Bush at War, Part II* (New York: Simon & Schuster, 2006), p. 408.
24. Rumsfeld, *Known and Unknown,* p. 429; Bush, *Decision Points,* pp. 234–35; Gordon and Trainor, *Cobra II,* pp. 31–32; Peter Baker, *Days of Fire: Bush and Cheney in the White House* (New York: Doubleday, 2013), p. 160.
25. Leon Fuerth, "Intoxicated With Power," *The Washington Post,* October 16, 2002, p. A25.
26. George W. Bush, State of the Union Address, January 29, 2002, *Public Papers of the Presidents,* http://www.presidency.ucsb.edu/ws/index.php?pid=29644&st=&st1; Melvyn P. Leffler and Jeffrey W Legro, eds., *In Uncertain Times: American Foreign Policy After the Berlin Wall and 9/11* (Ithaca, N.Y.: Cornell University Press, 2011), p. 111; "Foreign Policy Overview and the President's Fiscal Year 2003 Foreign Affairs Budget Request," Hearing Before the Committee on Foreign Relations, U.S. Senate, 107th Cong., 2nd Sess., February 5, 2002, Volume 4; Hillary Clinton, Speech on S.J. Res. 45 Authorizing the Use of Military Force Against Iraq, *Congressional Record* 148, no. 133 (October 10, 2002), http://www.gpo.gov/fdsys/pkg/CREC-2002-10-10/html/CREC-2002-10-10-pt1-PgH7739-6.htm.
27. Bush, *Decision Points,* p. 232.
28. Gordon and Trainor, *Cobra II,* p. 71; Brent Scowcroft, "Don't Attack Saddam," *The Wall Street Journal,* August 15, 2002.
29. Dick Cheney, *Defense Strategy for the 1990s: The Regional Defense Strategy,* January 1993, George Washington University National Security Archive, www2.gwu.edu/~nsarchiv/nukevault/ebb245/doc15.pdf, p. 4; Cheney, *In My Time,* p. 389; Feith, *War and Decision,* p. 301; Baker, *Days of Fire,* p. 211.
30. "Blair Arrives for Bush Talks," BBC News, April 5, 2002, http://news.bbc.co.uk/2/hi/uk_news/politics/1912050.stm; Gordon and Trainor, *Cobra II,* p. 95.
31. Bob Woodward, *Plan of Attack* (New York: Simon & Schuster, 2004), p. 315; Francis Fukuyama, *America at the Crossroads: Democracy, Power, and the Neoconservative Legacy* (New Haven, Conn.: Yale University Press, 2006), p. 100; Baker, *Days of Fire,* p. 246.
32. Abrams, *Tested by Zion,* p. 16; Gerson, *Heroic Conservatism,* p. 248; Bush, *Decision Points,* p. 333; Robert Zoellick, "Countering Terror with Trade," *The Washington Post,* September 20, 2011, p. A35.
33. Laura Bush, radio address, November 17, 2001, Radio Address Archives, White House, http://georgewbush-whitehouse.archives.gov/news/releases/2001/11/20011117.html; Gerson, *Heroic Conservatism,* p. 81.
34. Bush, State of the Union Address, 2002; Bush, "On the U.S. Response to the Terrorist Attacks of September 11."

35. Rice, *No Higher Honor,* p. 150.
36. Rice, "On Terrorism and Foreign Policy."
37. Packer, *Assassin's Gate,* p. 111.
38. Baker, *Days of Fire,* p. 216; "Bush Threatens: More Freedom," *Tagezeitung,* January 21, 2005, http://www.taz.de/1/archiv/archiv/?dig=2005/01/21/a0068.
39. Rumsfeld, *Known and Unknown,* pp. 95–96, 428; Dick Cheney, "The Statement of the Secretary of Defense Dick Cheney Before the House Armed Services Committee" February 6, 1992, www.dtic.mil/dtic/tr/fulltext/u2/a246700.pdf.
40. Franks, *American Soldier,* p. 466; Gordon and Trainor, *Cobra II,* pp. 87, 110, and chap. 2.
41. Gordon and Trainor, *Cobra II,* pp. 54, 98, 461.
42. Gordon and Trainor, *Cobra II,* p. 459.
43. Rumsfeld, *Known and Unkown,* pp. 457–58.
44. Thomas E. Ricks, *Fiasco: The American Military Adventure in Iraq* (New York: Penguin, 2006), p. 178; Bush, *Decision Points,* p. 258.
45. Gordon and Trainor, *Cobra II,* p. 12; Michael R. Gordon and General Bernard E. Trainor, *The Endgame: The Inside Story of the Struggle for Iraq, from George W. Bush to Barack Obama* (New York: Pantheon Books, 2012), p. 489.
46. Rumsfeld, *Known and Unknown,* p. 476; Gordon and Trainor, *Cobra II,* p. 464.
47. Feith, *War and Decision,* pp. 436–47; Rumsfeld, *Known and Unknown,* p. 488.
48. See Gordon and Trainor, *Cobra II,* chap. 23.
49. L. Paul Bremer, *My Year in Iraq: The Struggle to Build a Future of Hope* (New York: Simon & Schuster, 2006), pp. 9, 11, 12, 39; Gordon and Trainor, *Endgame,* p. 15; see also Feith, *War and Decision,* chap. 14.
50. Peter R. Mansoor, *Surge: My Journey with General David Petraeus and the Remaking of the Iraq War* (New Haven, Conn.: Yale University Press, 2013), pp. 11–12; Gordon and Trainor, *Endgame,* pp. 39, 57, 106.
51. Ibid., p. 131; Mansoor, *Surge,* pp. xvii, 21.
52. "American Forces in Afghanistan and Iraq," *The New York Times,* June 22, 2011, http://www.nytimes.com/interactive/2011/06/22/world/asia/american-forces-in-afghanistan-and-iraq.html; Gordon and Trainor, *Endgame,* pp. 115–120; Mansoor, *Surge,* pp. xvii, 21; Thomas E. Ricks, "General Failure," *Atlantic,* November 2012, p. 106; Baker, *Days of Fire,* p. 385.
53. George W. Bush, Inaugural Address, January 20, 2005, *Public Papers of the Presidents,* http://www.presidency.ucsb.edu/ws/index.php?pid=58745&st=&st1; Bush, *Decision Points,* p. 345; Rice, *No Higher Honor,* pp. 401, 438ff; Abrams, *Tested by Zion,* p. 150; Baker, *Days of Fire,* p. 385.
54. Gordon and Trainor, *Endgame,* pp. 160–61, 176; See also Andrew F. Krepinevich, "How to Win in Iraq," *Foreign Affairs,* September/October 2005; Rice, *No Higher Honor,* pp. 372–73; Fred Kaplan, *The Insurgents,* pp. 196–97.
55. Gordon and Trainor, *Endgame,* p. 193; Bush, *Decision Points,* p. 356; Baker, *Days of Fire,* p. 480.
56. Mansoor, *Surge,* p. 30; Gordon and Trainor, *Endgame,* p. 219; Bush, *Decision Points,* p. 371.
57. Rice, *No Higher Honor,* p. 410; Bush, *Decision Points,* p. 355; Thomas E. Ricks, *The Gamble: General David Petraeus and the American Military Adventure in Iraq* (New York: Penguin Press, 2009), p. 84; James A. Baker III and Lee H. Hamilton, *The Iraq Study Group Report* (New York: Vintage Books, 2006); Michael Dimock, "The Iraq-Vietnam Difference," Pew Research Center, http://www.pewresearch.org/2006/05/15/the-iraqvietnam-difference/; Baker, *Days of Fire,* p. 487.

58. Stephen Biddle, Jeffrey A. Friedman, and Jacob N. Shapiro, "Testing the Surge: Why Did Violence Decline in Iraq in 2007?" *International Security* 37, no. 1 (Summer 2012), pp. 7–40; Mansoor, *Surge,* p. 32; Peter Beinart, "To the Brink," *New Republic,* November 27 and December 4, 2006, p. 6.
59. Bush, *Decision Points,* p. 355; Ricks, *Gamble,* p. 122; Peter D. Feaver, "The Right to Be Right: Civil-Military Relations and the Iraq Surge Decision," *International Security* 35, no. 4 (Spring 2011), pp. 87–125.
60. Rice, *No Higher Honor,* p. 548; Ricks, *Gamble,* p. 185; Henry Kissinger interviewed by Andrew Marr, "U.S. Policy on Iraq," BBC, November 19, 2006, http://news.bbc.co.uk/2/hi/programmes/sunday_am/6163050.stm.
61. Bush, *Decision Points,* p. 376; Peter W. Rodman, *Presidential Command: Power, Leadership, and the Making of Foreign Policy From Richard Nixon to George W. Bush* (New York: Vintage Books, 2010), p. 268.
62. See Feaver, "Right to Be Right"; Fred Barnes, "How Bush Decided on the Surge," *Weekly Standard,* 13, no. 20 (February 4, 2008), http://www.weeklystandard.com/Content/Public/Articles/000/000/014/658dwgrn.asp.
63. Gordon and Trainor, *Endgame,* pp. 291; Rice, *No Higher Honor,* p. 544; Mansoor, *Surge,* p. 48; Rodman, *Presidential Command,* p. 267. The State Department favored an even more radical transfer of responsibility to Iraqi security forces than the Pentagon did.
64. George W. Bush, "On Military Operations in Iraq," address to the nation, January 10, 2007, *Public Papers of the Presidents,* http://www.presidency.ucsb.edu/ws/index.php?pid=24432&st=&st1; Bush, *Decision Points,* pp. 374–76; Gordon and Trainor, *Endgame,* p. 302.
65. Rice, *No Higher Honor,* pp. 544, 545; Baker, *Days of Fire,* pp. 500, 512.
66. For examples, see Peter Beinart, *The Icarus Syndrome: A History of American Hubris* (New York: HarperCollins, 2010); Michael Scheuer, "Anonymous," *Imperial Hubris: Why the West Is Losing the War on Terror* (Washington, D.C.: Potomac Books, 2004).

12: "NO WIGGLE ROOM"

1. "Presidential Job Approval Center," Gallup, http://www.gallup.com/poll/124922/Presidential-Job-Approval-Center.aspx; Rice, *No Higher Honor,* p. 734.
2. "Partisan Polarization Surges in Bush, Obama Years," *Trends in American Values: 1987–2012,* June 4, 2012, Pew Research Center for the People and the Press, p. 78, http://www.people-press.org/2012/06/04/partisan-polarization-surges-in-bush-obama-years/.
3. Barack Obama, "My Plan for Iraq," *The New York Times,* July 14, 2008, http://www.nytimes.com/2008/07/14/opinion/14obama.html; Karen DeYoung, "Obama Sets Timetable for Iraq Withdrawal, Calling It Part of Broader Middle East Strategy," *The Washington Post,* February 28, 2009, http://www.washingtonpost.com/wp-dyn/content/article/2009/02/27/AR2009022700566.html?hpid=topnews&sid=ST2009022700620; Greg Bruno, "U.S. Security Agreements and Iraq," Council on Foreign Relations, December 23, 2008, http://www.cfr.org/iraq/us-security-agreements-iraq/p16448.
4. James Mann, *The Obamians: The Struggle Inside the White House to Redefine American Power* (New York: Viking, 2012), p. 120; Fred Kaplan, *The Insurgents* (New York: Simon & Schuster, 2013), p. 296.
5. George Packer, "The Last Mission," *The New Yorker,* September 28, 2009, http://www.newyorker.com/reporting/2009/09/28/090928fa_fact_packer; Mann, *Obamians,* p. 128; Vali Nasr, "The Inside Story of How the White House Let Diplomacy Fail in

Afghanistan," *Foreign Policy,* March–April 2013, http://www.foreignpolicy.com/articles/2013/03/04/the_inside_story_of_how_the_white_house_let_diplomacy_fail_in_afghanistan?page=full.

6. Packer, "Last Mission."
7. Rajiv Chandrasekaran, *Little America: The War Within the War for Afghanistan* (New York: Knopf, 2012), pp. 107, 197.
8. Packer, "Last Mission."
9. David E. Sanger, *Confront and Conceal: Obama's Secret Wars and Surprising Use of American Power* (New York: Crown, 2012), p. 35; Bob Woodward, *Obama's Wars* (New York: Simon & Schuster, 2010), p. 192. See also General Stanley McChrystal, *My Share of the Task: A Memoir* (New York: Penguin, 2013).
10. Woodward, *Obama's Wars,* pp. 223, 292; Sanger, *Confront and Conceal,* p. 31.
11. Woodward, *Obama's Wars,* pp.135, 159–60, 247, 293.
12. Mann, *Obamians,* p. 128; Woodward, *Obama's Wars,* p. 251.
13. Woodward, *Obama's Wars,* pp. 253, 279, 301, 321.
14. Ibid., pp. 275–78, 302, 316.
15. Sanger, *Confront and Conceal,* p. 35; Woodward, *Obama's Wars,* p. 325.
16. Woodward, *Obama's Wars,* p. 329.
17. Ibid., p. 325
18. Packer, "Last Mission."
19. Woodward, *Obama's Wars,* p. 333.
20. Ibid., p. 324; Sanger, *Confront and Conceal,* p. 51.
21. Mann, *Obamians,* p. 110; Sanger, *Confront and Conceal,* p. 249; Thom Shanker, "A New Medal Honors Drone Pilots and Computer Experts," *The New York Times,* February 13, 2013, http://www.nytimes.com/2013/02/14/us/new-medal-to-honor-drone-pilots-and-computer-experts.html.
22. Sanger, *Confront and Conceal,* p. 262ff "Sustaining U.S. Global Leadership: Priorities for 21st Century Defense," January 2012, http://www.defense.gov/news/defense_strategic_guidance.pdf.
23. Vali Nasr, *The Dispensable Nation: American Foreign Policy in Retreat* (New York: Random House, 2013), p. 75.
24. Ibid., chapter 3; Sanger, *Confront and Conceal,* p. 51.
25. Mark Mazzetti, *The Way of the Knife: The CIA, a Secret Army, and a War at the Ends of the Earth* (New York: Penguin Press, 2013), pp. 234, 290–2.
26. Jeffrey A. Bader, *Obama and China's Rise: An Insider's Account of America's Asia Strategy* (Washington, D.C.: Brookings Institution Press, 2012), p. 113.
27. Ibid.; Sanger, *Confront and Conceal,* p. 375.
28. Bader, *Obama and China's Rise,* pp. 95–97.
29. Kim Ghattas, *The Secretary: A Journey with Hillary Clinton from Beirut to the Heart of American Power* (New York: Henry Holt, 2013), p. 185; Hillary Rodham Clinton, Remarks to the ASEAN Regional Forum, July 12, 2012, U.S. Department of State, http://www.state.gov/secretary/rm/2012/07/194987.htm; Bader, *Obama and China's Rise,* p. 105; Sanger, *Confront and Conceal,* pp. 394–95.
30. Bader, *Obama and China's Rise,* pp. 85–87.
31. Barack Obama, Remarks to the Parliament in Canberra, Australia, November 17, 2011, *Public Papers of the Presidents,* http://www.presidency.ucsb.edu/ws/index.php?pid=97064&st=&st1; Mark E. Manyin et al., "Pivot to the Pacific? The Obama Administration's 'Rebalancing' Toward Asia," March 28, 2012, Congressional Research Service, http://www.fas.org/sgp/crs/natsec/R42448.pdf.

32. Sanger, *Confront and Conceal*, p. xix.
33. Mann, *Obamians*, p. 247; Sanger, *Confront and Conceal*, p. 412; Hillary Clinton, "America's Pacific Century," *Foreign Policy*, November 2011, http://www.foreignpolicy.com/articles/2011/10/11/americas_pacific_century?page=full.
34. Mann, *Obamians*, p. xii; Ghattas, *Secretary*, p. 237; Ryan Lizza, "The Consequentialist," *The New Yorker*, May 2, 2011, http://www.newyorker.com/reporting/2011/05/02/110502fa_fact_lizza?currentPage=all.
35. Greg Jaffe, "In One of Final Addresses to Army, Gates Describes Vision for Military's Future," *The Washington Post*, February 26, 2011.
36. Mann, *Obamians*, p. xi; Sanger, *Confront and Conceal*, pp. 341, 342.
37. Sanger, *Confront and Conceal*, pp. 293, 343; Mann, *Obamians*, p. xii.
38. Sanger, *Confront and Conceal*, p. 348, 352; Lizza, "Consequentialist"; Mann, *Obamians*, p. 294.
39. Mann, *Obamians*, p. 301.
40. Paula Broadwell (with Vernon Loeb), *All In: The Education of David Petraeus* (New York: Penguin, 2012), cited by Thomas Powers, "Warrior Petraeus," *The New York Review of Books*, March 7, 2013, p. 43.
41. Sanger, *Confront and Conceal*, p. 56.
42. Michael Gordon and Mark Landler, "Senate Hearing Draws Out a Rift in U.S. Policy on Syria," *The New York Times*, February 7, 2013; Maggie Haberman, "Bill Clinton Splits with President Obama on Syria," *Politico*, June 12, 2013; Mark Mazzetti, Michael Gordon, and Mark Landler, "U.S. Is Said to Plan to Send Weapons to Syrian Rebels," *The New York Times*, June 13, 2013.
43. Obama presented his case for striking Syria to the American people even as he withdrew his request for Congressional approval, saying he wanted to test the Russian initiative. "Remarks by the President in Address to the Nation on Syria, September 10, 2013," Office of the Press Secretary, The White House.
44. Joe Klein, "Obama and Syria: Stumbling Toward Damascus," *Time*, September 23, 2013, p. 27; *The New Republic* print edition of October 7, 2013.
45. Barack Obama, "Remarks at the American Israel Public Affairs Committee Policy Conference, March 4, 2012, Public Papers of the Presidents, http://www.presidency.ucsb.edu/ws/index.php?pid=99935&st=1=; Joseph Biden, "Remarks by the Vice President to the AIPAC Policy Conference," March 4, 2013, www.whitehouse.gov/the-press-office/2013/03/04/remarks-vice-president-aipac-policy-conference; Evan Thomas, *Ike's Bluff: President Eisenhower's Secret Battle to Save the World* (New York: Little, Brown and Co., 2012).
46. Barack Obama, Remarks at the Pentagon in Arlington, Virginia, January 5, 2012, *Public Papers of the Presidents*, http://www.presidency.ucsb.edu/ws/index.php?pid=98803&st=&st1; Obama Remarks at National Defense University, May 23, 2013.
47. Office of the Under Secretary of Defense (Comptroller), *National Defense Budget Estimates for FY 2013*, Table 6–8. March 2012, http://comptroller.defense.gov/defbudget/fy2013/FY13_Green_Book.pdf.
48. Chuck Hagel, "Veterans of Foreign Wars National Convention Speech, delivered July 22, 2013, www.defense.gov/speeches/speech.aspx?speechid=1796.
49. Sanger, *Confront and Conceal*, p. 313.
50. Howard Schneider, "U.S.: No Plans to Join IMF Euro Fund," *The Washington Post*, December 9, 2011, http://articles.washingtonpost.com/2011-12-09/business/35287758_1_euro-crisis-imf-financial-crisis; "IMF Wins Pledges of $456bn for Crisis Fund," *Telegraph*, June 19, 2012, http://www.telegraph.co.uk/finance/financialcrisis/9340480/IMF-wins-pledges-of-456bn-for-crisis-fund.html.

51. Mann, *Obamians,* p. 72.
52. General Dempsey used this phrase in remarks at the Center for Strategic and International Studies, March 18, 2013; he repeated it in a press conference with Secretary Hagel. See http://www.defense.gov/news/newsarticle.aspx?id=119558 and http://www.defense.gov/transcripts/transcript.aspx?transcriptid=5211.
53. "Remarks by Secretary Hagel at the IISS Asia Security Summit, Shangri-La Hotel, Singapore, June 1, 2013," *U.S. Department of Defense News Transcript.* The cuts being considered in the summer of 2013 are described in Thom Shanker, "Hagel Gives Dire Assessment of Choices He Expects Cuts to Force on the Pentagon," *The New York Times,* August 1, 2013, p. A11. For General Odierno's lament, see Gordon Lubold, *FP Situation Report,* August 21, 2013.
54. Mann, *Obamians,* p. 72, 342.
55. Hillary Rodham Clinton, Forrestal Lecture at the Naval Academy, April 10, 2012, U.S. Department of State, http://www.state.gov/secretary/rm/2012/04/187693.htm; Hillary Rodham Clinton, "A Conversation with U.S. Secretary of State Hillary Rodham Clinton," September 8, 2010, Council on Foreign Relations, http://www.cfr.org/diplomacy-and-statecraft/conversation-us-secretary-state-hillary-rodham-clinton/p22896; Sullivan, Remarks at Center for a New American Security, June 2, 2012; see also Ryan Lizza, "Consequentialist."
56. Barack Obama, State of the Union Address, January 24, 2012, *Public Papers of the Presidents,* http://www.presidency.ucsb.edu/ws/index.php?pid=99000#axzz2h9MSLMq4.
57. Barack Obama, Remarks at the Pentagon in Arlington, Virginia, January 5, 2012, *Public Papers of the Presidents,* http://www.presidency.ucsb.edu/ws/index.php?pid=98803#axzz2h9MSLMq4; Obama Remarks at National Defense University, May 23, 2013; Barack Obama, Address to the United Nations General Assembly, September 24, 2013, http://www.whitehouse.gov/the-press-office/2013/09/24/remarks-president-obama-address-united-nations-general-assembly; Kaplan, *The Insurgents,* p. 356ff.
58. Ghattas, *Secretary,* p. 227.

EPILOGUE

1. Margaret MacMillan, *Dangerous Games: The Uses and Abuses of History* (London: Profile Books, 2009). See also Leslie H. Gelb, "The Horrible Libya Hypocrisies," *Daily Beast,* March 21, 2011, http://www.thedailybeast.com/articles/2011/03/21/the-horrible-libya-hypocrisies.html.
2. Peter Beinart, *The Icarus Syndrome: A History of American Hubris* (New York: HarperCollins, 2010), p. 139.
3. George H. W. Bush, State of the Union Address, January 28, 1992, *Public Papers of the Presidents,* http://www.presidency.ucsb.edu/ws/index.php?pid=20544&st=&st1.
4. *Foreign Relations of the United States, 1969–1973, Volume XIV, Soviet Union, October 1971–May 1972,* doc. 188.
5. Robert Dallek, *Nixon and Kissinger: Partners in Power* (New York: HarperCollins, 2007), p. 597; Barack Obama, Inaugural Address, January 21, 2013, http://www.presidency.ucsb.edu/ws/index.php?pid=102827&st=&st1; Kissinger, *White House Years,* p. 1476; *On China,* p. 214.
6. Office of the Under Secretary of Defense (Comptroller), *National Defense Budget Estimates for FY 2013,* March 2012, http://comptroller.defense.gov/defbudget/fy2013/FY13_Green_Book.pdf.

7. David E. Sanger, *Confront and Conceal: Obama's Secret Wars and Surprising Use of American Power* (New York: Crown, 2012), p. 417; George Tenet, *At the Center of the Storm: My Years at the CIA* (New York: HarperCollins, 2007), p. 191.
8. Carol E. Lee, Jay Solomon, and Lawrence Norman, "Two-Track Negotiations Led to Nuclear Deal," *The Wall Street Journal,* November 25, 2013, p. 10. Administration officials told reporters that "cutting out others eliminated the competing agendas that come with" multilateral talks. Mark Landler, "Obama Places an Emphasis on Diplomacy, *The New York Times,* November 26, 2013, p. A10.
9. *Foreign Relations of the United States, 1955–1957, Volume XIX, National Security Policy,* doc. 41; *Foreign Relations of the United States 1969–1976, Volume XVII, China, 1969–1972,* doc. 196; Kim Ghattas, *The Secretary: A Journey with Hillary Clinton from Beirut to the Heart of American Power* (New York: Henry Holt, 2013), p. 121.

INDEX

Page numbers in *italics* refer to photographs.

ABM (Anti-Ballistic Missile) treaty, 276
Abrams, Creighton, 172–3, 180, 181
Abu Ghraib, 293
Acheson, Dean, 10, *17*, 18–22, 33–8, 41, 85, 140
  defense spending and, 46, 99
  German rearmament and, 52, 53, 73
  on Johnson, 44, 48
  Kennedy administration and, 96, 99, 100
  Korea policy and, 50–5, 58–63, 282, 334
  Marshall's Harvard speech and, 24, 25
  NSC-68 and, 48, 207
  Paris Big Four meeting and, 33, 35, 40
  speeches of, 21–2, 37, 60
  Vietnam policy and, 159
Adams, Sherman, 68
Adelman, Kenneth, 234
Adenauer, Konrad, 5, 101, 102, 112
Afghanistan, 228, 230
  al Qaeda in, 265, 278–9, 281, 282, 304, 306, 307
  "freedom agenda" and, 286–7
  freedom fighters in, 211, 214, 229, 230, 232, 238, 279
  9/11 and, 278–9, 281, 282
  Pakistan linked with, 310
  Soviet invasion and occupation of, 8, 50, 214, 215–16, 224, 229, 232, 279
  Soviet withdrawal from, 238
  women and girls in, 286–7
Afghanistan War, 10, 150, 303–11, 317–18
  Bush Jr. and, 278–9, 281, 282
  cost of, 307, 308
  exit strategy in, 307–8
  innovative, low-cost and small-footprint approaches in, 309–11
  surge in, 305–9, 317
  as "war of necessity," 307
AFL-CIO, 200, 207, 229, 329
AfPak, use of term, 310
Africa, 205–6, 208, 286
  Carter policy and, 210
Agency for International Development (AID), 321
AIDS treatment, 286, 293
Air Force, U.S., 31, 44–5, 52, 136, 322
Air Force Academy, Nixon's speech at, 171
Albright, Madeleine, 11, 264, 267, 269, 270, 272
  military retort of, 260, 329
Alexander the Great, 289
Allawi, Ayed, 292
Alliance for Progress, 103
al Qaeda, 264–7, 277
  in Afghanistan, 265, 278–9, 281, 282, 304, 306, 307
  in Iraq, 281, 287
American University, Kennedy's speech at, 111
Amherst, Mass., Reagan's speech in, 239
Amnesty International, 200
Anbar province, 292
Andropov, Yuri, 228, 234
Angola, 205–6, 208, 228, 232
Annan, Kofi, 268–9
antiaircraft missiles, 232
anti-Americanism, 272
  of de Gaulle, 112
  Iraq War and, 286
  in Latin America, 87–8, 211
  9/11 and, 275
anti-Communism, 10, 11, 23, 74, 86, 200
  Johnson and, 123, 129, 140, 141
  negative effects of, 231
  of Reagan, 222, 227–33, 239, 240
  see also containment
antimissile technology, 235
antiwar sentiment, Iraq War and, 275

Arab-Israeli peace talks, 194–7, 211
Arab League, 318
Arab oil embargo (1973), 195–6
Arab Spring, 311, 314–18, 321
Arabs, Arab states, 81, 82, 103, 251
Árbenz, Jacobo, 75
Armitage, Richard, 278
arms control, 198, 201, 247, 276, 329
  Carter and, 210, 212, 214, 216, 217, 224
  Eisenhower and, 85–7, 327
  Johnson and, 123, 154
  Kennedy and, 105, 111–13
  Kissinger and, 201–3, 205, 207, 208, 217, 225, 235, 237, 303
  Nixon and, 171–2, 176, 181, 237
  Obama and, 302–3
  Reagan and, 223–8, 234–41
arms embargos, 5, 259
army, Iraqi, 292
Army, U.S., 31, 41, 52, 55, 62, 99, 276, 322
  Iraq War and, 289
  Nixon's Vietnam withdrawals and, 171, 172
  in Vietnam, 103–4, 168
Asia, 60–1, 238
  effects of Korean War on, 55, 62
Assad, Hafez, 195, 196, 318
Association of Southeast Asian Nations (ASEAN), 312–13
Aswan High Dam, 77
atomic bomb
  Soviet, 45
  U.S., 18, 31
Atomic Energy Commission, 44–5
"Atoms for Peace," 71–2
Attlee, Clement, 59–61, 345*n*
Australia, 313–14
authoritarian regimes, 210, 233
"axis of evil" phrase, 287

B-1 bombers, 212
B-29 bombers, 31
B-52 bombers, 181, 187
Baath Party, 292
Baghdad, 82–3, 290, 291, 292, 296
Baghdad Pact, 74–5
Baker, James, 245, 247, 252–7, 259
  Belgrade visit of, 257
  disengagement plan of, 295, 296
  first Gulf War and, 252–6
balance of power, 45, 106, 123, 224, 312
Balkans, 259–64, 267–70, 304, 316–17, 331, 332
  mass murder in, 8, 11, 259, 260, 267, 333
Ball, George, 11, 96
  on problems with allies, 112–13
  Vietnam policy and, 104, 115, 116, 128, 129, 135–6, 139, 141, 149, 153, 159, 311
ballistic missiles, 227, 235
Baltic states, 200
Bandar, Prince, 251
banking crisis (2008–9), 321
Barkley, Alben, 345*n*
Barshefsky, Charlene, 245
Bay of Pigs, 97, 106, 111
Begin, Menachem, 211
Beijing, 210, 214
  Kissinger's visits to, 175–80
  Nixon's visit to, 179, 180
Beirut, 81, 82, 348*n*
Belgrade, 257, 268
Benelux countries, 28
Berger, Sandy, 267
Berlin, 81
  division of, 98
  see also West Berlin
Berlin crisis (1961), 97–102, 104–7, 110, 111, 113, 119
Berlin crisis (Berlin blockade and airlift), 8, 28–34, 36, 42, 53, 66, 331, 332, 341*n*–2*n*
Berlin Wall, 100, 238, 244, 247, 248
Bevin, Ernest, 32, 33
Bidault, Georges, 20–1, 27
Biden, Joe, 204, 283, 306, 319, 334
Bien Hoa, 130
Big Four meetings
  in Moscow, 19, 20–1, 23
  in Paris, 33, 35, 36–7, 40, 86–7
bin Laden, Osama, 96, 232, 265, 266–7, 277
  raid against, 317
  WMD and, 280, 289
biological weapons, 279, 280, 281, 283
bipartisanship, 30, 37, 63, 283, 295, 296, 303
Blair, Dennis, 311, 333
Blair, Tony, 284
Blinken, Tony, 322

Bohlen, Charles "Chip," 30, 32, 47, 51, 62, 343*n*
 Berlin crisis (1961) and, 99, 104
 at London conference, 78
Bolton, John, 329
"bomb in the Waldorf" plan, 53, 73
bombs, bombing, 253
 atomic, 18, 31, 45
 in Balkans, 259, 261, 262
 of East African embassies, 264, 265
 of Golden Dome mosque, 294
 halt in, 158, 163–4, 165, 359*n*
 hydrogen, 46
 of Iraq, 265, 266, 267
 Korean War and, 51, 62
 NATO, 261, 262, 267, 268
 neutron, 212
 pauses in, 159
 strategic, 44–5
 in Vietnam War, 131, 132, 133, 147, 152, 155, 158, 159, 163–4, 165, 173, 180, 181, 187–9, 359*n*
Bosnia, 259–64, 316–17
"boy-commando" style, 94–8, 104
Bradley, Omar, 31, 40–1, 42, 50
 Asian tour of, 49
 on Johnson, 44
 Korean War and, 55–9, 334
Brazil, 321
Bremer, L. Paul, 292
Brezhnev, Leonid, 181–3, *191*, 194, 239, 331
 emigration policy and, 197, 198
 at Vienna talks, 211–14
 at Vladivostok meeting, 201
brinkmanship, 76, 85
Brown, Harold, 136, 139, 213, 214
Brzezinski, Zbigniew, 213–16, 225
Buddhists, 113, 114
Budget Bureau, U.S., 20
budget deficits, U.S., 70, 157
Bui Diem, 146
Bundestag, 112
Bundy, Bill, 130, 132, 164
Bundy, McGeorge, 94, 101, 143
 Cuba policy and, 97, 105, 106–7
 Rostow's replacement of, 151
 Vietnam policy and, 104, 114, 117, 118, 127–8, 129, 132, 133, 137, 139, 141, 159
Burma, 20
Burns, James H., 48
Bush, George H. W., 12, 203, 243–59, *243*, 260, 326, 327
 defense spending and, 244, 257, 258–9
 in election of 1992, 245, 257
 German reunification and, 247–50, 264, 333
 Gulf War and, 250–6, 283, 331, 332, 334
 maximalism and, 251, 331, 332
 speeches of, 244, 250, 251, 258
 as vice president, 227–8
Bush, George W., 5, 273–99, *273*
 Afghanistan War and, 303–4
 as "compassionate conservative," 275
 defense spending and, 274, 276, 328
 democracy promotion and, 276, 286–8, 293
 doing-less-abroad theme of, 275–6
 in election of 2000, 275–6
 "freedom agenda" and, 286–8
 hubris of, 298
 Iraq War and, 252, 275, 281–99, 302, 303, 334
 Johnson compared with, 297–8
 lack of confidence of, 298–9
 maximalism and, 275, 277, 283, 288, 291, 298, 310, 326
 9/11 and, 274–5, 277–83, 286–8, 298, 326
 Obama compared with, 302–6, 309, 310, 320, 323
 policy continuity and, 66–7
 speeches of, 275–6, 279, 283, 287, 293, 297, 326
 toughest and most unpopular decision of, 295–9
Bush, Laura, 286–7

Cairo, 314, 321
California, energy brownouts in, 277
Cambodia, 205, 228
 Vietnam War and, 152, 161, 172–4, 181, 184, 189
Campbell, Kurt, 314
Camp David, 86, 135, 136–7, 270
Camp David agreements, 211
Canada, 44
Carnegie Endowment for International Peace, 329

Carter, Jimmy, 7, 136, 193, 209–18, 229, 241
achievements of, 211
Afghan freedom fighters and, 211, 214, 229, 230
arms control and, 210, 212, 214, 216, 217, 224
bad luck of, 212
in election of 1980, 212, 215, 216, 222
human rights and, 210, 211, 240
ineffectuality of, 211–12
personal style's undercutting of leadership of, 212
retrenchment and, 9, 209, 211–12, 214–15, 217–18, 326, 329
speeches of, 209–14
spiritual side of, 211
at Vienna talks, 211–14
Carter Doctrine, 214
Casey, George, 294–5, 297
Casey, William, 229, 231
Castro, Fidel, 88, 89, 97, 105, 229, 230, 244
CBS News, 101
Central America
Reagan policy in, 229
Chamberlain, Neville, 212, 223
Chamber of Deputies, French, 32
Charette, Hervé de, 262
Charlie Wilson's War (movie), 230
chemical weapons, 279, 280, 283
Cheney, Richard, 12, 200, 205, 244, 258–9, *273*
energy brownouts and, 277
first Gulf War and, 251–3, 289
Iraq War and, 284–6, 289
9/11 and, 274, 277–8, 280
Chiang Kai-shek, 76
Chile, 231, 233
China, 193, 266
in Africa, 205
Carter policy and, 210, 214, 215
Clinton policy and, 263
Communism in, 45, 60, 76, 77, 140
Cultural Revolution in, 175–6
IMF and, 321
Japanese bogey and, 178
Korean War and, 54, 57–62, 68–9
NATO and, 268
Nixon policy and, 12, *167*, 175–84, 186, 189–90, 210, 263, 314, 335–6
Obama policy and, 311–14
Quemoy and Matsu and, 76
revolution in, 45, 46
Soviet relations with, 45, 60, 76, 176, 197
Syria's relations with, 318
Vietnam War and, 148, 153, 156
Chirac, Jacques, 260, 286
Christian Democrats, German, 112, 225
Christmas Bombing, 187–9
Christopher, Warren, 259, 262
Churchill, Winston, 27, 73, 74, 76, 77, 189
"Churchill speech, the," 251
CIA, 11, 82, 89, 203, 228–31, 318
al Qaeda and, 266–7
Angola and, 205–6
Bush Jr. and, 276–7, 279
Carter and, 211
Cuba and, 97, 105
Iraq War and, 282
Vietnam policy and, 115, 127, 133, 180
Clark, Dick, 329
Clark Amendment, 232
Clay, Lucius, 19, 31
Clayton, Will, 20, 23–6
Clifford, Clark, 95, 136–41, 146–7, 159–65, 359*n*
low-key approach advocated by, 149
McNamara replaced by, 159
policy review by, 160–1
South Vietnam's warning from, 164–5
war opposed by, 136–7, 149, 153, 159
climate change, 336
Clinton, Bill, *243*, 258–72, 318, 326, 329
Balkan wars and, 11, 259–64, 267–70316
Bush Jr. compared with, 279, 283
Bush Jr.'s criticism of, 275–6
China policy and, 263
defense spending and, 244, 246
in election of 1996, 263
globalization and, 245, 262–3, 265, 271
Iraq and al Qaeda and, 264–7, 281
Israeli-Palestinian peace efforts and, 270–1
Obama compared with, 306
Russia policy and, 263–4
speeches of, 271–2
U.S. global role and, 262, 269–72
Clinton, Hillary, 323, 324, 329
on failures in multilateral cooperation, 6
Iraq War and, 283

as secretary of state, 303, 306, 312–15, 317, 318, 323–4, 335
Clintonism, 303
Cold War, 3, 7–11, 45–9, 330–1
AFL-CIO and, 207
Africa and, 205–6
Carter's view of, 209
coinage of expression, 232
cost of, 40, 49, 70
Eisenhower's attempt to reduce tensions in, 71–2
Eisenhower's views on, 67
end of, 10, 11, 34, 70, 240, 244–6, 250, 257–8, 269, 314
escalation of, 41
in Europe, clashes over, 72–4
Johnson's easing of tensions in, 123
Kennan's view of, 36
Kennedy's efforts to reduce tensions in, 105, 111–13, 352*n*
moments of crisis in, 7–8
negative effects of, 232
NSC-68 and, 46–8
psychological stresses of, 71
start of, 247, 270, 333
in Third World, clashes over, 74–6, 203–6, 208, 213–14, 228–33
in Third World, U.S. unpredictable policies in, 76–8
U.S. global role in, 257
U.S. loneliness in, 102
victory in, 4
waning years of, 224
Cominform, 28
Comintern, 28
Committee on the Present Danger, 202, 329
"Committee to Save the World" cover, 245
Commonwealth Club of San Francisco, Shultz's speech at, 231
Communism, 23, 25, 42, 57, 72, 81, 138, 208, 210, 334
collapse of, 257, 331
in Eastern Europe, 80
in Greece, 19
Kennedy and, 94–5, 100
in Latin America, 88
in North Korea, 50, 55, 69
Reagan's views on, 222, 223, 224
in South Vietnam, 113, 114, 116, 118, 125, 140, 141–2, 151, 154, 159, 164, 174, 204, 355*n*
Third World advances in, 74–6
in U.S., 70
in Vietnam, 75, 132
in Western Europe, 28, 29
see also Soviet Union
Congress, U.S., 12, 345*n*
Acheson and, 10
Afghanistan War and, 317
Angola and, 206, 232
Bush Jr. and, 275, 287
Cheney's testimony to, 258–9
defense budget and, 42, 52, 53, 224, 244
Eisenhower and, 80, 85
election of 1966 and, 157
European defense and, 62
first Gulf War and, 251, 252, 253, 256
foreign aid and, 22, 26, 45, 50, 53, 73, 77, 244
Iraq War and, 275, 283, 294, 296, 297
Johnson and, 122, 129, 135, 141, 148, 149, 157–8
Kissinger's relations with, 197, 198–9, 204, 208, 329
Korea policy and, 50–3
Marshall Plan and, 22, 26
Obama and, 320, 321
Reagan and, 224, 226, 230–3
Soviet policy and, 197–8, 199, 208
Truman and, 19, 21, 23, 28, 42, 51
Vandenberg resolution and, 28, 30
Vietnam policy and, 129, 135, 148, 149, 158, 161, 162, 171, 173, 174, 184, 204
see also House of Representatives, U.S.; Senate, U.S.
Connally, John, 6
conservation, 211
conservatives, 10–12, 217
Reagan and, 223, 237, 240
containment, 10, 18–30, 245
Acheson's view of, 36
dissent from, 28–30
Marshall Plan and
retrenchment and, 72
contras, 229, 231, 232, 233, 236
Copenhagen conference (2009), 336

counterinsurgency
  in Afghanistan, 304–8
  in Iraq War, 294, 296
counterterrorism, 276–7, 287
Couve de Murville, Maurice, 100–1
covert action, 206, 208, 211, 212, 231, 240, 279, 311
crisis, Cold War and, 7–8
crisis management vs. strategy, 111
Croats, 259
Crowe, William, 252
cruise missile strikes, 265
Cuba, 229, 230
  in Africa, 206, 213
  Bay of Pigs landing in, 97, 106, 111
  revolution in, 88, 89
  Soviet relations with, 89
  U-2 flights over, 105, 111
  U.S. blockade of, 107–8
Cuban missile crisis, 8, 50, 98, 105–11, 113, 119, 138, 280, 331, 332, 351*n*
currency, 32, 161, 193, 260
  Nixon policy and, 169, 170
cyber warfare, 310, 319
Czechoslovakia, 28, 29, 42

Dayton talks, 261–2
decolonization, 67, 77
defense budget, U.S., 193, 269
  Bush, Jr. and, 274, 276, 328
  Bush, Sr. and, 244, 257, 258–9
  Carter and, 212–13, 214, 216
  Clinton and, 244, 246
  Eisenhower and, 67, 70, 83, 87, 143
  Ford and, 204
  Johnson and, 122–3, 147, 149, 274, 328
  Kennedy and, 99, 100, 122, 240, 274, 328
  Nixon and, 168
  Obama and, 309, 313–14, 320–1, 323, 328
  Reagan and, 216, 224, 240, 241, 274, 328
  Truman and, 40–6, 48–9, 52, 53, 62, 70, 73, 99, 328
Defense Department, U.S., 31, 40–6, 49, 75, 81, 202, 236, 237, 322
  Afghanistan War and, 307, 309
  Clinton and, 265
  first Gulf War and, 252
  German rearmament and, 52–3
  Iraq War and, 282, 288–92, 295–6, 304
  Korean War and, 52, 54–60
  Rumsfeld's goal of shaking up of, 277
  terrorist attack on, 281
  Vietnam policy and, 104, 113, 134, 138, 148, 151, 153, 158, 161, 164–5, 173, 181, 204
defense spending, in Europe, 72–3
de Gaulle, Charles, 5, 87, 100–2, 154
democracy, 23, 28, 29, 50, 57, 80, 83, 247
  human rights and, 210
  Johnson and, 123, 140, 141–2
  promotion of, 229, 231, 233, 242, 266, 276, 286–8, 293, 315
Democratic Congressional Conference, 22
Democrats, 12, 30, 94, 130, 140, 142, 159, 163, 164, 202, 206, 328
  conservative, 217
  first Gulf War and, 253
  Iraq War and, 283–4, 296
  retrenchment and, 327
  southern, 157
  working-class, 207
Dempsey, Martin, 322
Denfeld, Louis E., 45
DePuy, William, 147
Desert Shield, Operation, 252
Desert Storm, Operation, 255–6
détente, 9, 175, 194, 197, 329
  Carter's views on, 209, 213, 216, 217
  Cheney's views on, 200
  dropping of use of word, 207
  Kissinger and, 90, 171, 180–3, 189–90, 198, 199, 207, 208, 217, 239
  Nixon and, 90, 171, 180–3, 189–90, 208
  opposition to, 207, 208, 217, 329
  Reagan and, 239
Detroit, Mich., Eisenhower's Masonic Temple speech in, 68
Diem, Bui, 146
Diem, Ngo Dinh, 11, 103, 104, 113–18, 124–5, 131
Dien Bien Phu, 75
"diplomacy backed by force," use of phrase, 262
dissidents, Soviet, 200, 210, 211, 212, 239
Dobrynin, Anatoly, 108, 110, 171, 197
  Reagan's meeting with, 226–7
  recall of, 213

Doha Round, 286
dollar, U.S., 161, 169, 193
Dominican Republic, 88–9
domino theory, 138
Donilon, Tom, 314
Douglas, Lewis, 32
drones, 309, 310, 311
Duck Hook, 171
Dulles, John Foster, 6, *65*, 66, 67, 73–9, 85, 86, 101, 177
  brinkmanship and, 76
  death of, 89
  defense spending and, 70
  European tour of, 73
  Indochina and, 75
  Middle East policy and, 74, 77, 78, 81
  at Paris conference, 36–7
  Suez crisis and, 77, 78
  Truman criticized by, 66, 70–1

Eagleburger, Lawrence, 259
East Africa embassy bombings, 65, 264
East Asia, 322
  China's domination in, 311–14
East Asia Summit, 313
Eastern bloc, 247
Eastern Europe, 26, 28, 34, 80, 200
  collapse of Soviet control in, 247
  NATO and, 264
economic crisis, global, 302
economic growth, 4, 26–7
  in Vietnam, 126, 127, 133–4, 155
economic sanctions, 252, 319
economics, globalization and, 245, 262
economy, U.S., 4, 193, 196, 212
  oil embargo and, 195, 196
  Reagan and, 224
Eden, Anthony, 74, 76–9, 81
education, 274, 287
Egypt, 62, 103, 211, 321
  Arab Spring in, 314–15
  Soviet relations with, 77, 194–5
  Suez crisis and, 77–81
  Yom Kippur War and, 194–6
Eikenberry, Karl, 308
Eisenhower, Dwight D., 9, 65–90, *65*, 94, 175, 263
  attempts to reduce East-West tensions by, 71–2
  bluffing and, 320
  defense spending and, 67, 70, 83, 87, 143
  Diem's overthrow and, 11, 115
  European relations and, 72–4, 335
  Forrestal warned by, 41–2
  Franks's view of, 289
  Kennedy compared with, 94, 96, 97, 98, 102, 118–19
  Korea policy and, 50, 68–70, 164, 347*n*
  Latin American policy and, 87–9, 203
  Middle East policy of, 77–84, 203
  "missile gap" controversy and, 83–4, 203
  NATO and, 53, 66, 73
  nuclear weapons and, 69–72, 75, 76, 83–7, 327
  policy continuity and, 66–7
  as puzzle, 90
  retrenchment and, 67–72, 86, 90, 97, 143, 190, 217, 326–9
  speeches of, 67, 68, 71, 72, 84, 90, 320, 328
  Truman as viewed by, 7, 327
  Vietnam policy and, 147
Eisenhower Doctrine, 80–1
elections, U.S.
  of 1948, 31, 42, 43
  of 1960, 163
  of 1964, 127, 129–30, 131
  of 1966, 157
  of 1968, 151, 158, 162–5
  of 1972, 181, 184–7, 192
  of 1976, 202, 203, 209
  of 1980, 207, 212, 215, 216, 222
  of 1986, 236
  of 1992, 245, 257
  of 1996, 263
  of 2000, 271, 275–6
  of 2006, 294, 295
  of 2008, 302
El Salvador, 229
"emerging markets," 331
emigration policy, Soviet, 197–8, 199, 208
energy crises, 193, 195–6
energy issues, 211, 277
equal partnerships, 4–7, 168
espionage, 84, 87, 105, 111, 351*n*
Ethiopia, 213
Euromissiles, 224–8, 331

Europe, 19–38, 60, 77–81, 122, 238, 282, 331
Balkan wars and, 259–62
Bush Sr. and, 246–50, 257
collective defense in, 28, 45, 49, 62, 73
Communism in, 28, 29
dysfunction and weakness of, 20–1, 23–4, 35, 37, 38, 45, 46–7, 334
Eisenhower and, 72–4, 77–80, 85, 335
human rights and, 200
Iraq War and, 286, 291
Marshall Plan and, 19–20, 25, 26–7, 41
NATO enlargement and, 264
9/11 and, 283
oil embargo and, 195–6
recovery in, 26–7, 28, 32, 41
Soviet dominance in, 21, 22, 23
U.S. commitment to, 52–3, 99
U.S. troops in, 193
Vietnam War and, 138
European Common Market, 112
European Defense Community (EDC), 73
European Union (EU), 268, 321
eurozone, banking crisis in (2008–9), 320–1
Eveland, Wilbur Crane, 348*n*
ExComm (Executive Committee), 106–11, 116

Fahd, King of Saudi Arabia, 251–2
Fallujah, 293
farm lobby, U.S., 224
fertilizer, 126, 127
Fifteen Weeks, The (Jones), 27
finance, 4, 245
Ford, Gerald, 9, *191*, 193, 198–209, 217
in election of 1976, 202, 203, 207
policy continuity of, 326
retrenchment of, 326
speeches of, 205
Vietnam War and, 204–5
at Vladivostok meeting, 201
Foreign Affairs, 29–30, 175, 179, 202–3, 225
foreign aid, U.S., 19–27, 45, 53, 88, 204, 244, 321
to Afghanistan, 305
Angola and, 206, 232
Bush Jr. and, 286, 321
to Egypt, 77
Eisenhower's review of, 80
to freedom fighters, 229, 232, 238
to Guatemala, 75
Johnson and, 123, 126, 133–4
to Russia, 258
Foreign Intelligence Advisory Board, 136
foreign policy, U.S.
continuity in, 4, 7–10, 66–7, 122, 143, 209, 223, 224, 326, 353*n*
doubts about, 325–6
failure-induced directional change in, 7–8
global role and, 244–6, 257, 258, 262, 269–72, 276, 299, 308, 322, 333, 334
"good America" story in, 3, 5, 13
ingredients of previous success of, 4
isolationism in, 29, 66
leadership role and, 169–70, 177, 193, 195, 303, 316, 318, 322, 333
lessons to learn from history of, 4–12
maximalism-retrenchment cycles in, 9
morality in, 207, 211, 231
post-Cold War, 244–6
responsibilities of, 18–22, 47, 72, 80, 84, 246, 264
twenty-first century image change of, 3–4
Forrestal, James, 40–4, 46, 48
Forrestal, Michael, Vietnam policy and, 105, 114, 115, 117, 118, 128
Fox News, 329
France, 28, 46, 72–5, 266
Balkan wars and, 260, 261, 262
Berlin blockade and, 32–3
Big Four meetings and, 19, 20–1, 36, 37, 86–7
Communism in, 28, 29
defense spending of, 72–3
German rearmament and, 53, 73
German reunification and, 247–50
in Indochina, 62, 75, 103
Iraq War and, 286, 291
Libya policy and, 315, 316
Marshall Plan and, 26, 32
oil embargo and, 195
Program A and, 34–5
Suez crisis and, 77–80
U.S. animosity with, 5, 74, 75, 100–2, 111–13
Franklin, Ben, 131
Franks, Tommy, 282, 285, 289
free nations, use of phrase, 27

freedom, 199, 266, 313
"freedom agenda," 286–8
freedom fighters, 229–32
  Afghan, 211, 214, 229, 230, 232, 238, 279
Fuerth, Leon, 283
Fulbright, William, 85

"G-2," 312
G-8, 264
Gadhafi, Muammar, 315–18
Gaither, H. Rowan, 83–4
Gaither Commission, 83–4
Galbraith, John Kenneth, 11, 100, 104, 118
Gallup Poll, 149, 217
Gates, Robert, 211, 212, 228, 232
  in Obama administration, 303, 305, 306, 309, 315, 320
Gaza, 293
GDP, 26–7, 62, 72, 83, 147, 246, 269
General Conference of the United Methodist Church, 183
Geneva agreements (July 1954), 75
Geneva peace conference (1973), 194
Geneva summit (1985), 234
genocide, 315, 331, 333
  in Balkans, 11, 259–61, 267
Genscher, Hans-Dietrich, 247
Gephardt, Richard, 283
Germany, 27, 36, 40, 311
  French view of, 21, 32
  Iraq War and, 286, 288
  occupation of, 19, 28–34, 62
  reunification of, 33, 34, 36, 37, 112, 247–50, 264, 333
Germany, East, 36, 98, 100, 247–9
Germany, Nazi, 188, 199–200
Germany, West, 36, 37, 62, 73–4, 225, 246–9
  de Gaulle's treaty with, 112
  EDC and, 73
  formation of, 28, 35
  NATO and, 49, 74
  rearmament of, 49, 52–3, 73–4
  reunification and, 247
  U.S. animosity with, 5, 100, 101–2, 112
girls, Muslim, 274, 286–7
globalization, 245, 262–3, 265, 271
Golden Dome mosque, bombing of, 294
gold sales, 161
gold standard, 170
Goldstein, Gordon, 351*n*
Goldwater, Barry, 130, 231
"good America" story, 3, 5, 13
Gorbachev, Mikhail, 223, 227, 228, 234–41, 331
  Bush Sr. and, 246–9, 257, 264
  coup against, 257
Gore, Al, 276, 283
"gradual and sustained reprisal" strategy, 132
grain exports, 214, 224
Great Britain, 22, 28, 31, 59–62, 72–6, 101, 352*n*
  Africa policy and, 210
  Berlin blockade and, 32–3
  in Big Four, 19, 36, 37, 86–7
  in bombing of Iraq, 265, 266, 267
  Common Market and, 112
  decline in power of, 19, 46
  defense spending of, 72–3
  in German occupation, 19, 32
  German reunification and, 247–50
  Iraq War and, 284, 288
  Korean War and, 59–61
  Libya policy and, 315, 316
  Marshall Plan and, 20, 22, 26
  Middle East policy and
  Program A and, 34
  Reagan in, 230, 241
  Suez crisis and, 77–81
  U.S. "special relationship" with, 5, 60
Great Depression, 305
Great Society, 122–3, 157
  South Vietnamese version of, 126
Greece, 19–23, 25, 81
greenhouse gas emissions, 276
Greenspan, Alan, 245
Grenada, 230
Gromyko, Andrei, 101, 194, 197–200, 234
Guam meeting (March 1967), 152–4
Guam proposal, 152–5, 158, 161
Guatemala, 75
Gulf of Tonkin attack, 129
gunboat diplomacy, 263

Haas, Richard, 282
Hadley, Steve, 296–7
Hagel, Chuck, 296, 322

Haig, Alexander, 180–1, 184, 185, 187–8
  NATO resignation of, 217
  on Nixon's second term, 192
  as secretary of state, 224, 226, 229
Haiphong harbor, 155, 173, 182, 189
Haiti, 260
Halberstam, David, 95, 142
Haldeman, H. R., 169, 170, 173, 174, 183, 184
  China policy and, 176, 177
Hamilton, Lee, 295, 296
Hanoi, 184, 313
  bombing of, 173, 181
Harkins, Paul, 114
Harriman, Averell, 11, 55, 56, 58, 105
  Vietnam policy and, 104, 114, 115, 116, 118, 164, 359*n*
Harris, Louis, 130
Harris poll, 149
Harvard Club, 21–2
Harvard University, 187, 207
Havana, 88
Havel, Vaclav, 315
health issues, 286, 293
heavy missiles, 201, 210, 235
"hegemon problem," 272
Helena, USS, 70–2
helicopters, U.S., 147, 215
Helms, Jesse, 206, 237, 329
Helsinki Final Act, 200
Heritage Foundation, 329
Herter, Christian, 83, 89
Hilsman, Roger, 115, 117
Hitler, Adolf, 256
Ho Chi Minh, 129, 133, 152
Holbrooke, Richard, 261–2, 267, 304–5, 308–11
Hope, Bob, 131
hostage crisis, Iranian, 193, 212, 215
hostages, in Lebanon, 236
House of Commons, British, 81
House of Representatives, U.S., 44, 80, 157, 230, 232, 253
  Armed Services Committee of, 43, 59
  Ways and Means Committee of, 158
Hughes, Emmet, 67, 79, 83, 84
Hu Jintao, 313
humanitarian intervention, 11, 260, 267–9
human rights, 88–9, 197, 199–200, 205, 208–11, 263
  Carter and, 210, 211, 240
Humphrey, George, 70, 71
Humphrey, Hubert, 140–1, 164, 165
Hungarian revolution (1956), 80
Hussein, Saddam, 233, 264–7, 280–5, 288–90
  first Gulf War and, 251, 252, 254–6, 264, 331, 333, 334–5
  ouster of, 281, 285, 290, 292, 299
hydrogen bomb, 46
Hyland, William, 208, 225
hyperpower, use of term, 246

impeachment, 236
Inchon landing, 54, 56–7
India, 20, 270, 271, 293, 321
  Pakistan's relations with, 310
Indochina, 62, 75, 103
inflation, 32, 50, 193
INF treaty, 237, 238
"ink blot" strategy, *see* pacification
Inter-American Development Bank, 88
intermediate-range missiles, 225, 238, 331
International Criminal Court, 276
International Monetary Fund (IMF), 321
internationalism, 6, 11, 22, 115, 116, 142, 177
Iran, 74, 233
  hostage crisis in, 193, 212, 215
  nuclear weapons and, 311–12, 318–19, 320
  revolution in, 193, 212
Iran-Contra affair, 229, 236
Iraq, 80, 82–3, 233, 260, 280–99
  al Qaeda in, 281, 287
  civil war in, 294, 297
  Clinton policy and, 264–7, 281
  deterioration of, 292–3, 294
  economic sanctions against, 252
  Kuwait invaded by, 8, 250–6, 331, 332, 334
  UN weapons inspectors in, 265, 281, 284, 285
  U.S. occupation of, 284, 290–5
  WMD and, 255, 264–6, 281, 283–5, 287, 288, 334
Iraq Study Group, 295
Iraq War, 10, 160, 281–99, 334
  Baker-Hamilton plan in, 295, 296
  building support for, 286–8

casualties in, 295, 296, 298
cost of, 288–9, 291, 292
counterinsurgency strategy in, 294, 296
hit-and-run strategy in, 290
insurgency in, 292, 294
international debate over, 282–6
Obama and, 302, 303, 304
"off ramps" option and, 290, 292
opposition to, 275
planning of, 282, 285, 289–91
"running start" in, 290
"stand up" strategy in, 293
surge in, 297, 299, 304
unraveling of public support for, 295, 297
U.S. invasion in, 289–91, 293, 298
Vietnam War compared with, 294, 296, 297–8
Iron Curtain, 19
Islamabad, 214
Israel, 194–7
arms embargo against, 5
Egypt's relations with, 77, 211
Suez crisis and, 79
U.S. relations with, 5
U.S. sanctions against, 79
Yom Kippur War and, 194–6
Israeli-Palestinian peace efforts, 270–1
Bush Jr. and, 276, 286, 293
Italy, 261, 291
Communism in, 28, 29

Jackson, Henry "Scoop," 161, 197–8, 203, 329
Japan, 18, 34, 36, 168, 188, 311, 321
economy of, 178
oil embargo and, 195–6
U.S. occupation of, 51, 62
U.S. peace treaty with, 45, 66
Javits, Jacob, 204, 206, 329
JCS, *see* Joint Chiefs of Staff, U.S.
Jews, 77, 199
Jobert, Michel, 195
Johns Hopkins, Johnson's speech at, 133–4
Johnson, Louis, 40–1, 43–6, 48–50
firing of, 40, 43
Korean War and, 40, 56
Johnson, Lyndon, 9, 121–43, *121, 145*
ambitions of, 124, 143
anger of, 150
Bush Jr. compared with, 297–8
"can-do" spirit of, 139
debate of July 1965 and, 135–40
decision making problems of, 134–7
defense spending and, 122–3, 147, 149, 274, 328
despair of, 133
domestic programs of, 122–4, 143, 155, 157
election of 1964 and, 127, 129–30, 131
election of 1968 and, 151, 158, 162–5
failure to adjust Vietnam policy of, 154–7
governmental crisis and, 124
Gulf of Tonkin attack and, 129
as hands-on president, 137
insecurity of, 124, 141, 143
as man of peace, 123, 129–30, 143
maximalism and, 123–4, 147–8, 150, 156, 163, 298, 326, 328
NSAM 273 and, 125–6
Obama compared with, 306–7
policy continuity of, 122, 326, 353*n*
political vulnerability of, 140–2
retrenchment and, 123, 143, 163
right-wing backlash and, 124, 140, 141
"sotto voce" approach of, 148–50
speeches of, 122, 123, 130, 133–4, 157, 162, 163, 353*n*
as vice president, 103, 109, 126
Vietnam War and, 10, 103, 123–43, 145–65, 181, 297–8, 311
Joint Chiefs of Staff, U.S. (JCS), 11, 42, 45
Bush, Sr. and, 244, 252
Clinton and, 260
Eisenhower and, 81, 85
Johnson and, *121,* 155
Korean War and, 50, 52, 58
Vietnam policy and, 115, 186, 351*n*
Jones, James, 303, 306
Jones, Joseph, 27, 341*n*
Jordan, 82, 297, 316
Jordan, Hamilton, 213

Kabul, 279, 287
Karzai, Hamid, 304, 305
Kassim, General, 82–3
Keane, Jack, 295

Kennan, George, 8, 21–6, 34–6, 200, 264, 311
  dissent from containment of, 29–30
  Korea policy and, 50, 51, 53–4, 63
  Program A and, 34–5
Kennedy, John F., 7, 11, 93–119, *93*, 245, 306, 352*n*
  Bay of Pigs and, 97, 106, 111
  Berlin crisis (1961) and, 97–102, 104–7, 110, 111, 113, 119
  body language of, 96
  "boy-commando" style and, 94–8, 104
  Cuban missile crisis and, 98, 105–11, 113, 119, 138, 331, 332
  death of, 111, 113, 122
  defense spending of, 99, 100, 122, 240, 274, 328
  difficult relations with allies of, 5, 100–2, 111–13
  disdain expressed by, 95
  Eisenhower compared with, 94, 96, 97, 98, 102, 118–19
  Eisenhower's warning to, 89
  "good America" story about, 3, 5
  legacy of, 124
  maximalism and, 8, 9, 97–100, 106, 119, 163, 241, 277, 326, 329, 331, 332
  as senator, 95
  speeches of, 97, 99–100, 111, 113
  Vietnam policy and, 98, 103–5, 113–19, 126, 141, 351*n*
Kennedy, Robert, 349*n*
  Cuban missile crisis and, 108, 109–10
  Vietnam policy and, 116, 141–2, 157
Kennedy, Ted, 183, 253
Kenya, truck bombing in, 265
Khalilzad, Zalmay, 293
Khanh, Nguyen, 126, 128, 129, 131
Khomeini, Ayatollah, 315
Khrushchev, Nikita, 7–8, 80, 84, 86–7
  Berlin crisis and, 8, 98–101, 119
  Cuban missile crisis and, 8, 105, 107–10, 331, 332
  Johnson and, 123
Kiev, 257
Kim Il Sung, 69, 244
King, Martin Luther, Jr., 157
Kissinger, Henry, 5, 36, 169–90, 192–210, 226, 292, 327, 328, 329, 342*n*
  Africa policy and, 205–6, 208
  arms control and, 201–3, 205, 207, 208, 217, 225, 235, 237, 303
  China policy and, 175–84, 189–90, 197, 210, 314
  Clinton administration and, 245, 246
  Clinton compared with, 271
  debate over policies of, 207–9
  détente and, 90, 171, 180–3, 189–90, 198, 199, 207, 208, 217, 239
  election of 1976 and, 207
  in Ford administration, 198–209
  "heartland speeches" of, 199
  human rights and, 197, 199–200, 205, 208, 209
  Iraq War and, 296
  Middle East policy and, 194–7, 208, 210
  Moscow summit and, 181–4
  9/11 and, 274, 282
  Nixon's second term and, 192–6
  Obama compared with, 314
  outrageous statements of, 199–200
  power and autonomy of, 197
  Reagan criticized by, 223, 237, 238
  as secretary of state, 194–209
  shuttle diplomacy of, 194, 196, 210
  unilateralism of, 196
  Vietnam policy and, 171–4, 178, 182, 184–90, 203–8
Kohl, Helmut, 225, 249
Komer, Robert, 104, 155
Korea
  unification of, 54–5, 334
  U.S. indifference to, 49–50
  see also North Korea; South Korea
Korea, Republic of, *see* South Korea
Korean War, 7, 8, 10, 40, 41, 49–63, 66, 82, 140, 143, 147, 168, 241, 245, 256, 269, 282, 321, 333
  Eisenhower and, 68–70, 164, 347*n*
  Inchon landing in, 54, 56–7
  Kennan's views on, 53–4
  "limited engagement" ("police action") view of, 54
  NSC 81/1 and, 55–6
  policy changes triggered by, 52–3
  as policy setback, 54
  U.S. power and, 62
Kosovar Albanians, 268
Kosovo, 267–70, 331, 332

Krulak, Victor, 155–6
Kurds, 255
Kuwait, Iraqi invasion of, 8, 250–6, 331, 332–4
Kyoto Protocol, 276

Laird, Melvin, 173, 181
Lake, Anthony, 261
Laos, 104, 152, 161, 174–5, 189
Latin American, 87–9, 203, 211
  Nixon's trip to, 87–8
leadership
  Eisenhower's views on, 66, 72, 73
  U.S. role and, 169–70, 177, 193, 195, 303, 316, 318, 322, 333
leaks, 101, 201, 206, 259
Lebanon, 80–4, 233, 348*n*
  U.S. hostages in, 236
Le Duc Tho, 187
Lemnitzer, Lyman, 104
Libby, Scooter, 285
liberal internationalism, 6, 11, 115, 116, 142, 177
liberals, liberalism, 10–11, 30, 123
Libya, 315–18
Limited Test Ban Treaty, 111–13
"limited war," 132, 148
Lincoln, Abraham, 147
linkage, 171–2, 181, 182, 187
  oil embargo and, 196
Lippmann, Walter, 118, 128
Lodge, Henry Cabot, 79, 114–18, 125, 127, 128, 139
London, 98
  gold market in, 161
  multinational conference in (1956), 78
London summit (June 1990), 249
Lovett, Robert, 25, 30, 59
Luce, Henry, 77

MacArthur, Douglas, *39*
  firing of, 40, 43, 54
  Inchon landing and, 54, 56–7
  Korean War and, 40, 54–60, 63, 68, 334
  as manic-depressive, 41, 58
Macmillan, Harold, 5, 78, 81, 87, 98
Making of a Quagmire, The (Halberstam), 142
malaria, 293
Maliki, Prime Minister, 297
Malraux, André, 102
Malta meeting (Dec. 1989), 248
Mandela, Nelson, 316
Mansfield, Mike, 149
Mao Zedong, 45, 60, 156, 177, 179
Marcos, Ferdinand, 233
Marines, U.S., 289, 314
Marshall, George, *17*, 18–27, 29, 30, 32, 38, 73
  Acheson's replacement of, 33
  defense issues and, 42, 43, 56–9
  Harvard speech of, 24–5, 26
  Korea policy and, 50, 56–9
  at Moscow meetings, 19, 20–1
Marshall Plan, 19–27, 32, 35, 41, 47, 48, 66, 69, 139, 241
Marxism-Leninism, 230
Maryland Historical Society, 21
Mattis, James, 291
maximalist policy, 8–10, 12, 38, 49, 52, 189, 241, 326, 329–36
  Bush Jr. and, 275, 277, 283, 288, 291, 298, 310, 326
  Bush Sr. and, 251, 331, 333
  H. Clinton and, 323
  Holbrooke's views on, 308
  Johnson and, 123–4, 147–8, 150, 156, 163, 298, 326, 328
  Kennedy and, 8, 9, 97–100, 106, 119, 163, 241, 277, 326, 329, 331, 332
  Korean War and, 56–9, 63
  9/11 and, 275
  Obama and, 310
  Reagan and, 8, 222–3, 224, 233, 240, 277, 326, 328, 329, 331, 332
  Sputnik and, 83
  Truman and, 8, 38, 49, 52, 57–9, 241, 298, 326, 331, 332
Mayaguez (U.S. cargo ship), 205
McCain, John, 302, 303
McCarthy, Joe, 140
McCarthyism, 141
McChrystal, Stanley, 305–9
McCone, John, 11, 115, 127, 133, 354*n*
McConnell, John, 136
McConnell, Mitch, 295
McGovern, George, 207

McNamara, Robert, 94, 99, *121*, 349*n*
as can-do man, 95–6
Cuban missile crisis and, 107, 108, 111
ousting of, 158–9
policy failure predicted by, 151–2, 153, 158
Vietnam policy and, 117, 124–8, 132, 133, 135–9, 142, 148–9, 151–4, 156, 158–69, 351*n*, 354*n*
Meany, George, 329
Mediterranean, eastern, 19, 22
Mekong Delta, 126, 134, 135
Mexico, 260, 321
Middle East, 62, 103, 154, 181, 193, 314–20
Arab Spring in, 311, 314–18
Bush Jr.'s reformist vision for, 283, 286–8
Carter policy and, 210
Eisenhower and, 77–84, 203
9/11 in, 281
Reagan policy and, 233
Suez crisis, 77–81, 196
U.S. regional role in, 195
U.S. vs. British and, 5, 74–5
Yom Kippur War, 193–6
"mid-Pacific conference, the," 70–2
"military-industrial complex," 90
military intervention, 11, 12
military power, Soviet, 29, 30, 70, 71, 193, 202, 343*n*
military power, U.S., 4, 11, 31, 62, 86
Albright's retort about, 260, 329
British and French dependence on, 33
Clinton and, 262–3, 271
Iraq War and, 288
Vietnam War and, 128
Millennium Challenge Account, 286
Milosevic, Slobodan, 267–9, 331
"missile gap" controversies, 83–4, 94, 201–3, 330–1
Mitterrand, François, 247–50
Moch, Jules, 53
Mondale, Walter, 216
Morgenthau, Hans, 157
Moscow, 210, 211
Big Four meeting in, 19, 20–1, 23
Kissinger in, 198
Olympic Games in, 214, 215–16
Reagan's visits to, 223, 237, 239–40
Moscow State University, Reagan's speech at, 239
Moscow summit (1972), 181–4
most-favored-nation status (MFN), 197–8
Moyers, Bill, 131
Moynihan, Daniel Patrick, 200, 209, 231, 253
Mozambique, 205
Mubarak, Hosni, 314–15
mujahideen, Afghan, *see* freedom fighters, Afghan
Mullen, Mike, 311
Murphy, Robert, 24–5, 81–3
Muslim Brotherhood, 321
Muslims, 321, 331
Bosnian, 259–62
girls and women, 274, 286–7
Kosovo, 267–8
Shi'ite, 255, 296, 318
Sunni, 296, 297, 318
MX missile, 213

Nasser, Gamal Abdel, 77, 80, 81, 82, 103
National Assembly, French, 73
national consensus, 4, 10–12, 28, 66, 296, 303
National Farmers Union, 162
National Intelligence Estimate, 282
National Museum, Iraqi, 290
national security, U.S., 10, 12, 163, 208, 245
Clifford's policy review and, 160–1
Eisenhower-era debates over, 83, 90
Iraq as central to, 281, 283
Johnson's views on, 122–3
Kennedy's views on, 94–5
9/11 and, 274, 281, 282, 283
Obama and, 303, 306, 309, 310, 316
spending for, *see* defense budget
State Department's review of, 46–8
National Security Council (NSC), 46, 52, 54, 69, 79, 86
Bush Jr. and, 277, 278, 297
Bush Sr. and, 251
Clinton and, 259, 267
Obama and, 312
Reagan and, 227, 236
Vietnam policy and, 104, 105, 114, 117, 128, 134, 151, 173
nation-building, 323
in Afghanistan, 304, 305, 306

nationalism, "suicidal," 157
Nationalist Chinese, 76
NATO, 107, 154, 237, 316
Afghanistan War and, 307
Balkan conflicts and, 260–2, 267, 268
Congress and, 53, 62
Eisenhower and, 53, 66, 73
enlargement of, 263–4
Euromissiles and, 224, 225, 228
formation of, 28, 35, 44, 45
German reunification and, 248–50
Haig's resignation from, 217
Iraq War and, 291
weakening of, 246
West Germany and, 49, 74, 112
Naval Academy, Carter's speech at, 213
Navy, U.S., 40, 44–5, 52, 178, 263, 322
elite commando unit in, 96
Gulf of Tonkin attack on, 129
Nebraska, University of, 271–2
Negroponte, John, 292
neoconservatives, 207, 225
Neustadt, Richard, 96
neutron bomb, 212
New Frontier, 9
"boy-commando" style of, 94–8, 104
New Jewel Movement, 230
New Republic, 295
New York City, 226, 280
New Yorker, The, 245, 308, 326
New York Times, The, 20, 142, 206, 237, 259, 280, 281, 329
New York Times Magazine, The, 276
Newsweek, 237
Ngo Dinh Diem, 11, 103, 104, 113–18, 124–5, 131
Ngo Dinh Nhu, 114, 117
Nguyen Khanh, 126, 128, 129, 131
Nguyen Van Thieu, 164, 165, 184–7, 205
Nhu, Madame, 114
Nicaragua, 228–32, 238
9/11, 50, 277–83, 286–8, 298, 333
Afghanistan response to, 278–9, 281, 282
as foreign policy challenge, 274–5
see also Iraq War
Nitze, Paul, 25–6, 54, 56, 162, 329, 343*n*
Euromissiles crisis and, 226
on Kennedy, 96, 109
NSC-68 and, 46–8, 207
on nuclear weapons, 202–3
Nixon, Mrs., 87
Nixon, Richard, 167–90, 209, 217, 231, 239, 258
arms control and, 171–2, 176, 181, 237
China policy and, 12, *167,* 175–84, 186, 189–90, 210, 263, 314, 335–6
détente and, 90, 171, 180–3, 189–90, 208
election of 1968 and, 164, 165
election of 1972 and, 181, 184–7, 192
Foreign Affairs article of (1967), 175, 179
"go for broke" instinct of, 169–70, 173, 181, 183, 188
leaders admired by, 169
linkage and, 171–2, 181, 182
memoirs of, 169, 179–80
Moscow summit and, 181–4
as "Mr. Peace," 177, 327
Obama compared with, 314
Reagan compared with, 223
Reagan criticized by, 237
resignation of, 192, 196, 198, 237
retrenchment and, 9, 168–9, 170, 177–8, 183–4, 189–90, 217, 326, 327–8
second term of, 192–6
speeches of, 171, 172, 188, 192
as vice president, 79
Vietnam War and, 9, 168, 169, 171–5, 178, 180–90, 192, 204, 205, 208
Nixon Doctrine, 168
no-fly zone, Libya crisis and, 315–16
North Atlantic alliance, *see* NATO
North Atlantic treaty, 44, 45
Northern Ireland, 270, 271
North Korea, 54–8, 61, 68, 69, 104, 276, 313
Clinton policy and, 260, 270, 271
nuclear weapons and, 260, 293
South invaded by, 7, 50–2, 54, 57, 62, 99, 282, 333
North Vietnam, 75, 127–30, 142, 151, 154–6, 161, 203–4, 333
Diem's murder and, 125
disruption of supply chain of, 173
Easter offensive of (1972), 184, 188
mining of harbors of, 152, 173, 182, 189
Nixon policy and, 169, 171–5, 180–4, 187–9
Paris peace talks and, 163–5, 184–6, 204

North Vietnam *(continued)*
U.S. bombing of, 131, 132, 133, 147, 152, 155, 158, 159, 163–4, 165, 173, 187–9, 359*n*
NSAM 273, 125–6
NSC-68, 46–8, 71, 207
NSC 81/1, 55–6
"nuclear freeze" movement, 226
nuclear weapons, nuclear war, 42, 45–6, 68–72, 207, 260, 293
arms control and, 85–7, 105, 201–3, 210, 234–41, 302–3, 327, 329
Carter and, 214
Eisenhower and, 69–72, 75, 76, 83–7, 327
Kennedy and, 98, 99, 100, 105, 106, 107, 109, 111–13
Khrushchev and, 80, 100, 109
Korean War and, 59–62, 68, 69, 70
Limited Test Ban Treaty and, 111–13
"missile gap" controversies and, 83–4, 94, 201–3, 330
Nixon and, 168, 171–2, 176
Obama and, 302–3, 311–12, 318–19
proliferation of, 331
Reagan and, 222–9, 234–41
terrorism and, 279, 280
Vietnam War and, 148, 153, 162–3
Nunn, Sam, 303

Obama, Barack, 4, 301–23, *301*, 335
Afghanistan War and, 10, 303–11, 317–18
Arab Spring and, 311, 314–18, 320
defense spending of, 309, 313–14, 320–1, 323, 328
domestic focus of, 302, 323
East Asia policy of, 311–14, 322
innovative, low-cost and small-footprint approaches of, 309–11
Iran and, 311–12, 318–19
Iraq War and, 10, 302, 303, 304
Middle East and, 311, 314–20
retrenchment and, 302–3, 310–23, 326–9
speeches of, 313–14, 320, 328
visionary rhetoric of, 302
"off ramps" option, 290, 292
Ofstie, Ralph, 44–5
oil, oil issues, 74, 129, 253
oil embargo, Arab (1973), 195–6
"oil-spot theory," 126–7
Olympic Games, in Moscow, 214, 215–16
"Open Skies," 71–2
Organization of American States (OAS), 88–9, 107
Organization of Petroleum Exporting Countries (OPEC), 195
Orszag, Peter, 307
overcommitment, 8, 67, 149, 217

Pace, Peter, *273*
pacification (HOP TAC; "ink blot" strategy), 126–7, 155
Pacific fleet, 44
Pakistan, 229
U.S. relations with, 214, 230, 270, 271, 310–11
Palestine, 20
Palmer, Bruce, 181
Panama Canal treaties, 211
Panetta, Leon, 306, 318, 320
Paris
Big Four meetings in, 33, 35, 36–7, 40, 86–7
Rusk in, 101
Vietnam peace talks in, 163–5, 184–9, 204
Paris conference (1947), 26
Parliament, Australian, 313–14
Parliament, British, 59, 230
Parliament, Irish, 230
Paul, Rand, 329
Peace Corps, 103
peaceful co-existence, 239, 241
"peace through weakness" strategy, 30
Pearl Harbor, 50
Pelosi, Nancy, 283
perestroika, 228
Perle, Richard, 235–6
Perry, William, 263
Persian Gulf
as U.S. national interest, 214, 215
U.S. troop presence in, 255
Persian Gulf War (1991), 246, 250–7, 264, 283, 331, 332, 334
cost of, 289
Vietnam War compared with, 147, 256
Peru, 87
Petraeus, David, 304, 306, 309, 317, 318
Philippines, 62, 168, 231, 233
Pickering, Thomas, 254–6

Pinochet, Augusto, 233
planes, U.S., 147, 194
Pleiku, 133
Poland, 8, 211, 228, 229, 264
Politburo, 108, 181–3, 216, 234–6, 239, 240
Pompidou, Georges, 195
Portugal, 205, 291
poverty, 122
Powell, Colin, 11, 12, 230, 244, 277, 293
  Balkans conflict and, 260, 332
  first Gulf War and, 251–6, 332
  Iraq War and, 252, 284, 285, 289, 334
power, U.S., 113, 119, 140, 143, 178, 192, 325
  Clinton and, 245, 262–3, 271, 272
  9/11 and, 278–9, 282, 283, 298
  Obama and, 302, 316, 322–3
Present at the Creation (Acheson), 35–6, 63
presentism, 325
Program A, 34–5
public opinion, 84, 85, 100, 276
  Carter and, 215
  end of Cold War and, 244
  first Gulf War and, 246, 251, 253, 255, 256
  global, 106–7, 151
  Iraq War and, 295, 297
  Korean War and, 54
  Obama and, 302
  Reagan and, 236
  Vietnam War and, 148, 149, 151, 157–61, 163, 172, 173, 188–9
Putin, Vladimir, 276

Qatar, 316
Quemoy and Matsu, 76, 85

Radford, Arthur, 44
Rambouillet multilateral conference (1998), 267
Reagan, Ronald, 7, 9, 221–42, *221*
  arms control and, 223–8, 234–41
  Clinton compared with, 271
  critics of, 223, 236–7
  defense budget and, 216, 224, 240, 241, 274, 328
  in election of 1976, 203
  in election of 1980, 207, 215, 222
  empathy of, 222, 240
  on end of Cold War, 244, 246
  Euromissiles crisis and, 226–8, 331
  at Geneva summit, 234
  hanging tough and, 226
  Iran-Contra affair and, 229, 236
  maximalism and, 8, 222–3, 224, 233, 240, 277, 326, 328, 329, 331, 332
  Middle East policy and, 233
  policy continuity and, 223, 224
  at Reykjavik summit, 235–8
  speeches of, 227, 229, 230, 231, 233, 237, 238, 239
  Third World policy of, 228–33
  zero option of, 225–7, 238–9, 332–3
Reagan Doctrine, 228–33, 238–9
realpolitik, 175
recession, 193, 196, 257
Red Army, 33, 80, 229, 240
refugees, Vietnamese, 204
regime change, Iraq and, 265, 267, 283, 284
Reid, Harry, 296
Republican Guards, Iraqi, 254
Republicans, 22, 30, 116, 141, 165, 202, 203, 217, 327, 345*n*
  Angola policy and, 206
  conservative, 217
  Eisenhower and, 66, 70, 72
  in election of 1964, 130
  in election of 1966, 157
  in election of 1976, 203, 207
  in election of 2006, 295
  Iraq War and, 295, 296
  playing to the public's interest in peace by, 11–12
Resor, Stanley, 136
"responsibility to protect" principle, 269
retrenchment policy, 8–10, 12, 193, 326–39
  Carter and, 9, 209, 211–12, 214–15, 217–18, 326, 329
  Eisenhower and, 67–72, 86, 90, 97, 143, 190, 217, 326–9
  Ford and, 326
  Johnson and, 123, 143, 163
  Kissinger and, 203, 205, 208
  Korean War and, 68–70
  Nixon and, 9, 168–9, 170, 177–8, 183–4, 189–90, 217, 326, 327–8
  Obama and, 302–3, 310–23, 326–9
  post-Cold War, 244–6, 269
revolt of the admirals, 40, 44–5
Reykjavik summit (Oct. 1986), 235–8

Rhee, Syngman, 69, 70, 164
Rhodes, Benjamin, 322
Rhodesia (now Zimbabwe), 210
Rice, Condoleezza, 274, 277, 284, 287–8, 302
  as secretary of state, 293, 294, 297
Ridgway, Matthew, 41, 62
Riyadh, 255
Robertson, Walter, 69
Rodman, Peter, 231
Rogers, William, 173
rogue states, 265, 266
Rolling Stone, 309
Rolling Thunder, 133, 181
Romania, 25
Romans, ancient, 105
Roosevelt, Franklin D., 7, 305
Roosevelt, Theodore, 169
Rostow, Mrs. Walt, 94
Rostow, Walt, 6, 94, 96, 97, 102–5
  Vietnam policy and, 103–5, 132, 143, 151, 162, 355*n*
Rostropovich, Mstislav, 217
Royal Navy, British, 20
Rubin, Robert, 245
Rumsfeld, Donald, 12, 200, 202, 203, 207, *273,* 275–82, 329, 349*n*
  cost consciousness of, 276, 277, 289, 292
  Iraq War and, 289–92, 294, 296, 297
  9/11 and, 275, 278–82
  ouster of, 296, 297
Rusk, Dean, 6, 11, 102
  Berlin crisis (1961) and, 100, 101, 105
  Cuban missile crisis and, 105, 106, 107, 351*n*
  problems with allies and, 112, 113
  Vietnam policy and, 104, 115, 127–8, 138, 141, 142, 149–50, 161, 162
Russell, Richard, 161
Russia, 266, 321
  Bush Jr.'s policy and, 276, 279
  Clinton policy and, 263–4, 268
  Syria's relations with, 318
  U.S. aid to, 258
Russian Revolution, 46
Rwanda, 260

SA-7 missiles, 182
Sacirbey, Mohammad, 261
Sadat, Anwar, 194–5, 211
Safire, William, 234
Saigon, 116, 117, 125, 126, 139, 184
  bombing in, 131
  fall of, 205
  Johnson's visit to, 103
  McNamara's visit to, 153–4
  Tet Offensive in, 159
Sakharov, Andrei, 200, 210
SALT, 202, 216, 217
SALT II, 214, 224
Sarajevo "marketplace bombing," 261
Saturday Evening Post, 111
Saudi Arabia, 61, 82, 287, 288, 321
  first Gulf War and, 251–2, 255, 334
Schlesinger, Arthur, Jr., 96, 326
Schlesinger, James, 200, 202, 203, 207, 329
Schmidt, Helmut, 225
Schorr, Daniel, 101
Schröder, Gerhard, 268, 286
Schuman, Robert, 53
Schwarzkopf, Norman, 255–6
Scowcroft, Brent, 250–1, 263–4, 284
"search and destroy" missions, 147, 150
security forces, Iraqi, 293, 294
Senate, U.S., 18, 77, 80, 214, 253, 296
  Angola and, 206, 232
  arms control and, 201
  Finance Committee of, 199
  Foreign Relations Committee of, 113, 283
  Intelligence Committee of, 231
  Kissinger and, 198–9
  Vietnam policy and, 158, 161
September 11 terrorist attacks, *see* 9/11
"sequestration" plan, 320
Serbia, 259, 267–9
Serbs, Bosnian, 259–62
Shevardnadze, Eduard, 247
Shi'ites, 255, 296, 318
Shultz, George, 226, 230, 234–7, 244, 303
  Commonwealth Club speech of, 231
shuttle diplomacy, 194, 196, 210
Singapore, 314, 322
"situations of strength" strategy, 27
Six-Day War, 154
Smith, Walter Bedell, 28
Snow, Edgar, 156
Social Democrats, German, 225
Soldier's Story, A (Bradley), 58

Solidarity, 229
Solzhenitsyn, Aleksandr, 200, 207
Somalia, 260
Sorensen, Ted, 352*n*
  Cuban missile crisis and, 108
  "good America" story of, 3, 5
  Vietnam policy and, 113, 116
"Sources of Soviet Conduct, The" (Kennan), 29–30
South Africa, 205, 231
South America, 278
South Asia, 310, 311
South China Sea, 313
South Korea, 68, 69, 231, 276, 313, 321
  North's invasion of, 7, 50–2, 54, 57, 62, 99, 282, 333
  U.S. troops in, 168, 178, 212
South Vietnam, 75, 113–19, 124–9, 131–42, 150–62, 297, 311
  Bundy-McNamara "total collapse" memo on, 132, 133
  Clifford's warning to, 164–5
  collapse of, 204–5, 208
  Communists in, 113, 114, 116, 118, 125, 140, 141–2, 151, 154, 159, 164, 174, 204, 355*n*
  Diem overthrown in, 11, 113–18, 124–5, 131
  Johnson's trips to, 103, 126, 150
  Kennedy and, 95, 103–4, 126
  McNamara's trips to, 124–5, 126, 135, 151, 153–4
  Nixon policy and, 171–4, 178, 180, 181, 184–8, 205
  NSAM 273 and, 125–6
  pacification in, 126–7, 155
  Tet Offensive in, 159–60, 163
  U.S. troops in, 103–4, 113, 133, 134, 137–8, 146, 148, 151, 152, 154, 158, 161, 162
  "Vietnamization" and, 171
Southeast Asia, 125, 129, 138, 278
South-West Africa (now Namibia), 205
Soviet bloc, 212, 264
Soviet Union, 26–38, 60–1, 98–102, 105–13, 193–204, 311, 343*n*
  Afghanistan invaded and occupied by, 8, 50, 214, 215–16, 224, 229, 232, 279
  in Africa, 205–6, 213
  arms control and, 86–7, 105, 111, 154, 171–2, 176, 198, 201–3, 210, 214, 216, 224–8, 234–41, 247, 327
  Berlin crises and, 8, 28–34, 36, 42, 98–101, 341*n*–2*n*
  Big Four meetings and, 19, 33, 36–7
  Bush Sr.'s policy and, 246–9
  Carter policy and, 209–17
  China's relations with, 45, 60, 76, 176, 197
  Cold War and, 7–8, 45–9, 330–1, 334
  collapse of, 244, 257, 331
  Cuban missile crisis and, 105–11, 331, 332, 351*n*
  Cuba's relations with, 89
  détente and, 171, 175, 180–3, 189–90, 197, 198, 199, 200, 209, 213, 216
  dissidents in, 200, 210, 211, 212, 239
  Egypt's relations with, 77, 82, 194–5
  emigration policy of, 197–8, 199, 208
  European dominance and, 21, 22, 23
  as "evil empire," 222, 227, 237
  first Gulf War and, 253
  French relations with, 112
  German reunification and, 247, 248, 249
  Guatemala and, 75
  Iran's relations with, 74
  Korea policy and, 50–1, 55, 68–9
  Middle East policy of, 193–7
  military power of, 29, 30, 70, 71, 193, 202, 343*n*
  "missile gap" controversies and, 83–4, 94, 201–3, 330
  most-favored-nation status of, 197–8
  Nixon policy and, 169, 171–2, 175, 176, 180–4, 186, 187
  Reagan policy and, 222–41, 331
  "reverse linkage" and, 172
  Suez crisis and, 79–80
  Truman's peace initiatives and, 71–2
  U-2 spy flights over, 84, 87
  U.S. fears about, 21, 37, 38, 42
  U.S. grain embargo against, 214, 224
  Vietnam War and, 148, 153, 156, 171–2, 175, 180, 181, 182, 183, 187, 204
Spaak, Paul-Henri, 87
Special Operations, 279, 309
Sputnik, 7, 83–94
Srebrenica, 260
SS-20s, 224–5

Stalin, Joseph, 18, 22, 24, 26–9, 37, 200
Berlin blockade and, 28, 29, 31, 33, 331
death of, 71
Marshall's meeting with, 21
State Department, U.S., 19, 20, 29, 59, 83, 199, 216, 244, 259, 272, 310
Africa policy and, 206
Berlin blockade and, 30, 341*n*–2*n*
East Asia policy and, 314
German rearmament and, 52–3
Johnson's speech at, 123
Korea policy and, 50, 55, 69
national security policy reviewed by, 46–8
policy-planning staff in, 21, 25, 46–7
Vietnam policy and, 115, 125, 130
Stennis, John, 161
Stevenson, Adlai, 94, 95
Cuban missile crisis and, 107, 108, 109, 111
Stingers, 232
strategic bombing doctrine, 44–5
Strategic Defense Initiative (SDI; Star Wars), 227, 234, 235, 238
Strauss-Kahn, Dominique, 286
Sudan, 265
Suez Canal, 194
Suez crisis, 77–81, 196
Sullivan, Jake, 323
Summers, Lawrence, 245
Sunnis, 296, 297, 318
Symington, Stuart, 43
Syria, 81, 195, 196, 318

Taft, Robert, Jr., 206
Taiwan, 176, 178, 263
Taiwan Strait, 178, 263
Taiwan Strait standoff, 84–5, 203
Talbott, Strobe, 262, 268, 272
Taliban, 278–9, 282, 286, 304, 305, 307
Tanzania, truck bombing in, 265
taxes, 43, 70, 150, 157–8, 161
cuts in, 224, 276
Soviet exit, 197
Taylor, Maxwell, 108
Vietnam policy and, 103–5, 114, 117, 125, 126, 127, 129, 131–2, 134, 139, 141, 146, 150–1, 156, 164, 351*n*, 355*n*
technological change, 262
technological superiority, 278–9
Tehran, 212
television, 188
Johnson on, 135
Kennedy on, 99–100, 116
Tet Offensive on, 159, 160
Westmoreland on, 159
Tenet, George, 266–7, 276–7, 333
Tennessee Valley Authority (TVA), 133, 135
"terrorist universities," 293
terrorists, terrorism, 236, 331
Bush Jr.'s lack of urgency towards, 276–7
in Iraq War, 294
training camps for, 280
war on, 277–99
see also al Qaeda; 9/11
Tet Offensive, 159–60, 163
Thatcher, Margaret, 225, 234, 247–50
Thieu, Nguyen Van, 164, 165, 184–7, 205
Third World, 98, 118, 182, 203
clashes over conduct of Cold War in, 74–6, 203–6, 208, 213–14, 228–33, 238, 240
Kennedy policy makeover in, 102–5
nuclear reactors in, 71
U.S. unpredictable policies in, 76–8
Thompson, Llewellyn, 109, 111
Time, 77, 245, 277
Together Forward, Operation, 294
Together Forward II, Operation, 294
Tokyo Bay, 263
Tonkin, Gulf of, 204
trade, 245, 263, 286, 313
Indo-Pakistani, 310
U.S.-Soviet, 197–9
trade agreements, 245
trade deficit, 27
Trans-Pacific Partnership, 313
Treasury, U.S., 157
Treaty of Amity and Cooperation, 312
"Trollope ploy," 109
Troubled Partenership, The (Kissinger), 5
Trujillo, Rafael, 88–9
Truman, Harry, 7, 17–63, *17, 39*, 95, 96, 311, 335, 344*n*
Clinton compared with, 270
defense spending and, 40–6, 48–9, 52, 53, 62, 70, 72, 73, 99, 328

Eisenhower compared with, 66–7, 70, 72–3, 76, 81, 84, 327
election of 1948 and, 31, 42, 43
internal battles over military issues of, 40–6, 48–9
Kennedy compared with, 104
Korean War and, 10, 40, 50–63, 68, 70, 140, 241
March 12 speech of (1947), 19, 21, 23, 28
maximalism and, 8, 38, 49, 52, 57–9, 241, 298, 326, 331, 332
State of the Union message of (1949), 43
successes of, 37–8
"year of decisions" of, 18, 340*n*
Truman Doctrine, 19–20, 25, 47, 66
Tulane University, 205
Turkey, 19, 20, 22, 23, 25, 81
U.S. missiles in, 109–11, 332
Twining, Nathan, 81, 85
Two Plus Four, 248–9

U-2 spy flights, 84, 87, 105, 111
Ukraine, 257
UNITA, 232
United Arab Emirates (UAE), 316
United Nations (UN), 18, 25, 81, 262
Balkan conflicts and, 259, 268–9
Eisenhower's speech at, 71
first Gulf War and, 253, 254, 256
Iraq War and, 283–6, 299
Johnson and, 123
Korean War and, 51, 55, 59, 60, 61
Relief and Rehabilitation Agency (UNRRA), 20, 25
Security Council of, 51, 75–6, 79, 108, 194, 253, 268, 269, 284–6, 299, 316, 318
Vietnam policy and, 127
weapons inspectors, 265, 281, 284, 285

Valenti, Jack, 135, 136, 143
Vance, Cyrus, 210
Vandenberg, Arthur, 25, 30, 63
Vandenberg, Hoyt, 31
Vandenberg resolution, 28, 30
Venezuela, 87–8, 89
Vienna
Carter-Brezhnev talks in, 211–14
Kennedy-Khrushchev meeting in, 98–9
Vietcong, 103, 125, 130, 133, 134, 185
pacification and, 126
Tet Offensive and, 159
Vietnam, 75
Kennedy and, 98, 103–5, 113–19, 126, 141, 351*n*
partition of, 75
Vietnam War, 12, 70, 82, 203–8, 245, 269, 270, 333, 354*n*, 355*n*
Afghanistan War compared with, 304–5
"Americanization" of, 136–40, 146, 297
Bien Hoa attack in, 130
bombing in, 131, 132, 133, 147, 152, 155, 158, 159, 163–4, 165, 173, 180, 181, 187–9, 359*n*
bombing pauses in, 152
casualties in, 135, 147, 153, 160, 173
Clifford's policy review of, 160–1
costs of, 147, 148, 152–3, 157
debate of July 1965 and, 135–40
domino theory and, 138
Duck Hook in, 171
end of, 171, 181, 205, 208, 314
escalation and de-escalation combined plan in, 155–6
escalation in, 127–9, 134, 137–8, 146, 151–5, 171, 174, 180
expansion of, 152, 161, 172–5, 181, 184
first Gulf War compared with, 147, 256
"gradual and sustained reprisal" strategy in, 132
Guam proposal and, 152–5, 158, 161
Gulf of Tonkin attack in, 129
interagency working group for, 130–1
Iraq War compared with, 294, 296, 297–8
Johnson and, 10, 103, 123–43, 145–65, 181, 297–8, 311
Johnson's failure to adjust policy in, 154–7
linkage and, 171–2, 181, 187
as "longest war," 150
McNamara-Westmoreland prediction of policy failure in, 151–4
Nixon and, 9, 168, 169, 171–5, 178, 180–90, 192, 204, 205, 208
NSAM 273 and, 125–6
nuclear weapons and, 148
opposition to, 136–7, 148, 157, 159, 160, 173, 245

Vietnam War *(continued)*
optimism in, 150–1
pacification in (HOP TAC), 126–7, 155
peace talks in, 157, 163–5, 184–9, 204
public opinion and, 148, 149, 151, 157–61, 163, 172, 173, 188–9
Rolling Thunder in, 133, 181
"search and destroy" missions in, 147, 150
Tet Offensive in, 159–60, 163
U.S. honor and, 138
U.S. troop withdrawals in, 171, 172, 178
"Vietnamization," 171
Vladivostok, 201
Vladivostok framework, 201–3
Voting Rights Act (1965), 122

wage and price controls, 70, 170
Wake Island, 57
walk-in-the-woods formula, 226
Wall Street Journal, The, 230–1, 284
Warsaw Pact, 249
Washington Post, The, 188, 253, 283
Washington summit (1987), 237, 238, 239
Washington Times, The, 223
Watergate, 192, 207, 208
weapons of mass destruction (WMD), 255, 264–6, 279–81, 283–5, 287, 288, 334
Weinberger, Caspar, 226, 237
West Berlin, 8, 203
Khrushchev's threats against, 84–5
Reagan in, 238
see also Berlin crisis
Western Union, 28
Westminster, 241
Westmoreland, William, 126, 127, 131, 133–6, 138, 146, 151–6, 158–62
Guam proposal and, 152–5, 158, 161
removed as Vietnam commander, 162, 172
Wheeler, Earle, 129
White House, firings in, 236
Wilson, Charlie, 230
Wise Men, the, 159, 163
WMD, *see* weapons of mass destruction
Wolfowitz, Paul, 278
women, Afghan, 286–7, 304
Woodcock, Leonard, 210
World Bank, 77, 158
World Trade Center, 281
World Trade Organization, 263, 264
World War I, 3, 46, 200
World War II, 3, 18, 20, 25, 46, 50, 102, 118, 188, 200, 248
drift and ambivalence after, 269–70
end of, 169, 170, 177, 196
first Gulf War compared with, 256
Korean War compared with, 54, 62
Wright-Patterson Air force Base, 261–2

Yang Jiechi, 313
Yeltsin, Boris, 264
Yemen, 265
Yom Kippur War, 193–6
Yugoslavia, 25
breakup of, 257, 259, 269

Zarqawi, Abu Musab al-, 281
zero option, 225–7, 238–9, 332–3
Zhou Enlai, 76, *167,* 176–80, 187, 335
Zia ul-Haq, Mohammad, 229

ILLUSTRATION CREDITS

CHAPTER 1: Copyright Unknown, Courtesy of Harry S. Truman Library

CHAPTER 2: Fotosearch/Getty Images

CHAPTER 3: © Bettmann/CORBIS

CHAPTER 4: Paul Schutzer/Time and Life Pictures/Getty Images

CHAPTER 5: LBJ Library photo by Yoichi Okamoto

CHAPTER 6: LBJ Library photo by Jack Kightlinger

CHAPTER 7: Ollie Atkins/Time and Life/Getty Images

CHAPTER 8: Courtesy Gerald R. Ford Presidential Library

CHAPTER 9: Courtesy Ronald Reagan Library

CHAPTER 10: Paul J. Richards/AFP/Getty Images

CHAPTER 11: Eric Draper/Courtesy George W. Bush Presidential Library and Museum

CHAPTER 12: United States Government Work